Cockburn Library, Yorkhill

T05429

KU-467-552

Techniques of Grief Therapy

Creative Practices for Counseling the Bereaved

EDITED BY

Robert A. Neimeyer

 Routledge
Taylor & Francis Group

NEW YORK AND LONDON

First published 2012
by Routledge
711 Third Avenue, New York, NY 10017

Simultaneously published in the UK
by Routledge
27 Church Road, Hove, East Sussex BN3 2FA, UK

Visit the Taylor & Francis Web site at
www.taylorandfrancis.com

and the Routledge Web site at
www.routledgementalhealth.com

Routledge is an imprint of the Taylor & Francis Group, an informa business

© 2012 Taylor & Francis

The right of the editor to be identified as the author of the editorial material,
and of the authors for their individual chapters, has been asserted in
accordance with sections 77 and 78 of the Copyright, Designs and
Patents Act 1988.

All rights reserved. No part of this book may be reprinted or reproduced or
utilised in any form or by any electronic, mechanical, or other means,
now known or hereafter invented, including photocopying and recording,
or in any information storage or retrieval system, without permission in
writing from the publishers.

Trademark notice: Product or corporate names may be trademarks or registered
trademarks, and are used only for identification and explanation without
intent to infringe.

Library of Congress Cataloging in Publication Data
Includes bibliographical references and index
ISBN 978–0–415–80725–8 (pbk.)
Grief therapy. 2. Bereavement. I. Neimeyer, Robert A., 1954–
RC455.4.L67T43 2012
616.89'147—dc23   2011043910

ISBN: 978–0–415–80725–8 (pbk)
ISBN: 978–0–203–15268–3 (ebk)

Typeset in Minion
by RefineCatch Limited, Bungay, Suffolk, UK

Printed and bound in the United States of America on acid-free paper.

Contents

Figures and Tables

FIGURES

TABLES

Prologue

Viewed from an "outsider" perspective—and ironically this perspective includes many helping professionals—grief therapy can seem like a deceptively simple affair. It seems *simple* because it addresses a presumably universal human experience, that of bereavement, and does so using a basic repertory of techniques, consisting mainly in lending a sympathetic ear, "normalizing" the client's response, engaging in "psychoeducation" and offering some generic form of "support" through grief's stages or passages. But it is *deceptively* simple because, as most grief counselors and therapists can attest, the life-altering experience of loss shakes and sometimes shatters survivors in all their human complexity, which can involve complicated clients undergoing complicated ways of losing complicated relationships, often in a complicated social field. In such instances, which may encompass perhaps 20–25% of cases of bereavement,[*] a well-meaning listener seeking to normalize and support the mourner can find that much more than that is required. This book is about that "much more."

I decided to compile this book because the sophistication, thoughtfulness and technical versatility of the grief counselors and therapists[†] alongside whom I work, and whom I often

---

[*] I base this estimate on numerous studies of complicated, prolonged grief as a form of problematic response to loss that differs from its "near neighbors" of depression and anxiety disorders, which consistently place estimates of this reaction in the range of 10–15% of bereaved adults, the great majority of whom have lost partners or parents to natural causes (Prigerson et al., 2009; Shear et al., 2011). However, the incidence of complicated grief among parents who have lost children (Keesee, Currier, & Neimeyer, 2008) or who struggle with the death of a loved one to violent causes (McDevitt-Murphy, Neimeyer, Burke, & Williams, 2011) is substantially higher, potentially in the vicinity of 30–50%. Add to this the approximately 10% of bereaved spouses who respond with chronic depression (Bonanno, Wortman, & Nesse, 2004) and the countless other mourners experiencing severe anxiety and posttraumatic responses, and an estimated 20–25% of the bereaved experiencing significant long-term struggle may be conservative.

[†] In this book, the terms "bereavement counseling" and "grief therapy" will be used more or less interchangeably. Sometimes, however, the former is used to connote more straightforward support, counsel and ritualization offered to apparently adaptive mourners grieving a normative loss, whereas the latter is reserved for more specialized interventions, often by more highly trained professionals, for more complicated cases struggling with highly traumatizing loss, or against the backdrop of personal or systemic vulnerability. While acknowledging the legitimacy of this distinction—particularly in establishing boundaries of competence for working with very challenging cases—I am concerned here with representing the substantial overlap in technical resources from both domains, with the understanding that individual therapists will naturally choose to utilize those that are within their range of competence.

have the privilege to train in professional workshops, routinely exceed their characterization by the media. Far from the stereotype of naïve would-be helpers informed only by outdated stage models of grief, and simply pressing clients to share their painful feelings, the thousands of therapists with whom I have worked typically are aware of and interested in learning of more recent conceptual and empirical advances in the field, and modulate their approach to clients based on a delicate reading of the resources and vulnerabilities of particular individuals and families. Moreover, and still more impressively, they draw on a vast panoply of practices, which range from research-informed treatments for specific problems (e.g., traumatic responses, attachment issues) to creative adaptations of narrative, artistic and ritual forms to address common or unique client needs. Of course, no given therapist in my acquaintance practices the full range of possible interventions, not even the most eclectic or exploratory among us. But collectively, the community of grief counselors and therapists has crafted a rich repertoire of methods for assisting the bereaved, and a major goal of this volume is to share these practices, both within and beyond the field of specialists who have devised them.

A second goal of the book is more subtle: to continue to foster an interchange between the field of bereavement research and scholarship, on the one hand, and of clinical and counseling practice, on the other. Of course, this intent is hardly new with this volume, inasmuch as serious efforts to advocate cross-fertilization of the two have characterized both scientific work groups (Bridging Work Group, 2005) and professional organizations (such as the Association for Death Education and Counseling) for some time. Indeed, the present project extends my own recent effort with colleagues to foster just such bridging through the publication of a major volume in which every chapter was co-authored by a prominent bereavement scholar or researcher, on the one hand, and clinician, on the other (Neimeyer, Harris, Winokuer, & Thornton, 2011). In the current context I have therefore recruited contributions from three constituencies:

1. visible theorists or scholars who have published extensively in the field of bereavement and grief therapy;
2. leading clinical researchers who are enlarging the body of knowledge on bereavement interventions through quantitative or qualitative studies; and
3. practitioners in the field, many with limited opportunities to share their craft beyond their own institution, who are nonetheless frequently innovating on traditional practices.

I will count this project a success if this book brings to the attention of practitioners a burgeoning set of concepts and methods with origins in the academy or laboratory that could inform and extend their work, and if it awakens researchers to the often greatly more creative practices that animate the field, beyond those they have investigated to date.

Before closing, it would perhaps be useful to say something about the character of the invitations to contributors that resulted in the present compilation. First, I invited a few chapters for a preliminary section of the book whose goal is to "frame" the many contributions to follow, by discussing the relational matrix of grief therapy within which specific techniques are utilized. At least optimally, this frame features a therapist animated by deep empathy and responsiveness, able to offer unflinching presence to the pain of loss and the person experiencing it, in a state of mindfulness, and with some discernment about whether to focus attention on the client's biopsychosocial challenges or on struggles in reworking his or her relationship to the deceased. Because of the breadth of this cluster of issues, I relaxed somewhat the structure of the resulting contributions, though encouraging succinctness overall to keep the chapters "user-friendly" for the reader.

Second, and predominantly, I invited a great range of chapters on grief therapy techniques, broadly defined to include specific procedures, modalities and ways of working with particular clinical issues, or more rarely, certain kinds of losses or clients. Here, I mainly sought out methods that, with appropriate adaptation, could be used across a vast spectrum of bereavement situations or populations, recognizing that most practices are somewhat elastic, and can be extended judiciously beyond the focal context in which they were first formulated. However, I also take it as axiomatic that few if any interventions can claim universal applicability, at least when used by a clinician humble and astute enough to recognize their limitations. For this reason I asked each author to address honestly and succinctly the issue of the "indications and contraindications" of his or her particular method, that is, under what circumstances it is and is not appropriate. I then requested a clear description of the technique, ideally expressed in a set of procedures for implementing it, though realizing that for some broad categories of methods (e.g., consultation/liaison, the use of metaphoric reframes), this could be accomplished only suggestively. The use of this technique then was to be anchored in an illustrative case, which, readers should be warned, occasionally makes for emotionally strong reading, reflecting the sometimes grievous losses brought forward by the clients we serve. Because any distress in reading such cases pales by comparison with the rigors of bereavement care itself, attention is also given in various chapters to self-care for the therapist—both in opening and closing contributions to this volume. Finally, in my request to contributors, the case example was to be followed by concluding thoughts noting any research relevant to the procedure, any significant variations on the method or qualifications to it, and a few carefully selected references to further document the technique, offer an entry point into relevant research or theory, or point toward related resources for practitioners. In all of this I pressed for brevity, recognizing that busy professionals are more likely to be interested in substantial kernels of helpful techniques vetted in the laboratory or field than in elaborate scientific or conceptual justifications of the author's preferred practices. The goal, then, was to present a rich and representative smorgasbord of methods for engaging grief and its complications with greater creativity and awareness of alternatives, perhaps particularly when our usual ways of working *aren't* working. The sheer scope of the offerings to follow gives me hope that this goal has been achieved, and that this selection of techniques of grief therapy will spur further innovation and more informed and informative research in the practices that constitute our field.

References

Bonanno, G. A., Wortman, C. B., & Nesse, R. M. (2004). Prospective patterns of resilience and maladjustment during widowhood. *Psychology and Aging, 19,* 260–271.

Bridging Work Group (2005). Bridging the gap between research and practice in bereavement. *Death Studies, 29,* 93–122.

Keesee, N. J., Currier, J. M., & Neimeyer, R. A. (2008). Predictors of grief following the death of one's child: The contribution of finding meaning. *Journal of Clinical Psychology, 64,* 1145–1163.

McDevitt-Murphy, M. E., Neimeyer, R. A., Burke, L. A., & Williams, J. L. (2011). Assessing the toll of traumatic loss: Psychological symptoms in African Americans bereaved by homicide. *Psychological Trauma,* in press.

Neimeyer, R. A., Harris, D. L., Winokuer, H., & Thornton, G. (Eds.). (2011). *Grief and bereavement in contemporary society: Bridging research and practice.* New York: Routledge.

Prigerson, H. G., Horowitz, M. J., Jacobs, S. C., Parkes, C. M., Aslan, M., Goodkin, K., Raphael, B., et al. (2009). Prolonged grief disorder: Psychometric validation of criteria proposed for DSM-V and ICD-11. *PLoS Medicine, 6*(8), 1–12.

Shear, M. K., Simon, N., Wall, M., Zisook, S., Neimeyer, R., et al. (2011). Complicated grief and related bereavement issues for DSM-5. *Depression and Anxiety, 28,* 103–117.

Acknowledgments

The present project has a long past, but a short history. That is, the formal story of this volume's development from my initial conception of it to its visible birth in print has been surprisingly swift, as scores of clinical collaborators eagerly joined in sharing their research-honed procedures and clinical creativity in the conduct of grief therapy. Editing these into a coherent project and supplementing them with my own best efforts to "unpack" my favorite therapeutic practices has been a joy. But in a larger sense, *Techniques of Grief Therapy* reaches back to my earliest engagement with clients struggling with loss, as well as with the courageous cadre of colleagues who counsel them. To a greater extent than any other clinical handbook I've encountered, this volume therefore represents a chorus of clinicians and their clients whose voices resonate in these pages, sometimes harmonizing, sometimes offering contrapuntal elaboration of the shared themes of loss and emergent hope in the context of bereavement. I am indebted to each member of this chorus, many of whom I am privileged to call friends.

I am equally indebted to other colleagues whose silent presence nonetheless made the project possible. Among them is Anna Moore, my capable acquisitions editor for the *Routledge Series on Death, Dying and Bereavement*, who trusted me to craft the volume as I saw fit with her full support. Every volume editor with a vision should enjoy such freedom. I also appreciate the tireless (or at least uncomplaining!) efforts of Elizabeth Crunk, my onetime student who has gone on to pursue her own dreams of becoming a counselor, but who selflessly contributed countless hours of administrative and editorial support for this immense project. Those readers who find the index to be a trove of useful connections will owe a debt to her. Kirsty Holmes likewise ensured that the typeset book was as visually appealing and free of errors as conscientious attention to the manuscript could make it, and a special thanks is due to my artist friend, Lisa Jennings, for her generous willingness to share her visually intriguing, spiritually inflected art as the cover of this book, invoking not only the hardship of the sojourn through grief, but also the companionship and hoped-for destination that make it sustainable. Her work calls to me like a song, as I hope it will as well to other readers of the volume. Finally, and fundamentally, I want to express my heartfelt gratitude to the hundreds of clients who have allowed me to walk alongside them through the darkest valleys of their despair, and especially to those who gave explicit permission for me to include their stories, and sometimes their words, in the vignettes that animate several of the chapters. It is their voices that will carry the emotional truth of loss and its transcendence beyond the pages of this clinical anthology and into the lives of others who struggle with similar decimation, across the bridge of inspired practice by the clinicians who read these accounts. It is deeply satisfying to anticipate this outcome.

Robert A. Neimeyer, PhD
February, 2012

Part I
Framing the Work

Presence, Process, and Procedure
A Relational Frame for Technical Proficiency in Grief Therapy

Robert A. Neimeyer

In an important sense, it is not a question of what grief therapy techniques do for a bereaved client; it is the question of what bereaved clients (and therapists) do with the techniques that counts. And so it seems appropriate to open this book with a consideration of the broader relational framework that provides a "container" not only for our client's grief, but also for the specific procedures we offer to express, explore and ease the experience of loss. My goal in this chapter is therefore to suggest that therapeutic *presence* provides the "holding environment" for a responsive grief therapy, within which attention to therapeutic *process* attunes the therapist to that unique juncture where a client's need meets his or her readiness for a particular intervention in a particular moment of interaction. Nested within these larger and more ample containers like Russian dolls, specific *procedures* have a potentially powerful place in the overall project of counseling or therapy. Divorced from these larger contexts, however, stand-alone techniques lose much of their potency; they become merely a random concatenation of methods whose relevance to a particular loss remains uncertain, uncoordinated and unconnected to the durable thread of coherence that characterizes effective therapy.

My goal in these pages is to frame these issues, in keeping with the spirit of the broadly humanistic and specifically constructivist tradition of psychotherapy that is my home base (Neimeyer, 2009a). I trust, however, that readers from many disciplines will recognize the counterparts of these concepts in their own traditions, be they analytic, systemic, cognitive behavioral, spiritual or simply grounded in their intuitive sense of the common factors that tend to underpin healing human interactions, across and beyond the counseling professions as such. I will begin with the most fundamental of these factors, therapeutic presence, and progress to process and procedure in turn.

PRESENCE

Therapy begins with who we are, and extends to what we do. That is, bringing *ourselves* to the encounter, as fully as needed, is the essential precondition for all that follows, that distinctive blend of processes and procedures that broadly defines a given therapeutic tradition and more specifically defines our own therapeutic style. Here, I want to emphasize the foundational quality of therapeutic presence, the way in which the offer of full availability to the client's concerns, undistracted by other agendas, grounds the work by offering a reflective audience to the telling and performance of the client's grief narrative, allowing both (or in the case of family or group therapy, all) participants to take perspective on current conundrums in fresh ways.

Attending from self to other

In this conception, the presence of the therapist does not "crowd out" attention to the client, or even compete with it in a direct sense, as in implying that therapists should be particularly self-disclosing in their work, or offer clients object lessons from their own lives and losses. Instead, it more typically implies a kind of *from–to* attention, as the therapist attends from his or her sense of self to the person of the client. It is precisely this form of "personal knowledge" that is described by the philosopher of science Michael Polanyi, in which the knower holds him- or herself in subsidiary awareness while retaining a focal attention on the other (Polanyi, 1958). For example, in one memorable grief therapy session I found myself conducting a (minimally) guided imagery exercise with a client who was grieving the loss of her mother (Neimeyer, Burke, Mackay, & Stringer, 2010). Inviting her to close her eyes with me, I asked her to scan her body for a felt sense (Gendlin, 1996) of how she was holding the loss, slowing the pace of my instructions to encourage a "loosening" of her meaning-making from the more clipped, "tightened" discourse of our previous therapeutic conversation (Kelly, 1955/1991). What emerged was remarkable: with a beatific smile she quickly gestured toward the space around her head, and described a radiant, warm light that seemed to be coming to her from above, beginning to shroud her head and shoulders. Noticing tingles of warmth rippling down my own spine and into my body, I then invited her to allow the light to enter her and envelop her body more completely. As she did so, she brightened still more, nearly laughing, and described a delightful tickling in her abdomen, a sensation strongly reminiscent of how her mother would tickle her when she was a little girl. As we closed this period of inward attention, she described the remarkable sense of peace and connection to her mother that she felt and voiced a clear conviction that her mother was with her still, but in an oddly spiritual/corporeal way. I would argue that my own sympathetic "channeling" of the client's experience—something that occurs for me in the great majority of sessions at cognitive, emotional, and often palpably physical levels—represents precisely the sort of *from–to* knowing that usefully orients me to the client's position and to potentially therapeutic "next steps" in our work together.

Relating respectfully

In keeping with the collaborative, reflective and process-directive approach that is central to a meaning reconstruction approach to grief therapy (Neimeyer & Sands, 2011), the stance of the therapist is one of respectful, empathic engagement in the client's evolving narrative of self and world. The therapist does not decide what meanings will be reconstructed and which will be reaffirmed in the wake of loss, but instead assists clients in recognizing incompatible old meanings or constructs and works with them as they endeavor to find alternatives. Significantly, this is not typically a very "cognitive" process in the usual sense, as the assumptive world that is challenged by profound loss scaffolds our core sense of identity, purpose and relationship. In particular, for clients with deeply disturbed personal histories, the heart of psychotherapy may consist in offering them a reparative relationship in which they are able to risk letting the therapist have access into their core understanding of self (Leitner & Faidley, 1995). The creation of this *role relationship* (in which one person attempts to construe the deepest meaning-making process of another) is vital, as both client and therapist seek to establish a reverential relationship that acknowledges the uniqueness of the other. This reciprocal connection does not necessarily imply that the therapist discloses personal *content* in the therapeutic relationship—although this is not precluded when clinic-ally or humanly indicated. But it certainly makes room for the disclosure of the therapist's *process responses* to the client's behavior (e.g., feeling moved by a bereaved client's coura-geous acknowledgement of his profound loneliness, or feeling distanced by a client's shift toward apparently superficial content), which can play a useful role in fostering client aware-ness and enhancing the intensity of the therapeutic connection.

Although this sort of receptive presence might seem to have mystical overtones, it can be rendered in other terms as well. Among the most adequate is Buber's evocation of an *I–Thou* relationship with the other (Buber, 1970), which presumes an essentially sacred attribution of full personhood to the other, in contrast to an *I–It* relationship which casts the other as simply an object to be acted on for our own purposes. In more secular terms it also resonates with the cardinal role of therapeutic *empathy, genuineness* and *unconditional positive regard* given particular emphasis by the honored tradition of humanistic psychology, and most especially by Carl Rogers (Rogers, 1951). But I find that Polanyi's description adds usefully to such formulations because it highlights the necessary presence of the self in the relational knowing that is therapy, as the implicit *ground* from which our awareness is directed to the explicit *figure* of the client's words or actions. Interestingly, I think that the self of the thera-pist functions in a similar way for the client as well, as he or she attends from the therapist's questions or instructions to his or her own material. Thus, for both, the therapist's presence serves as a clarifying lens that brings into greater focus (inter-)personal patterns and processes that are more difficult to observe in the client's private reflections. Contributions to the present volume that underscore the importance of mindfulness in both therapist and client clearly resonate with this conception.

Some relevant data

Interestingly, empirical research on a large number of bereavement and end-of-life profes-sionals accords with the centrality of therapeutic presence as a foundational feature in responsive grief therapy (Currier, Holland, & Neimeyer, 2008). Responding to open-ended questioning about how they helped bereaved clients make sense of their losses, nearly half (41.2%) of the participants discussed ways that they practice presence with mourners by emphasizing the quality of the relational environment as a crucial determinant of meaning-making. In particular, 16.0% of the participants explicitly stressed the quality of the relation-ship with the bereaved, noting that "I let the client know that they can tell me anything" and "I provide for my patients and their families a safe holding environment." About a quarter of the sample (26.1%) highlighted the relevance of empathic attunement. Examples of responses that fell within this second basic category included: "Listen, listen, listen;" "I attempt to validate the patient's feelings;" and "Being present to their pain." Lastly, 15.1% of the participants emphasized the centrality of respect and not casting judgment. For instance, practitioners shared that "[meaning-making] is all dependent on the degree of the client's readiness" and "I try to go to where the person is in their journey rather than where I might want them to be." By offering a safe container for the client's grief and its expression, therapists offer the precondition for its transformation as well.

PROCESS

If therapist presence sets the stage for psychotherapeutic work, *process* is the medium in which the drama of therapy unfolds. Extending this metaphor, an effective grief therapist attends to unfolding action in the consulting room much as a director might attend to a theatrical performance, with the crucial exceptions that the director him- or herself is also an actor on the stage, and there is no script for the enactment! Instead, in the improvisational theatre that is counseling, the therapist subtly directs the process by attending to signals of possible extension, elaboration or intensification of the action or emotion in promising directions, sometimes through explicit instructions or suggestions, but more commonly through her or his own responsiveness to the client's "lines" or performance. This attention to the unfolding "give and take" of interaction is what opens the possibility for timely suggestions regarding therapeutic techniques, like many of those included in this volume.

Following the affect trail

A basic orientation to process carries several implications for the practice of grief therapy as a moment-to-moment transaction between two (or more) people. The first can also be stated as a guiding principle: *Follow the affect trail.* That is, significant emotion, even (or especially) when subtly present, typically defines the growing edge of the client's experiencing—the shadow of sadness that portends looming loss, the static of anxiety that announces a sense of abandonment, the spark of pride that attends a client introducing us to stories of a deceased loved one. In each instance the feeling tone underpinning the client's experience in the moment is palpably present in his or her language of gesture, proxemics, verbal, co-verbal and nonverbal expression. Simply articulating this implicit emotion and inviting elaboration ("I notice that your jaw is trembling as you say that. What's happening for you right now?" or "If those tears could speak, what would they tell us?") is often enough to deepen the client's self-awareness, prompting symbolization of new meaning as a precondition to its further negotiation. Contributions in subsequent chapters that focus on sensing, labeling and modulating significant emotion accord with this principle, as do those that foster attention to the body as a locus of felt meanings.

At some points, however, emotion and other modalities (such as imagery or narrative) can be so closely inter-braided that drawing forth one automatically brings with it the other(s). An illustration of this arose for me in a recent session of therapy with a lonely client grieving the death of her father after a long lapsed relationship that recently had been rekindled (Neimeyer et al., 2010). Altered by her statement that she felt like there was "a sheet of Plexiglas" between herself and others, I asked her to close her eyes and visualize that Plexiglas and her relation to it. As she did so, she described it as an "octagonal enclosure" in which she found herself alone, with others as shadowy figures passing by on the outside. When I enquired whether the enclosure had a ceiling of some sort, she replied that it did not, that it was open at the top. Visualizing the scene myself, and getting more details of her positioning in relation to the walls ("sometimes touching them, but never able to get through"), I inquired as to their height. She responded without hesitation: "Eight feet." "Hmm . . ." I wondered, "Eight feet, and eight walls in the enclosure . . . Does the number *eight* have a special significance for you?" Immediately my client burst into tears with a slight gasp, and responded, "Yes—my father died on the 8th!" The seemingly unbreakable, unbridgeable walls in which she felt encased were the walls of her grief, cutting her off from other human contact. Elaborating the image a bit more, she described the enclosure as an aquarium and herself as the fish observing and being observed by a world beyond her reach. She eagerly accepted my suggestion as the session ended that she might write a short metaphoric story with the title *Life in the Fishbowl* as a means of extending the image, its associated feelings and meanings into our conversation the following week.

Whether emotion is given attention in its pure physical expression or in the way it resonates through a significant story or image shared in therapy, it is viewed as being rich in significance from a meaning reconstruction standpoint. For example, personal construct theorists interpret emotions as clues to incipient shifts in our core constructs for maintaining a sense of self and relationships (Kelly, 1955/1991), as when a client's anxiety in the aftermath of loss suggests that he or she is confronting life as a bereaved person without the necessary means of anticipating or making sense of it. More generally, this conception views emotion as a form of intuitive knowing (Mahoney, 1991), rather than as an irrational force to be brought into line with rational evaluations of a situation. In this way we need not see affect, even negative affect, as a problem to be eliminated, controlled, disputed, minimized or simply coped with through distraction, but rather respected as a source of understanding to be validated and explored for what it says about what a client now needs. Several of the expressive interventions outlined later in this volume resonate with this conception.

Privileging experience over explanation

A corollary to the principle of following the affect trail is that *all therapeutic change is initiated in moments of experiential intensity*; all the rest is merely commentary. That is, potent grief therapy interventions need not be heavy-handed, but they entail ushering a client into new awareness, clarity and possibility by engagement in an emotionally significant *experience* of something, not merely a cognitive discussion of it. My imagery work with the woman bathing in radiant connection with her mother was a case in point: once she had had this experience, consolidating it descriptively by (her) framing it as connection with her mother was relevant and useful, harvesting its implications for further reflection. But absent the experience, mere discussion of changed connection with her mother would have been simply abstract discourse, divested of concrete referents or novelty, and ephemeral in its effect. Many strategies to follow in this book, such as those involving imaginal dialogues with the deceased or restorative retelling of the event story of the loss, place a premium on vividly experiential work as a prelude to deeper integration of a loss.

Catching the wave

A further principle governing the therapeutic use of process is *timing*. Descriptively the principle is easy enough to grasp: seek the right intervention at the right moment. Pursuing something too soon, before the client's growing edge is receptive to it, will produce resistance at worst or intellectual or behavioral compliance at best, and pursuing it too late will halt the client's forward momentum and redundantly reaffirm what is already clearly enough grasped or accomplished. The latter represent the cardinal constructivist "sin" of therapeutic *tracking errors* (Neimeyer, 2009a), in which the therapist loses the leading edge of the client's meaning-making, like a surfer who leans too far forward on a wave's crest and is dashed beneath it or who falls too far back, loses momentum, and ends up in a lull. An example of this occurred in my otherwise effective work with a bereaved mother, Darla, who 10 minutes earlier in the session had described how other members of her family retreated in silence from the pain of their shared grief, leaving her alone in wanting to introduce her son back into the family conversation, sharing his memory and the feelings it evoked (Neimeyer, 2004). At the later therapeutic point she had moved beyond this topic to the issue of finding some new way to relate to her suffering, to "not treat it as the enemy." Still preoccupied at some level with the family's lack of openness to sharing the loss, I paused and then said, "It seems important to have people who respect your suffering, the way [your son] might have respected it." Even if the statement were true in some sense, it was poorly timed, and Darla rightly looked at me blankly, added a "Huh . . ." with diverted eyes that suggested she was continuing to pursue her own line of thought. When I then joined her in fuller presence to her process and inquired, "What's the '*huh*'?" she readily accepted my prompting to extend the implications of her comment in strikingly fruitful directions, leading us to enact a dialogue with the suffering, personifying it in keeping with the implicit anthropomorphism with which she had spoken of the need to find a way to "work with" this seeming antagonist. Only with appropriate timing, derived from a close attunement to the client's process, can an intervention find the fertile soil it requires to germinate into fresh possibilities.

Cultivating a sense of timing, as opposed to simply *describing* it, is harder, however. I find that establishing presence, as discussed earlier, goes some distance in this direction, allowing me to notice clearly the gaps, leads, implications and prospects inherent in the client's presentation in each and every speaking turn, at levels that are enacted as much as narrated. But in addition to this basic noticing I find it useful to orient to the implicit question, "What does my client need, now, in this moment, to take a further step?" Sometimes, of course, the answer is *nothing*—merely permitting a productive silence to ensue, giving the client space for further processing, in keeping with the careful psychotherapy process research of my colleagues, Frankel, Levitt, Murray, Greenberg, and Angus (2006). But even this form of patient waiting is a response, as is the raised eyebrow, the knowing smile, the forward lean, the wrinkled brow that in their various ways represent an invitation to continue or say more. Like the more obvious interventions of questions, prompts or instructions, all of these require an intuitive read of their appropriateness in the present moment with and for the client. I find Jung's definition apt here: "the intuitive process is neither one of sense-perception nor of thinking, nor yet of feeling . . . [but rather] is one of the basic functions of the psyche, namely *perception of the possibilities inherent in a situation*" (Jung, 1971). Therapy is most effective when it intuitively seeks, finds and grafts onto this emergent sense of possibility. Methods covered in the following pages that inquire about what the client is ready or unready to change or engage respect this principle of timing, just as many of the indications and contraindications that preface each technique attend to its appropriateness at a given point in the grief journey.

Harnessing the power of the poetic

A further principle of process might be phrased as: *Speak poetically, rather than prosaically, for maximum impact.*[*] Of course, much of therapeutic discourse is necessarily practical, descriptive and representational—staying close to the language of everyday life (and of the client) in order to intelligibly engage the mundane realities of the client's life world. But a therapy that does not at least occasionally lift above this to highlight or offer a less literal, but richly imagistic depiction of the client's problem, position or possibilities fails to *transcend the obvious* (Kelly, 1977), that is, not merely to map current realities, but rather to foster their transformation by casting them in fresh and figurative terms.

Although the therapist's use of poetically vivid formulations can often be powerful in this sense, they can also fail if they do not meet the twin tests of following the client's affect trail and being well timed, as elaborated earlier. An antidote for this over-eagerness on the part of the therapist is to attend to the *quality terms* resident in the client's speech,[†] those turns of phrase that reveal his or her position with special clarity and precision. Such terms are typically signaled in any or all of three modalities: the client's use of metaphor, coverbal inflection (as through variations in prosody or intensity of speech), or nonverbal

---

[*] In recent years I have been taking myself more literally in this respect, out of the therapy room as well as in it. Two results are *Rainbow in the Stone* (Neimeyer, 2006) and *The Art of Longing* (Neimeyer, 2009b), both collections of poems that often arise from my clinical contact with bereaved clients, as well as with the broader world.

[†] I owe this term to my colleague, Sandy Woolum, a practicing therapist and trainer in Duluth, Minnesota.

underscoring by facial expression or gesture. An example arose in my therapy with Susan, who was speaking of the unfamiliar sense of confidence she mustered as she served as family caregiver to her dying mother. In response to my question of how her mother responded to this self-presentation, she acknowledged that her "mom had a hard time accepting, umm . . . this new *façade* of me." Allowing her to finish her elaboration of her new strength, I then returned to the quality term in her statement, signaled by both vocal emphasis and by its highly figurative quality. I began, "A moment ago, you said your mother had a difficult time accepting this new *façade* of you . . .," when she interrupted, "Did I use that word, *façade*?" I assured her she did, and suggested that the word implied a kind of *mask*, something that was only *surface deep*. She replied, "That's true, that's true . . . It was like a new . . . *garment*. But now it's becoming more comfortable" (moving her shoulders and arms, as if breaking in a new jacket). We went on to acknowledge explicitly how the mantle of confidence was now feeling more like *her* and to explore the validation she had subsequently received for this enduring strength from her strongly independent sister and daughters. Methods that harness imagery of a non-literal visual, narrative, theatrical or poetic kind in the chapters that follow extend figurative work with a client's position in useful directions.

Some relevant data

How commonly do bereavement counselors attend to the emotional, narrative, temporal and figurative dimensions of the therapy process? Data from the study cited earlier suggest that they do so frequently (Currier et al., 2008). Among those surveyed, 13.4% discussed integration or finding meaning in the loss in broad terms. For example, one participant reported using "integrative work to help patients process their loss and to incorporate the meaning of that experience into their cognitive and spiritual schemas." Almost a quarter (23.5%) relied on storytelling, such as those who help the bereaved to "share stories of life together before the death and life since the loss" and "encourage them to tell their stories and to describe the actual death." A smaller percentage of the sample (7.6%) focused on uncovering benefit or a paradoxical silver lining that can sometimes be found in the loss experience: "I try to evaluate what sense of fulfillment can be gathered from this loss." Several participants (9.2%) stressed the centrality of emotional expression in their work, stating that "I facilitate the sharing of feelings regarding the loss." A larger percentage (16.0%) reported focusing on the spiritual or existential significance of the loss by encouraging the client or patient to "look at their own mortality in the spiritual realm" or "fit [the loss] into their picture of God and the world." EOL practitioners (9.2%) also reported transmitting a sense of hope by "punctuating choices or new directions," "moving or looking to the future," and "goal setting." Finally, others (5.0%) attempted to facilitate a continuing bond or lasting connection for the bereaved: "I focus on the individual's relationship with the deceased person and how the relationship may be continued." Numerous techniques in the chapters that follow reflect attention to these processes.

PROCEDURE

Finally, of the triad of therapeutic practices outlined here, procedure is the most concrete. Whereas *presence* places the alert and responsive therapist fully in an intersubjective field shared with the client, and attention to *process* characterizes their subtly shifting ongoing communication, concrete therapeutic *procedures* address specific goals and draw upon identifiable change strategies. These, of course, are the focus of the cornucopia of techniques of which this volume is chiefly comprised, each accompanied by an illustration of its use in a concrete clinical context.

The range of techniques considered and the scope of their application are impressive, and subject to any of a number of means of organizing them by population, purpose or procedural features. Here, I have grouped them into clusters based on their "family resemblance" under broad headings bearing mainly on their therapeutic intention or goal, more than surface characteristics of the techniques themselves (e.g., whether they involve writing or imagery, apply to adults or children, or represent one theory or another). Hence, after Part I, Framing the Work, subsequent chapters on technique are aggregated into sections: Part II, Modulating Emotion, Part III, Working with the Body, Part IV, Transforming Trauma, Part V, Changing Behavior, Part VI, Reconstructing Cognition, Part VII, Encountering Resistance, Part VIII, Finding Meaning, Part IX, Rewriting Life Narratives, Part X, Integrating the Arts, Part XI, Consolidating Memories, Part XII, Renewing the Bond, Part XIII, Revising Goals, Part XIV, Accessing Resources, Part XV, Grieving with Others, Part XVI, Ritualizing Transition, and Part XVII, Healing the Healer.

Some relevant data

The findings of Currier and his colleagues suggest that techniques such as those covered in these pages are popular among practitioners. About a quarter of the sample surveyed (26.9%) mentioned using specific narrative techniques, such as journaling, life review or letter writing, or made use of empty chair or imagery-based dialogue with the deceased. Over a tenth (11.8%) reported implementing rituals around death and dying, which included both religious and secular memorial services such as planting a bulb or rosebush in honor of their loved one. Of those who espoused a particular theoretical orientation in the sample, 4.2% discussed cognitive-behavioral therapy techniques (CBT; e.g., "relaxation training and guidance," "thought diaries and positive self-talk"), 3.4% expressed an allegiance to psychodynamic methods (e.g., deriving from object relations or attachment theories), and 3.4% made use of a humanistic perspective (e.g., "looking at personal constructs," gestalt, client-centered). A significant minority (10.9%) assumed a pastoral care role or what was often a distinctively Christian approach. For example, one participant shared using "guided meditation on what the Lord was doing at the time of their loss, guided meditation on the Lord going before them into difficult situations, and inspiration from the Holy Spirit." A similar percentage of practitioners (9.2%) reported focusing on brief practical interventions, including "physical care," helping the client to "sort out their needs," and "practical strategies as needed for living." Finally, of those surveyed, 12.6% indicated implementing procedures that allow for the symbolic expression of thoughts and feelings, including art and play therapy techniques. Thus, there is reason to hope that the current generous trove of technical resources, which encompass each of these methods and many more, will offer a convenient and creative resource to aid professionals of many disciplines seeking a larger toolkit with clients whose lives have been disrupted by loss.

References

Buber, M. (1970). *I and thou*. New York: Charles Scribner's Sons.

Currier, J. M., Holland, J. M., & Neimeyer, R. A. (2008). Making sense of loss: A content analysis of end-of-life practitioners' therapeutic approaches. *Omega, 57*, 121–141.

Frankel, Z. F., Levitt, H. M., Murray, D. M. Greenberg, L. S., & Angus, L. E. (2006). Assessing psychotherapy silences: An empirically derived categorization system and sampling strategy. *Psychotherapy Research, 16*, 627–638.

Gendlin, E. T. (1996). *Focusing-oriented psychotherapy*. New York: Guilford.

Jung, C. G. (1971). The structure of the psyche. In *The portable Jung* (pp. 23–46). New York: Viking.

Kelly, G. A. (1955/1991). *The psychology of personal constructs*. New York: Routledge.

Kelly, G. A. (1977). The psychology of the unknown. In D. Bannister (Ed.), *New perspectives in personal construct theory* (pp. 1–19). San Diego, CA: Academic.

Leitner, L. M., & Faidley, A. J. (1995). The awful, aweful nature of ROLE relationships. In R. A. Neimeyer, & G. J. Neimeyer (Eds.), *Advances in personal construct psychology* (Vol. 3, pp. 291–314). Greenwich, CT: JAI Press.

Mahoney, M. J. (1991). *Human change processes.* New York: Basic Books.

Neimeyer, R. A. (2004). *Constructivist psychotherapy* [video]. Washington, DC: American Psychological Association.

Neimeyer, R. A. (2006). *Rainbow in the Stone.* Memphis, TN: Mercury.

Neimeyer, R. A. (2009a). *Constructivist psychotherapy.* London & New York: Routledge.

Neimeyer, R. A. (2009b). *The art of longing.* Charleston, SC: BookSurge.

Neimeyer, R. A., Burke, L., Mackay, M., & Stringer, J. (2010). Grief therapy and the reconstruction of meaning: From principles to practice. *Journal of Contemporary Psychotherapy, 40,* 73–84.

Neimeyer, R. A., & Sands, D. C. (2011). Meaning reconstruction in bereavement: From principles to practice. In R. A. Neimeyer, D. L. Harris, H. Winokuer, & G. Thornton (Eds.), *Grief and bereavement in contemporary society: Bridging research and practice.* New York: Routledge.

Polanyi, M. (1958). *Personal knowledge.* New York: Harper.

Rogers, C. (1951). *Client-centered therapy.* Boston: Houghton Mifflin.

2

The Empathic Spirit in Grief Therapy

Jeffrey Kauffman

Like the previous chapter, this one is concerned with presence in grief therapy, emphasizing the empathic spirit of the therapist as the foundation of the clinical process of facilitating mourning. This stance is the ground of the therapeutic relationship, constituting the therapeutic space within which diverse techniques may be deployed to focus and carry out the specific work of processing the experience of loss. My primary concern in this chapter is to describe the empathic presence of the grief therapist, and how it functions as an intervention, while also framing other specialized techniques.

THE THERAPEUTIC MATRIX

Above all else, the therapist's presence is grounded in his or her openness, receptivity and attunement to the client's grief. Within the matrix of the therapeutic relationship, the client experiences his or her grieving self through the therapist's responses—a potentially powerful point of connection between one suffering human being and a responsive witness. This empathic grasping of the client's experience of loss is the most implicit and fundamental dimension of the therapeutic process.

"Being there" with the mourner is sometimes called listening or empathic listening, but the receptive organ is not merely the ear that hears the words of the patient. Instead, this is the therapist's disciplined receptivity to the grief the client brings to treatment, through the way in which the mourner experiences the grieving self in his or her relationship with the grief therapist. The presentation of grief by the client—overtly and in the shadows, verbally and between the lines, silently and through speech, in words and in action—in conjunction with the reception of grief by the therapist—this is the "scene of presence" where the therapeutic pair meet. In this meeting place, the client is present in bringing his or her grief and in experiencing the therapeutic partner's experience of the grief. This empathic engagement between the grief therapist and the mourner is a process in which the therapist, in being open, receptive and attuned to the client's distress, provides a container in which the client may safely experience a pain that had in some way been closed off and stuck within.

THE MYSTERY

The relational dynamic activated by the therapist's receptivity to the client's grief operates as the ground for therapeutic interaction. However, the relationship itself and the client's experience of self in the presence of the therapist are an implicit dimension, and this does not disclose itself explicitly. Being open to and respecting the implicit and hidden dimension is the chief concern of this account of presence. The being or meaning of presence turns out to be a mystery, beyond what we can see or say. And the "being there" of the grief therapist for the client, being near to the great mystery of being human, is an openness to a sacred space, a space in which the mourner wanders, disconnected from everyday, professional, scientific and commercial worlds and their meanings. In the therapist's empathic presence, the self searching and wandering inwardly in an ineffable space of grief, is helped to find itself and to find its way.

The pain of grief also involves a dimension that is beyond symbolization. The particulars of grief-related pain articulated over the course of grief therapy are expressions of a wound that goes to the invisible core of existence. In being present to the other in grief, the therapist stands in the presence of the mystery of loss and bonding, of death and life. The client's pain has a dimension that is too sacred, powerful and frightening to show itself, but that is grief's invisible core. Likewise, the therapeutic relationship involves a dimension that stands outside the symbolic representations of thought and language. This is not to treat a natural process of human connectedness as something exotic or mythic, but simply to acknowledge the depths and mysteries occurring live, as it were, in this relational field for processing grief.

As a receptive organ, the grief therapist is attuned with what Freud dubbed "free-floating attention," which is a technique of listening in which attention is not attached to particular meanings, but instead is open to meanings only indirectly suggested by the client's speech. It is listening for what is there but not present in the client's consciousness of him- or herself. Free-floating attention describes a way of receiving the unknown calling forth from the presence of the grieving client.

Being receptively present involves absorption in the emotional narrative of the mourner, attuned to what is emotionally expressed by the client. Being present with the mourning client involves a tolerance for not knowing, for being close by the mystery, the unknown, merely adumbrated by the story and the emotions of the client. It is not just the object of attention in grief therapy that retains a mysterious horizon; the process is itself full of mysteries. While filled with the presence of the grieving client, the therapist is in the surround of mysteries. In the presence of the power hidden in and defining the therapy relationship, grief therapy is awake to the mystery that informs, yet exists outside of art and science. The presence of the grief therapist is awakened in openness, love and awe by the nearness of the unknown that overwhelms consciousness and sets mourning in motion.

MIRRORING, HOLDING AND BEARING WITNESS

This view of therapeutic presence resonates with a view of the basic human bond as the medium through which identity is formed and social connection is nurtured. Like a mirror, the other's experience of us lets us experience ourselves, and when those selves are grieving, we receive this attention as permission to mourn and ultimately to transform the pain into a new sense of self. By being receptive to and registering the client's grief, as a mirror through which the client may experience his or her grieving self, the therapist validates, authenticates and sanctions the pain of grief and the self of the griever.

Such attentiveness may also be understood as *bearing witness*. Even with social support, the pain of grief may exist in a deeply isolating way. Bearing witness liberates the client from the shame and aloneness grief can engender, and this facilitates mourning. From another angle, Winnicott (1960, 1967) names this relationship "holding"—a relationship between a holder (that is, a mother or a therapist) and the other who is becoming, that is, developing or healing. The grief therapist as a "holder" or container embraces the emotional life of the grieving client. The guiding question of the therapist in holding the grief of the client is, "What is the pain?" The empathic presence of the therapist to the pain of the client is the necessary and sufficient condition of grief therapy, as in Rogers' (1961) account of psychotherapy in general. "Being present, fully present and fully human with another person [is] healing in and of itself" (Gellar & Greenberg, 2002; also, cf. Sheppard, Brown, & Graves, 1972).

THE SELF-CARE OF THE GRIEF THERAPIST

This work requires taking care of oneself as a therapeutic instrument. But it is not the instrumentality of the therapist's self so much as its presence to the client that concerns us here. In "being there" with the client, we are moved. Our own wellbeing and our ability to be receptive and attuned are two edges of the same self-care process of staying open to and in touch with oneself in experiencing the pain of the client.

Taking care of oneself is built into the process of being present. Self-care work is based in being in touch with oneself, open within oneself to the fullness, the nuances, the dissonances, the pain that is there in one's experience of the client's grieving self. Inwardly, as needed, during, and between treatment sessions, the therapist is attentive to his or her own reactions—sometimes implicit in our perceptions, sometimes as an affect or thought or afterthought and, sometimes as an anxiety or a defense. By regarding these self-observations as questions to be answered, the therapist sets in motion a process of self-care. For the grief therapist, this is a site of open-ended personal and professional growth and learning possibilities. Taking care of oneself helps to develop and maintain the ability to be present with the client's grief. We all have anxieties, defenses, blind spots and dead spaces, and places where we are closed to the pain and meaning of the client's grief. Being open to awareness of this and processing these clinical experiences, strengthens presence, tunes intuition, and improves the flexibility of responsiveness. The spirit of presence in the grief therapist needs to be cared for by processing one's own experience, so that one's own needs, anxieties and defenses do not close off pathways of receptivity.

IN THE SPIRIT OF GRATITUDE

The vital principle, the spirit that animates the grief therapist's receptivity, presence, openness, interest and concern in relationship with the mourner is *gratitude*. Gratitude entails appreciating the meaning and value of the client's grief. As host, the therapist welcomes the client just as he or she is, full of grief; assuring the stranger that this pain is welcome and safe, that the vulnerable self has a place to be, and the mortal humanity of the griever will be sheltered. Gratitude is a spirit of receptivity that does not defend itself against the grief of the client; it welcomes and provides grief with a safe haven. Gratitude expresses giving *and* receiving a gift in reciprocity. In receiving from the client expressions of grief, the very reception is giving a gift in return. Receiving with gratitude expresses to the client a sense of the value and meaning of his or her grieving self. The receptive spirit of gratitude provides a place and a container.

There is a *reciprocity* of gratitude in honoring the other—in being privileged to receive the opening up of the griever and in the privilege of having one's opening up implicitly received as an honor. Gratitude sustains reciprocal obligations, observes Simmel (1950); that is, gratitude is a way of receiving that gives back. It is a prosocial emotion that begets prosocial behavior (Bartlett & DeSanto, 2006). The therapist's spirit of gratitude helps to sustain both the grieving client and the therapist.

Gratitude is a sanctuary for the fear and shame of the mourner, and helps to de-stigmatize the mourner; the therapist's gratitude in receiving the grief of the mourner helps provide safe passage for the mourner on their mutual journey of processing loss. It may affect not only the loss that is acutely grieved, but also the life processing of loss that is at the heart of meaning-making and identity. In this sense, the empathic spirit with which the therapist receives the presence of the grieving client is an opening of the heart, which honors the other and helps to secure and maintain their connection. In the end, the mutuality of gratitude in grief therapy is like a state of grace; it operates in a gift economy in which there is no debt. Embodied, and in relation to our own death, we are, however, in need of recognizing imperfections of our gratitude and its limits, including the inevitable limits in our capacity as therapists to hold empathically the suffering of our grieving clients.

References

Bartlett, M. A., & DeSanto, D. (2006). Gratitude and prosocial behavior. *Psychological Science, 17*, 319–325.

Gellar, S. M., & Greenberg, L.S. (2002). Therapeutic presence: therapists' experience of presence in the psychotherapy encounter. *Person-Centered and Experiential Psychotherapies, 1*, 71–86.

Rogers, C. R. (1961). *Becoming a person*. Boston: Houghton Mifflin.

Sheppard, I., Brown, E., & Graves, G. (1972). Three-on-ones (Presence). *Voices, 8*, 70–77.

Simmel, G. (1908/1950). *The sociology of Georg Simmel* (K. H. Wolff, ed. and trans.). Glencoe, IL: Free Press.

Winnicott, D. W. (1960). The theory of the parent–child relationship. *International Journal of Psychoanalysis, 41*, 585–595.

Winnicott, D. W. (1967). Mirror-role of the mother and family in child development. In P. Lomas (Ed.), *The predicament of the family* (pp. 26–33). London: Hogarth.

3

Selah

A Mindfulness Guide through Grief

Joanne Cacciatore

Since the 1990s, a burgeoning number of clinicians have actively engaged in mindfulness-based interventions (MBI), to improve outcomes both for clients and for themselves. While initial evidence of the efficacy of MBI was primarily anecdotal (Kabat-Zinn, 1982), the empirical data in its support is gradually mounting in the areas of mindfulness-based stress reduction, dialectical behavioral therapy, acceptance and commitment therapy, and mindfulness-based cognitive behavioral therapy (Hoffman, Sawyer, Witt, & Oh, 2010). Yet, despite the potential for its utilization, few mindfulness-based paradigms have been proposed for bereavement counseling. The Selah Grief Model is a mindfulness-based, guided intervention that recognizes two foci: self and other. The term *selah* itself derives from the Hebrew word *celah*, often noted in the book of Psalms to remind the reader to pause, reflect, and contemplate meaning.

Generally, traumatic grief during early therapy manifests in a state of intense existential suffering. It is imperative, then, that clinicians establish, first and foremost, a safe place wherein clients are able to *be with* their grief, turning toward the loss, allowing the loss to find expression. Here, the goal for the client is to enter an endogenous state of pause, becoming fully attuned to—mindful of—their changing emotional processes through intentional solitude (contemplation), emotional transparency with self and other, and self-compassion and awareness. Self-compassion, for example, has been shown to reduce self-criticism and ruminative tendencies. This may improve an individual's ability to reflect and learn from an experience. A client can be aided toward expression, when ready, through mindfulness-based activities such as weeping, meditation and prayer, bibliotherapy, emotion journaling, eco-connection through "barefoot walkabouts" (see Chapter 88 in this volume), three-minute breathing space or conscious, deep breathing, creative arts (music, arts, poetry, symbols), and help-seeking. Significantly, the cultivation of these capacities for mindful awareness in the client requires a similar cultivation of a grounding mindfulness in the therapist as a foundation for their mutual work (Cacciatore & Flint, 2012).

Once clients have become attuned to their experience, they may be better able to enter a state of therapeutic reflection with the clinician by surrendering to the grief. The mourner's focus vacillates between self (client) and other (children, partner, parents, and others). Often, it is in this state of mind and heart that the client will also learn to trust themselves: they can *be with* their grief, surrender to it, and find their way toward a new normal. Clients, with the gentle shepherding of clinicians, may wish to actively approach the often evolving emotional states, recognizing and honoring each as valid and remaining mindful of the present moment.

This can be achieved through many of the practices described in this volume, such as narrative therapy—telling and retelling the story—and focusing on the associated feelings during each telling of the story more than the facts. Writing out the story, in as much detail as possible, can be a useful clinical homework tool. Alternatively, this can be achieved through a feelings or adjective journal, wherein the client hones in specifically on descriptive words and emotions. A clinician may want to encourage community support groups or faith-based groups (when appropriate) as a way for clients to begin to see the suffering of others. This process can aid in helping the client's heart open to the other. Genograms can be useful in understanding family patterns, and the clinician can engage in empathic mimicry, particularly in family systems which may have been dysregulated or dysfunctional. Many bereaved parents struggle with issues of guilt and shame, thus, one of the most expiating strategies may be reconciliation methods. For example, I use a technique I call *the apology letter*. Here, the bereaved parent writes a letter to the child who died, explaining, with specificity, what he or she would redress, how things could or should have been different, expressing to the child everything that the parent feels went wrongfully unspoken. Then after a period of often profound introspection, the parent begins a letter to him or herself, 'authored' by the child who died. Often the letters are full of forgiveness and compassion directed toward the parent absolving them of responsibility with assurances of an enduring and loving bond.

When parents feel ready, their perspective begins to change, and the emotions surrounding their child's death become qualitatively different. Meaning begins to—very gradually— unfold from the suffering, and having gained some psychological equilibrium, they feel better equipped to turn the heart toward the suffering other or toward a greater calling. It is a process of transforming, not abandoning, painful emotional states. Clinicians can help the bereaved explore and discover, when they are ready, their call toward the greater good. Practices such as random acts of kindness, leading a support group, volunteering, fellowship with like others, gratitude journals, and psychoeducation may all inspire responsible action. The heart is now ready to turn more fully to service toward the other. In a support group, for example, a client may focus on others' stories of loss with less impulse to divulge his or her own story. It is this transformation that will, in the end, help the traumatically bereaved come full circle in the aftermath of the unthinkable. Figure 3.1 summarizes the Selah model.

CASE EXAMPLE

Jim is a 50-year-old father who lost his eldest son, age 23, to suicide nearly three years before seeking therapy. He had attended several support groups in the immediate weeks following his son's death, but never returned because he felt awkward. Jim described himself as dysfunctional, noting that he went to his job every day but had withdrawn from friends and social activities because of what he perceived to be the insensitivity of others toward his loss. Jim had lost considerable weight over the past few years, and suffered from insomnia, nightmares, intense emotional outbursts, paralyzing anger, and intrusive thoughts of the death. Jim often avoided thinking about his son, and even had great difficulty looking at photographs of him, to the point of removing them from the walls of his home. He sought therapy when he realized that the relational quality with his surviving child was diminishing. Jim's first visit lasted two and a half hours, as I focused on listening mindfully to his story, paying homage to the moments of emotional silence between his thoughts, and being mindful not to interrupt his deliberate and unhurried communication style. This helped build trust in this new therapeutic relationship so that Jim felt unrushed, "finally heard and seen," and aware that I was able to tolerate his emotional state, which he described as overwhelming to most others. At last, Jim had his willing witness.

Our first eight to ten sessions focused on allowing Jim to be with his grief unconditionally and non-judgmentally, willing to join him even in what he called the dark places. He learned to be

Cacciatore's Selah Model of Grieving

Self focus	Other focus

Being with grief	Surrendering grief	Doing with grief

State: Pause Goal: Attunement	State: Reflect Goal: Trust	State: Meaning Goal: Responsible action

- solitude
- self-awareness
- self-compassion
- emotional transparency
 	
Practices such as:
- radical mourning
- meditation and prayer
- bibliotherapy
- emotion journal
- barefoot walkabout
- 3 MBS
- autogenics
- sunshine/nature
- telling the story
- poetry, music, chanting,
  symbology, or art
- yoga or qi gong
- gardening
- help seeking
- soma care (nutrition,
  exercise, massage)
	- approaching grief
	- honoring emotional self
	- heightened awareness
	
	Practices such as:
	- radical tolerance
	- radical acceptance
	- retelling the story
	- writing the story
	- ritualizing
	- waking up (living with
	  intention)
	- letters to the dead
	- letters to the living
	- support group for self
	- remembering journal
	- community support
	- remunerative work
		- seeing others' suffering
		  (longlen)
		- calling to a greater
		  cause
		- posttraumatic growth
		
		Practices such as:
		
		- radical change
		- seeking kindness
		- opportunities
		- offering social support
		- support groups for others
		- community service
		- volunteerism
		- seeking awake others
		- gratitude journal
		- psychoeducation

Figure 3.1 The Selah grief model

honest about his current emotional state, trusting that I would accept anything he presented. He began daily quiet time—meditation—starting with ten minutes in both the morning and evening. He kept an emotion journal and realized that a certain symbol, the firefly, represented his son and had special meaning. He began to intentionally look for them throughout the day. During the fifth session, he focused on an amorphous rage he felt. We discussed what mindful rage might look like: (1) recognizing anger/rage as it arose within him while it was happening; (2) approaching the anger with curiosity and openness; (3) asking the question: What is this anger in this moment really about for me?; (4) taking three or more deep, slow breaths; and (5) if those things don't work at that time, walk away from the situation/person. He began using progressive relaxation during times when he felt like "blowing up." By the tenth session, Jim felt substantial relief from the rage, confirmed by his emotion journal, which we reviewed weekly. His sleep patterns began to improve and nightmares ceased. By the 13th session, he had regained eight pounds.

When Jim felt he was ready, we began to more actively approach his grief. This included becoming increasingly aware of the nuanced, sometimes conflicted, feelings around his son's death. In his retelling of the story, Jim recognized a previously undiscovered sense of guilt and shame around his son's suicide. He realized he held a belief that others perceived his son as "weak" and that he hadn't done enough to help him. This unearthed a strong sense of parental responsibility, culminating in a very emotional disclosure: Jim felt his son's death was ultimately his fault. We began a new series of apology letters to Mark wherein Jim expressed his feelings of failure. He detailed the times he wasn't there for Mark and wrote about all the events he'd missed during Mark's childhood. He expressed his regret for not having answered his phone on the day of Mark's suicide. Then he asked Mark's forgiveness. I asked Jim to wait at least 30 minutes, and in the same journal, write a reply from Mark to him. "What would Mark say to you," I asked, "now that you've asked his forgiveness?" This was a seminal and compelling exercise for Jim. He said he "cried until he had no tears left," and that "it felt so good, I could almost hear his voice, saying, 'Dad, I love you.'"

As Jim surmounted some of the guilt and shame, his relationship with his surviving son improved and he began making new friends. He also began attending a support group for bereaved parents every month. He eventually regained all the weight he had lost, and was able to talk about Mark freely, even putting his photos up around the house. About two years after Jim's intake, he expressed a desire to help other bereaved fathers, and he is now a regular volunteer, helping many other grieving parents since. While Jim's journey through grief has not ended, and it likely will never reach a final conclusion, he has developed the skills necessary to allow him to be with his grief, surrender to it, and then do something with it. He has a better chance of living a fulfilling life, one dedicated to serving others. And guiding him mindfully through the process, seeing him through to the other side of traumatic grief, has helped inspire me to continue this very difficult work.

CONCLUDING THOUGHTS

Recent studies have shown that mindfulness-based interventions (MBI) have been used effectively to treat depression, anxiety, and other mood disorders (Hoffman et al., 2010) as well as a host of physiological ailments such as hypertension, chronic pain, and improved brain functioning and immune responses (Davidson, Kabat-Zinn, Schumacher, et al., 2003; Kabat-Zinn, 1982). However, to date, the treatment of clients with traumatic bereavement has been overlooked in the literature on MBI. The Selah Grief Model is such an MBI that promises an enriching relationship between grieving clients and their clinicians: One that unites them during suffering in pause, reflection, and meaning, as mourners find their own path in their own time.

References

Cacciatore, J., & Flint, M. (2012). ATTEND: Toward a mindfulness-based bereavement care model. *Death Studies*, in press.

Davidson, R., Kabat-Zinn, J., Schumacher, J., Rosenkranz, M., Muller, D., Santorelli, S., Urbanowski, F., Harrington, A., Bonus, K., & Sheridan, J. (2003). Alterations in brain and immune function produced by mindfulness meditation. *Psychosomatic Medicine*, 65(2), 564–570.

Hoffman, S., Sawyer, A., Witt, A., & Oh, D. (2010). The effect of mindfulness-based cognitive therapy on anxiety and depression: a meta-analytic review. *Journal of Consulting and Clinical Psychology*, 78(2), 169–183.

Kabat-Zinn, J. (1982). An outpatient program in behavioral medicine for chronic pain patients based on the practice of mindfulness meditation: Theoretical considerations and preliminary results. *General Hospital Psychiatry*, 4, 33–37.

4

Tracking through Bereavement
A Framework for Intervention

Simon Shimshon Rubin

As this book amply demonstrates, there are myriad methods on which clinicians can draw in working with bereaved clients. These range from emotion modulation strategies and mindfulness practices through techniques for renegotiating the continuing bond and honoring the loved one's memory with expressive arts modalities. But given the great range of techniques, how can professionals choose one that is appropriate with a given client, suffering a specific loss, at a particular moment in therapy? My goal in this brief chapter is to illustrate how the Two-Track Model of Bereavement (TTMB; Rubin, 1999) can help therapists coordinate therapeutic interventions in light of the client's needs, by drawing on it for conceptual, assessment and intervention purposes. Bereaved individuals and families typically find this framework helpful as well (Rubin, Malkinson, & Witztum, 2012).

The Two-Track Model of Bereavement looks at the response to loss as requiring people to find a way to continue their lives, as well as to renegotiate the psychological relationship to the person who has died. Track I of the model addresses *biopsychosocial functioning* and Track II focuses on the past and ongoing *relationship to the deceased*. An adaptive response to bereavement will balance attention to the challenges of life with a flexible connection to the deceased. When difficulties in the response to loss occur, they typically reflect some degree of interdependence of the tracks, which is often the case early in bereavement, as well as in a more persistent fashion in cases of complicated grief. Alternatively, difficulties may be manifest on only one of the tracks and assessment and intervention should take this into account. One implication of this is that even in the absence of biopsychosocial difficulties, we cannot assume the bereavement response is adaptive without information on the pre-loss and post-loss experience of the relationship with the deceased. If functioning appears adequate and yet memories of the deceased are rigidly avoided, the determination of positive outcome applies only to Track I. If a full and balanced bond with the deceased is described and yet there are indications of significant difficulty in one or more areas of biopsychosocial functioning, one may speak of positive outcome on Track II and difficulties on Track I. Relationships may seem to be set aside and deactivated, but this is not equivalent to having grieved and reorganized the relationship to the significant person who has died. Assessing for relevant problems in both domains (see Table 4.1) can assist the therapist in conceptualizing the case in a more comprehensive manner, and using this to identify an appropriate intervention, as illustrated in the case example to follow.

Table 4.1 Brief orientation to the Two-Track Model of Bereavement

Track I: Biopsychosocial functioning	*Track II: Relationship to the deceased*
Distressing affects and cognitions (e.g. anxiety, depression)	Degree of preoccupation with loss event and/or the deceased
Somatic distress (e.g. appetite, sleep, sexual dysfunction)	Problematic and/or avoided recollections about the deceased
Trauma indicators (e.g. PTSD)	Over- or under-emotional involvement, closeness vis-à-vis the deceased
Interpersonal problems (in family and other circles of connection)	Negative and conflictual features associated with the deceased
Disruptions in self-esteem, self-system, and self-compassion	Indications of pronounced shock, searching, disorganization and/or minimal reorganiza-
Challenges to general meaning structure	tion when describing the relationship and
Difficulties at work, school and in investment in life tasks	the death
	Diminished or disorganized sense of self when thinking of deceased
	Lack of progress towards memorialization and transformation of the relationship

CASE EXAMPLE

Dan came for therapy two years after losing his son Uri in a car accident to an unlicensed driver with multiple previous driving offenses. A retired government worker, he had few hobbies. Dan suffered from feelings of great sadness, a sense of lethargy, a tendency to anger, sleep difficulty, and general fatigue. He had formerly been a member of a bereaved parents therapy group, and he reported that he had made friends in the organization. Dan had become a public advocate for changes in public safety and driver education. He was a frequent speaker at local and national events connected to driver safety. Dan made it a point to begin his lectures and interviews with stories about his son Uri's accomplishments and the importance that this kind of preventable tragedy be curtailed as much as possible. Dan felt alive and energized only when dealing with his efforts at memorializing his son or acting to change public attitudes to driving. Dan seemed to have relied on these activities to maintain a kind of relationship with Uri, which also reinforced a positive sense of himself.

However, this heavy focus on keeping the memory of Uri alive also had its costs. In particular, Dan's high investment in the relationship with his son placed him at an emotional distance from his other child and from his wife. The preoccupation with his deceased son and the sense of longing were pronounced, but the sense of needing to keep his son in the public eye was most predominant. Dan reported great closeness to his son Uri, with positive emotions and frequent thoughts about him. He was able to give a full and rich story of their lives together with emphasis on the closeness and pleasure they enjoyed together. Dan had little interest in anything that did not relate to Uri.

Formulation and treatment focus

Dan's difficulties on Track I Biopsychosocial functioning difficulties were pronounced. His family interpersonal relationships were impacted by his predominant focus on Uri, he had somatic

complaints, he wept frequently and his sadness was never far from consciousness. The ways he organized his life's meaning and his investment in life tasks were heavily concentrated on things related to the memorialization of his son. His broad biopsychosocial functioning had coalesced in a way that was thoroughly intertwined with his son. On Track II, the ongoing relationship to Uri revealed a rich tapestry of their relationship. His preoccupation and longing were pronounced but these occurred in the context of a positive and rich experience of the years spent together. There was clear access to Uri's life story and to their relationship as parent and child over the years.

On Track I, treatment involved targeting interpersonal relationships with other family members to redirect his focus to close persons. It also involved a plan to include physical activity, exercise, and mindfulness to give him alternative activities and ways to regulate his emotion. The encouragement of the therapeutic relationship also provided him a secure base and emotional support. The focus was on expanding Dan's areas of life interest to provide for a more variegated openness to life. On Track II, treatment left much room for the description and retelling of various aspects of his relationship with Uri and of Uri himself. Individual treatment continued weekly for 1 year and once every two weeks for the second year. With the strengthening of the therapeutic alliance and relationship, Dan became calmer emotionally and less depressed. He worked on his relationship to his wife and some of the pre-loss problems they had were sufficiently resolved to allow them to provide greater support to each other. Dan was able to add some physical exercise to his routine and had taken up gardening as a hobby to calm him. He had also become an advisor to the government commission on pedestrian safety. Dan experienced treatment as a safe place where he could share the things that preoccupied him from session to session. In that supportive context, he renegotiated a number of areas of functioning that broadened his life and gave him a greater sense of calm, even though he continued to feel understandable sadness at the loss of Uri.

CONCLUDING THOUGHTS

In a case such as that of Dan, the Two-Track Model of Bereavement suggests a tapestry in which the strands of biopsychosocial functioning and the relationship with the deceased are interwoven. In this case, the relationship and focus on Uri had come to dominate many areas of Dan's life. His wish to keep alive his son's memory left him in a constant state of alarm and mobilization. Finding ways to recalibrate the resulting emotional dysregulation was part of the Track I intervention. In addition, therapy focused directly on the domains of Track I through emphasizing other aspects of life separate from his connection with Uri, which was also explored and supported (Track II). Without a significant therapeutic focus on his relationship with his son (his feelings of loss and wish to keep alive his memory), Dan would not have been invested in treatment despite his difficulties in functioning. At the same time, a primary focus on his relationship with Uri would not have been sufficient to facilitate many of the behavioral changes that helped Dan emerge from treatment a different man than the one who entered.

Clinical and research utilization of the Two-Track Bereavement Questionnaire (Rubin, et al., 2009) can further our understanding of the interconnection and distinctness of the two domains discussed here and their implications for treatment. Weaving and attending to both tracks in our work in bereavement is recommended, with differing emphases varying depending on the case at hand. Tracking through bereavement using the Two-Track Model of Bereavement as a conceptual aid, clinicians are in a better position to select from the toolbox of techniques offered in this volume those that meet the genuine needs of the clients they are serving.

References

Rubin, S. S. (1999). The Two-Track Model of Bereavement: Overview, retrospect and prospect. *Death Studies*, *23*, 681–714.

Rubin, S. S., Bar Nadav, O., Malkinson, R., Koren, D., Gofer-Shnarch, M., & Michaeli, E. (2009). The Two-Track Model of Bereavement Questionnaire (TTBQ): Development and findings of a relational measure. *Death Studies*, *33*, 1–29.

Rubin, S. S., Malkinson, R., & Witztum, E. (2012). *Working with the bereaved: Multiple lenses on loss and mourning*. New York: Routledge.

Part II
Modulating Emotion

5

Grief Monitoring Diary

Nancy Turret and M. Katherine Shear

CLIENTS FOR WHOM THE TECHNIQUE IS APPROPRIATE

Most bereaved people who experience painful emotions that wax and wane in intensity. The diary is not appropriate for clients who cannot read or write. It should be modified for people who are so avoidant that they feel worse when they monitor their grief, such as by initially monitoring only periods of lowest grief.

DESCRIPTION

The waxing and waning grief emotions are a part of the natural process whereby a person learns to comprehend the finality of the death and its consequences, and to re-envision a future without the loved one. For a minority, this learning process is derailed as they perseverate in the seemingly endless loop of intense longing, yearning, sadness and guilt or frustration that is complicated grief (CG). We use a grief monitoring diary as a core component of Complicated Grief Treatment (CGT) (Shear & Mulhare, 2008; Shear & Gorscak, in press), for clients who experience unremitting suffering and preoccupation for six months, a year or more beyond the death, to a point that it compromises their social or occupational functioning and poses medical and psychological risk. Diaries may also be helpful for clients earlier in the mourning process.

The grief monitoring diary is a table with days of the week listed on the left, as labels for rows, and 5 columns labeled on the top as "Lowest grief," "Situation," "Highest grief," "Situation" and "Average grief" (see Table 5.1). Clients rate their grief intensity on a scale of 0–10, where 0 = no grief at all and 10 = the most grief they have ever felt. We provide a sample diary so people can see what we are looking for. Clients are instructed to observe their grief intensity during the day and then, each evening, to record the highest level of grief, the lowest level of grief and the average level for that day. They are further instructed to make a brief note of the situations in which the highest and lowest levels occurred. Average grief intensity refers to clients' estimates of the overall average for the day and is usually not the arithmetic average of the highest and lowest levels. We discuss the diary in treatment sessions, exploring various emotions that grief typically holds, both negative and positive. We also discuss situations in which a surge in grief occurs as well as those in which grief is lower. Monitoring grief levels helps bring the treatment into the client's daily life. Monitoring also helps people identify negative self-judgments about grief levels and gives the therapist a

Table 5.1 Partially completed Grief Monitoring Diary

Date	Lowest Grief (0–10)	Situation	Highest Grief (0–10)	Situation	Average Grief
8/14	3	Biking in evening	7	Going to bed alone	5
8/15	2	Playing with grandkids	5	Organizing family photos	4
8/16	0	Getting a good night's sleep after working out	4	Finishing photos and sharing them with sister	2

chance to normalize the observation that there are times when grief is higher and lower, and explain that this is the way successful mourning usually progresses. We encourage clients to allow themselves to both experience painful feelings and also to set them aside.

When clients record grief levels, it sometimes becomes apparent that they are confusing feelings of grief with periods of depression or anxiety. Some clients start by labeling any negative feeling as grief, and may be unclear about the distinctions (Zisook & Shear, 2009). We want to discriminate emotions a client is experiencing because we work with them differently. In CGT, we acknowledge and validate feelings of longing and yearning for a deceased loved one, and sadness that they are gone. Memories of the person will always be tinged with these feelings, though over time, memories naturally become more positive and comforting. On the other hand, we work to resolve feelings of guilt, anger, anxiety and depression. Feelings of sadness occur in both grief and depression. However, sadness with grief is focused on missing the person who died. Sadness in depression is focused on a sense of hopelessness and helplessness about oneself, the world and the future. Sadness is a very natural component of grief, while feelings of depression can make it very difficult to come to terms with a loss and renew a sense of vitality in ongoing life. The grief monitoring diary is one way we work with clients to discriminate these different feelings.

CASE EXAMPLE

Helen had been struggling for five years with the death of her 87-year-old mother. She began grief monitoring in session 1 and reported in session 2 that completing the diary had "opened up a Pandora's box of memories." She had noticed frequent fleeting thoughts of her mother that left her feeling badly and worried that recording this was not such a good thing to do. The therapist validated her feelings and suggested that they look at the diary together. As it turned out, the diary helped them identify "stuck points" in her grief. For example, folding a pair of slacks in the laundry reminded Helen of a similar pair of slacks her mother wore when taken to the hospital after a bad fall. When the clothes were returned, they were badly cut. Helen did not see the necessity of cutting the clothes and felt a surge of anger at the hospital. She was very troubled by the apparent disregard for her mother's property. As they discussed this incident, Helen realized that anger about her mother's care often dominated her thoughts. Thinking that her mother was disrespected and treated roughly by medical personnel confused her, increased her sadness about her mother and led her to feel helpless and hopeless about the world.

As Helen and her therapist continued to work with diaries over the ensuing weeks, she became aware that dealing with insurance companies, paying bills, seeing a medical doctor and hearing an ambulance siren similarly triggered anger, along with grief-related sadness. These situations triggered thoughts of her mother's death and evoked a troubling thought that no one really cared. Helen further realized that she felt a great deal of shame and guilt in acknowledging these feelings. Discussion of her shame and guilt brought up memories of traumatic childhood events and Helen talked about how she had struggled all her life to feel comfortable in her own skin. She began to differentiate feelings associated with her mother's death and ones that belonged to other significant life events. As she observed, "I was putting everything in the grief bucket. Feelings of shame and guilt don't belong there. They come from a different place." As treatment progressed, she began to see how shame and guilt affected her self-esteem and feelings of worth, which, in turn, affected her mood. She always thought of her mother when she felt sad, and this tended to bring up the anger with uncaring people, and then the shame and guilt about these feelings.

The diary was also helpful in discussions of positive emotions. Helen could be distracted by activities such as movies and shopping, but disparagingly reported that she was just "escaping into mindless activities" and was ashamed that she let herself do this. Again, her feelings of shame could be linked to her early trauma, and the therapist helped Helen see that pleasant activities were not shameful and were things she had always genuinely enjoyed and that had enriched her life. The therapist shared her own interest in similar activities and they laughed together about a shopping story. The therapist explained that positive emotions are very healthy and encouraged Helen to open herself to experiencing them without self-criticism. They discussed how Helen could use these activities to comfort or reward herself.

CONCLUDING THOUGHTS

Most people with CG are so caught up in the experience of grief that they don't have a clear idea of the variability of grief intensity or the situations in which these occur. When they begin to observe their grief levels, they usually find it interesting and reassuring. Monitoring daily panic results in a moderate, statistically significant reduction in panic frequency. Our experience with conducting evidence-based Complicated Grief Therapy (Shear et al., 2005) suggests that monitoring grief intensity has a similar effect. Reviewing a grief monitoring diary further enables a therapist to validate and support natural grief feelings, clarify and help resolve those issues that lead clients to be stuck in the mourning process, and help people problem solve barriers to fully engaging in ongoing life, especially with respect to openness to positive emotions.

References

Shear, M. K., Frank, E., Houch, P. R., & Reynolds, C. F. (2005). Treatment of complicated grief: A randomized controlled trial. *Journal of the American Medical Association, 293*, 2601–2608.

Shear, M. K., & Gorscak, B. (in press). *Complicated grief treatment.* New York: Guilford.

Shear, M. K., & Mulhare, E. (2008). Completed grief. *Psychiatric Annals, 39*, 662–670.

Zisook, S., & Shear, M. K. (2009). Grief and bereavement: What psychiatrists need to know. *World Psychiatry, 8*, 67–74.

6

Mapping the Terrain of Loss
Grief and Not Grief

Phyllis S. Kosminsky

CLIENTS FOR WHOM THE TECHNIQUE IS APPROPRIATE

Adolescents and adults whose grief experience includes intense and unrelenting emotions that can be differentiated from the pain of loss *per se*, for example, fear, guilt, anger. It may not be suitable in cases of unrelenting guilt concerning the manner of the deceased's death if that guilt is reality based.

DESCRIPTION

Grief is a state that encompasses many emotions: sadness and longing, certainly, but also rage, guilt and fear (Lichtenthal, Cruess, & Prigerson, 2004). Research documents that such feelings as anger are particularly elevated when losses occur through violent death, as in suicide, homicide and fatal accident, when they can often eclipse core emotions associated with grief such as yearning for the deceased (Holland & Neimeyer, 2010). But even when people have experienced a more normative loss, their pain may be compounded by feelings that are not directly related to the death at hand. For example, there may be echoes of earlier losses, or fears triggered by early experiences of neglect. I became aware of how these kinds of feelings can increase the pain of grief when our family dog, our much loved golden retriever Cookie, died at the age of seven, of cancer. We had done everything we could to save Cookie. At the time I told myself that this all-out effort was for my children's sake, but I can easily admit now that I too was willing to try anything to keep her alive. When she died, I was more bereft than I would have imagined possible, truly heartbroken. As I thought about Cookie's life, what came to me repeatedly were memories of her with my children. Throughout his childhood, my son would appear at my bedside every morning with Cookie, and the sight of them side by side never failed to make me feel like the luckiest person in the world. That memory, which had been such a happy one, was now bittersweet. What I came to understand was that my grief was not just about Cookie, but about the end of that golden time in my children's lives—the end of childhood. When I thought about this, I was able to separate the pain of losing Cookie from my pain about my children no longer being little. I was able to feel sadness about missing Cookie, and separately, sadness in knowing that it would not be long before my son and daughter both left for college. When I realized this, my sadness about Cookie became more bearable.

I often reflect on the fact that people who come to us after the loss of a loved one are bringing us a problem that we cannot solve. Perhaps because of the inherent impossibility of relieving the focal point of their pain, I try to find pieces of that pain that I *can* help them resolve. This technique fits in with that orientation. In simple terms, the technique of mapping the terrain of loss involves a series of questions aimed at "separating out" feelings that are experienced (as my feelings about Cookie/my children) in an undifferentiated way. While the questions used are of necessity specific to the client, the following list illustrates the types of questions that would elicit information needed to guide the mapping process.

> *Step 1: Describe the parameters of the present experience:*
> • Who or what has been lost, and what feelings are evoked by the loss?
> *Step 2: Identify related feelings connected with past and/or anticipated events or circumstances:*
> • Besides sadness and missing X, what else are you feeling? When you think about that feeling, what else does it connect with; what else comes to mind? (Maybe another time you felt lonely, or afraid, or something you worry could happen in the future?)
> *Step 3: Amplify the above memory or future fear to connect with the feelings it triggers:*
> • Tell me a bit more about that other experience, or memory, or fear.
> *Step 4: Distinguish feelings that are specific to the current loss and feelings that are intensified by past experience or fears about future difficulties:*
> • Do you think it's possible that some of what you're feeling now might be related to that other, earlier experience? Is it possible that some of what you're feeling now might be fear about the future? How might we help you feel less of that fear? When you think about being more in control of the future, how does that feel?

Needless to say, this process, like much of the work we do, is as much an art as a science. In the case example presented below, the reader will note the point at which the opportunity to "figure out what's grief and what's not" arose, and how the client was encouraged to notice that while her sadness about losing her father was unavoidable, her feeling of fearful powerlessness was not.

CASE EXAMPLE

Joanne was a 52-year-old woman grieving the loss of her father, who had died of a heart attack the previous year. Although she had intermittent periods of engagement with life since his death, as in the completion of a satisfying oral history project some months earlier, she continued to feel "very low" much of the time—a feeling of stagnation, or "just kind of blah," which sapped her enthusiasm and sense of purpose. Exploring this, we soon recognized that her habit of retreating to bed in the face of this feeling provided at best a short-term respite, and in the long term simply reinforced her sense of disengagement. It wasn't that she couldn't identify what might be helpful, such as closer engagement with a new church group focused on prayerful outreach to those in need; it was that, when she focused on it, she began to identify an edge of fear in undertaking new activities. Prompted by our further conversation, Joanne tearfully linked the fear to the absence of her father, who had long been the voice of encouragement for her to try new things, to take risks, to embrace future possibilities.

With this emotional self-awareness in clearer view, Joanne was better able to separate the feeling of missing her father from that feeling of being scared and unsettled when she had to "figure something out for herself," and risk behavioral commitment to it. With this greater clarity she was able to understand that missing her father was an appropriate expression of her grief, and something that need not disable her from confronting her fear of change. Instead, she quickly came to recognize fear as simply the discomfort of having to figure something out, and that discomfort was something she could manage. Having mapped and differentiated her emotional reaction to her father's death, Joanne discovered that the two different feelings, longing for her father and fearing change, called for different solutions: acceptance in the first instance, and recruiting other support figures and drawing on her own resilience in the second. As we looked more closely at current situations where fear was contributing to Joanne's stagnation, she volunteered that she had been considering moving to a new house, but in her father's absence had been too anxious and intimidated by that prospect to take action. However, when we considered who in her life might give her the "push" she needed to begin looking for a new place, Joanne easily identified her friend Linda, whom she imagined would enjoy the process of brainstorming and checking out potential houses. In a single therapeutic session, the static stance associated with Joanne's previous emotional muddle was resolved, and she began searching for a home and engaging with the prayer group soon after.

In this case, differentiating the feeling of loss from the feeling of fear and focusing on the client's personal and relational strengths enabled Joanne to shift her attention from what she had lost to what she still had, and could have, in the future. She was able to identify feelings that had to do with the loss of meaning in her life and fear about not being able to make decisions without her father. While her sadness was an inescapable feature of losing him, her feelings of meaninglessness and fear could be addressed, and at least to a considerable extent, moderated.

CONCLUDING THOUGHTS

In differentiating empirically between grief and depression, Prigerson and her colleagues (2009) have identified yearning for the deceased as the signal characteristic of grief. When we help clients "map" their grief, we are inviting them to treat yearning as its own emotional experience, with a weight and texture different from any of the other emotional components of bereavement. The implicit message is that although the pain associated with yearning is unavoidable, the inescapable consequence of lost attachment, there are, in any loss, factors that contribute to the bereaved individual's suffering that call for different forms of adaptive responding. Guiding clients toward recognition of what they can and cannot change in relation to their loss can produce a subtle but crucial shift in the balance of despair and hope, helplessness and strength. For Joanne, the realization that there were things she could do to help herself feel better provided the spark of motivation she needed to determine a course of action.

References

Holland, J. M., & Neimeyer, R. A. (2010). An examination of stage theory of grief among individuals bereaved by natural and violent causes: A meaning-oriented contribution. *Omega, 61*, 103–120.

Lichtenthal, W., Cruess, D., & Prigerson, H. (2004). A case for establishing complicated grief as a distinct mental disorder in DSV-V. *Clinical Psychology Review, 24*(6), 637–662.

Prigerson, H. G., Horowitz, M. J., Jacobs, S. C., Parkes, C. M., Aslan, M., Goodkin, K, Raphael, B., Marwit, S. J., Wortman, C., Neimeyer, R. A., Bonanno, G., Block, S. D., Kissane, D., Boelen, P., Maercker, A., Litz, B., Johnson, J. G., First, M. B., & Maciejewski, P. K. (2009). Prolonged Grief Disorder: Psychometric validation of criteria proposed for DSM-V and ICD-11. *PLoS Medicine, 6*(8), 1–12.

7

Experiencing the Pain of Grief

Howard R. Winokuer

CLIENTS FOR WHOM THE TECHNIQUE IS APPROPRIATE

This technique can be effective for adults who are working through their grief after the death of someone whom they love, as well as those who are working though non-finite, non-death-related losses. It is most appropriate in early bereavement, when the pain of grief may be most intense, and may be less appropriate at later points, when people have confronted the pain and are attempting to reorganize their lives as survivors.

DESCRIPTION

It seems clear that people can cope effectively with difficult times in their lives; however, there are also times when that just is not the case. An individual may experience a wide range of losses and life events that tax his or her ability to maneuver that difficult road of grief. These losses may include: the death of a loved one, divorce and troubled relationships, losing one's job, traumatic events, miscarriages, infertility and reproductive loss, chronic illness, brain injury, a change in sexual orientation (coming out), etc. (Harris, 2011). It is also important to understand that loss is inevitable; no one is immune. Loss begins at birth with the loss of the security of mother's womb and the cutting of the umbilical cord. We experience many of these losses throughout our lives, people we love die, and then eventually, we die. Again, although coping with some of these issues might not be too difficult, other losses may shock our system so that without professional help our lives spiral out of control and we have a difficult time functioning.

When someone is going through a difficult grief reaction, there can be a wide range of feelings and emotions associated with that loss (Worden, 2009; Worden & Winokuer, 2011). These emotions often throw one out of control and affect a person on a number of different levels: emotional, physical, cognitive, behavioral, and spiritual. This leads many individuals to ask, "Are all these feelings and emotions normal? And, am I going crazy?" Normalizing and expressing such feelings play an important role in Worden's (2009) task model of grieving. Using this framework, the counselor can assess whether the client is stuck in one of four tasks: (1) acknowledge the reality of the loss; (2) experience the pain of grief; (3) adjust to the world without the deceased; and (4) find an enduring connection with the deceased in the midst of embarking on a new life. When one suppresses troubling emotions, they can manifest themselves in physiological symptoms. On many occasions, my clients have difficulty with the second task, in both feeling their pain and expressing their emotions.

One technique I often use with these clients is therapeutic writing. There are many forms that writing make take, including but not limited to letter writing, journaling, storytelling, essays, and more:

> The combination of therapy and writing helps bring out individuals' natural capacities for healing and change. When writing is used as an adjunct to the therapeutic process or as a therapeutic process in and of itself, it is possible to cathart, process, reflect, integrate.
> (Adams, 1999, p. 2)

I typically suggest cathartic, emotionally expressive writing as a homework assignment in order to give clients an opportunity to get in touch with their feelings in a private setting and express things they normally would not when in the presence of another. I then ask the client to bring the writing to the following session and read it aloud. This exercise can promote healing by:

- Helping the bereaved to accept the loss.
- Helping the bereaved to identify and express feelings related to the loss (for example, anger, guilt, anxiety, helplessness, and sadness).
- Providing the bereaved a safe place to share their experiences and feelings.
- Helping the bereaved to separate emotionally from the person who died.
- Providing support and time to focus on grieving.

CASE EXAMPLE

Mr. R., a 70-year-old businessman, came to counseling because of the death of his wife of over 40 years. Mr. R. had struggled with the death because, as a highly successful executive, he felt strongly that he should have done a better job monitoring her illness and caring for her during her dying after a long battle with breast cancer. Mr. R. was a very stoic man who had little use for emotions, let alone expressing his feelings. After his wife's death, he found himself experiencing symptoms of depression. He was very uncomfortable with these feelings and had very little experience in knowing how to process them. He didn't have a vocabulary to verbalize how he felt and his pain seemed to be deeply locked inside of him. It was clear that he had no difficulty acknowledging the reality of his loss, but he had no tools to enable him to express his feelings. With that in mind, I encouraged him to write a letter to his wife telling her about how he felt about her dying, his inability to be there for her and how he has been doing since her death; in reality, this was also a way for Mr. R. to reestablish an ongoing connection with his wife that he so desperately needed to make. He brought in a four-page, heartfelt letter that provided him an opportunity to share with her the thoughts and feelings he had been holding on to since her death. Mr. R. surprised himself as he read the letter out loud and began to cry. This proved to be a very effective technique to help Mr. R. express his feelings. However, he still had a great deal of guilt about the fact that he hadn't been available for Mrs. R. during her dying. I therefore asked him to write a second letter; this time from his wife to him in response to the initial letter that he had written her. When he read the letter at his next session, this three-page letter once again brought tears to his eyes. In this letter, his wife forgave him for his behavior and thanked him for the wonderful years they had together. Over the course of the next two months, Mr. R. drafted six more letters between him and his wife; three from him to her and three from her to him. This release of feelings and emotions was cathartic for Mr. R. Having allowed himself to feel the pain, he was now able to put his wife in a place where he could begin reinvesting himself in living. Since then he has started working as a volunteer executive for a local non-profit organization. He has gained some needed weight, resolved his depression and once again found meaning in his life. This is another example of how helping a client work through the tasks of mourning can provide the foundation for an individual, in spite of a painful loss, to have a full and meaningful life.

CONCLUDING THOUGHTS

Expressing one's feelings after the death of a loved one can be a healing process for the grieving individual and a very effective tool to use in therapy is letter writing (Worden & Winokuer, 2011). This technique has proven effective with many of my clients. One woman wrote a letter to her son who died by suicide and another letter to herself from her son in response to her initial letter. Although this did not alleviate her pain or bring her son back, this exercise provided her with the opportunity to understand why her son made the decision that he made. I'm pleased to say that in each of the previous mentioned cases, the client was able to work through the pain of grief and reinvest in living.

References

Adams, K. (1999). Writing as therapy. *Counseling and Human Development, 31*, 1–16.

Harris, D. L. (2011). *Counting our losses*. New York: Routledge.

Worden, J. W. (2009). *Grief counseling and grief therapy* (4th ed.). New York: Springer.

Worden, J. W., & Winokuer, H. W. (2011). A task based approach to counseling the bereaved. In R. A. Neimeyer, D. L. Harris, H. R. Winokuer, & G. F. Thornton (Eds.). *Grief and bereavement in contemporary society: Bridging research and practice* (pp. 57–67). New York: Routledge.

8

Psychotropic Medication for Grieving Adults

Laura E. Holcomb

CLIENTS FOR WHOM THE TECHNIQUE IS APPROPRIATE

Psychotropic medication can be helpful for some grieving adults experiencing moderate to severe depression, anxiety or insomnia. Medication may also help some adults to better tolerate and complete certain intensive psychotherapy approaches for treatment of complicated grief. However, psychotherapy, not psychotropic medication, is the first line treatment for grief and related psychological difficulties. Psychotropic medication should cautiously be considered as an adjunct for some grievers for whom therapy alone is not adequately addressing symptoms.

DESCRIPTION

Therapists often have concerns about the use of psychotropic medication for grieving adults. They may fear that medication will prevent important processing of grief from occurring. However, available studies suggest that antidepressants do not interfere with the "normal" grieving process (Hensley, 2006; Simon et al., 2008).

About 40% of people meet criteria for a major depressive episode one month after a loss, while about 15% meet criteria one year after a loss (Hensley, 2006). Moderate to severe depression or anxiety after loss may respond best to a combination of psychotherapy and antidepressant medication. Antidepressants may also help some grieving adults to complete some forms of psychotherapy, such as Complicated Grief Therapy, developed by Shear and colleagues, which includes adapted exposure methods that can be challenging for some with high levels of anxiety or depression to tolerate (Simon et al., 2008).

Few studies have focused on the use of psychotropic medication for grieving individuals. The existing research has typically included small sample sizes and has not involved a randomized controlled trial (RCT) model, the gold standard for this type of research. Keeping these limitations in mind, available research suggests that the following types of psychotropic medications may be helpful for some grieving adults (Simon et al., 2008):

- *Selective Serotonin Reuptake Inhibitors (SSRI)*: This class of medication treats both depression and anxiety. SSRIs that have been found effective for bereavement-related Major Depressive Disorder include escitalopram (Lexapro) and paroxetine (Paxil). Other SSRIs, including sertraline (Zoloft), citalopram (Celexa), and fluoxetine

(Prozac), would, theoretically, be just as effective. SSRIs are rarely lethal in overdose. They typically take several weeks or more before improvement is noticed. They can cause sexual side effects (e.g. decreased libido, difficulty having orgasm).

- *Norepinephrine Dopamine Reuptake Inhibitor (NDRI)*: Buproprion (Wellbutrin) treats depression. It can be especially helpful for those who experience lethargy but can exacerbate psychophysiological anxiety. Bupropion does not typically cause sexual side effects. This medication typically takes several weeks to take effect.
- *Tricyclic antidepressants*: Nortriptyline has been found to reduce symptoms of bereavement-related Major Depressive Disorder (Hensley, 2006). Other tricyclics (e.g. imipramine, desipramine) would, theoretically, be just as effective. Tricyclics have often been used at low doses to treat chronic pain. Amitriptyline can also treat insomnia, given sedative effects. Higher doses of tricyclics are generally necessary to treat depression and anxiety. Anticholinergic side effects, such as dry mouth, constipation, dizziness and coordination problems, may be more pronounced in older adults. Tricyclics should be avoided or used with great caution in those with risk for suicide, as they can be toxic in overdose.

Other psychotropic medications which have not been studied specifically for grieving individuals but which may be helpful, include the following:

- *Serotonin Norepinephrine Reuptake Inhibitors (SNRI)*: Venlafaxine (Effexor) and duloxetine (Cymbalta) treat depression and anxiety. They may also be helpful for chronic pain. SNRIs can take several weeks to take effect.
- *Mirtazapine*: This medication treats depression and anxiety. Lower doses are more sedating and can also treat insomnia. It can be good for those with nausea, decreased appetite and associated weight loss but should be avoided in those where weight gain is undesirable. It can take 2–3 weeks to take effect. It does not cause sexual side effects. This medication can be good for older adults.
- *Benzodiazepines*: Clonazepam (Klonopin), diazepam (Ativan), alprazolam (Xanax), and other benzodiazepines are sometimes used for short-term treatment of insomnia or anxiety associated with grief. Risk of physical and psychological dependence, rebound anxiety upon discontinuation, and potential for abuse should be considered. Side effects of cognitive and memory impairment, lightheadedness, and daytime sedation may be more pronounced in older adults because of age-related changes in medication metabolism, and a risk of falls should be considered. Research by Simon, Shear and colleagues (2008) suggested benzodiazepines may be helpful for adults participating in interpersonal therapy (IPT) for grief. However, randomized controlled trial (RCT) research is required to further investigate this possibility.
- *Trazodone*: This is an antidepressant often used in low doses for insomnia. It may be a better choice than some other options (e.g. tricyclics, hypnotic sedatives, benzodiazepines) for insomnia, as it does not result in dependence and is less likely to cause falls in older adults.
- *Hypnotic sedatives*: Medications such as zolpidem (Ambien), eszopiclone (Lunesta) and zaleplon (Sonata) are used for short-term insomnia. The most common side effect is headache. Dizziness, daytime sleepiness, nausea, and memory loss can also occur.

CASE EXAMPLE

Ms. Bee Reaves is a 73-year-old whose husband of 50 years died 6 months ago. The Reaves never had children. They had a number of close friends and sang in their local church choir prior to

Mr. Reaves being diagnosed with colon cancer. Bee was a devoted caretaker during the last year of Mr. Reaves' life. Since Mr. Reaves died, Bee has felt guilty for experiencing a sense of relief from the caretaking role. She has avoided social activity, believing that to resume enjoyable activities would mean that she was forgetting about her husband. She has rarely felt hungry since Mr. Reaves' death, and has lost 20 lbs. She has had trouble sleeping, worrying about finances and taking care of the house by herself, as well as thinking about her husband not being there next to her in bed. She frequently has awoken at 4:00 a.m. and has not been able to return to sleep. Bee admitted to her primary care provider that she was still crying daily, feeling there was nothing to look forward to, and was thinking about ending her life in order to be with her husband. Her primary care provider referred her for psychotherapy, and prescribed a low dosage of mirtazapine. Her sleep and appetite improved. The therapist saw her twice per week during the first 3 weeks to help to manage suicidal ideation. They began work on problem solving related to finances and home maintenance, and on resuming social activity without guilt. After 2 to 3 weeks of taking mirtazapine and working with the therapist, Bee noticed that she was crying less, feeling more hopeful, and no longer had thoughts of killing herself. Her primary care provider discontinued the mirtazapine 6 months after Bee was no longer depressed, and she continued to maintain progress.

CONCLUDING THOUGHTS

Bereaved adults often first seek help from a primary care provider. They or their loved ones may be surprised or even frightened by the intensity of the "normal" grief experience, which can include periods of uncontrollable crying, insomnia, psychophysiological anxiety, and even hallucinatory experiences. These symptoms can be difficult for the primary care provider to distinguish from Major Depressive Disorder, and sometimes may be comorbid. Ideally, a referral to a psychologist or counselor with expertise in grief and loss would occur for further evaluation of symptoms prior to consideration of psychotropic medication. Such a referral may not take place because of patient-perceived stigma of mental health treatment or lack of primary care provider education. Therefore, there is a potential for over-prescribing of psychotropics and under-use of psychotherapeutic treatment for grieving adults. However, psychotropic medications can be helpful when used judiciously.

References and further reading

Hensley, P. L. (2006). A review of bereavement-related depression and complicated grief. *Psychiatric Annals, 36*(9), 619–626.

Lexi-Comp, Inc. (Lexi-Drugs™). Lexi-Comp, Inc., June 25, 2011.

Simon, N. M., Shear, M. K., Fagiolini, A., Frank, E., Zalta, A., Thompson, E. H., Reynolds, C. F., & Silowash, R. (2008). The impact of concurrent naturalistic pharmacotherapy on psychotherapy of complicated grief. *Psychiatric Research, 159*(1–2), 31–36.

9

Mindfulness Training

Barbara E. Thompson

CLIENTS FOR WHOM THE TECHNIQUE IS APPROPRIATE

Clients experiencing traumatic or complicated grief may benefit. However, a focus on establishing a sense of safety or restoring basic daily routines, or other approaches to self-regulation may be more appropriate for some in the initial phases of traumatic grief.

DESCRIPTION

Mindfulness training teaches people to direct their attention to the contents of experience, such as thoughts, emotional states and bodily sensations, with an attitude of nonjudgmental openness and curiosity (Kabat-Zinn, 2005). Mindfulness practice also directs attention to the absence of feelings, such as an experience of emptiness, without trying to fill it up, flee, or fix it (Epstein, 1998). Acceptance, a closely related construct, suggests a willingness to attend to experiences that are unpleasant or unwanted without attempting to avoid, control or escape them. Experiential avoidance perpetuates suffering and prevents people from living fully in the present with a sense of empowerment and hopefulness regarding their future. Another related construct is decentering, which refers to the capacity to view the contents of experience as passing events rather identifying with self-limiting conceptions or labels (Baer, Walsh, & Lykins, 2009). For instance, "I am depressed" might become "I am noticing a feeling of heaviness, sadness, and a stream of harsh comments." Mindfulness involves an ability to attend to the changing contents and process of moment-to-moment experience without dissociating or being carried away, even when grief is vivid. Subtle sensations and shifts in experience are equally important to notice in order to recognize grieving as an active process rather than a fixed, impenetrable, passive or permanent state, even though it may appear so initially. It can be fruitful, for instance, to explore subtle contours with the experience of "stuckness" or "emptiness." Attending to the felt sense of these experiences may reveal moments of movement in the stuckness or fullness in the emptiness. Likewise, complicated grief can be accompanied by an acute sense of aloneness or abandonment. Bringing attention to the sense of connection between the skin and the environment, such as noticing the texture of one's clothing or the temperature of the air on the skin, can provide an opening, however momentary, to a direct experience of being alive and in relationship with the surrounding environment.

Mindfulness as a therapeutic approach with grief and loss is not a relaxation exercise nor is it about achieving a particular state of mind, a different set of thoughts, or an improved mood. Rather, it is a skill that can be learned through practice as a way to experience grief with less struggle and attempts at escape. Mindfulness is also a way to reconnect with everyday life, learning ways to expand attention outward, for example, noticing the taste of one's food, the sound of a bird, the color of the sky, a cool breeze, sensations in the feet while walking, or a soothing fragrance (Kabat-Zinn, 2005). In the midst of grief, paying attention to pleasant as well as unpleasant experiences can help to ground people in the midst of experiencing disorienting and destabilizing loss. Moreover, it can help to create a space for people to unwind and open to a broadened view and new way of being with themselves and others.

CASE EXAMPLE

As a child, Diana coped with her father's suicide and her mother's depression by "becoming self-sufficient" and focusing on her schoolwork and artistic endeavors. Diana completed her graduate studies with distinction, then married a fellow graduate student. While she continued to work part-time in her field, most of Diana's attention centered on raising her children and supporting her husband's career goals. When her husband asked her for a divorce 15 years later and told her that he was involved with another woman, the life that Diana had known fell apart and with it the future that she had imagined with her husband. For Diana, the end of her marriage and a protracted divorce constellated her father's suicide and its difficult aftermath. Methods for surviving catastrophic loss that had served her as a child now isolated Diana. In therapy, she described being caught in a maelstrom of self-criticism and self-doubt, working herself even harder in her daily life in an attempt to be seen, heard and appreciated. If she had been good enough, her father would not have left her. Diana felt similarly responsible for the ending of her marriage and ruminated on perceived failures in the past as well as fears of being alone in her future. Diana described a sense of "being divided head and heart, body and mind" and utterly alone even in the midst of caring family and friends.

A body scan was the first mindfulness approach introduced to Diana. After an overview, Diana was invited to assume a comfortable but upright posture. Closing her eyes helped Diana to focus on bodily sensations. For the first few moments, I asked Diana to just notice the experience of sitting in the room, the sensation of her feet on the carpet, the feeling of support from the chair, the sounds in the environment as well as anything else that was present. Then, I asked Diana to let her attention rest on the experience of inhaling and exhaling, without trying to change her breathing whatsoever. If her mind wandered off, or if she found herself thinking about something in the past or future, she was asked to label these thoughts "thinking" and return to the movement of the breath. After settling in through this short breathing meditation, I guided Diana through a body scan, asking her to notice whatever she was experiencing in her body without interpretation, slowly moving her attention from her toes to her head. Initially, Diana reported feeling like her "head was in a vice" and that she was "disconnected from her body." With practice, Diana was able to access more bodily sensations as well as latent emotion, which helped her to integrate loss-related experiences more fully and develop new ways of being in the world that didn't require her to split off from a range of feeling, whether pleasant, unpleasant or neutral.

Along with abbreviated forms of the body scan and breathing meditation, Diana practiced other mindfulness methods, such as becoming aware of the environment through her senses and mindful walking when she found herself ruminating or feeling disconnected. She also resumed her artwork, with the instruction to attend to the sensory experiences and the process associated with art making rather than approaching her work more analytically or with the goal of achieving some perceived standard of success. Mindfulness applied in this way helped Diana to rediscover the pleasure of art making. In addition, her pieces became metaphorical expressions of the changes she was experiencing in her life and therapy. Currently, Diana is working on a series of works entitled "out of the rubble," using naturally colored bits of broken egg shells to reconstruct three-dimensional forms that in her own words "are coherent in their own way" and "emergent." Uncharacteristically, she has also invited several friends to her studio to view her artwork, something she avoided in the past due to fear of criticism. Like her artwork, Diana is beginning to allow herself to become visible, to emerge from the rubble of her past, working with the broken pieces of previous shells to create new forms that can be appreciated by herself and others.

CONCLUDING THOUGHTS

Mindfulness practices can complement and potentiate other psychotherapeutic approaches that address complicated grief and loss. Of great value is the potential for mindfulness approaches to restore a connection between body and mind, and to revivify the experiences of daily life. The approach itself is quite gentle, and can help people to befriend the most painful and alienating of experiences. Fundamentally, mindfulness training and practice rest on the assumption that people have innate resources for learning, growth, and personal transformation. While many mindfulness approaches are delivered in a group format, they also can be integrated into a more traditional psychotherapeutic framework. There is debate regarding the necessity for personal training and experience on the part of the therapist. I believe that it is important for the therapist to have some direct training and experience with mindfulness in order to guide others through the pitfalls and possibilities of practice. According to Epstein (1998), mindfulness meditation, like psychotherapy, "hinges on showing us a new way to be with ourselves, and with others" (p. xx). For this, there is no time to lose and now is the only time that we have.

References

Baer, R., Walsh, E., & Lykins, E. (2009). Assessment of mindfulness. In F. Didonna (Ed.), *Clinical handbook of mindfulness* (pp. 153–168). New York: Springer.

Epstein, M. (1998). *Going to pieces without falling apart.* New York: Broadway.

Kabat-Zinn, J. (2005). *Full catastrophe living.* New York: Delta.

10
Multiple Losses and the Circle of Significance

Jane A. Simington

CLIENTS FOR WHOM THE TECHNIQUE IS APPROPRIATE

Adolescents and adults who have difficulty resolving multiple and compounded losses benefit most from this technique. This activity is not designed for the newly bereaved and I caution its use with those who are dissociative, unless the therapist is skilled at working with dissociation.

DESCRIPTION

While the impact of any loss and the difficulty with its resolution can be compounded by a variety of factors, including timing and tragedy, many experience multiple major losses, each infused with associated and subsequent losses. In group therapy, especially in a work-shop setting, I find the Circle of Significance a valuable experiential activity for those who are bereaved in these ways. Multiple and compounded losses can saturate consciousness, keeping grievers from being able to individualize their losses, and interfering with their ability to comprehend any possibility of healing, thus perpetuating continued confusion and grief. The Circle of Significance exercise allows for the identification of both aspects of grief: the destructive aspect, acknowledgement of the losses, and the transformative aspect, recognition of any resulting positive growth.

I introduce the Circle of Significance exercise by discussing multiple losses and how associated and subsequent losses are often contained within a major loss. I illustrate this by outlining a large gold circle on a whiteboard. Participants are encouraged to envision themselves as an incredible being of golden light, as they might have been prior to any of their losses. I invite one participant to describe a major loss and to portray that loss by drawing a wedge on the Circle in the size and color that best describes the impact. A second, third and fourth participant are also asked to each describe a significant loss and to add their wedges to the Circle.

As a way to illustrate the impact of multiple losses, participants are encouraged to observe how each new loss piles up against earlier unresolved losses. By comparing unresolved grief to a physical wound I explain how fragile tissue over a new wound can be easily torn, and even though as healing happens tissues become less fragile, a hard bump can rip away scar tissue, and cause the wound to once again bleed freely.

Using colored pencils and a 9" × 12" sheet of gold colored paper, each participant creates a Circle of Significance by portraying each loss and any associated and subsequent losses. They are encouraged to journal their process and emotional responses.

In the second portion of the exercise, which is to recognize any healing that has taken place, participants choose a variety of stickers that represent their healing and place them on the appropriate wedges. They journal the reasons for their choice of stickers and their emotional responses to the process.

When verbally processing the exercise, participants describe each loss, its impact and any related healing. They identify their emotional reactions to the various processes they engaged in while doing the exercise and identify any outcomes they believe the exercise produced for them.

CASE EXAMPLE

Margaret was 67 years old when her husband, Gerald, died from pancreatic cancer. She came two years later for grief counseling emphasizing that she felt a sense of failure and shame for being stuck in her grief process and for not being able to recover, as did her sister Rose whose husband had died two weeks before Gerald.

I invited Margaret to participate in a grief-healing workshop and during the workshop to complete a Circle of Significance. Margaret spent a lengthy time pondering, writing in her journal and carefully designing each wedge. When we processed her Circle of Significance, Margaret described how the first wedge represented a 3-year-old daughter who had died of pneumonia. The size of this wedge and the emotional load that accompanied the story indicated considerable unresolved grief around a death that occurred 40 years previously. A second wedge depicted a farm the couple had lost from an unpaid mortgage. Margaret attributed the loss of the family farm to her husband's heavy drinking which had started after their daughter's death. She labeled this wedge, "Alcohol." It had multiple subdivisions identifying her losses of dreams, respect, admiration and love for her husband. The third wedge represented the death of her close friend. This wedge too had several subdivisions. Margaret wept as she described how this woman friend had been her only companion and confidante during the difficult years when her husband had emotionally withdrawn due to his own grief and alcoholism. A fourth wedge portrayed the death of her adult son from liver cirrhosis. His death preceded Gerald's by only three years. This wedge was also subdivided. As Margaret processed the subdivisions she talked about the numerous losses she had grieved as she witnessed her only son lose so much due to his uncontrollable drinking. The final wedge was placed for her husband. In response to my invitation to tell me about this wedge, she replied, "There is little left to say. I have just discovered it is not really him I am grieving. I grieved for him many years ago. It is all the other things that I could not, dared not, ever before, let myself grieve. I guess I thought everything would fall apart if I did. I now know that Gerald's death has opened all these old wounds. His death has brought me to a standstill. It has forced me to look at these things and find a way to heal them before I can ever hope to go on."

When I asked Margaret to go back over the Circle of Significance and tell me about the stickers she had placed in each wedge to describe the healing she had done, she noted how affirming it was to know that even though she had a lot of grieving still to do, she was pleased and surprised to be able to honor that she had made progress along the journey.

CONCLUDING THOUGHTS

As Margaret did, most people who complete the Circle of Significance exercise find that when they finish the portion of acknowledging all they have lost, there is a huge recognition of why they may have felt unable to move beyond their grief. Many respond as Margaret did. "It is no wonder I feel so much grief; I have so much to heal from. I never realized the toll all of this has taken on my life." Margaret also made a comment I commonly hear when I asked her how it felt to acknowledge the grief by getting it outside of her and onto the paper. She noted that while the entire process allowed her to be gentler with herself, the act of putting all the losses on paper where she could actually identify them in a visual way would help in her process. "I am now able to recognize what I am trying to heal from." When asked to describe the greatest benefit of the exercise, Margaret emphasized that "It taught me to celebrate as much as I mourn."

Margaret's sister Rose had attended the same workshop, hoping to be of help to her. Rose listened intently as Margaret described her Circle of Significance. In response, Rose communicated that she had underestimated her sister's strengths, but also her need for support. Rose noted that the exercise had moved her from anger and frustration, to caring and empathy, thus adding an unforeseen benefit to the use of this technique.

Further reading

Simington, J. (1999). *Listening to soul pain* (Audiovisual). Edmonton, Alberta: Soleado Productions, Taking Flight Books.

Simington J. (2010). *Setting the captive free: A guide for soulful change and transformation*. Edmonton, Alberta: Taking Flight Books.

11

Reconstructing Nightmares

Courtney Armstrong

CLIENTS FOR WHOM THE TECHNIQUE IS APPROPRIATE

Adults, adolescents, or children who are disturbed by nightmares symbolizing unresolved issues around the death of a loved one or nightmares replaying disturbing aspects of the way someone died. The technique may be contraindicated for clients who report having difficulty visualizing. Clients who have internal conflicts about resolving the issue being played out in the dream, such as a client who is not ready to relinquish anger or guilt, may also have difficulty with this exercise until the internal emotional conflicts are resolved. Then again, reconstructing nightmares can also help with the resolution of these emotional conflicts.

DESCRIPTION

Initially, I reassure grieving clients that nightmares after the death of someone close are not unusual, especially when there are unresolved issues in the relationship with the deceased or when the deceased has died suddenly or violently. Clients are often relieved to hear this and it helps to normalize their experience.

Next, I explain to clients that dreams are the mind's attempt to make sense out of something troubling or disturbing. I suggest they can stop the nightmares and help the mind find peace and resolution by intentionally rewriting the dream-script and changing the dream-scene in any way they would like.

To demonstrate this, it is best to have the client first imagine changing another scene that is unrelated to the nightmare because it is less anxiety-provoking and increases their sense of mastery. For example, I have the client close their eyes and imagine being chased by a fictitious monster. Then I tell the client to turn around to face the monster and invite the monster to approach them. Frequently, clients are surprised to see that when they stop running and face their scary dream-monster, the creature spontaneously disappears or walks away. If this does not occur, I remind the client that they are the movie directors of their dreams and have "superpowers" in the dream-world, so they can change the scene however they would like. With this suggestion, clients might imagine flying away or having the monster disappear in some other way.

After the client gets comfortable adjusting this imagined scene, I encourage them to replay the nightmare scene that has been haunting them. We first discuss the nightmare and explore some possible variations the client would like to make to the dream. Often the ideas that come to the client are better than the therapist's suggestions, as the client's ideas usually have metaphorical relevance to the problem being expressed in the dream.

CASE EXAMPLE

Lydia's son Logan died of a violent suicide after a long battle with bipolar disorder. Lydia made the decision to have Logan's body cremated, but had some guilt about this because she wasn't sure if her son wanted cremation. Shortly after his death, Lydia had recurring nightmares of her son strapped to a gurney and reaching out to her as he was rolled into a flaming furnace. Lydia understood the nightmares symbolized her guilt about not being able to save her son from emotional suffering when he was alive, as well as the guilt she felt over having his body cremated. As she was deeply religious, the dream also symbolized her fear that her son was now eternally suffering in hell.

I suggested Lydia replay the dream in her mind a few times during our session, noting the part of the mind that creates dreams also can come up with the solution. I encouraged her to let her imagination just show her a new ending as the imagination often integrates wisdom from the subconscious mind.

Lydia re-imagined the dream ending with Logan jumping off the gurney before it went into the flames and coming to stand beside her. Putting his arm around her, Logan reassured Lydia that he would be alright. He then kissed her and said, "Goodbye, Mom. I love you." From this experience, Lydia realized that she just wanted the opportunity to say "goodbye" to Logan as they affirmed their love for one another. After replaying the dream in this way, Lydia also got the sense her son would be okay and that God would likely understand how deeply troubled Logan was and offer him compassion, not punishment. Lydia imagined the dream playing out this way several times before she went to sleep that night. To Lydia's delight, her dream changed just as she imagined it and the nightmares have not come back.

CONCLUDING THOUGHTS

Although people are fascinated by their dreams and are often eager to analyze their content and symbols, discussing nightmares provokes anxiety. Re-imagining the nightmare with a new outcome before having the client reflect on the detailed content of the dream makes the process much less scary and helps put symbols or metaphors from the dream into clearer context.

This technique is most effective when you have clients close their eyes and vividly imagine and *experience* the feelings associated with the changed outcome of the dream. Just discussing a new outcome is not sufficient to change the dream content. Neimeyer (2009, p. 69) notes, "[P]otent interventions need not be heavy handed, but they entail ushering a client into new awareness, clarity, and possibility by engagement in an emotionally significant *experience* of something, not just a cognitive discussion of it."

Although the client's suggestions for new dream outcomes are often relevant and insightful, occasionally a client may suggest a dream outcome that does not provide a peaceful resolution. When this occurs, I explain to the client why the solution may not be advantageous and discuss ways we might improve it.

For example, a client who had nightmares in which her deceased mother chased her with a knife decided she would shoot her mother with a gun in the dream to stop her mother from chasing her. However, the client's mother had died from a suicidal gunshot wound. Although the client and I realized shooting her mother symbolized the anger the client felt she could not express to her mother regarding the suicide, we also agreed that metaphorically shooting her mother in the dream-state exacerbated the client's feelings of sadness and guilt. Therefore, I suggested the client stand still peacefully knowing that her dream-body could not be hurt and let her dream-mother come toward her with the knife. When the client played the dream this way, she was astonished that her dream-mother appeared confused, dropped the knife, and hugged the client instead. Not only did changing the dream this way stop the client's nightmares, but it also helped the client begin to release guilt and anger, finding a new sense of compassion for her mother.

References

Danlen, P. (1999). Follow-up counseling after disaster: Working with traumatic dreams towards healing. *Traumatology, 5*(3), 28–33.

Neimeyer, R. A. (2009). *Constructivist psychotherapy*. New York: Routledge.

Siegel, A. (1996). *Dreams that can change your life*. New York: Putnam.

12

Visualization for Anticipatory Grief

Robert F. Morgan

CLIENTS FOR WHOM THE TECHNIQUE IS APPROPRIATE

Clients experiencing apparently unspecific and random fits of anxiety who have suppressed traumatic or anticipatory grief can benefit from this technique. However, it is contra-indicated for psychotic individuals.

DESCRIPTION

Visualization in a safe setting may be a treatment of choice for those who readily do this, such as artists or writers, or those who can use this approach to create a safe distance from upsetting material. In hypnosis parlance, it creates (or is an indicator of) light trance (Morgan, 2004). Introducing the concept of anticipatory grief into the trauma literature suggests a fresh perspective for the treatment of debilitating anxiety. Anticipatory grief occurs when a catastrophic or death-related outcome is assumed to be beyond intervention or, at times, conscious comprehension.

CASE EXAMPLE

James had black polish on his fingernails and very long hair. He was in his thirties and was calmly discussing his art and his communal life in his new San Francisco home. James had left Buffalo, New York, the month before although he could not say exactly why. He was in my clinic office because, for no apparent reason, he would from time to time start shaking uncontrollably.

James was tall and athletic, self-assured, and utterly mystified by these shakes. He wanted me to solve the mystery for him and banish the problem. I asked him to do some deep breathing exercises and then to visualize what was causing the anxiety. He complied but in seconds was vibrating in a near epileptic fit. I changed the focus and asked him to visualize his best art. The shaking stopped.

I decided to work on trust and relaxation for a while, being clear that we would not address the cause any more that session. He relaxed completely. Rapport was easy, as we had grown up in the same town and he had sought me out after reading a light novel I once wrote about it (Morgan, 1964). He agreed to return the following week at the same day and time.

Visual and relaxation exercises were used over several sessions. Gradually he was able to realize and acknowledge that he had left his home at the other side of the country because he was running away from some traumatic grief and it was "lethal." Each session we gave a little more time to these exercises but none were devoid of shaking. He did eventually feel safe enough (an essential condition) in my office to make use of a proffered "distancing" technique: to visualize a photograph of a painting of a medical document that underlay his anxiety. The words standing out above the rest were terminal cancer.

At this point we could begin the reality phase of our work. He was able to fully recall the diagnosis and his running away from it. Now he no longer shook because he knew what the catastrophic fear was based on. It was anticipatory grieving for his own demise.

With my support he agreed to get an immediate and complete medical examination. He brought the report to me somewhat embarrassed. The cancer was in complete remission. He was healthy. Had he not confronted his catastrophic fear, he likely would have lived out a full life with constant anxiety attacks from anticipatory grieving. Facing the origin of his traumatic grief in the softened form of distancing imagery—inviting him to view it as a photograph, or artwork, or both—mitigated his terror sufficiently to allow us to address it in therapy (Morgan, 2008).

CONCLUDING THOUGHTS

Traumatic or anticipatory grief, when overwhelming, may be suppressed. This at first glance might be considered by some practitioners to be classic repression in a psychoanalytic sense. In these cases, particularly with artists or good visualizers, the paradigm of hypnosis seems a better fit (Morgan, 2004). Visualization creates a light trance state and, given trust and safety, can often lead to the understanding and resolution of the traumatic anticipatory grief.

References

Morgan, R. F. (1964). *The muddy chuckle.* New York: Exposition.

Morgan, R. F. (2004). *Training the time sense: Hypnotic and conditioning approaches.* Chico, CA: Morgan Foundation.

Morgan, R. F. (2008). *Opportunity's shadow and the bee moth effect: When danger transforms community.* Fairbanks, AK: Morgan Foundation.

13

Intuitive Humor

Robert F. Morgan

CLIENTS FOR WHOM THE TECHNIQUE IS APPROPRIATE

My experience with the International Congress of Applied Psychology (Morgan, 2008) has led me to appreciate the humor that often is used as a test of trust among indigenous people such as the Maori in New Zealand, the Senoi in Malaysia, the Aboriginal People of Australia, and the original tribes of the Native Americans, Canadians, and Mexicans. For them and for those clients from any culture where humor and irony are to be found, the initial rapport so essential to psychotherapy can be enhanced as a treatment for either genuine or factitious grief. However, therapist humor is contraindicated when its timing is inappropriate, merely sustains a client's defensiveness, or is incongruent with the client's emotional tone.

DESCRIPTION

When an apparently spontaneous and unconventional intervention occurs to a psychotherapist, it is important to subject it to an immediate tripartite test: (1) *Is it legal?* (2) *Ethical?* (3) *In the client's best interest?* From Hippocrates on, we know we must above all "do no harm." The entire field of prevention of iatrogenic practice rests on violations to this standard (Morgan, 2004). Yet, if none of the barriers apply, it is often useful to go ahead with the intervention. Intuitive humor or irony certainly falls into this category and can be an effective treatment, particularly in reframing seemingly overwhelming grief. This is one of my favorite techniques (Morgan, 1982). On the other hand, a client may present factitious or pseudo-grief as a test for safety and as a cover for more genuine grieving to be accessed later in treatment. This is not unknown as a client-produced method from native peoples and the therapist's response needs to be congruent. Intuitive humor can be one such response.

CASE EXAMPLE

Now that my husband has shot him, I don't know what to do with the body.

In the mountains of Northern California, in counties where only one or two psychologists may be found at best, live the Maidu Indian people, side by side with scatterings of settlers from European cultures. The nearest town is Reno, Nevada, about a two-hour drive from there.

Some years ago my wife and I moved to Greenville, California, in the heart of Maidu country, because my wife was promised a job as the sole librarian for the town's tiny library—a job that failed to materialize. So there we were, moved into a small community and completely unemployed. Knowing that there were absolutely no psychologists in the area, I walked in to the tribal health center, one covering the needs of the residents of that remote but beautiful region of the county.

Did they need a psychologist to help out? Yes, they did. Desperately. And a substantial amount of money was promised for every hour of service. I quickly concluded that it was a good cause and a way to pay the rent. I agreed immediately and was given an empty office just off the waiting room.

A day went by with no clients, no hours, no stipend, no rent. I asked the director if she would be willing to run an announcement in the local paper to let potential patients know I was there. "No need," she said. "They know you are here." The situation was interesting, to say the least.

No patients came the next day either. By the morning of the third day, I was walking to work with some real concern. I was prepared to be the psychological equivalent of the country doctor, a real need there, but the clients were not apparent. And then, within sight of the health center, a woman in her forties walked up to me and asked if I was Dr. Morgan. I was. She asked if she could ask me a question.

I said: "Yes, did you have another question?" Clearly this was an out-of-the-office free consultation coming up, but it beat having no clients at all. She cleared her throat.

"My husband shot our dog today."

"Why did he do such a thing?"

"Well, the dog is a loving dog and walks the children to their school bus every morning. But our neighbor hates children. So when they come by his house he yells at them and throws things. Once the children are safe away and on the way to school, our dog goes on this neighbor's porch and relieves himself in front of his door. Then the neighbor keeps calling my husband and complaining. Says his front porch is not a bathroom for puppies. My husband got one telephone call too many and so he took the dog out in the back yard and shot him to death."

As she said this, her nonverbal behavior was completely incongruent. She was smiling, almost seeming to hold back laughter, and her "tells" suggested less than an honest description. Of course, this can be a trap. If you smile back in the midst of a sad story, your client might feel you are not taking them seriously. The normal response for a clinician is just to point out that the smile doesn't match the story and is that how they feel? But I wasn't sure about this culture. Maidu and many other tribal people have a rough sense of humor, somewhat akin to that of the inhabitants of Manhattan or Auckland. So I asked a question instead.

"Well, that is very sad. What is your question, then?"

"Now that my husband has shot him, I don't know what to do with the body."

Humor can be a very powerful way to help clients in trauma. Or, badly timed or poorly thought through, it can create trauma or grief, for both parties. But, after engaging in my internal tripartite test, I took a chance that the story was a complete fabrication.

I said: "Well, my advice is to take the dog's body and leave it on your neighbor's porch with a suicide note. Sign it with a paw print."

She studied me for a minute and then said: "You're not from around here, are you?"

She turned and walked away slowly. Just before turning the corner, she started laughing.

That afternoon, the waiting room was full and I never had a shortage of clients thereafter.

For herself, she soon came to terms with her genuine loss and anticipated loss—neither of which had to do with her healthy pet dog. These losses were both true and overwhelming. It took a year for her to surmount them but that she did. In a five-year follow-up she was still doing quite well.

CONCLUDING THOUGHTS

It is crucial to have some understanding of our client's culture and values, particularly when different from our own. Then there will often be a test for safety and trust, occasionally with fictitious information, even pseudo-grieving. Humor and non-defensive patience can move you quickly past that point and into genuine therapeutic work with the genuine grief.

References

Morgan, R. F. (1982). Balloon therapy. *Canadian Psychology*, *23*, 45–46.
Morgan, R. F. (2004) *The iatrogenics handbook: A critical look at research and practice in helping professions*. Chico, CA: Morgan Foundation.
Morgan, R. F. (2008) *Opportunity's shadow and the bee moth effect: When danger transforms community*. Fairbanks, AK: Morgan Foundation.

Part III
Working with the Body

14

Analogical Listening

Robert A. Neimeyer

CLIENTS FOR WHOM THE TECHNIQUE IS APPROPRIATE

Analogical listening is suited to adults who are experiencing an unclear sense of malaise, sadness, grief or other strong feeling, and are uncertain about its meaning or how to respond to it. For clients who resist introspection or have extreme difficulty acknowledging emotion, a more external, action-oriented approach to therapy could be indicated.

DESCRIPTION

At a deep level, we know more than we can say, so that therapists often must assist a client with the delicate process of meaning symbolization. Ironically, this is sometimes true even when we think we know what our clients are saying, as when they are using public language to refer to private feelings associated with their presenting problems. Almost always, there is more to be discovered in a simple description of an internal state like *grief, fear, emptiness* or *tightness* than meets the ear. When clients are uncertain about what they sense or feel, it is even clearer that a literal discussion of the problem is unlikely to access a novel and useful description of it, or provide direction for therapy. Simply put, we need to find a way to listen beneath the stories that clients tell us and themselves about their predicament in order to find a fresh way forward.

At such moments, it can be helpful to attend to preverbal and often somatic sensed meanings that are unique to that person, in that specific moment of experiencing. Like Gendlin's (1996) focusing-oriented psychotherapy, my use of *analogical listening* is intended to assist with this process, often lowering the barriers that make problem specification and solution impossible in straightforward "rational" terms.

In my typical clinical use of this procedure, I invite my clients simply to close their eyes with me for a moment, as I do the same, giving them tacit "permission" to join me, rather than their having the sense of my staring at them as they engage in the awkward act of closing their eyes for an extended period in the presence of another. Slowing my voice to induce a more relaxed and attentive state, I encourage them to allow their attention to shift from the outer world to their body, perhaps prompting them with a question that contains the feeling word they had just used in connection with a distressing situation. For example, for a client who describes a sense of deep grief over the death of her son, I might prompt her in this quiet, inwardly attentive state to ask herself, "Where do I hold my grief?" and then allow her body to respond, perhaps with a sense of a void in her abdomen, or constriction around her heart. This would then become the image we would "unpack" as I ask other questions slowly, opening my eyes to catch her nonverbal expressions, and listening analogically, non-literally, to her answers. My goal in this is not to "solve" the feeling or get the person beyond it, but simply to sense its meaning as fully as possible. From there, the path forward will open.

Some possible questions to guide you in this process include:

- Can you think of a recent time when you felt _____ keenly? Without describing the situation, can you close your eyes for a moment and go back there, now?
- What are you aware of when you feel _____? If you focus your attention in your body, what do you notice?
- If you can identify a bodily feeling associated with _____, where is it located? If it had a shape, form or color, what might it be?
- Is there a movement, or a clear blocking of movement, associated with ____? Can you let it move forward in this direction a bit? What happens?
- What do you find yourself doing or wanting to do when in touch with this feeling? Are other people aware of how you are responding to it? If so, what do they do?
- What do you need to do to integrate or understand this feeling more fully? What would help with it in some way? What would you need from others in this process?

CASE EXAMPLE

An illustration of analogical listening arose in a recent first session with a 50-year-old client, Darla, who was experiencing a complex grief following the death of her 22-year-old son, Kyle, some 7 months earlier from an aggressive bile-duct cancer. Gesturing with her hands, she described both an enveloping and energy-vitiating pain that surrounded her, and that led her to lay down and rest herself, as well as a void pain, signaled fleetingly by hands holding an empty sphere, situated at the level of her abdomen, at the level of her womb, where she once carried her son. As the proud story of Kyle's achievements melded into the more tragic tale of his diagnosis and death, I queried about where she felt the pain now, in this present moment. "Deep in my abdomen, deep in my chest," was her reply, and she confirmed my impression that this was the void pain she had spoken of earlier. This then became the starting point for analogical listening.

I began by closing my own eyes, and inviting Darla to do the same, finding a comfortable way of sitting in the chair, and just allowing her attention to enter her body, seeking where she held that pain now. Speaking slowly as I opened my eyes to track her nonverbal responses, I invited her to draw close to the pain, just off to one side of it slightly, and from that position to describe what it would look like. Darla responded that it "was something with a lot of texture . . . like a really fine sandpaper." "A fine sandpaper," I intoned, "And if you reached out and touched it lightly, what would it be like?" "Just kind of rough," Darla replied. "Rough . . ." I echoed, "and how would your hand feel after touching it, that sandpapery roughness?" "Like it would burn, and want some lotion or something," she answered, tears flowing. "A lotion, like a balm almost, something to soothe that burning sensation." Darla nodded, noting further that the ball of sandpaper was "something with a dimension to it." "A dimension . . ." I reflected, "as if it has other 'somethings' beneath it, or is it all of the 'something?' " "I think there might be more there," she replied with hesitation. "If you draw close to it, and look, and listen quietly, what else might you find there, wrapped in that sandpaper?" "Just all of the hopes, all of the dreams for what might have been," she sobbed, her voice breaking, and tears flowing now heavily, ". . . the possibilities." "The possibilities," I whispered, "buried there, there beneath that sandpaper." She nodded, adding that they seemed "compartmentalized." "Do you think that you can continue to hold them in that way, or does that seem to be changing?" I asked, as Darla opened her eyes. Darla affirmed that she couldn't keep holding the burning pain of her grief in that way, because it hurt too much. Further processing the experience, she recognized the need to reach into the pain and through it, to contact again "all those memories, all those hopes for that young man, buried within that sandpaper." This then became the work of the session.

CONCLUDING THOUGHTS

Because of its non-literal, highly sensory quality, analogical listening commonly evokes imagery of a figurative kind that captures a feeling: hot lava, a binding constriction, a ball of lead, a black mass, something struggling to emerge from a restrictive container. A common error in working with such images is to follow or inadvertently prompt a client's shift to a more logical, historical, literal level—the conflict with another that engendered the feeling, the circumstances of the loss, etc. However, I would advise against such shifts during the active unfolding of the imagery and feeling, which commonly requires 10 minutes or more to be done fully and unhurriedly. Such contextual and conceptual processing of the external realities associated with the feeling is better left for subsequent, open-eyed processing, after the therapist gently ushers the client into more conventional reflection on what has arisen analogically. Alternatively, further imagistic processing of the feeling can be fostered through conjoining such listening with expressive arts media, especially free-form painting or coloring within the outline of a human body, with or without subsequent commentary or journaling about the experience.

Therapists interested in watching the use of this method with grieving clients can consult either of the video recordings of actual sessions noted below (Neimeyer, 2004, 2008). A fuller discussion of therapeutic imagery, complete with case illustrations, can be found in Neimeyer (2009), alongside many other meaning-oriented techniques.

References

Gendlin, E. (1996). *Focusing oriented psychotherapy*. New York: Guilford.

Neimeyer, R. A. (2004). *Constructivist psychotherapy* [video]. Washington, DC: American Psychological Association.

Neimeyer, R. A. (2008). *Constructivist psychotherapy over time* [video]. Washington, DC: American Psychological Association.

Neimeyer, R. A. (2009). *Constructivist psychotherapy*. New York: Routledge.

15
Clapping Qigong

Cecilia Lai Wan Chan and Pamela Piu Yu Leung

CLIENTS FOR WHOM THE TECHNIQUE IS APPROPRIATE

Bereaved persons who find it difficult to express grief or are unwilling to talk about their feelings of loss and sadness. Clapping qigong works particularly well on clients who somaticize grief through the manifestation of insomnia, fatigue, bodily pain and other physical symptoms. However, it should only be used as an adjunct to more intensive therapies when grieving is complicated.

DESCRIPTION

Physical exercise can enhance bereaved persons' capacity to manage their grief, especially those who are overwhelmed with loss and emotionally fixated in great sadness. In traditional Chinese medicine, the mind and the body are interconnected; emotions and physical health are interwoven and inseparable. Distressing emotions such as grief and bereavement may cause stagnation in the energy flow in the body resulting in physical and emotional disharmony (Ng, Chan, Ho, Wong, & Ho, 2006). Twelve of the 14 *meridians* (key energy pathways in the body) pass through our hands, our ears and our feet. Exercises with our hands in particular can significantly facilitate the flow of *qi* (energy) in the meridians. The improvement of energy flow can promote the internal harmony of bodily function, reduce negative emotions of grief, anger, sadness, frustration, and hopelessness, as well as bring on more positive thoughts and emotions (Lee, Ng, Leung, & Chan, 2009).

Clapping qigong is a set of mind–body techniques that is specifically designed for exercising our hands. It is one of the simplest forms of *qigong* (*qi* exercise) that can be easily learned through observation and repetition. Through practicing a short routine of "one-second techniques" (Chan, 2006), clients will be empowered by regaining a sense of control over their mind–body conditions through simple physical exercises that do not require verbal articulation of their emotional and spiritual pain. These techniques also provide clients with a concrete way to relieve their sorrows. In order for clapping qigong to be effective, clients will need to practice at least three times a day for 5 to 10 minutes each time. Sharing success stories of clients using these simple techniques to overcome their grief can increase exercise compliance, while using a log book to record practice times and mood levels can also enhance motivation and track improvements.

Clapping qigong can be taught during one-to-one counseling situations or in therapeutic groups as a self-help empowerment intervention. The following series of exercises can be practiced as single technique or as a set of hand exercises. They are best practiced in a park, under trees or in an open space with fresh air. To begin, clients should be standing upright with shoulders and bodies relaxed; stand with feet apart at shoulder width, toes gripping firmly on the ground, and with knees slightly bending (for those who are wheelchair-bound or are too frail to stand up, the exercises can be performed in a sitting position):

1. *Palm rubbing*: This is a warm-up exercise. With palms facing one another in front of the chest, finger to fingers, palm to palm, rub the two hands with some force, about 50 times, until they are warm. Palm rubbing facilitates energy flow through the 12 meridians that go through various parts of the body, fostering general well-being of the person.

2. *Hand clapping*: With fingers and palms facing each other in front of the chest, fingers pointing upwards and in a prayer position, spread the two palms to one and a half times shoulder width and open the chest by squeezing the shoulder blades, then bring the two palms back together through loud forceful claps of the hands. A sharp but brief pain should be felt with every clap. Hand clapping should be performed three times a day for 5 minutes each time, about 300–500 claps each time. The palms may likely turn blue after clapping every day for 1 to 2 weeks. The physical pain can serve to release the emotional and spiritual pain of loss and grief. This single technique can be sufficient to improve the physical and psychosocial conditions of bereaved persons.

3. *Pulling energy ball*: After rubbing and clapping, with shoulders and arms relaxed, palms facing each other and fingers pointing out front from the abdomen, slightly cup the palms and fingers as if holding an invisible energy ball. Slowly separate the palms by pulling and squeezing the energy ball horizontally from shoulder width to about 4 to 6 inches. Keep eyes closed and feel the tingling sensation between the palms; this invisible energy is the *qi*. The pulling energy ball exercise should be practiced at least three times per day for 5 to 10 minutes each time.

4. *Compassionate breathing*: After practicing the entire routine or any one of the techniques, take in slow deep breaths for a few minutes. With a smile and the thought of love and compassion, breathe in a beautiful calming light that spreads slowly throughout the entire body.

CASE EXAMPLE

Josie lost her husband, Lee, at the age of 67. Lee was a retired teacher who was very caring and protective. He was not only a husband, but also her best and only friend, soul mate, true companion and greatest source of joy. Throughout their long marriage, Lee pampered and spoiled Josie like a princess whose only job was to enjoy life. Josie was deeply devastated when Lee died from a sudden heart attack two years ago. Since then, Josie had been living alone and wanting her married daughters to spend more time with her, but this was becoming increasingly difficult if not impossible as they were both working mothers. Consumed by feelings of anger, frustration, betrayal and abandonment, Josie experienced insomnia, lost her appetite and suffered from the constant fear of illness and heart attack. She cried all the time and refused to leave her house.

Josie consulted Chinese Medicine doctors who referred her to participate in an integrative body–mind–spirit group for persons with mood disorders. She shared her grief and how her daughters were being unhelpful, with strong self-pity and bitterness. She learned clapping qigong during the first group session. She reported to the group that hand clapping was very useful and she could sleep for five hours every night since she started the practice.

Josie learned the energy ball technique during the second session. She started taking morning walks to a park and practiced 5 minutes of clapping and 10 minutes of energy ball pulling exercise every day for a few times per day on the second week. She found that the hand exercises could improve the quality and quantity of her sleep.

Compassionate breathing was taught during the third session. Josie began to understand the importance for her to develop her own social networks instead of relying fully on her daughters. She was more willing to make friends and participate in community activities for elderly persons in her neighborhood. The practice of hand clapping, pulling the energy ball and compassionate breathing actually helped her to appreciate that her health is in her own hands. She had to take responsibility for her own wellbeing.

Clapping qigong and each of the body–mind techniques were used as part of the counseling group. Josie made the decision that she had to relinquish bitterness and to start a new life on her own after the six-session group. She continued her daily practice of clapping qigong and regained new strength as she adjusted to a life without her husband.

CONCLUDING THOUGHTS

Clapping qigong is a pain-inducing exercise. The physical pain could actually serve as a distraction for the bereaved person from their emotional and spiritual suffering. A full set of mind–body exercises can be found in the training manual and video-CD noted below (Chan, 2006). Moreover, a detailed case report of how the body techniques as applied in the case of a bereaved mother can be found in Leung, Chan, Ng and Lee (2009).

References

Chan, C. L. W. (2006). *An Eastern body–mind–spirit approach: A training manual with one-second techniques.* Hong Kong: Resource Paper Series No. 43, Department of Social Work and Social Administration, The University of Hong Kong.

Chan, C. L. W., Chan, C. H. Y., Tin, A. F., Chan, W. C. H., & Ng, P. O. K. (2009). *In celebration of life: A self-help journey of preparing for death and living with loss and bereavement.* Hong Kong: Centre on Behavioral Health, University of Hong Kong.

Chan, C. L. W., & Chow, A. Y. M. (eds.) (2006). *Death, dying and bereavement: The Chinese experience.* Hong Kong: Hong Kong University Press.

Lee, M. Y., Ng, S. M., Leung, P. Y. & Chan, C. L. W. (2009). *Integrative body–mind–spirit social work: An empirically based approach to assessment and treatment.* New York: Oxford University Press.

Leung, P. P. Y., Chan, C. L. W., Ng, S. M., & Lee, M. Y. (2009). Towards body–mind–spirit integration: East meets West in clinical social work practice. *Clinical Social Work Journal, 37*(4), 303–311.

Ng, S. M., Chan, C. L. W., Ho, D. Y. F., Wong, Y. Y., & Ho, R. T. H. (2006). Stagnation as a distinct clinical syndrome: comparing '*yu*' (stagnation) in traditional Chinese medicine with depression. *British Journal of Social Work, 36*, 1–17.

16
Hands in the Sand

Darcy L. Harris

CLIENTS FOR WHOM THE TECHNIQUE IS APPROPRIATE

Bereaved clients of all ages. However, this technique should not be introduced until the therapeutic relationship is well established, and the client is able to tolerate the possibility of strong emotions arising in the process.

DESCRIPTION

Sand Tray Therapy (or "sandplay") is a technique based upon practical, creative work in a sand tray. Use of sand as a therapeutic method was originally developed by Dr. Margaret Lowenfeld, who formalized the technique with miniature figures, sand, and water in a blue-bottomed, aluminum container to help children to express and work through emotionally-charged issues (Lowenfeld, 1979). The current use of the sand tray with adults began with the work of Dora Kalff, a student of Carl Jung, who also studied Lowenfeld's work. She recognized that the archetypal content and symbolic process involved in this medium could make it readily adaptable to Jungian theory and she used the term "sandplay" therapy (Kalff, 2003). Sandplay therapy is now used with both adults and children.

Most clinicians who incorporate sandplay therapy with adults still use figures as representational models of either intrapsychic processes or of situations that are brought up in verbal (talk) therapy prior to the work in the tray. Sand can be either dry or wet. Some clients talk as they work and others remain silent. The meaning of the work emerges as the client experiences it and shares it with the therapist. For the client, working in a sand tray translates personal experience into a concrete, three-dimensional form. Just as a picture can say more than a thousand words, a figure or scene can express feelings, emotions, and conflicts that previously had no verbal language. Thus, the sand-worlds that are created can offer a rich and highly personalized vocabulary for pre-verbal or non-verbal experience. Without having to depend upon words, clients can increase their capacity for expression through the tray. Often, clients experience a sense of awareness and clarity that was not possible in talk therapy alone (Ammann, 1991).

In the current application, it is suggested that the tray be approximately 14" in diameter and at least 2" deep. Round plastic trays that fit under large plants work well for this purpose. The sand should be fine, soft, and clean. If using sand from a beach or a natural area, the sand should first be sifted through a fine mesh strainer, and then treated by heating it in an oven for 30 minutes at 300 degrees Fahrenheit once before use in a tray. Reptile sand that is available at pet supply stores is a good substitute due to its fine, soft texture. For the representational work, various natural objects should be available to the client, such as rocks, shells, pieces of wood, leaves, or feathers, especially if they have a unique or distinct shape, color, or feel. Some clients may choose to bring in their own objects for this work as well.

HANDS IN THE SAND

In this type of sand tray work, clients are simply asked to immerse their hands in the sand and to work with the sand in whatever way comes to them intuitively. The tray is most often placed on the floor for this work, but clients can also have the tray in their laps or on a low table situated in front of them. The exercise is nonverbal; clients are asked to enter the sand with their hands as they choose, to focus on their hands and the sensations that their hands experience, and upon what they are feeling as they do the exercise [see Figure 16.1(a) and (b)]. They are usually given about 5 minutes to work the sand with their hands. The therapist observes the client's process, paying careful attention to body language and how the client uses the sand. The therapist's role is to quietly bear witness to this process.

(a)

Figures 16.1 (a) and (b) "Hands in the Sand." Clients place their hands in the sand and work the sand as they feel drawn to do so, while the therapist remains silent and fully present to the client's work. Evocative music is often used in this process. After five minutes, the client is gently asked to complete the work and the therapist asks the client to describe the thoughts and feelings that arose during this process.

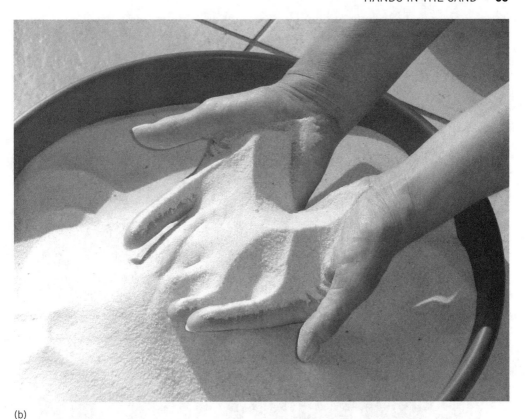

(b)

Figures 16.1 *Continued.*

When the client's hands enter the sand, deeper thoughts and feelings often come quickly to the surface. The tactile sensation of the sand may also remind some clients of their desire to be touched or of missing touch—something that may be absent after the loss of a loved one. For some, the act of immersing their hands in the sand or feeling it as they lightly touch the surface changes the tone of the session immediately, often intensifying it, and focusing it completely on the client's experience. The use of music during this time can help to foster the process of the client nonverbally. Music can be chosen by the client in advance, or the therapist can choose a piece that may fit the client's situation or mood, or a piece that may have a special association for the client with a deceased loved one. At the end of the session, the client is invited to integrate the affective and tactile experience with his or her own personal story of loss.

Another use of the "hands in the sand" approach is to help a client remain grounded when there has been a tendency to dissociate in the session, or the client begins to feel overwhelmed by the material that has arisen in the session. Clients who become familiar with the use of the sand tray may begin to instinctively reach for the tray in subsequent sessions, working their hands in the sand while they are talking as a means of feeling "grounded" and more present.

THE TRAY AS METAPHOR

Another way to use the sand tray is by having a client place representational figures into the tray to better visualize a situation or to better describe it. This method has been very helpful

(a)

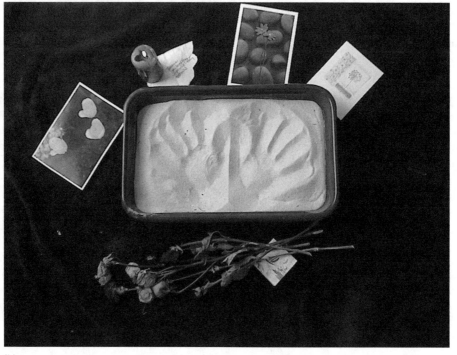

(b)

Figures 16.2 (a) and (b) Tray as metaphor. Clients may place symbolic objects in the sand, manipulate them and optionally discuss their meanings and associated feelings with the therapist, or may simply use their hands to create or discover meaningful patterns in the sand, perhaps configured with other objects.

when clients remain "stuck" on a particular issue or situation. Rather than stockpiling specific representational figures, therapists can simply ask clients to choose from the natural objects that are in a bowl or spread out on a tray that is kept nearby. The sand tray itself may be seen as their life, their loss, their family, or whatever topic is the focus of that session [see Figure 16.2(a) and (b)].

Clients can then choose the objects and place them in the tray as they wish to situate them. The advantage of this method is that it allows clients to project their own interpretations onto the objects themselves and this becomes part of the "process" of the tray.

CASE EXAMPLE

Anna's 24-year-old daughter was found dead in her apartment, apparently from complications to her diabetes. Anna was engulfed in guilt, feeling responsible for not monitoring her daughter more closely because of her health condition. She would often come to the session and weep, unable to verbalize her feelings because they were so intense and deep. Anna struggled with images of what her daughter's body looked like when it was found by her husband, apparently several days after she had died.

In one of her sessions, Anna stated that she just felt overwhelmed, and could not speak. I suggested that she place the sand tray in her lap, and place her hands in the sand. She was hesitant to do so at first, but she agreed to give it a try. I suggested that she take a deep breath and focus only on her hands and what they felt in the sand. She moved her hands in the sand for a minute, and then recounted a story of being at the beach with her daughter when she was young and how they made sand castles together. After she told this story, I suggested that she close her eyes and let her hands feel the sand. She wept quietly and became engaged in the tray, moving the sand in patterns, pouring the sand from one hand to another, and finally, resting with both hands buried in the sand. At the end of the session, she told me that she felt better.

The next session, Anna asked to try the tray again. After a few minutes of working with her hands in the sand, she lifted her hands out of the tray and noticed the pattern looked like a butterfly. She then took some items that she had brought to the session with her—the last birthday card her daughter had given her, dried flowers from an arrangement that her daughter had sent to her, a candle, another card that she had given to her daughter, and a picture that reminded her of her daughter. She arranged these around the tray and asked to take a picture of the tray. We spent the rest of the session talking about the objects around the tray and her relationship with her daughter. Anna stated that doing this tray helped her to connect again with the healthy part of her daughter, who wanted her independence, knowing that her health issues were significant.

CONCLUDING THOUGHTS

Both ways of working in the tray often help to slow the session down, especially when there is a lot of anxiety or intense emotion present. The "hands in the sand" method is very tactile for clients who need touch to stay "connected" to their emotions. The metaphor method allows clients to be "outside" of the situation or relationships that are being represented while having an opportunity to focus directly upon them. Often, subtleties in the situations that are being represented in the tray may not be readily accessible for the client in typical talk therapy, and the sand tray seems to give expression to words, events, feelings, and experiences in a way that might otherwise have been difficult for the client to name or describe.

References

Ammann, R. (1991). *Healing and transformation in sandplay: Creative processes become visible.* La Salle, IL: Open Court Publishing.

Kalff, D. (2003). *Sandplay: A psychotherapeutic approach to the psyche.* Cloverdale, CA: Temenos Press.

Lowenfeld, M. (1979). *The world technique.* London: Allen & Unwin.

17
Moving and Breathing Through Grief

David C. Mitchell

CLIENTS FOR WHOM THE TECHNIQUE IS APPROPRIATE

Adolescents and adults who are processing an experience of loss or transition, and particularly the bereaved. Participants would need to be able to share and discuss topics in a group. The physical limitations of some clients may limit participation.

DESCRIPTION

Grief demonstrates the integral connection between mind and body. Wolfelt notes that "one literal definition of the word 'grievous' is 'causing physical pain,' suggesting that, we mourn life losses from the inside out" (2009, p. 1). I have observed in my clients how grief can be physically felt and evoke a bodily reaction. For example, clients often make remarks such as:

I feel like there is a brick at the back of my neck.
I feel a heaviness in my chest.
My back has begun aching.
My whole body feels tense.

Often clients are surprised that grief can manifest so physically. I recently noticed on a handout our agency uses for grief education listing "grief responses" that the category with the most examples is "physical reactions." Whether these are direct responses to stress related to grief or psychosomatic manifestations, they are experienced as real physical responses for the person and can further complicate their grief process. Sometimes those reactions precipitate an initial visit for grief counseling. In other cases, they can simply make the whole grief process more difficult to manage. As one client shared, "It is bad enough my mother died, now my stomach aches, I feel like there is a brick in the back of my neck and I catch every disease I come in contact with."

Sometimes these somatic reactions lead to significant health problems. Our immune system is compromised allowing for infection and other issues. Physical stress reactions lead to chronic conditions potentially leading to serious consequences (Kabat-Zinn, 1990, p. 265). Poor diet, sleep and intensive care taking schedules can lead to exhaustion affecting most areas of life. I have seen such reactions create a "feedback loop" where the physical reactions validate how "bad" clients' grief is, especially if they are not able to connect well to their emotions. This could be verbalized as, "My body's breaking down really tells me how serious my grief is, and I feel worse knowing this."

The frequency of these reactions in my practice led me to begin addressing some of the physical needs of our bereaved clients by offering yoga within the context of a supportive grief therapy group. This began as part of a six-week group called *Moving and Breathing through Grief*. This 90-minute closed group begins with a 15-minute "check in" and 15-minute reading/discussion of a grief-related poem, which is facilitated by a grief counselor. These poems promote "mindfulness" concepts such as equanimity, impermanence, and appreciation of the moment. I have found that this initial phase allows participants to settle down, connect with the group through story sharing and rapport, and explore a perspective conducive to the goals of the yoga portion.

The next hour of the group is led by a certified yoga instructor (who is also a trained Hosparus volunteer). I have found it beneficial for the yoga instructor to be present during the first part of the group. This allows her to adjust the postures to the needs of the group by having a sense of their issues, mood, and energy level on that day. The type of yoga movements are intentionally quite gentle, in order to accommodate as many physical abilities as possible. Props are also used to help extend the range of available postures. Participants are frequently reminded to coordinate the breath with each yoga movement. This serves to increase their sense of mindfulness, body awareness, and relaxation through each movement. "In fact, in Sanskrit, yoga means to 'yoke,' in this case bringing together the body and mind . . . a rejuvenating practice that offers many other health benefits" (Stahl & Goldstein, 2010). Indeed, after the group, members talk about feeling refreshed, calmer, rejuvenated, and feeling "alive again."

CASE EXAMPLE

As members participate in this setting, I have noticed a variety of beneficial effects. On a symbolic level, one is "moving through grief" and is asked to "extend oneself," to "move in a new way," and to "become more flexible," all the while being supported by the yoga instructor and the group members. Certain poses suggest strength and dignity, such as "The Warrior." Others suggest "opening" and "release," and even "holding tension." As the group progresses, each participant becomes more flexible, able to relax more into the process, and to become more adept performing the movements. The vehicle of the body informs the griever, allowing exploration of connections between body and mind.

One common exclamation is, "I didn't know I could calm down. This is the first time in (weeks, months, years) that I have actually felt calm for even a moment, and I didn't know I could do this." Realizing that one can achieve even a momentary calm can be powerful for a griever who has become accustomed to stress, rumination, and anxiety. For one client this "discovery" became a turning point in her grief process, as she stated, "Now that I know if I can feel this, I will be OK. I felt that was a bit of the old me [the calm]. I know it will take a while, [to get back to my old self] but now I know it is not lost." The calm sensation in the group allowed her to have hope, which became an important step in her recovery.

Another group member experienced an emotional release related to her grief process. The class ends with a relaxation period as members lie calmly on their yoga mats. The member began to cry, and shared that the moment reminded her of being calmed by her mother as a child. She cried gratefully as she had not been able to express her grief through tears up to this point, and that was a relief for her. Because the yoga practices can induce a sense of nurturing calm, connections to positive moments with the person who died can arise.

Self-esteem of the group members can be enhanced as well. A male participant in his sixties said, "I am just glad to be doing something good for myself." He related to the physical nature of the yoga practice, and he liked the clear, concrete directives. Over the six-week course, improvement and competency increase, giving participants a sense of accomplishment that can be translated to the grief journey as a whole.

CONCLUDING THOUGHTS

The combination of mindful breathing and yoga movements within a therapeutically supportive environment appears to be beneficial to a grieving person's process. Our bodies can do much to inform us. Establishing a "dialogue" between our mind and body facilitates opening one to physically stored memories and emotions related to the deceased, allowing for healing with the support of the yoga practices, group members and counselor. Although the yoga is limited to individuals who can perform the movements, adjustments can be made that extend the range of those who can participate (e.g., chair-based yoga). Some participants become inspired to seek out more formal practice in yoga centers. Others find the breathing awareness aspect of the practices worthy of further exploration. There is little research available directly about the benefits of combined grief counseling and yoga. However, one may find related research through studies in "mindfulness and depression." In our program, all of the participants noted a "better" or "much better" reduction in the "pain of their grief" in post-group anonymous surveys. Group therapeutic discussion joined with gentle yoga appears to provide effective relief for the griever's painful journey.

References

Kabat-Zinn, J. (1990). *Full catastrophe living*. New York: Bantam Dell.
Stahl, B., & Goldstein, E. (2010). *A mindfulness-based stress reduction workbook*. Oakland, CA: New Harbinger Publications.
Wolfelt, A. (2009). *Healing your grieving body*. Fort Collins, CO: Companion.

18
Body Imagery for Sustaining Connections

Lara Krawchuk

CLIENTS FOR WHOM THE TECHNIQUE IS APPROPRIATE

Grieving clients who have lost someone or something dear to them and are struggling to maintain a connection with that which feels lost. Body-centered imagery of this sort may be less appropriate for clients who are newly bereaved, as it may prove too intense to focus on physically sensed reconnection.

DESCRIPTION

After significant loss, grievers often struggle to learn how to sustain new, meaningful connections to a person no longer physically present (Neimeyer, 2001). Longing to literally touch, hear and feel a loved one who has died can feel torturous to those left behind. Many feel confused, isolated, disconnected, and deeply alone in the wake of a great loss. For some, body imagery can open a pathway for building new connections with a loved one who remains deeply cherished, but no longer physically accessible. Body-centered guided imagery is a technique that gently steers the imagination to see, hear, taste, touch, smell, and feel images that hold deep meaning, retain questions, or need further exploration. In the past 25 years, imagery has been increasingly established as having a positive impact on physical and emotional healing. One of the most appealing features of imagery is that, to the body, images raised by the mind can be as real as actual external events (Naprastek, 2004; Rossman, 2000). For example, if one constructs a detailed image of a favorite food, it is quite common to literally salivate, even though this mental food could not actually be touched or consumed. For a few moments the mind is eating that favorite food! For grieving clients, entering into a relaxed, gently altered state of guided body imagery offers a chance to experience powerful reconnection with a loved one who has heretofore felt completely absent. This can, in turn, foster a lasting sense of relational connectedness that both reflects the reality of physical absence and offers a potent experience of sharing space for brief moments in time. For grievers, this imagery connection can provide a powerful balm to tired, lonely, and wounded souls.

To practice body imagery with clients, I first explain that we are simply exploring their inner world and that there are no "rights" or "wrongs" to the practice. I encourage clients to allow themselves to relax and to stay open to whatever comes up. I remind them that my words are a gentle prompt, but that their minds will take them wherever they really need to go in that moment. I urge them to allow the process to unfold without judgment and inform them that they are in total control of the experience. They may simply stop, at any time, if they want or need to. After offering a brief overview of what to expect, I ask them to close their eyes (or focus on a fixed point on the floor), breathe at a comfortable pace and allow their bodies to unwind. I ask them to take note of the feel of their bodies in the chair, feet on the floor, and a connection to all the wisdom of the universe. I then do a brief body scan to note where grief "lives" in their body and how it presents itself. We take some time to experience images of pain and eventually shift to explore inner connections with a lost loved one. The following case exemplifies the power of this technique.

CASE EXAMPLE

Debra was a 60-year-old, Catholic woman who, eight months prior, lost her 28-year-old daughter, Lindy, to a terrible autoimmune disease. Though the illness was long, filled with extreme pain and physical degeneration, the actual death was sudden and unexpected. Debra had, a year before, quit her job to become the full-time caregiver for her daughter and was proud of the excellent 24-hour care she provided. Throughout Lindy's illness, Debra often recounted to me her gratification over finding a good balance between being her daughter's primary care giver and also her mother and friend. The sudden death of her daughter caught her completely off guard and she was totally devastated by the loss of her child and her role as caregiver. She was deeply hurt by friends' attempts to console her by stating that "Lindy was in a better place" and that she needed to "Let Lindy go and be happy again." She repeatedly reported that her heart was totally broken and that she was forever changed by the experience. The loss of Lindy took a huge emotional toll on Debra and also seriously compromised her physical health. Due to ongoing health problems, Debra was only able to attend therapy sporadically.

One Spring day, Debra returned to therapy after a month-long absence. She dragged herself into the office and dropped heavily into the chair, her face already soaked by tears. Her face was grim, eyes sunken, and deep frown lines were etched around her eyes and mouth. She simply looked at the floor and cried. After some time she whispered "I can't do this. I just miss her too much." I quietly validated her deep pain, inquired briefly about her safety and listened deeply to the story of terrible anguish she was living every single day. It quickly became clear that one of the hardest parts for Debra was her inability to feel a connection with Lindy anymore. This was intolerable for Debra who had spent so long virtually connected at the hip to Lindy, throughout her terrible physical ordeal. Debra longed to touch, smell and literally feel Lindy again, but instead she felt nothing but unbearable emptiness.

I asked if Debra would like to practice body-centered imagery (something we had done several times before) in an attempt to explore a new kind of connection with Lindy that might exist inside of her. Debra readily agreed. I reminded her that there were no set goals to our exploration and that she could stop at any time. We began by doing calming breathing and when Debra's posture indicated to me that she was feeling relaxed, I led her through a simple body scan to notice how each part of her body was feeling. The pain was so intense that several times Debra made wrenching choking noises, but indicated that she wanted to continue. After spending some time with the pain, I asked Debra to notice her body in a different way by noticing any parts in her body where Lindy or Lindy's spirit might feel most present. Right away Debra smiled and moved both her hands to her heart. I invited Debra to take a moment to breathe with the feeling of presence. Debra's entire face softened and a smile played on her lips. I urged Debra to take her time exploring this image of her daughter that lives within her, to notice small details, breathe in any smells, listen to offered wisdom. I repeatedly asked Debra to breathe deeply and "drink in the experience of being with Lindy in this moment." I noticed Debra's fingers caressing her heart and asked if she might create an even larger space for Lindy by expanding the space between her hands. Slowly Debra's hands separated as if being pushed gently apart by an invisible balloon. Her fingers continued to caress the space between and her smile widened. Little by little we expanded the space between her hands and ultimately I asked Debra to move her hands to best reflect her experience of being with Lindy in this moment. Instantly Debra's arms shot out, parallel to the floor, and she moved them delicately like soft wings. Debra's smile lit up the entire room and I again repeated the instruction to "drink in the experience of being with Lindy in this moment." As I led Debra through the rest of our guided imagery, I felt a peaceful energy radiating from her. I instructed Debra to share a few last minutes with Lindy, absorb the detail of the moment, and finally to say goodbye for now. I reminded Debra that this part of Lindy lived within her and that she could visit again any time she wanted. I asked Debra to take five deep breaths to seal in her experience and return to our shared space when she felt ready. I used a Tibetan singing bowl to call her back to my office, and when Debra opened her eyes she looked absolutely transformed. She was joyous and radiant. It took my breath away. Debra shared that through our guided imagery she was able, for the first time since Lindy's death, to feel connected to her again. She felt Lindy's literal presence in her heart. She saw that Lindy now had the wings of an angel and that her body was no longer deformed or wracked with pain. She reported that Lindy asked her to trust that she was safe and also shared that it was okay to be sad, but also important to find moments of joy once again. Debra stated that she was able to wrap her arms around Lindy and felt her baby in her arms once again. It felt wonderful. Debra profusely thanked me for assisting in this experience, but in truth her joyful smile was more thanks than I could ever desire! I, like Debra, felt transformed by this experience.

Two weeks later, I saw Debra again and she reported that after our imagery experience she felt drawn to a little church she passes on her way home from work. Several times since, she has entered the church, knelt to pray quietly, and each time she felt a deep connection to Lindy. She reported that her pain still cut deep, but that she now felt a new kind of bond to Lindy, in her heart, that she felt would live with her for the rest of her life. Debra credited our work with body imagery with opening her heart to the meaningful connections with her beloved daughter that lay within.

CONCLUDING THOUGHTS

Anyone can learn how to do body imagery and it can be safely practiced with a trusted therapist, in a group setting, or alone in the privacy of one's personal space. Because connecting with a loved one who is lost or has died can be very intense and emotional, it is imperative to build a deep foundation of trust before embarking on this kind of imagery journey. Offer, never require imagery work and proceed at a slow, comfortable pace based on visual and verbal clues provided by the client.

References

Naprastek, B. (2004). *Invisible heroes: Survivors of trauma and how they heal.* New York: Bantam Dell.

Neimeyer, R. A. (2001). *Meaning reconstruction and the experience of loss.* Washington, DC: American Psychological Association.

Rossman, M. L. (2000). *Guided imagery for self-healing.* Novato, CA: H.J. Kramer Inc.

19
Written on the Body

Jane Moss

CLIENTS FOR WHOM THE TECHNIQUE IS APPROPRIATE

Adolescents and adults following the loss of a parent or significant elder relative. It may be of help to those who wish to remember and write about someone who has died, but who find photographs too emotive to contemplate. Those who find the physical detail of remembered characteristics or appearance too raw to approach in the early stages of grieving may also find it difficult. The facilitator should be alert to those who may access memories of an abusive family relationship.

DESCRIPTION

We are all products of our upbringing and of the people who have made us. When we are bereaved, the story of our lives is disrupted (Bowman, 2000). When parents or other loved ones die, the memory of their physical presence, their voice, their laugh, their distinctive scent or the way they walked, fades. Photographs can capture the still image, but the nuance of physical detail can be hard to recall. In early bereavement, the child (adult or younger), will hear relatives say "You're so like her" or "You have your father's smile." This can bring comfort but may also underline the pain of separation. The adult's transition to bereaved child entails a process of remaking one's own image as an individual stepping out of the parent's shadow, while also wishing to honour his or her memory. A period of biographical adjustment is required (Walter, 1996), before the bereaved are able to move on with their own life narratives.

This creative writing technique uses guided imagery to generate a written character sketch of a parent or other significant elder. It uses the starting point of a physical feature, for example, hands. Adapting this from creative techniques commonly used in writing biography, I have found this to be a supportive way to enable bereaved people to explore memories about a family member who is dear to them and to reflect upon the similarities and differences inherent in the relationship. It is worth considering whether or not to encourage people to write specifically about their most present loss. Some will wish to; others will benefit from switching attention to a different family member; perhaps a cherished grandparent or someone from further back in childhood, as a form of respite from present distress. The choice should be offered and the technique structured in a way that the participants can make use of their choice.

I begin by inviting participants to close their eyes and picture a pair of hands. I suggest that these be the hands of someone who has been dear to them; whether the person for whom they are now grieving or someone else who has been significant in their past. I invite them to study the hands closely; to note their age and appearance, the shape of wrist and fingers, and any marks or scars. I suggest they observe any rings, bracelets, or perhaps the colour of nail polish or the pattern of a tattoo. I ask them to consider whether the hands are soft or rough; the hands of someone who has known manual or domestic work, or who has enjoyed leisure. You can read the story of a person's life and occupation in their hands.

Moving on, I invite them to see what these hands are doing and where they are. Perhaps they are at rest or at work, making something or holding something. I suggest they look now at the rest of the person. Whose hands are these? In their mind's eye, they can continue to regard the owner of the hands and to enjoy a memory of them. Ideally they will be able to picture themselves with the person in this memory and be able to describe their feelings about them alongside their recollection. When they are ready, I invite them to open their eyes and begin writing the story of those hands and their treasured memory of the person. I would offer 15 minutes for this writing, with a 5-minute prompt before the end. If people are still writing after 15 minutes, offer them a further minute or two in which to finish off and perhaps make notes so they can continue in their own time. This is not to hurry them, but to provide an end point for the exercise and permission to stop writing (Thompson, 2010, pp. 44–45).

Inviting the writers to share what they have written, I reiterate the ground rule that everyone should feel free to decline the offer. If they do not wish to read out, perhaps they will be encouraged instead to talk about it, or to have someone else (the facilitator, perhaps) read it for them. With this safety net in place, participants rarely decline.

Where a desire has been expressed to capture in writing the character and life history of someone who has died, this technique provides a supported way into memory. It enables the writer to capture the close physical and sensory detail that can lend richness and texture to expression, whether in talking or writing about the person. Occasionally, it can stimulate the writer to describe people they have not expected to write about. This can give rise to pleasure, both in the experience of recovering a positive memory, and in sharing with others in the group. The facilitator can comment on this and on the palpable presence of vividly described individuals in the room as stories are shared. This affirmation enhances the therapeutic value of the writing. There may be scope for further self-reflective writing about the relationship between the writer and the person they are describing. This can be followed up in personal journal writing or in one to one counselling.

CASE EXAMPLE

Judith produced her poem about a mother and daughter using her mother's hands as a metaphor through which to explore difference and similarity. As a piece of biographical story telling in blank verse, the poem incorporates elements of life history (with references to WWII), and acknowledges the sometimes difficult relationship between mother and daughter ("imagined hurt"). The poem has a satisfying circularity in its structure, beginning and ending with the image of the hands and their signs of ageing ("Small, cold and old the hand was hers, that now I see is mine ... at least we share the vivacity of wrinkles") which finds reconciliation in similarity.

> ### Keepsake
> *Small, cold and old the hand*
> *was hers, that now I see is mine:*

the nails are pale, gently smooth –
but I bite mine – the knuckles proud
and like their owner independent;
nimble and sure the fingers loop and twist,
knit up all inconsistencies from the past
in cosy cardigan, intricate shawl.

Veins – French navy or Paynes grey?
spread in a maze of rootlets
under transparent, thin layered
skin like parachute silk
from the airfield
still flecked with blood
to swell the tears:
we sewed soft knickers and slips.

I like to think myself more capable,
more worldly than she, and wiser,
yet called a true daughter of her mother.
At best spring follows winter
in spite of time's eccentricities
of melting hours, grey heads, imagined hurt,
and at least
we share
the vivacity of wrinkles.

Sharing her poem, which was written at home following the stimulation of the guided writing exercise and brought to the group, Judith commented that for her the poem was both a memorial for her late mother and her own meditation of the passage of time, her own changing status as daughter of a mother no longer living, and a way to record details of biography and shared memory in a contained form. She reported that the writing came quickly and that she felt calm and absorbed while writing and redrafting it. The affirmation she received from the group on reading it aloud gave her pleasure.

CONCLUDING THOUGHTS

In this example I have offered hands as the starting point. You may feel free to suggest eyes, a smile, a voice or laughter, or some other physical attribute. Participants may of course choose their own. This approach to self-expression provides a contained way into writing about the subject. The invitation to "write about your uncle" or "describe your mother for me" may be too blunt or loose for some. A hook is required to draw writers in and to enable them, perhaps, to make something that is unbearable to contemplate in its entirety, manageable through the detail.

References

Bowman, T. (2000). Bereavement and shattered dreams. *Bereavement Care, 19*(1), 3–5.
Thompson, K. (2010). *Therapeutic journal writing*. London: Jessica Kingsley.
Walter, T. (1996). A new model of grief: Bereavement and biography. *Mortality, 1*(1), 7–25.

20
The Body of Trust

Diana C. Sands

CLIENTS FOR WHOM THE TECHNIQUE IS APPROPRIATE

The body of trust is used in traumatic bereavement when the griever's ability to story the loss is disrupted with distressing ruminations that do not eventuate in adaptive narrative development and integration of grief. It is probably less appropriate in the context of support groups for more normative bereavement experiences.

DESCRIPTION

One of the fundamental issues for those traumatically bereaved is a sense of fractured or broken trust with the way the world is known and understood. Particularly for those bereaved through suicide, issues of volition provoke intense distress and are frequently perceived as a breach in relational trust between the griever and deceased that can disrupt the formation and adaptive functioning of the continuing bond. These and other issues in traumatic bereavement can provoke a crisis in meaning, challenging beliefs and values that form the bedrock of the griever's assumptive world and the framework through which the griever makes meaning of life events (Neimeyer & Sands, 2011). For some of those bereaved, retelling the loss story assists grief integration, but when there is a severe disjunction between the griever's assumptive world and the loss, the story becomes disrupted and rigid, yielding no relief, and exhausting both griever and caring listener. The intervention known as "the body of trust" draws on narrative and body-focused methods to facilitate the integration of challenging embodied sensory, emotional and cognitive material, to assist adaptive meaning reconstruction.

In traumatic bereavement there is a tendency for the deceased's pain and the griever's pain to become undifferentiated (Sands, Jordan, & Neimeyer, 2011). Stepping into the story from a first-hand perspective provides opportunities for the bereaved to identify and make meaning of their own heavily embodied pain. Revisiting the death story through the body of trust can help soothe and introduce new insights and perspectives. The intervention enhances narrative flexibility through the use of spoken and written words, expressive art, symbol, metaphor and enactment—a menu of possibilities to allow for the various ways people interpret their world. The pace of the intervention is slow and unfolding, allowing time for the bereaved to sit with grief and listen to their body. It provides opportunities to add information not available at the time of death, to order and sequence events, and to enact undone actions. The counselor paces with the clients, breathing with them, attentive to nuances in body language and the spaces between words. Deepening questions about the position, size, shape, weight, color, texture and feeling senses associated with pain and wounding prompt exploration of challenging material. It is important to remember that for all violent deaths, the place of death is a crime scene, and investigation protocols prevent holding and touching the body of the loved one and other expressions of grief. Shock also interferes with the ability of the bereaved to perform actions at the time of the death, which can give rise to deep regrets. A simple form of enactment can be used to address these concerns. The intervention should take place within an established therapeutic relationship after identifying and strengthening resilience and support resources. It can be used in both bereavement groups and clinical settings.

The first step is to trace around the bereaved person's body on a large sheet of paper. The intervention proceeds with the bereaved person talking, while the clinician responds and writes, draws, or places symbolic objects onto the drawing that express the bereaved person's experience. In a group context, members can fulfill some of these functions. For example, a griever's spoken words at that time, "No, no, no!" can be written on the outline next to the mouth. The body's shut-down, freeze responses associated with shock can be represented by blue coloring in relevant parts of the body. Flames symbolic of anger can be drawn, and objects such as stones can be used to represent the weight of grief. It is important to represent the griever's relational, spiritual and other resources on the body outline. The deceased loved one's presence can be added, and the state of the griever's heart and elements of the grief experience, such as walls of protection, can be drawn around the outline.

There are three salient, over-arching time points that gently guide and facilitate this intervention, beginning with Time 1, setting the context just before the bereaved found out about the death: What day and time was it? Where were they and what were they doing? Who was with them? Was there something they were looking forward to? Time 2 is concerned with how they found out about the death: Did they find the body? If not, how did they come to be told? When they found out, where were they? What happened at that time—thoughts, feelings, words, sensations within their body, perhaps shaking, screaming, vomiting, hyperventilation, collapse? Time 3 is concerned with the current time and how they are experiencing their grief now: What do they notice in their heart and body that is different? Have some of the things indicated on the drawing healed?; are some the same?; do certain aspects of their grief seem more intense? How do they understand these differences? How can their resources help to soothe, heal and comfort?

CASE EXAMPLE

Edouard, grieving the loss of his son to suicide, was consumed with themes of bitterness and frustration with the health professionals in whose care his son was being treated. His intense rumination on these issues dominated, excluding other elements of his grief. Participating in the body of trust in the context of group therapy with other suicide survivors, he talked of driving home on the day his son died, leaving the early morning Christmas church service with a sense of pleasant anticipation of a day of celebration with his family. He spoke of his mounting anxiety when his son did not arrive and the cold clenching fear in his stomach when he could not reach him on the phone. As he drove to his son's apartment, a deadening numbness descended over his body. He used his key to unlock the door and found his son. The shock and horror were so overwhelming that he felt he "was out of this world" and went "completely blank." His son's body was cold and he recalled repeating his name "over and over." It seemed only moments before the paramedics were on the scene working to save his son, as he stood helpless, crying and praying to God, barely daring to breathe. He broke down as he recalled the paramedic turning towards him, knowing his son was dead before the words were uttered. He told of his wife's arrival, her heart-wrenching screams and collapse. Shaking his head, he sobbed, "His body—his beautiful body—so terribly scarred." Haltingly Edouard related how previously his son had set himself on fire, suffering burns to over 60% of his body. Hands over his face he told of their anguish, the countless hours, days and months at the hospital, and the slow process of rehabilitation. "I feel he died that day—he never healed inside." Sobbing, he cried, "But why, why Christmas Day?" His son's action seemed to negate all the years of happy family Christmas celebrations. For Edouard, Christmas represented the essence of everything that was good about the family and home he and his wife had created together in this new country they had come to just after the birth of their first child.

The body of trust provided opportunities for him to sit and unpack this deeply distressing emotional, physical and cognitive material in a different way, with time, safety and support, as he permitted group members to inscribe his outline on a large sheet of paper placed on the floor. As Edouard told his story, group members captured its vivid imagery on the drawing: a cold blue mass in the center of his stomach, the black question marks surrounding his head. His son's terrible burn wounds that the father carried on his own body were drawn as a mass of red, jagged lines onto the outline. In an enactment, holding a pillow proffered by the therapist, Edouard held and rocked his son in a way he had not been able to do at the death scene, telling him of his love and pride in him, the joy and light his being had brought into his life. As a group member depicted a golden light radiating on the client's outline from above, the therapist invited him to imagine the spirit of family Christmases past and to share about the many wonderful times, such as when his son was given his first musical instrument, and the love of music that father and son shared. A beautiful Christmas tree with presents and gathered family were added silently to the body drawing by another group member, placed close to his heart. His wife who was present spoke of her son's long and exhausting struggle with mental illness, and how she soothed herself thinking of "her boy at peace—no longer in pain." The father shared his philosophy on love and the way he had parented his children: "Love is understanding, love is caring. If you believe in love, you can survive many difficulties." Reverently, a group member wrote these words within his heart on the drawing. Together husband and wife began to weave a new way of making meaning of their son's death on Christmas Day, as a time in the year that epitomized the very heart of love for this family. Paradoxically, sitting with and visualizing their pain allowed them to sense the possibility that at the end of his long struggle their son was comforted by these warm memories of happy times. A group member gently wrapped a length of soothing, blue green material like a healing cloak around Edouard's shoulders as the felt sense of their son's words, "I couldn't stay any longer—I love you," was written above the body image, releasing tears, peace and shared grieving. Mother and father talked of how "their boy" would have known they would come and take care of him in death with all the understanding and love that they had cared for him throughout his life. It was a beginning for them of finding a way to live with all that had happened, a story that allowed into the darkness and despair crucial resources and emotional nourishment for life. The tiny shoots of new beginnings in this reconstructed story, represented by fragile green around the edge of the figure, offered subtle transformations, choices that opened pathways for change and growth. As the narration and drawing reached a natural stopping place, both parents noted tearfully how grateful they were for the experience, and other group members offered affirmation and support for the moving story they had shared. The group concluded with the gifting of the drawing to the couple from the group members.

CONCLUDING THOUGHTS

The body of trust is grounded in research into meaning reconstruction in the context of traumatic loss, and significantly the "walking in the shoes" phase of the tripartite model of suicide bereavement (Sands, Jordan, & Neimeyer, 2011). The intervention is also supported by research by Ogden, Minton and Pain (2006) and other researchers, confirming the effectiveness of body-focused approaches for integration of traumatic sensory experiences to assist adaptive narrative reconstruction. As an accompaniment to verbal processing of traumatic deaths, it can play a useful role in sense-making in the face of senseless loss.

References

Neimeyer, R. A., & Sands, D. C. (2011). Meaning reconstruction and bereavement: From principles to practice. In R. A. Neimeyer, D. L. Harris, H. R. Winokuer, & G. F. Thornton (Eds.), *Grief and bereavement in contemporary society: Bridging research and practice*. New York: Routledge.

Ogden, P., Minton, K., & Pain, C. (2006). *Trauma and the body: A sensorimotor approach to psychotherapy*. New York: Norton.

Sands, D. C., Jordan, J. R., & Neimeyer, R. A. (2011). The meanings of suicide: A narrative approach to healing. In J. R. Jordan, & J. L. McIntosh (Eds.), *Grief after suicide*. New York: Routledge.

Part IV
Transforming Trauma

21
Complicated Grief and Trauma
What to Treat First?

Stephen Fleming

CLIENTS FOR WHOM THE TECHNIQUE IS APPROPRIATE

This approach is appropriate with bereaved adults who are experiencing traumatic symptoms following the loss of a loved one. This intervention is contraindicated when there is a risk for self-harm, social support is weak or non-existent, there are severe comorbid conditions that must be addressed first (e.g. major depressive disorder), or where intense arousal is medically injudicious.

DESCRIPTION

Succinctly stated, grief is the price we pay for loving and, in most instances, it does not present the survivor with insurmountable obstacles to integrating the loss, nor is professional intervention indicated. However, particularly when the death has been traumatic, complications in one's grief response may develop. Characteristics of a traumatic death include such factors as the suddenness of the death, deaths that occur "out of time" (e.g. the death of a child), deaths involving violence or mutilation, multiple deaths, random deaths, and deaths perceived as unnecessary or preventable (Worden, 2009). When working with survivors of traumatic loss, or if one suspects the existence of Axis I or Axis II disorders that might complicate adjustment to loss, the prudent clinician will conduct a comprehensive personality assessment to enhance diagnostic accuracy and inform and direct intervention strategies.

One ticklish diagnostic and treatment issue for clinicians is the distinction between grief symptoms (affective, cognitive, physical, social, and spiritual) and posttraumatic stress disorder or PTSD. There is a striking similarity between the symptom presentation of grief and PTSD. PTSD symptoms of re-experiencing (e.g. dreams, nightmares, and perturbation when exposed to reminders of the trauma) are not uncommon in bereaved individuals. Similarly, PTSD avoidance and emotional numbing responses (e.g. distancing from painful reminders of the deceased, loss of interest in previously enjoyed activities, feelings of detachment or not belonging, restricted range of affect, and thoughts of a foreshortened future) are often reported by those whose loved ones have died. Finally, PTSD symptoms of hyperarousal (constant vigilance, difficulty falling and/or staying asleep, irritability and anger, concentration difficulties, and an exaggerated startle response) are frequently reported by those grieving a loss, particularly the death of a child (Buckle & Fleming, 2011). Awareness of the distinctive features of PTSD (e.g. the unbidden nature and intensity of the re-experiencing and the persistence of the numbing/avoidance response) and the use of reliable and valid psychometric tools can assist in determining the presence or absence of PTSD symptoms in the midst of grief (Buckle & Fleming, 2011).

A trauma overlay has the potential to hamper or interfere with the emergence of one's grief response, e.g. if the traumatic circumstances of the death are so aversive that the mourner struggles to actively avoid thinking or speaking about the deceased, then trauma material effectively impedes the emergence and experiencing of sadness, pining, and reminiscing. When PTSD symptoms complicate the grief response, it is recommended that such symptoms be addressed prior to targeting the impact of the loss.

Although there are a number of recognized intervention strategies for the treatment of PTSD, I would like to discuss trauma-focused exposure therapy. Exposure therapy involves the careful, repeated, detailed imagining of the trauma (exposure) in a safe, controlled environment to help the survivor face and gain a sense of mastery over the fear and distress associated with the traumatic event. In most instances, a titrated approach is recommended, i.e., the therapist gradually exposes the client to the most severe trauma by using relaxation techniques and by starting with less upsetting life stresses, or by taking the trauma one piece at a time ("desensitization").

CASE EXAMPLE

Lisa, a 34-year-old mother of three, was standing at the roadside to greet the school bus transporting her 4-year-old daughter, Emma, from school. As Emma stepped from the bus, a gust of wind caught a paper in her hand and blew it to the front of the bus. Emma impulsively ran to fetch her drawing. Unable to see the child, the driver moved the vehicle forward and it struck and fatally injured Emma—and her mother watched in horror, and helpless, as this scene unfolded. Along with her debilitating grief, Lisa presented with classic PTSD symptoms of intrusion, avoidance, and hypervigilance.

In addition to the unbidden and intrusive traumatic scenes from the road, it became obvious that Lisa had a powerful, competing motivation to share fond memories of Emma, to discuss her impish qualities, and to illustrate the love and laughter she brought to the family. In therapy, Lisa's longing, pining, and missing Emma were followed, in rapid succession, by disruptive traumatic memories of what happened on "the road." Increasingly, I found it artificial and disruptive to gently keep her focused on the trauma work and nudge her away from the painful but important reflections of Emma's legacy. I abandoned the decision to deal with the trauma first and decided to follow Lisa's lead. When she was exploring her grief, that became the focus and, alternatively, when material from "the road" would suddenly intrude, I adopted a non-titrated approach to exposure therapy.

During one session Lisa reflected, "You know, I used to love going shopping for girl's stuff with Emma—I'll really miss that." After a comment on the joys of "retail therapy" with her daughter, traumatic images suddenly emerged as Lisa recalled the dress Emma was wearing as she held her on the road. Rather than evaluate the intensity of emotional distress created by this imagery and its relative position on a desensitization hierarchy, I facilitated the bringing of this traumatic material to consciousness through the repeated reliving, reconstructing, and re-experiencing of this particular traumatic event and the horror, fear, guilt, rage, and helplessness associated with it. With a titrated approach, exposure is prolonged to extinction, in this instance the traumatic scene was followed to its conclusion (and, of course, repeated as it emerged during the course of psychotherapy). I don't think extinction is a realistic goal in such situations, rather, the best one can hope for is a reduction in stress level and the enhanced ability to discuss the trauma without becoming destabilized and having this material derail the grief process.

In following Lisa's lead the flow of therapy was not interrupted, and no attempt was made to construct a hierarchy of distressing recollections for desensitization. Lisa had been taught anxiety management strategies to facilitate a calming response and understood that, at any time, she could stop the exposure if she felt threatened. At the conclusion of therapy, psychometric testing revealed a sharp reduction in intrusive symptoms (e.g. flashbacks, nightmares), significant decreases in Lisa's avoidance behavior. She was able to discuss what happened on "the road," she was also able to travel on a school bus and, importantly, she was able to allow her other children to travel by bus to various school outings.

CONCLUDING THOUGHTS

In my experience, it is not uncommon for psychotherapy with traumatized bereaved individuals to proceed along two avenues simultaneously, i.e. adaptation to grief and trauma. In moving from a titrated to a non-titrated intervention, I had to attend to Lisa's lead into the traumatic material; of course, such rapid transitions put the therapist's response agility to the test as I struggled to effectively keep pace with Lisa. Prerequisites for this type of intervention would include a thorough psychometric assessment of the presenting symptoms, a sound therapeutic relationship, adequate training and skill level and, since one is a participant in traumatic material, the monitoring of one's vicarious traumatization.

With respect to the question, "What to treat first: complicated grief or trauma?", the answer is an unequivocal "*Yes.*"

References

Buckle, J. L., & Fleming, S.J. (2011). *Parenting after the death of a child: A practitioner's guide.* New York: Routledge.

Worden, J. W. (2009). *Grief counseling and grief therapy* (4th ed.). New York: Springer.

22

Retelling the Narrative of the Death

Robert A. Neimeyer

CLIENTS FOR WHOM THE TECHNIQUE IS APPROPRIATE

Adults and adolescents who struggle with intrusive thoughts and images concerning the death, particularly from violent causes. However, re-narration of the death should be preceded in most cases by interventions that stabilize the bereaved and provide coaching in emotion modulation, and that facilitate meaning-making following imaginal exposure. Intense retelling may not be needed in some cases of even violent death when the client is primarily concerned with attachment issues with the deceased, rather than with the dying *per se*.

DESCRIPTION

From a meaning reconstruction perspective, integrating the reality of a loved one's loss commonly involves two forms of narrative processing, centered on the *event story of the death*, on the one hand, and the *back story of the relationship* with the loved one, on the other (Neimeyer & Sands, 2011). In the natural accommodation of loss, mourners commonly tack back and forth between these two stories, sharing them with receptive others in an effort to weave the death narrative into the larger story of their lives as a sad, but necessary transition, while drawing on and finding sustenance in the back story of their loved one's life, which continues to provide a sense of attachment security as they reconstruct, rather than relinquish, their continuing bond. In most cases as this process proceeds, the raw grief of the loss becomes less preoccupying, and the survivor gradually reestablishes a sense of meaning and coherence in a changed life.

Nothing, however, assures this outcome, as circumstances associated with the death, with the relationship, or with their interaction can interfere with integration of the loss and reorganization of the bond. Among these factors are situations associated with the dying itself, ranging from a precipitous change in a loved one's health that challenges the survivor's attempt to make sense of it, ambiguous causes that lead to the death, and especially death by homicide, suicide and fatal accident, particularly of a grotesque kind. In such cases the mourner may ruminate continually, even if privately, on the death narrative, or be repeatedly assaulted by unbidden traumatic imagery, whether the death was witnessed or the body was discovered, or whether the loved one's final moments were vividly dreamed or imagined. All of these circumstances represent an assault on mourners' worlds of meaning, frequently shattering assumptions that the universe is benevolent, that others can be trusted, and that they themselves can shield those they care for from harm. When this occurs, the event story of the death can become preoccupying, to a degree that reworking the attachment to the loved one and seeking new meaning in one's life are greatly impeded.

It is not surprising, therefore, that leading attachment and coping, cognitive-behavioral and meaning reconstruction models of grief therapy converge on certain principles and practices, among which is "fostering confrontation with the event story of the death in an attempt to master its most painful aspects and integrate its finality into the mourner's internalized models of the deceased, the self, and the world" (Shear, Boelen, & Neimeyer, 2011, pp. 158–159). Like evidence-based treatments for other traumatic experiences featuring prolonged exposure to the feared situation under conditions of safety, "restorative retelling" of violent death also entails countering ineffective avoidance coping with direct engagement with the story of loss, but under conditions that foster emotional accommodation and reconstruction of meaning (Rynearson, 2006). The following guidelines for "revisiting" or "retelling" the narrative of the death represent a distillation and integration of features of Shear's, Boelen's, and Rynearson's models with my own, along with constructivist practices for promoting review and reconstruction of affect-laden autobiographical material (Guidano, 1995). The goal of such work is not simply "habituation" to the trauma of the loss, but also integration of the experience into autobiographical memory in a way that fosters deeper sense-making regarding the death and its meanings for the life of the survivor. Guidelines for therapeutic retelling include:

- *Construct a safe container for experientially intense work.* Ensure the presence of a strong therapeutic alliance marked by trust and the capacity of the therapist to tolerate and help modulate the client's arousal before prompting retelling.
- *Anchor in strengths and competencies.* Before reviewing in detail the event story of the dying, invite the client to introduce you to the deceased in life by sharing who he or she was as a person, and who they were as a family (or other close relation) prior to the death. Likewise, consider coaching the client in mindfulness techniques, relaxation methods involving breathing, and soothing imagery to build a repertoire of skills for managing the intense emotion that retelling the death narrative can arouse.
- *Concentrate on significant episodes in the account.* For example, begin with the moment when bad news was delivered, death was imminent, or the body was discovered, and continue until a point of natural closure, such as with the funeral or memorial service, or the end of the first day. Subsequent episodes in a more complex dying trajectory can be retold in later sessions, separated by periods of meaning making about each.
- *Invite the client to close his or her eyes to visualize the scene vividly.* Alternatively, photographs of the dying (as with photos of the delivery and stillbirth of a baby or a death in hospice) can be used to enhance engagement with the account. Note that graphic photographs of a crime scene, accident or suicide should probably be avoided as overly traumatizing, however.
- *Slowly pan the "camera" of attention over the visual details of each scene, noting emotionally significant sights, sounds, smells, and other stimuli.* This "slow motion" review of relevant scenarios, punctuated by "close-ups" of pertinent details (expressions on the face of the doctor or police officer, the image of mechanical ventilation) and "panning" across the scene (looking up from the bed of the loved one to the faces and eyes of others present) typically lasts at least 10–15 minutes per episode, and often much longer, depending on the client's level of tolerance and need for periodic processing.
- *"Tack" naturally among different narrative voices.* Elicit the external, objective account of the death, the internal, emotional response to it, and the reflexive, meaning-making

narrative that promotes perspective taking. Ask, "*What caught your attention first when you walked into the room?*" "*What did you see that you wish you had not?*" "*What do you recall was happening for you emotionally or in your body at that moment?*" "*What sense did you make of that at the time?*" "*Did that change, and if so, when?*" Braiding the three strands of narration together in the course of the retelling can help mitigate the sense of silent terror, providing a "through line" that gives a potentially fragmentary, incoherent experience greater intelligibility and wholeness.

- *Repeatedly review "hot spots" associated with the break through of strong emotion.* When a client signals a sharp escalation in distress marked by a flood of tears, sobbing, or an inability to speak (or an escalation of 2 or more points on a 10-point SUDS scale rating prompted by the therapist periodically in the revisiting, as in the Shear protocol), allow a moment of quiet and then encourage the client to retell the immediately preceding material once more, as if "rewinding" the video of the scene several seconds. Repeating this procedure three or four times at such junctures helps permit mastery of the difficult material, and commonly fills in the "narrative gaps" in the account by providing important details omitted from the first telling, but implicitly troubling for the client.

- *Process the experience thoroughly, allowing the client to take the lead.* After the retelling reaches a stopping point, invite the client to slowly open his or her eyes and reorient to the therapeutic space you share. Ask what the client observed in the retelling that seemed new or important, what sense he or she made of the event at the time, and what further sense, if any, he or she makes of it now. Follow the client's lead toward hopeful reappraisals of the experience (such as that the loved one is beyond pain), expressing appreciation for his or her courage in confronting extremely difficult material without suppressing it. Optionally, arrange an audio recording of the retelling to send home with the client to review between sessions to promote further mastery and integration, but only after emotion modulation skills are firmly established and a clear transition is constructed to conclude the revisiting and shift to another engaging activity (e.g., lunch with a trusted friend, listening to soothing music).

- *Set aside the death narrative for later revisiting.* Typically this follows a period of days or weeks devoted to journaling about the experience with an emphasis on sense-making and adaptive coping as well as additional discussion with the therapist.

Note that although clients commonly provide a cursory account of the death narrative in bereavement support contexts, this is usually a carefully edited version designed to spare the listener the hardest parts of the story, those that are the source of wordless torment for the client. Companioning clients through an uncensored telling of the troubling imagery and anxieties that haunt their days and nights is therefore strong medicine, which should be administered only by professionals with substantial training, supervision or experience in prolonged exposure and related experientially intense interventions. Transformative retelling is critically different from both narrative fixation on a "broken record" account of the death and a re-traumatizing re-immersion in its horror, and it is largely the therapist's sense of presence, attunement to the client's process, and command of emotion modulating and meaning-enhancing procedures that ensure that revisiting the story will allow it to evolve in healing directions.

CASE EXAMPLE

An illustration of retelling the event story of death arose in my work with a client, Theresa, whose son, Michael, was killed in a vehicular accident several months earlier while returning to college.

Our early conversations centered on Michael's remarkable character—his orientation to serving others in need, his genial disposition, his spiritual quest that had deepened after an earlier accidental brush with death. While giving ample voice to her own "broken heart," Theresa understandably concentrated in our initial sessions on the practical necessities of managing the distress of other family members, modulating her own grief in a way that permitted her to function in her home and in her work, and striving to connect with her son in intangible, but critically important ways that gave her hope of some form of eventual reunion. In this, her eclectic but deep spirituality was a great resource, encouraging her to discern broader cosmic reasons for her son's dying so young, both to release him from the inevitable suffering entailed in every earthly incarnation, and to teach her and others who loved him important lessons about the nature of impermanence and the value of compassion in this life.

Ultimately, however, Theresa acknowledged that this spiritual narrative, crucial though it was, told only half the story. The silent story, she confessed, was far more anguishing, wordless, filled with a jumble of painful imagery and emotion, much of it centered on the events surrounding Michael's final hours. It was this story, I recognized, that needed an audience, someone who could stand alongside her and hear what others could not, who could help her confront the pain, tolerate it, and piece together a more coherent account of what both she and her son had suffered. I briefly outlined for her the procedure and goals of retelling, and addressed her questions about it before securing her consent. Theresa herself suggested we schedule 90 minutes for the next session to give us ample time to engage the story and regroup, and opted to accept my suggestion that she bring an audio recorder to capture the story for later revisiting if she chose.

We began the next session with a centering meditation, closing our eyes together, focusing on the shared intent to give voice to her experience of Michael's death, asking her to begin at the beginning, when a phone call interrupted her participation in a staff meeting at work. The call, from the highway patrol office of a distant state, informed her that her son had been in an accident, and was being transported by helicopter ambulance to the nearest trauma center. As Theresa, in a controlled voice, described the call, I opened my eyes, tracked her nonverbal displays of emotion, and prompted gently for what happened next. She then described the flurry of calls to and from members of her family and various supporters, with each of whom she concluded, "Please pray, please pray." It was when she related the agonizing call to Michael's brother, whom she reached as he himself was making a long interstate drive home, that her voice broke, pain breaking through into deep sobs. As I gently inquired what made that call the most difficult of all, Theresa replied, as if recognizing it for the first time, "Because I can't protect him from this. I needed him to be there." Tacking between the raw emotion and the associated relational meanings of the unfolding events, Theresa moved forward to other episodes of organizing herself to fly to her son's side, noting the fear in the eyes of other family members, the extraordinary kindness of members of the hospital staff who met her at the airport, the dissociative blur of walking through the hospital corridor, bright with anonymity. Play by play the scenes unfolded, yielding up the forgotten details—the doctor's words before she saw her son, "This is not a survivable event;" her urge to vomit; the tenderness of the nurse caressing her son's broken and misshapen face—all underpinned by the shifting emotional score, with its crescendos of fear, hope, love and grief. As she pieced together the shattered jigsaw puzzle of the previously mute experience, we looped repeatedly through the hardest parts—her first sight of Michael's body on the gurney, the impossible decision the following day, surrounded by friends and family, to withdraw life support on the advice of the compassionate physician, as she collapsed onto her son's lifeless form, shaking him, sobbing, begging him to breathe. It was with that fateful scene that we concluded the retelling after 75 minutes, shifting through a state of mindful breathing together for a few minutes, before "re-entering" the room, opening our eyes and beginning to process the experience, something we continued for the next few sessions in both our dialogue and in her therapeutic journal. The result was significant: in Theresa's words, it left her feeling more "whole," less "reactive," and more "at peace" that she had made the necessary decision, and had discovered deep reserves of strength in her and around her that helped her bear the unbearable with less raw anguish and more understanding. Following this period of consolidation, she requested that we return to the retelling, beginning with the withdrawal of Michael's life support, moving through the funeral service, and concluding with her placing the first shovelful of dirt on her son's grave.

CONCLUDING THOUGHTS

As an experientially evocative therapeutic intervention, detailed retelling of the event story of the death can allow the client to recruit a witness in the therapist to what was previously a largely silent story, sharply edited with others, in the service of articulating, validating, integrating and ultimately renegotiating its meaning. In the process, clients commonly achieve greater clarity and coherence in the account, and are able to accredit their own courage in facing down an anguishing experience in the presence of a responsive other. While not erasing the pain, narration of the loss in all of its cruelly objective and deeply emotional detail also allows clients to begin to glimpse more affirming meanings and possibilities in the wake of the horror, seeing how they responded lovingly to the deceased, or imagining more clearly how they would have, had they been given the chance. Retelling therefore both assists with a more self-compassionate integration of the death into the client's self-narrative, and affirms the challenged relational bond that is at the heart of many of grief's complications.

In addition to the general literature on the efficacy of exposure interventions for trauma, use of retelling or revisiting protocols, whether spoken to the therapist or written in a private journal, is receiving increasing research support in the context of grief therapy (Neimeyer, van Dyke, & Pennebaker, 2009). Such interventions are a mainstay of both "restorative retelling" procedures (Rynearson & Salloum, 2011), which have been found effective in open trials, and complicated grief therapy (Shear, Frank, Houch, & Reynolds, 2005), which outperforms alternative therapy in randomized controlled research. Although more remains to be learned about the "active ingredients" in this intervention, it seems clear that it has an important place in the repertory of skilled and experienced grief therapists.

References

Guidano, V. (1995). Self-observation in constructivist psychotherapy. In R. A. Neimeyer, & M. J. Mahoney (Eds.), *Constructivism in psychotherapy* (pp. 155–168). Washington, DC: American Psychological Association.

Neimeyer, R. A., & Sands, D. C. (2011). Meaning reconstruction in bereavement: From principles to practice. In R. A. Neimeyer, D. L. Harris, H. Winokuer, & G. Thornton (Eds.), *Grief and bereavement in contemporary society: Bridging research and practice*. New York: Routledge.

Neimeyer, R. A., van Dyke, J. G., & Pennebaker, J. W. (2009). Narrative medicine: Writing through bereavement. In H. Chochinov, & W. Breitbart (Eds.), *Handbook of psychiatry in palliative medicine* (pp. 454–469). New York: Oxford University Press.

Ryenearson, E. K. (Ed.). (2006). *Violent death*. New York: Routledge.

Rynearson, E. K., & Salloum, A. (2011). Restorative retelling: Revisiting the narrative of violent death. In R. A. Neimeyer, D. L. Harris, H. Winokuer, & G. Thornton (Eds.), *Grief and bereavement in contemporary society: Bridging research and practice* (pp. 177–188). New York: Routledge.

Shear, K., Boelen, P., & Neimeyer, R. A. (2011). Treating complicated grief: Converging approaches. In R. A. Neimeyer, D. L. Harris, H. Winokuer, & G. Thornton (Eds.), *Grief and bereavement in contemporary society: Bridging research and practice* (pp. 139–162). New York: Routledge.

Shear, K., Frank, E., Houch, P. R., & Reynolds, C. F. (2005). Treatment of complicated grief: A randomized controlled trial. *Journal of the American Medical Association, 293,* 2601–2608.

23

Invoking an Alliance with the Deceased after Violent Death

E.K. Rynearson

CLIENTS FOR WHOM THE TECHNIQUE IS APPROPRIATE

Invoking the presence of the deceased is easily mastered by clinicians and readily accepted by clients who maintain an internalized memory and connection with their loved one's violent dying. The technique may be included in the treatment protocol of children, adolescents and adults unable to accommodate to prolonged trauma distress associated with intense and frequent reenactment imagery (flashbacks and recurrent nightmares). However, it may be unsuitable in circumstances in which an abusive or oppressive relationship with the deceased is itself a source of distress.

DESCRIPTION

The violent death of a loved one is traumatizing beyond the event of death itself because of the suddenness of violent dying combined with its three V's: *violence, victimization* and *violation* (Rynearson, 1987a). Those emotionally attached to and identified with the victim are vulnerable to high levels of both *separation distress* (pining and searching) related to the loss, as well as *trauma distress* (intrusive reenactment imagery, avoidance, hyper-arousal) and secondary thoughts of remorse, retaliation and fears of recurrence related to the reenactment imagery. Persistent intrusive reenactment imagery of violent dying can be psychologically disabling and associated with non-accommodation and treatment seeking (Rynearson, 1995). Moderating trauma distress and the frequency and intensity of reenactment imagery is a clinical priority in recent protocols and manuals of treatment designed specifically for traumatic grief after violent death in children, adolescents and adults, including a modified technique of "exposure" to the dying imagery (Rynearson, 2001).

A dynamic framework of the effects of violent dying reenactment on loss and restoration may be included within the Dual Process Model of Bereavement (Stroebe & Schut, 1999) where grief is theorized to be a dynamic imbalance between the dialectic confrontation of death (loss-oriented) and life (restoration-oriented) restored through irregular oscillations. The dynamic effects of violent dying may be represented in the illustration of DPM as an accessory to the loss-oriented referent, as depicted in Figure 23.1.

As Figure 23.1 visually suggests, the violent dying orientation may overshadow the loss orientation and interfere with the loss/restoration dynamic. It is difficult to process the more

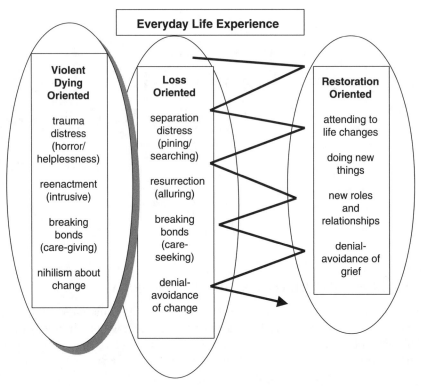

Figure 23.1 The Dual Process Model of Bereavement in the context of violent death

vulnerable ruminations of loss when the mind is fixated within a helpless entrapment, struggling to save and survive the intrusive killing of the loved one associated with intense remorse and nihilistic despair because the dying was so utterly meaningless.

The projected "presence" of the deceased may be actively enlisted during the intervention so the therapy frame becomes triadic as well as dyadic by invoking the voice of the deceased through an imaginary conversation as a resource of stability and meaning (Rynearson, 1987b). This triadic frame of exposure (patient, therapist and "presence" of the deceased) initiates a restorative ingredient during the retelling (exposure) of prolonged and intense reenactment imagery. The projected presence of the deceased joins the therapist and patient as a helpful ally in revising the reenactment narrative by introducing themes of rescue, respect, relinquishment and forgiveness—themes that widen and deepen the reenactment story so it becomes psychologically bearable, more coherent and no longer "possesses" but rather can be released and summoned with a greater sense of personal agency and control.

CASE EXAMPLE

Mary, a 17-year-old student, was violently raped and murdered 14 months before her mother, Ellen, was referred to our center. At the beginning of the first session with Ellen, she could not stop herself from crying, "... and I don't want to talk about her dying. It's all I think about and it just makes me feel worse to tell." This disinhibition had been noted by her referring psychiatrist and listening and empathizing with her reenactment retelling had not been helpful.

I interrupted Ellen and told her we needed to talk about her daughter's living before we talked about her dying. At my urging she retrieved pictures from her purse and grew more animated as the pictures passed between us. She was convinced that her daughter's spirit was in heaven awaiting a reunion.

I asked Ellen if she continued to have conversations with her daughter.

"Yes, I talk to her every day."

I asked if she could imagine a three-way conversation—how would Mary feel about her seeing me as a therapist, and what suggestions would she give us to help her mother?

"She would want me to work with you to stop missing her so much and stop me from blaming myself."

We mutually agreed with Mary's advice and ended that first session with resilience reinforcement; building Ellen's skills in deep breathing, muscle relaxation and guided imagery (she selected a comforting image of sitting beside a mountain stream) and I suggested that she actively divert her mind when the reenactment flashbacks arose by concentrating on Mary's photo and hearing her say, "Stop blaming yourself, Mom, I'm OK now."

By invoking Mary's reassuring presence and message of safety, Ellen felt more detached from the daily flashbacks, but they persisted and she agreed to join a closed group composed of survivors of violent death in a ten-session focused protocol, the structure of which is available online (www.vdbs.org; simply download pdf of Restorative Retelling Manual).

The group support and reinforcement of Ellen's resilience strengthened her stability but the active retelling of the reenactment imagery during session five was particularly helpful in transcending her self-blame for her daughter's dying. With the group's encouragement Ellen made a drawing of her reenactment imagery. The image of Mary's dying was represented as a blackened circle with Mary's spirit as a winged angel transcending the death scene. She could not allow herself to "see" the actual events of rape and murder and we did not encourage its explicit representation. The therapist noted that Ellen's drawing did not include her own presence and asked where she would introduce herself. She placed herself at Mary's side in the dark circle, sacrificing herself to the murder. The therapist invited Mary's voice into that revised image. "Mary" protested, saying her mother's sacrifice would not have stopped the killing, both would have been murdered together, and reminded her mother that her father and two siblings needed her strength and attention and Mary would not want her to continue suffering.

At the completion of the group therapy the reenactment flashbacks of Mary's dying were now counterbalanced by memories and images of her enlivened and supportive "presence." In the final group session as members constructed a farewell message to their loved ones and one another, Ellen included Mary's voice in a written message that read, "Thanks for helping my Mom. She's doing a lot better and she needs to get back to work and living for herself."

A year after treatment, Mary's mother reported that the flashbacks and dreams of her daughter's dying were infrequent and that the therapy had helped her remember Mary's living more than her dying but felt that returning to her work as a nurse and her older daughter's delivery of Ellen's first grandson were of equal importance in her restoration.

CONCLUDING THOUGHTS

The technique of invoking the deceased in a triadic therapeutic alliance initiates a restatement and revision of the reenactment imagery through a process of shared narrative deconstruction and reintegration. By establishing a collaborative and reconstructive retelling with the deceased, a role for the client as active narrator begins to materialize within the fixation. And once the client becomes narrator, "ownership" of the story follows: the retelling belongs to the teller instead of autonomously intruding.

References

Rynearson, E. K. (1987a). The psychotherapy of pathologic grief: Revisions and limitations. *Psychiatric Clinics of North America, 10*(3), 487–499.

Rynearson, E. K. (1987b). Bereavement after unnatural dying. In S. Zisook (Ed.), *Advances in bereavement* (pp. 77–93). New York: American Psychiatric Press.

Rynearson, E. K. (1995). Bereavement after homicide: A comparison of treatment seekers and refusers. *British Journal of Psychiatry, 166*, 507–510.

Rynearson, E. K. (2001). *Retelling violent death*. New York: Brunner-Routledge.

Stroebe, M., & Schut, H. (1999). The Dual Process Model of coping with bereavement: Rationale and description. *Death Studies, 23*(3), 197–224.

24

Eye Movement Desensitization and Reprocessing (EMDR)

Phyllis Kosminsky and Raymond McDevitt

CLIENTS FOR WHOM THE TECHNIQUE IS APPROPRIATE

Clients with unresolved trauma related to loss, early relational trauma, unremitting guilt, anger, or other emotions that compromise their capacity to adapt to bereavement. While EMDR has been found to be safe and tolerable for most clients, those with medical concerns such as high blood pressure, heart conditions, seizures or a history of stroke should consult with their physician before treatment. Clients who experience dissociation should only be treated by EMDR clinicians trained to work with this population. Those with substance abuse issues should have appropriate supports in place prior to EMDR.

DESCRIPTION

"I know intellectually that what you're saying is true, but I still feel like it was my fault." "I can't get those images out of my head and it's driving me crazy." "Even though it happened two years ago, it feels like it happened yesterday." These are the kind of statements that an EMDR-trained clinician listens for, because they are indications that the speaker is suffering from unresolved trauma. It need not be a major trauma—being witness to a car crash or finding a loved one dead. Something seemingly small—the memory of not getting an elderly parent a glass of water, an argument that occurred shortly before the loved one died— can take up residence in a survivor's mind and crowd out other, more positive memories. The inability to access these positive memories of the relationship and the person who died is but one of the ways that unresolved trauma complicates the grieving process (Rando, 1993). As clinicians, we want to help, but there are times when nothing we do seems to be working, when our clients seem locked into their experience or belief and their sense of powerlessness threatens to overtake us. This is where EMDR comes in. The following description is meant as an introduction to EMDR, but in no way prepares the reader to practice the technique. Practice requires training and supervision, the details of which can be obtained from the EMDR Association.

  Developed by Francine Shapiro (Shapiro & Forrest, 1997), EMDR is a combination of elements from cognitive and body-related approaches, along with the unique feature of bilateral stimulation: the "eye movement" contained in the name. EMDR is conducted according to a protocol consisting of several phases, each of which builds on the previous ones. The client is asked to recall the "worst part" of the event (the moment when she saw the body; the moment when he heard the scream) and is then asked to describe what he saw, felt, etc. A core feature of EMDR is eliciting the "negative cognition" associated with the event (e.g., "It was my fault" or "I am a bad mother"). EMDR is based in learning theory, and the assumption is that what keeps a person locked in a traumatic memory is that by its nature trauma overwhelms the brain's capacity for processing information. Our beliefs about what happened—often beliefs generated by a lack of information, or by a false sense of our ability to alter the course of what occurred—create a kind of prison, and it is a prison we cannot be talked out of. What EMDR does is to allow for the integration of new information, a shift in how the individual views the event and their own role in relation to the event. The survivor does not forget the event, but through EMDR "processing" is able to remember it without the attendant feelings of terror, guilt, etc. The following summary provides a general sketch of the phases of EMDR:

Step 1: History taking. As with any client, gather background information. If the client is presenting with a specific trauma, discuss the nature of the trauma.

Step 2: Client preparation. Introduce EMDR, and describe its procedures.

Step 3: Target assessment. Ask the client to recall the "worst part" of the loss experience, with all its attendant physical, emotional and cognitive aspects. In addition to the "negative cognition," obtain a "positive cognition" ("What would you like to believe now when you think about what happened then?") to elicit hope and belief in potential change.

Step 4: Desensitization:
- Ask the client to bring up the disturbing picture and negative thoughts and to become aware of any feelings or body sensations that are evoked.
- Request the client to rate the "level of disturbance" evoked by the memory, on a scale from 0 to 10.
- Provide some form of alternating stimulation: in the case of eye movements, instruct the client to hold his or her head still and "follow my fingers" as they pass back and forth in front of the client's eyes. Other forms of "bilateral stimulation" including auditory or physical cues can also be used.
- Throughout processing, track the client's level of disturbance in response to the original target image, with the goal of reducing the subjective level of disturbance to a 0.

Because EMDR is unlike the therapeutic modalities most of us employ in our work, and because it involves a "mechanical" aspect (the bilateral stimulation), the reader may be disinclined to consider it. The authors have found that EMDR can be integrated into the treatment of clients who are suffering from acute, as well as longstanding trauma, and that the relief clients experience serves to strengthen the therapeutic bond and facilitate related work.

CASE EXAMPLE

Gary, a 50-year-old auto mechanic, entered therapy to address the death of his brother and the profound effect the incident was having on his life. He felt hopelessly mired in the circumstances around the death, unable to move on or "get over it". His brother had died more than two years earlier, but the impact had acutely resurfaced due to the similar circumstances of the sudden death and discovery of Gary's best friend, two months prior to seeking treatment.

Gary had found both his brother, and later his friend, several days after they died in their respective apartments. Both deaths were the result of natural causes but were sudden and unexpected. Gary's brother Jack was single and had long been estranged from family. The friend was recently divorced and isolating himself. Both Jack and the friend were without support systems other than Gary.

Jack, a recovering alcoholic, had worked at Gary's auto shop for many years. He had maintained sobriety for over ten years while there. Several days before he found his brother, Gary and Jack had an altercation at work. Nasty words were exchanged and the two needed to be separated by co-workers. Jack stomped off and failed to return to work the next day (not an uncommon occurrence for him following these types of incidents). Unable to contact Jack for several days, Gary entered his brother's apartment to find him slouched in his recliner. He had been dead for three days.

About eighteen months after Jack's death, Gary's best friend stopped contacting him. After finding the friend's car in the driveway, Gary had the police investigate and they found the man, two days dead. This incident re-triggered Gary's emotional memories of his brother's death. He started experiencing flashbacks, anxiety bordering on panic, anger issues, nightmares and deep debilitating sadness. He felt hopelessly mired in the circumstances around the deaths and unremittingly guilty and upset about his last, angry exchange with his brother.

At the time, I (RM) was a relatively inexperienced EMDR practitioner, but was fortunate to have several highly experienced clinicians as EMDR supervisors. I used the standard EMDR protocol, which focuses on negative cognition, images, feelings, and somatic stress points as targets for bilateral stimulation. I used auditory bilateral stimulation, tones alternating right and left through headphones.

Gary's negative cognition was that his brother's death was his fault, that he should have done more. His negative image was the sight of his dead brother and the smells in the apartment. Gary felt horribly ashamed and guilty. He experienced tightness in his chest and throat. On the scale used to measure subjective distress, Gary assessed his belief in his negative cognition and his anger and upset as being at the maximum levels.

Gary processed the target at a rapid pace. After the first session, his belief that the death was his fault was down two-thirds and his upset was halved. Chest tightness was almost gone. The second session's end found him with no belief that the death was his fault and no upset. He'd remembered an image of a whiskey bottle next to his brother, which he hid when the ambulance came. Gary also recalled strange behavior from Jack preceding their last fight. He was angry that his brother relapsed, but forgave him. "I don't feel guilt about it, just sad. We had good times over the years and I love him." The third session started with a re-check of the measures of belief in negative cognition and degree of upset. Both were still zero. The tension he had felt had dissipated, the nightmares had stopped, anxiety had disappeared, his temper was controlled and he was no longer sad. He next processed the death of his friend in a half hour.

Gary stayed in therapy working on other issues for a year. He never experienced recurrence of the trauma and debilitating grief over his brother's or his friend's death. However, there are no "typical" cases. People process traumatic loss at their own rate, some faster than others. EMDR is not a shortcut, but it is a very helpful tool.

CONCLUDING THOUGHTS

EMDR is a therapeutic technique that has attracted attention because of its effectiveness in helping people recover from the effects of traumatic events. As Solomon and Rando (2007) have noted, the death of a loved one, while ubiquitous throughout all human life, is nonetheless distressing, even traumatic. Additionally, we know that many of our clients come to us having experienced trauma, either early in life or as an adult. Research has shown us that when a client has traumatic memories that are interfering with normal grief, EMDR can be helpful (Sprang, 2001). EMDR can provide much-needed relief from unremitting feelings of guilt, anger and fear, and can facilitate access to positive memories of the deceased, where those have been blocked by trauma. We encourage readers who have not explored EMDR to learn more about it and to consider adding it to their therapeutic repertoire (for training information, see www.emdria.org). We also hope that clinicians will consider seeking consultation with an EMDR-trained clinician for clients who seem "stuck" or who seem caught in unhealthy rumination about the deceased or about the death itself. Used in this way, EMDR can facilitate resolution of trauma and foster healthy mourning.

References

Rando, T. (1993). *Treatment of complicated mourning*. Champagne, IL: Research Press.

Shapiro, F., & Forrest, M. (1997). *EMDR: The breakthrough therapy for overcoming anxiety, stress, and trauma*. New York: Basic Books.

Solomon, R., & Rando, T. (2007). Utilization of EMDR in the treatment of grief and mourning. *Journal of EMDR Practice and Research, 1*(2), 109–117.

Sprang, G. (2001). The use of eye movement desensitization and reprocessing (EMDR) in the treatment of traumatic stress and complicated mourning: Psychological and behavioral outcomes. *Research on Social Work Practice, 11*, 300–320.

25
Making Meaning of Flashbacks

Susan Roos

CLIENTS FOR WHOM THE TECHNIQUE IS APPROPRIATE

Those who, in the aftermath of a traumatic loss of a loved one, are experiencing triggers and flashbacks, and who, though intensely grieving, are functioning adaptively and productively. The method is not relevant for grievers who are experiencing mainly strong separation distress, without traumatic intrusions.

DESCRIPTION

As right brain phenomena, flashbacks are customarily understood as posttraumatic stress disorder symptoms. As a consequence of experiencing a traumatic loss, even when criteria of PTSD are not completely met, flashbacks may begin to occur at variable times and frequency. As frightening as they may be, one could speculate that the brain is attempting to help the person deal with "unfinished business" or to understand more deeply crucial life events. One could also speculate that flashbacks may cease when critical experiences are fully processed and integrated into the personal narrative. At that point, flashbacks may be stored in the brain like all other memories and retrieved when wanted or needed.

Although energy psychology is currently revealing that flashbacks can at times be appreciably alleviated, medication for flashbacks has not resulted in a utopian cure. There is also a risk that medication may increase the likelihood of overuse or substance abuse. I have found that *making meaning* of flashbacks is an option that is feasible, effective, and beneficial. Within a relational context, the technique includes: mutual reflectivity (analogous to contrapuntal music and art), psychodynamic, and cognitive-behavioral components.

CASE EXAMPLE

Genna was referred to me by her physician because of anxiety related to her 21-year-old daughter Heather's death as a result of a car wreck a few months earlier. This loss had left extensive trauma in its wake, and her physician felt her lupus was worsening due to her anxiety. A therapeutic alliance was quickly established, perhaps abetted by Genna's great distress and hope for relief. There were open and loving relationships within her family of four: Genna, her husband, Heather, and Heather's younger brother. Genna was seen for 15 months, once weekly for three months and once every two weeks thereafter until termination. As expected, she began therapy by describing the sad circumstances of Heather's death. She was anxious and tearful, but she did not meet all criteria for PTSD.

From childhood, with parental support, Heather was determined to become a law enforcement officer. Her younger brother also wanted to become a police officer. Heather had obtained a B.S. in criminal justice and shortly before the wreck had completed the academy of a small police department. At the time of the crash, her field training officer was driving, and she was in the front passenger seat. The training officer swerved to the right to avoid collision with an automobile, and the squad car hit a utility pole that crushed the area where Heather was sitting. Heather had multiple severe injuries and was unconscious. The training officer had very minor injuries. Heather's parents were notified when she was transported to a trauma center. A few broken bones were repaired, but further treatment was considered detrimental. On life support, she languished in a coma for three weeks. She had three options: (a) coming out of coma with significant disabilities; (b) entering a vegetative state; or (c) she could die.

Genna described the three weeks of coma as "feeling like years." She did not know if Heather was aware of her parents' presence. Each moment seemed interminable and overwhelming. Genna's anxiety worsened day by day. The day came when physicians reported that Heather was "brain dead." Life support was removed, and a decision to donate usable organs for transplantation was made.

A police funeral was impeccably handled. Genna knew the funeral was "just as Heather would have wanted," but rather than being comforted, Genna remarked that she was "even more distraught." She rejected the training officer's attempts to console her and stated she "couldn't look at him!" After the burial, she felt somewhat more at ease. In her family's home, Heather's room was untouched, including a few boxes that were packed in preparation for moving into her own apartment.

In a relational context, I engaged Genna in integrated eclectic therapy. She made measurable progress. She met Heather's organ recipients and remained in contact with one of them. She socialized with friends. She and her husband travelled to Austin and to Washington, DC, to ceremonies where police officers who died in the line of duty the previous year were commemorated by having their names added to a wall of remembrance. A plaque honoring Heather was placed in her department's administrative office. Genna felt good about honoring Heather and began to talk to others about her.

Genna stopped going to Heather's gravesite every day (and some evenings). When she seemed receptive to the idea, I asked if she would benefit from making peace with the training officer. She indicated readiness, and he was invited to her next session. In the beginning, she and the training officer were tense, speaking almost inaudibly. I asked Genna if she wanted to say anything about Heather. She immediately told the officer she no longer blamed him for her daughter's death and that she knew he had visited Heather in the hospital and appreciated his respect and caring. He shared his deep sorrow and regrets and stated he was considering leaving police work entirely. They tearfully exchanged hugs. Genna said she hoped he would continue in police work. We all experienced relief, and the "bad blood" between them was resolved. Genna and her husband also talked with their son about becoming a police officer. He was confused, as he still wanted this future but did not want to be a source of his parents' misery. His parents gave him their full approval, encouragement, and support.

When Genna said she felt she was on the "right path," we considered termination and did so at that time. I indicated my availability to her if needed in the future.

Six months later, Genna made an appointment with me. She reported that she wanted to return to her church (where Heather's funeral was held) and had tried to do this every Sunday for two months. When she got a glimpse of the church, she would have unbidden images of the *officers making the long salute at either end of the coffin. She would begin to sob and then return home. At the funeral, this salute had been made just before the closing of the coffin.*

I knew this client very well and felt she needed quality of life as well as symptom relief. I chose not to refer her to another therapist for energy psychology such as thought field therapy, EMDR, perturbation, and so forth (Weinstock, 2010). Improvisationally, I asked if together we might think of potential meanings of the imagery. As we simultaneously searched internally for possibilities, she said, "The salute is just too long. I think it will never end. It's too much to bear. It feels like years." I asked if she felt similar to how she'd felt during Heather's coma. "Absolutely," she said. "We've got it." I asked if this were "the point of no return." She nodded and cried and then began to relax. We were silent for several minutes. We then worked together on covert rehearsal and rational self-statements to make as she approached the church. She said she felt "less crazy" and "more self-confident." She would go to church the following Sunday and would call me in a few weeks as a follow-up on the status of her disturbing imagery. Two months later she called. She reported she had been going to church, that her friends were happy to see her, and since our most recent session, she had not experienced intrusive images.

I have not talked with her since that time. As a result of my "take" on the most recent session, I feel rather confident that she is doing well and that, although continuing to grieve the loss of her daughter, the salute imagery has ceased or has been considerably reduced.

CONCLUDING THOUGHTS

While this technique was useful for eliminating flashbacks, factors other than the association of death following a three-week coma with the long salute (both symbolizing the end of hope for her daughter's survival) could be considered. These factors include intervention timing following the trauma, resilience, various kinds of support, and others. My impression is that establishment of a firm therapeutic alliance may be essential to favorable therapy results. Information supporting this impression has generally been consistent over the years. If energy techniques are used for flashbacks, I tend toward the recommendation that they not be used in isolation but within the context of an ongoing therapeutic relationship.

Reference

Weinstock, D. (2010). *Neurokinetic therapy*. New York: Random House.

26

Trauma Dialogues

Nita Mehr and Theresa L. Blakley

CLIENTS FOR WHOM THE TECHNIQUE IS APPROPRIATE

Adults who report experiencing distress from intrusive symptoms of traumatic stress following sudden, violent loss. The technique is appropriate for use in both individual and group settings and should be considered only after therapeutic rapport has been strongly established. The trauma dialogues should not be utilized with persons within six months of their loss, or those whose current level of symptom distress threatens to overwhelm the person's sense of safety and stability.

DESCRIPTION

In the aftermath of sudden, violent death, *separation distress* and *trauma distress* are two overarching stressors that can dominate the psychological landscape of surviving loved ones. Trauma distress can supersede separation distress, as rumination on the violent death scene is played out through a host of intrusive psycho-physiological symptoms (Rynearson, 2001). The grief experience can feel contaminated, or at times, supplanted, by experiences of trauma distress, challenging familiar streams of coping and interfering with everyday life.

The trauma dialogues technique was developed as a therapeutic exercise aimed at helping homicide-loss survivors cope with traumatic loss as repetitive and intrusive symptoms were demonstrated or reported in the course of therapy. The technique augmented and enhanced the more traditional methods of psycho-education in explaining the nature and function of posttraumatic stress symptoms.

Use of the trauma dialogues technique follows in the tradition of psychodrama as participants actively engage in dialogue with the clinician who takes on the role of the personified symptom. For example, after sudden, violent loss, a person may feel compelled to tell the dying story repetitively to anyone who will listen. This obsessive retelling can become a preoccupying and endless tale of horror as the client is caught in what Rynearson (2005) depicts as a "metaphor for the hopeless confusion" (p. 355). A trauma dialogue in such a context of distress may sound like this:

Client: I don't know why I do it, but I can't seem to help myself. I was telling my aunt the story of how Sam was murdered for the fourth time, and she just held up her hands and told me to stop. She said she couldn't take it anymore. So, I sat down with my uncle and told him the whole story all over again. What's wrong with me?

Therapist: That's what we call *obsessive retelling*. It's normal for people to feel the need to tell their traumatic loss stories over and over.

Client: Really? I thought I was going crazy.

Therapist: To help us better understand this behavior, let's do a little exercise. Let's pretend for a moment that I am obsessive retelling, and you are having a discussion with me. Is that all right with you?

Client: Yes. I wish you would leave me alone. I won't have any friends or family left to support me if you don't stop pushing me to tell Sam's story over and over again.

Therapist: I'm obsessive retelling, and I say good for you. Good for you for telling Sam's story again and again. If they don't like it, they can go fly a kite.

Client: But I'm chasing away the people that mean the most to me. They are avoiding me, and I think it's because they don't want to hear one more time how Sam died.

Therapist: But maybe they are not the ones the story telling is for. Maybe it's really for you.

Client: For me?

Therapist: Yes, you. If you keep telling your story over and over again, maybe you'll begin to figure out *why* it happened, *how* it happened. Maybe you'll finally begin to figure out something that, so far, hasn't made any sense to you at all.

Client: And that's the thing. I just don't know why Sam was murdered. How could this have happened to Sam? To me?

Therapist: Right, and by going over and over it out loud, maybe you will discover the how and why to Sam's murder. So, go ahead. Tell the story of Sam's death a thousand times. Then maybe you will find the answers to the questions why and how.

Client: But I keep saying the same thing over and over. These are unanswerable questions. That Sam was murdered has no rhyme or reason. Telling the story won't ever change the fact that Sam was murdered no matter how many times I tell it.

Therapist: Oh. So what do you want to do with me? Don't you want me to push you to tell and tell and tell and tell? I'm sure I could find someone else to listen to you.

Client: No, I think I'm done with you now that I know what you are all about.

Therapist: Are you sure, because there are people in your neighborhood you haven't told yet?

Client: No, I'm sure. I don't want to chase away everybody I know. I don't need you anymore. You can go now.

In this example, facilitation of a dialogue between the affected person and the clinician in the role of the personified symptom invited open exploration and discovery of the meaning of the unwanted symptom. Giving voice to the symptom offered moments of clarity and at times unexpected relief through humor. This normalization and explanation of the behavior helped to demystify and strip the symptom of its power.

Just as a trauma dialogue can emerge within the individual session, the technique can be utilized in group settings. The "me too" moments of realization occur within the group as internalized symptoms are given an active voice and members discover they are not alone in their horror and loss.

Step-by-step guidance in the technique

1. Clinician assesses client's global stability to engage in the trauma dialogues.
2. The client reports or demonstrates distress due to a repetitive, intrusive, and unwanted symptom of traumatic stress from loss. The clinician clarifies the symptom with the client, inquiring as to the nature, frequency, context, and triggers of the target symptom.
3. Clinician facilitates a review of the client's past coping strategies. What has worked and what was the client's understanding of it?
4. Transition, orientation, and invitation to engage in a trauma dialogue might sound like:

   Therapist: Would you like to look at this distressful experience from a different perspective? Yes? This is how it works. I will take on the role of a symptom that is distressful to you. For example, I could personify the trauma symptom known as *intrusive crying*—that is, I could pretend to be the symptom of intrusive crying, and you and I could have a little conversation together. And the conversation might sound like this:

   I am intrusive crying. And I'm telling you to go ahead cry some more. I own you, Betty. You might as well face it—you are going to cry like this forever.

   What would you like to say back to me, Betty?

   The clinician as personified symptom and the client as self converse until the clinician notes an empowered voice and increased insight into the distress caused by the symptom.
5. After a quiet moment of transition to indicate the fictive conversation is over, the clinician facilitates reflection on the experience with emphasis on insights gained, demystification and empowerment over target symptom, and new insights of coping.

CASE EXAMPLE

Betty was referred to counseling by the Victims Advocate program following the recent murder of her husband, John. His unsolved case has resulted in intrusive symptoms of hyper-vigilance. Betty describes her constant fear and need to protect her family. After assessment of her readiness to participate in a trauma dialogue, the clinician offers Betty a different perspective on the symptom, and the clinician begins a dialogue in the role of hyper-vigilance:

Therapist: Do you realize you've been here thirty minutes and you haven't checked in with your children?

Betty: I better call home right now to check on things. I am getting a security system.
You know, I can't understand why the police can't track down the person who murdered my husband. What if he comes back? There is no way that I am going to let this happen to my family again.

Therapist: You're right. You better not let your guard down. You've got to personally monitor what goes on 24/7, Betty. And surely you're not thinking of getting any rest?

The clinician pauses here to let Betty reflect on the sense of urgency and breathlessness of the clinician as personified symptom before debriefing.

Betty: *Is that how I sound to others? No wonder the kids want to go to a friend's house right now. I am so tired. I just wish John were here to take care of everything.*

CONCLUDING THOUGHTS

The trauma dialogues technique is a therapeutic one with underpinnings in psychodrama. Clients actively engage in role-play scenarios in which intrusive symptoms are explored and insight is gained (Casey, 2001). Clinicians who are willing to model symptoms through this psycho-educational and cognitive-behavioral technique offer traumatized clients a safe way to speak back to intrusive symptoms.

References

Casey, A. (2001). Psychodrama: Applied role therapy in psychotherapeutic interventions. *Journal of Heart Centered Therapies, 4*(1), 67–84.

Rynearson, E. K. (2001). *Retelling violent death.* New York: Routledge.

Rynearson, E. K. (2005). The narrative labyrinth of violent dying. *Death Studies, 29,* 351–360.

27

Treating Traumatic Bereavement in Conflicted and Inter-Generational Families

Robert F. Morgan

CLIENTS FOR WHOM THE TECHNIQUE IS APPROPRIATE

Immediate or inter-generational families experiencing second-order guilt, fear, and grief based on a traumatic death of a feared or disliked but key family member. It is contraindicated for grieving traumatized individuals so close in time to the original trauma that therapy would be premature until adequate safety and trust are established.

DESCRIPTION

Application of a blend of psychodynamic, existential and family-oriented psychotherapy to vicarious traumatic grief offers some alternate possibilities for the treatment and understanding of secondary traumatic grief. The key to this method is realizing the ecological impact of death-related unresolved events on families, groups, and even generations. It entails first identifying unresolved grief based on underlying fear and dislike of the deceased family member or relief at the passing of this individual, feelings not sanctioned by their family or culture. This traumatic and unresolved grief can be magnified in a violent death in which guilt is shared by the innocent who still are shamed or frightened by their perceived indirect responsibility or relief. Although safety, trust, and timing are crucial, the treatment involves psychotherapy habituating to the passage and acceptance of their own feelings, diminishing any traumatic fear or shame, and ultimately forgiveness of themselves and the deceased. This will allow the traumatic grieving to proceed into a normal phase in which the client can move on with their own functional life. The case history features an extreme circumstance but demonstrates the dynamics and the approach.

CASE EXAMPLE

As soon as Mikael killed his father, he was able to love him again. But now that his anger was satisfied, he had a larger problem. Putting down the shotgun, he called the police and said, "I killed my father. Come get me." Then, immobilized by grief at what he had done, he said nothing more: not when they came, not in jail, and not when he was carried off the plane frozen to his chair en route to Hawaii State Hospital. He took up residence in his catatonic state and remained in apparent safety there for the duration.

Only days after his arrival, his younger brother Alberto was also flown in for hospitalization. Alberto was the youngest of several children, a stocky teenager, and, far from catatonic, was swearing vengeance to his father's ghost, or so he said. Mother, the sole survivor in the family home, had decided Alberto needed to be flown to Oahu to be with his catatonic brother and away from her. She was considered to be mentally disabled but she wasn't stupid. Speaking to invisible beings, after Mikael's action, just didn't seem right to her, and she decided her children needed to be elsewhere. Alberto was assigned to my Young Adult Day Program while Mikael was taken under the care of a psychoanalytical psychiatrist who began coordinating the treatment of the brothers with me. This was not always easy. Meeting with me, Alberto was quite friendly and rational with two exceptions. The first was whenever he saw the psychiatrist, who resembled his deceased father. At this time, he would bellow and chase this physician into his office. The doctor found it difficult to relate effectively to Alberto from the safe side of his locked office door.

The second stressor was the monthly visit of his mother. On viewing her, Alberto would punch the air and loudly swear vengeance for his dead father. Soon Mother was only visiting Mikael, even though these visits were somewhat unusual: Mikael sat frozen in his chair where he had been carried outside to the front grass and sunshine. For hours Mother would sit quietly next to him along with some local relatives. Not a word was ever said beyond, "Hello, Mikael" and "Goodbye, Mikael."

The psychiatrist and I sifted through the family history. Mikael and Alberto were the youngest of a large Portuguese family on a small rural island. Their mother was barely functional, her great achievement being the household cooking and cleaning. Her husband had been an absolute tyrant, completely controlling all under his roof with regular beatings. He alone would go into town and shop. His children were discouraged from going to school and were not allowed to speak unless spoken to first by him. The expression 'poor communication' does little justice to the managed silences under this father's regime. The children left home as soon as they could: most boys joined the army while girls got pregnant and married. Eventually only Mikael and Alberto remained.

Of these, Mikael was his father's favorite. They worked together in the fields in rare and quiet harmony. Alberto, at 15 the youngest, was another story. Although he was as large as Mikael, he had a heart murmur. Mother kept Alberto close. So close in fact, he slept with her right up to the day he was hospitalized. Father wanted Alberto to work in the fields with his brother but, apparently for the first time in their marriage, his wife refused to permit it, saying she would leave if Alberto had to do such dangerously vigorous work. The patriarch possibly did not see himself doing cooking or cleaning. He gave in.

Alberto went to public school and did reasonably well. This favoritism was not missed by Mikael. One day Mikael himself ordered his brother to come out to the fields and work. Alberto declined and their parents supported him. The next day Mikael went into town to enlist in the Army. Unfortunately for him, the recruiters were required to give an intelligence test, and he returned home in a foul mood. He once again worked with his father in the fields but began muttering that his father was a "communist" and a "revisionist," words heard on the family radio. It may well be that taking Alberto's side was a revisionist thing for his father to do, given Mikael's former status as his father's favored child. The father did not know what a revisionist was but he knew that a "communist" was supposed to be something very bad. He beat Mikael until he fell into the fields, covered with blood and bruises. That night Mikael borrowed his father's shotgun and killed him in his sleep.

As time went by, the psychiatrist's psychoanalytic work with Mikael paid off. Mikael began moving again and in a few weeks he was one of the happiest residents in the hospital. He worked hard at what the hospital termed "industrial therapy" (which for him meant hospital garbage collection) and developed a close bond with his psychiatrist, who was also his therapist and father figure. ("But I'll never take him on a hunting trip," said the psychiatrist.)

Alberto, for his part, thrived in my Young Adult Program. Despite his harsh background, he was of normal intelligence and made many new friends. Oh, he still chased the psychiatrist into his office (but now smiled when he did so) and became quietly anxious when Mother visited. But that was all. He also spent time with his brother and often left him gifts. Asked about Alberto, Mikael would smile and say, "My brother loves me now." Asked about Mikael, Alberto would say, "He killed him for me."

Why had Alberto been so belligerent at home, hallucinating a dead parent? The psychoanalytic psychiatrist believed it was grieving guilt for wishing his father dead. This may be but certainly there was traumatic grief involved. Eventually, Alberto explained it to me. He believed in an afterlife in which his father's malevolent ghost was still around. Only this ghost was worse than his father had been before: Father was now invisible and with ghostly powers, Father could tell that Alberto wanted him dead more than Mikael did. Father would hurt him if he didn't swear vengeance and be convincing in his grief. On the plus side, Alberto believed that his father's ghost could only be found in his old house or by his mother's side. So he enjoyed his new life on Oahu without traumatic grief.

And why chase the psychiatrist? "At first, I didn't like the way he looked." "Like your father?" "Yes." "Now you know he's not your father." "Oh yes. But now I like the way he runs." And Alberto smiled.

The children of loving and competent parents normally experience a rivalry for parental affection. This "sibling rivalry" is quite normal. On the other hand, children of abusive or non-competent parents may band together against the common enemy but this is a relationship based on trauma and danger. As such, it can be handicapping or even violently destructive. This has been termed "sibling bondage" (Moulon & Morgan, 1967). The destruction of the feared parent, directly or even indirectly or vicariously wished for, can generate a traumatic grief, even to the point of dysfunction and hospitalization.

If our perspective was correct, then the older siblings would soon also be in distress. Checking with the local clinic on the Mother's island, within weeks of the death of their father, every one of the grieving brothers and sisters had been in for treatment. The eldest daughter had recurring nightmares of an open coffin in her living room into which she dared not look. Under the hospital psychiatrist's supervision, all received therapist encouragement to accept their anger and its shadow, a death wish for their father, as a normal traumatic reaction to his brutality, and in their grief to face his memory without guilt or fear. Today, in any grieving work of this kind, I would add forgiveness as well, but in this instance the psychiatrist's therapy was effective. Shadows lose their power when a light is shone on them. All the brothers and sisters grieved successfully and recovered.

CONCLUDING THOUGHTS

Vicarious fear and grief can be transmitted across generations (Duran, 2006; Morgan, 2007). Even an entire community can be led into sibling bondage, transformed by trauma, members bound together unified against a common enemy, but ultimately into a closed system of unresolved grief. This bond can be pathological and responds to resolution.

References

Duran, E. (2006). *Healing the soul wound: Counseling with American Indians and other native peoples.* New York: Teachers College.

Morgan, R. F. (2007). Eduardo Duran's trilogy. *Journal of Transpersonal Psychology, 38*(2), 242–245.

Moulon, R., & Morgan, R. F. (1967). Sibling bondage: A clinical report on a parricide and his brother. *Bulletin of the Menninger Clinic, 31,* 229–235.

Part V
Changing Behavior

28
Behavioral Activation

Laura E. Holcomb

CLIENTS FOR WHOM THE TECHNIQUE IS APPROPRIATE

Many bereaved adults who have moved past challenges with basic self-care but who are not yet participating in a full range of life activities may benefit from behavioral activation work. This technique may be especially helpful for those who are clinically depressed or who have been avoiding activities because of grief. However, behavioral activation does not replace loss-oriented grief work or specialized methods for treatment of traumatic symptomatology following tragic loss.

DESCRIPTION

Behavioral activation treatments address the vicious cycle of depressed mood leading to avoidance of activity, in turn leading to further increased depression related to lack of positive reinforcement, by providing a framework for increasing activity level and reducing avoidance. Behavioral activation treatments have strong research support for treatment of depression (Dimidjian et al., 2006; Mazzucchelli, Kane, & Rees, 2009). For those with severe depression, Dimidjian and colleagues (2006) found behavioral activation comparably effective to antidepressant medication, and superior to cognitive therapy.

For the bereaved, withdrawal from a range of life activities may occur, not necessarily in the context of depression, but directly as a result of the grieving process. If the bereaved do not begin, in a reasonable time frame, to gradually re-engage in life activities that bring pleasure and a sense of purpose, they may be at increased risk for depression. Therefore, though there is not currently a body of research investigating this theory, it logically follows that some form of behavioral activation may be useful to prevent depression in the bereaved, and certainly can be helpful as part of treatment of depression triggered by bereavement.

Behavioral activation involves monitoring of behavior. Activity logs are available for this purpose. However, use of a day planner (either paper or electronic) with room for recording information at least hourly may be more helpful. A day planner is less likely to be misplaced or forgotten than individual pieces of paper, and allows patients/clients to integrate behavioral activation homework with their work schedule (if employed), medical and mental health appointments, as well as reminders of important life events such as birthdays of loved ones and holiday events. Use of a day planner also helps with relapse prevention, as it is more likely for the bereaved to continue with use of a day planner indefinitely than to continue to use individual log sheets.

The bereaved spends the first week simply recording their activities and moods in the day planner, with the instruction not to alter their recent routine in order to get a baseline of activity. This instruction makes the task seem less overwhelming. However, because of purposeful focus on logging activity and anticipation of sharing the log with the therapist, the bereaved may begin to initiate positive changes the first week. This self-motivated progress provides an opportunity for praise from the therapist and encouragement of self-reinforcement by the bereaved.

The therapist can then assist the bereaved in brainstorming to create a list of activities currently being avoided. Pleasant activities have traditionally been a focus of behavioral activation, given their potential to improve mood. Other activities that are consistent with core values and long-term life goals should also be included, as well as activities of daily living not yet resumed (e.g., housework and other chores, exercise). Predictions of enjoyment of each activity can be made in order to compare these predictions with actual experience. The list may also be rated according to anticipated difficulty, so less challenging activities can be incorporated earlier in the process, to increase probability of success and decrease chances of drop-out.

The therapist then guides the bereaved in selecting and scheduling activities for the following week in the day planner, with the goal of optimizing chances of success. To further increase chances of success, the bereaved are encouraged to alternate chore-type tasks with pleasant activities and/or rest periods, as well as to be realistic about the amount of time any given activity may take and the amount of energy required to complete the activity.

The bereaved may be asked to rate levels of enjoyment and mastery (sense of accomplishment) of each activity from 0 to 10, where 0 indicates they did not experience any enjoyment or sense of accomplishment and 10 indicates extreme enjoyment or perception of accomplishment. By providing such ratings, the bereaved may discover that avoided activities result in unexpected reward, encouraging engagement in further activities. The bereaved should also make notes in the day planner about any obstacles encountered to specific activities, and any ideas for improving upon the schedule for the following week.

Activities, ratings and notes in the day planner are reviewed with the bereaved, observing patterns in the impact of activities on mood and quality of life. The bereaved should be encouraged to congratulate themselves on progress, to continue with activities that were reinforcing, and to incorporate at least one new activity into the schedule each week until life feels full and rewarding.

CASE EXAMPLE

Mary was a 47-year-old woman, self-referred to therapy six weeks after her 53-year-old sister, with whom Mary had lived since her divorce five years ago, died unexpectedly of a heart attack. She had returned to work as a receptionist but found that she did not feel up to doing much after work. She had been eating regularly, though mostly fast food, as she had not felt like going to the grocery. She had fallen behind in general house cleaning and paying bills. She avoided answering the phone when friends called, and had not socialized since her sister died.

Mary had benefitted from therapy for adjustment to her divorce, so she sought therapy to cope with the death of her sister. She felt that she might be mildly depressed, as she had been after her divorce. She was able to understand and agree that in addition to loss-oriented grief work, she needed to gradually re-engage in life activities, in order to prevent herself from becoming more depressed.

Mary recorded her activities and mood levels in a day planner for a week. Her therapist reviewed her day planner, and noted to her that her mood had improved at work and when she accepted a call from a friend. She was receptive to the idea that while she could not replace her sister, additional contact with friends would help with loneliness. Mary was concerned she might not be good company but agreed to schedule into her planner calling a friend that evening at 7:30 p.m. to ask her over for coffee later in the week. She found that her level of enjoyment of the visit with her friend was 7 out of 10, and her level of mastery was 6 out of 10.

Mary also agreed to schedule time on Friday evening from 7:00 p.m. to 8:00 p.m. to work on paying bills. Though not an enjoyable activity (level of 2 out of 10), her mastery level was 6 out of 10. However, being very tired on Friday night after the work week, she made a note in her planner to schedule bill paying for another night in the future. Mary was encouraged by her therapist to follow chores with pleasant activities. So after paying bills, she had scheduled watching a favorite funny movie at 8 p.m. (enjoyment level of 7 out of 10, mastery level of 5 out of 10).

The following week, Mary felt that her mood and energy levels had increased somewhat. She scheduled cleaning the bathroom for 20 minutes on Tuesday night after dinner at 6:30 p.m. (enjoyment level 3 out of 10, mastery level 8 out of 10), followed by reading a new mystery novel at 7:00 p.m. (enjoyment level 8 out of 10, mastery level 6 out of 10). As she had enjoyed the visit with a friend in the past week, she scheduled calling that friend on Wednesday at 7:30 p.m., and suggested they carpool to church on Sunday morning (enjoyment level 6 out of 10, mastery level 7 out of 10). She scheduled grocery shopping on Saturday afternoon from 2 p.m. to 2:30 p.m. (enjoyment level 5 out of 10, mastery level 8 out of 10) in order to be able to start preparing meals at home.

Mary continued use of the day planner, with the help of her therapist, to maintain reinforcing activities she had incorporated into her schedule, and to gradually incorporate other activities that brought her pleasure or purpose. She referred to her possible activity list and made sure that she had scheduled at least one brief pleasant activity each day. Her mood continued to improve, and she felt she was starting a new, exciting phase in her life. She continued to use her day planner long-term.

CONCLUDING THOUGHTS

Behavioral activation techniques are easy to implement, and have been proven effective for depression (Dimidjian et al., 2006; Mazzucchelli et al., 2009). Therefore, these techniques can be a good choice for the bereaved, for prevention or treatment of depression and to facilitate re-engagement in a full range of activities to promote quality of life. Use of behavioral activation to help the bereaved is an area worthy of research investigation. Behavioral activation techniques go hand in hand with goal-setting techniques described by this author in Chapter 73 in this volume.

References

Beck, J. S. (2011). *Cognitive behavioral therapy* (2nd ed.). New York: Guilford.

Dimidjian, S., Hollon, S. D., Dobson, K. S., Schmaling, K. B., Kohlenberg, R. J., Addis, M. E., Gallop, R., McGlinchey, J. B., Markley, D. K., Gollan, J. K., Atkins, D. C., Dunner, D. L., & Jacobson, N. S. (2006). Randomized trial of behavioral activation, cognitive therapy, and antidepressant medication in the acute treatment of adults with major depression. *Journal of Consulting and Clinical Psychology*, 74(4), 658–670.

Mazzucchelli, T., Kane, R., & Rees, C. (2009). Behavioral activation treatments for depression in adults: A meta-analysis and review. *Clinical Psychology: Science and Practice*, 6(4), 383–411.

29
Working with Difficult Times

Nancy Turret and M. Katherine Shear

CLIENTS FOR WHOM THE TECHNIQUE IS APPROPRIATE

Clients struggling with or anticipating difficulties with significant periods such as holidays or anniversary occasions that evoke loss and avoidance. However, planning to cope with such periods may be less relevant when clients are experiencing profound and unremitting grief, irrespective of the date, in which case, more intensive treatment for debilitating daily symptoms may be indicated.

DESCRIPTION

This technique was developed as a component of complicated grief treatment, an evidence-based treatment for bereaved people with complicated grief (CG; Shear & Shair, 2005). There are certain calendar days, like family holidays or the anniversary of the death, that are especially painful for many bereaved people, and people with complicated grief often experience these days as even more emotionally activating than other bereaved people. Sometimes people cope with the stress of these times by trying not to think about them. They may shut down emotionally, withdraw socially and just try to get through the difficult period. There is no right way to mourn; however, it is usually more helpful in coming to terms with a loss to use other, more active strategies to manage the pain of reminders. Planning for difficult times gives people more of a sense of control and can help them work toward making peace with a painful loss. The approach we suggest can help people with complicated grief, and may also be helpful for other bereaved people experiencing an upsurge in grief on certain calendar days.

Working with difficult times is part of the procedure used in complicated grief treatment (CGT) called *situational revisiting*. This procedure entails encouraging people to revisit places and activities that they are avoiding because they evoke painful reminders of the loss. A particular kind of revisiting is a calendar day from which it is impossible to escape. Examples include the anniversary of a loved one's death, the person's birthday or one's own birthday, or family holidays. Some times are more idiosyncratic. For example, a client who always shopped on the biggest sale day of the year with her deceased friend found the sale day particularly difficult each year. Someone who lost a child found the first day of school each year especially painful. Different people have their own pattern of times that are changed forever by the loss. These highly emotional times also provide opportunities to reflect on the loss, to honor the deceased person and to think about one's own future. Work in CGT with difficult times follows four simple principles that help people develop more adaptive strategies:

Principle 1: Anticipate and plan for difficult times. The therapist invites the client to identify times during the year that are especially difficult. Anticipating and planning for these times enables the bereaved person to increase her or his sense of control and lessen feelings of powerlessness in the face of the loss. The common attempt to control feelings by avoidance can have the unintended consequence of increasing feelings of being overwhelmed and out of control. By contrast, confronting these times, anticipating and actively planning for them, can help people feel less helpless and this, in turn, can lower the intensity of the grief.

Principle 2: Expect to be sad and focus on self-care. It is best to acknowledge that sadness and longing will be intensified and then to decide what to do about it. People do not need to be passive about the fact that they are facing an upsetting time. It may be helpful for clients to give themselves permission to feel sad. Often people are thinking that they should be past this. They may be self-critical or they may focus on how others don't understand. It is better to accept the sadness and decide how to manage it. Some people prefer to just let themselves be sad. Others may wish to plan activities or mental strategies that can help them feel less so. Some people prefer to engage in distracting activities. It is a good idea to try to be with others, even though doing so can make a bereaved person feel lonelier. Others often want to help. We encourage people to be as open as possible to this caring attention.

Principle 3: Keep some focus on your own life and find something as interesting or pleasurable as possible. Part of the struggle during complicated grief is finding a way to live a satisfying life without the deceased person. Complicated grief treatment maintains a focus on both dealing with the loss and figuring out how to live without the deceased person in a way that still holds the potential for joy and satisfaction. During a difficult calendar day, a person's thoughts and emotions naturally focus on the loss. So it is a good idea to be sure to build in some time to focus on oneself. People solve tough, long-term problems better when they are in a positive rather than a negative emotional state. Difficult times can be viewed as an opportunity to try being open to positive emotions about the person who died.

Principle 4: Try to find ways to honor or care for the person who died. When an adult loses someone close, it is almost always someone they have taken care of. Most people find that one of the troubling aspects of bereavement is that caregiving for a loved one is over. This assumes that caring for loved ones stops when they die. It is helpful to consider that it is possible to take care of people you love, even though they are gone. We can and do take care of people who died, though doing so is very different than when they are alive. A deceased parent, child, friend, or lover has a need to be remembered and honored. Sometimes there is a need to carry on with a very important activity. For example, a woman whose husband has died may feel that taking care of his business is something she can do for him. For most bereaved people, it is very important to remember their loved one and to cherish the memories. Difficult times are opportunities to honor the memory of someone we love. People might plan to visit the cemetery or place of final rest, to light candles or spend time in prayer or other religious activity. Some people honor a loved one by doing something the person liked to do. Some people write about the person or gather others to celebrate the life of the person who died.

CASE EXAMPLE

Martha, a 69-year-old widowed, retired woman lost her 30-year-old daughter, Jane, in a car accident when she was returning home from a business trip in another city. The date of her daughter's death, her birthday and wedding anniversary were very difficult for Martha, as were the winter holidays with their many memories of times with her daughter during the school holiday. Martha could not visit Jane's grave often because it was in a distant city. Therefore she had made an arrangement with a florist who placed flowers at the gravesite and sent a photograph of the floral arrangement to Martha afterward. However, this provided little solace, as Martha hated the reminder of her daughter's death and berated herself for not doing more. The therapist talked with her about the principles of difficult times. They discussed how she could anticipate the day and participate in selecting the flower arrangement. She began to see that her floral plan was a way to take care of her daughter. She could show these arrangements to her friends and family and light a candle with them in honor of Jane. Anticipation and acceptance of difficult times enabled Martha to experience these painful holidays in a different way. Additionally, toward the end of her treatment, she was worried that she would miss the therapy each Wednesday at the time she had been coming. She decided to anticipate this, let herself feel sad about it, and create a plan to take care of herself. She decided to go to church every Wednesday and light a candle for her daughter. She also decided to add this ritual to other times in the future.

CONCLUDING THOUGHTS

Most people with CG struggle to get through difficult times. These can be conceptualized as situations they would like to avoid but cannot. Given the inevitability of occurrence of calendar days, it is a good idea to plan for them and to follow the principles reviewed above, which are incorporated in evidence-based treatment for complicated grief (Shear, Frank, Houch, & Reynolds, 2005; Shear & Gorscak, in press). When clients actively cope with difficult times, they generally feel a greater sense of wellbeing, have more hope for the future and find this useful in helping them come to terms with the painful loss.

References

Shear, M. K., Frank, E., Houch, P. R., & Reynolds, C. F. (2005). Treatment of complicated grief: A randomized controlled trial. *Journal of the American Medical Association, 293,* 2601–2608.

Shear, M. K., & Gorscak, B. (in press). *Complicated grief treatment.* New York: Guilford.

Shear, M. K., & Shair, H. (2005). Attachment, loss, and complicated grief. *Developmental Psychobiology, 47,* 253–267.

30

Assertiveness Training

Rafael Ballester Arnal and Beatriz Gil Juliá

CLIENTS FOR WHOM THE TECHNIQUE IS APPROPRIATE

Bereaved adolescents and adults who need help expressing their feelings and needs with others around them. However, assertion training does not in itself resolve conflicted internal feelings about the loss that deserve attention using other therapeutic techniques.

DESCRIPTION

The grieving process never happens in a vacuum. Those who have lost loved ones are typically part of a family, social and work environment where neither their feelings nor ways of coping with the new and painful situation are always understood and respected by the people around them. Assertiveness training therefore can be a useful technique when the bereaved must assert their right to experience their own emotions in an appropriate manner and pace, expressing their suffering and devoting time to recalling the lost person.

Grounded in the pioneering work of Wolpe (1958) and popularized by Alberti and Emmons (1978), the concept of assertiveness refers to people's ability to convey to another person their views, opinions, beliefs or feelings effectively and without discomfort (Kelly, 2000). It is important to remember that there is a continuum from passive to aggressive behavior, with assertiveness lying in the middle. At the passive end, people place too little value on their own rights, being unable to set limits or ensure that their own needs are given equal priority to those of others. At the aggressive end, the person places too little value on the needs and rights of the other person. Midway between passivity and aggression lies assertiveness, which entails communicating one's own position and expressing how one wants to be treated, all reported firmly and convincingly but without hostility. In contrast to other social skills training, the aim of which is to help people meet others and interact with them more comfortably in a range of settings, the goal of assertiveness training is to decrease the number or impact of interactions that frustrate the individual's wishes.

Assertiveness training has been used in countless settings ranging from schools and workplaces to communication skills programs for couples and private psychotherapy. Curiously, however, it has rarely been used systematically in the context of grief therapy, even though loss ends up affecting the whole social environment of bereaved people, interfering with many aspects of their social functioning. Our goal here is to describe and illustrate the specific relevance of this intervention for people in mourning.

Several decades have passed since Parsons (1958) coined the term "sick role" to refer to the socially institutionalized role given to people considered "sick." According to Parsons, the sick role was characterized by two rights and two duties. First, the patient had the right to be exempted from usual responsibilities as well as to no longer be considered responsible for his or her condition. In return, the patient had two obligations, that is, to consider his or her status undesirable and to make efforts to surmount that condition. Likewise, in the case of bereavement, people have the right to grieve and to assert their reasonable need to remember the deceased in a healing way. Not infrequently, however, those who live and work with people who have experienced a significant loss, in their well-intentioned desire to help the mourners suffer less, do not give them opportunities to express their pain or even recall their loved ones with pleasure, as they gradually adjust to the loss, assimilate grief at their own pace, and learn to live without the loved one. By criticizing or discouraging expressions of grief, they inadvertently blame the bereaved for their suffering, thereby compounding it or reinforcing the mourners' sense of being misunderstood or isolated. The result can be aggressive responses on the part of the bereaved, or alternatively, passive retreat, creating cycles of pernicious interactions that wound all members of the family or social system. In such cases, providing coaching in assertiveness to the bereaved can reverse this dynamic.

CASE EXAMPLE

Maria was a 45-year-old woman who three months earlier had lost her father, with whom she had a strong bond. She was married to Juan and had two children, aged 8 and 12 years. Deeply immersed in grief, she had withdrawn from many family activities, and her husband complained of her emotional and sexual distance from him. Maria acknowledged her tendency to get lost in her own thoughts and memories, although she was able to manage basic responsibilities to her children and housework. As this situation continued, Juan reproached Maria's expressions of pain, and chided her not only for crying, but also for simply sharing memories of her father, her relationship with him and what he meant in her life. With Maria's grief disallowed, the relationship eventually built to an angry standoff, as Juan accused her of prolonging the process of grieving, while ignoring his needs and those of the children. What she needed to do, Juan argued, was to control her grief by thinking about her father as little as possible. This counsel was delivered with what Maria felt were a series of rebukes: "You act like you're the only person who has lost a loved one," "Your father is dead but it's not the end of the world," "Seeing you in that state, why would I want to come home?," "You could control yourself so that the children do not notice anything, otherwise they are going to end up with psychological problems because of you." Maria was crestfallen, and alternated between angry retorts and resentful and guilty withdrawal.

At this point, the therapist arranged a meeting with Juan in order to ask him what Maria's grieving process meant for him and the children. The clinician also offered psycho-education on bereavement, that is, what it is considered normal and acceptable in the process of loss assimilation and what might be a facilitative attitude on his part. Despite these efforts to arouse his empathy, Juan, who was emotionally much cooler than his wife, had serious difficulties in understanding her behavior, since according to him, when he lost his parents, he had never behaved in such a way. He did not understand how different bereaved people have their own process after the loss of a loved one, that is, how grief is unique to each person. Given his lack of interest and involvement in the treatment of his wife, the therapist decided to raise in a subsequent meeting with Maria the issue of her right to experience and express the suffering caused by the loss of her father. The therapist explained to the patient both the concept of assertive behavior and the continuum of passivity–assertion–aggression, and asked her to make a list of different situations in which she felt her behavior was not accepted by Juan and his comments in those situations. Through behavioral experiments and coaching in assertive responses, therapist and patient

Table 30.1 Example log of assertive responses to conflict situations

M's behavior	Husband's response	Possible passive response	Possible aggressive response	Assertive behavior
I was relating a story of walking with my father while we talked about the things we shared.	Juan said, "With these comments you only hurt others and yourself and wallow in your suffering."	"Okay, sorry. I will try to avoid making any comment like this in the future."	"You're the most insensitive person in the world! If you loved me even a little, you would not say this to me. I *hate* you!"	"I just don't agree with that. I have no intention of forgetting my father, and recalling those times makes me feel better. I think I have the right to do so, but if it bothers you I will try to share these stories with other people."

tested possible verbal and nonverbal answers that Maria could give to her husband so that he would respect her own process. Finally, they collaborated in drafting a list of "rights of the bereaved," including, for example, the rights to mourn, to cry, to leave for a few minutes or hours in order to think, to recall moments lived with the loved one and to accept both a temporary reduction in sexual desire and the lack of interest in some activities. With this consistent focus across a few sessions the situation at home improved, and with that, Maria began to make progress in adapting to her loss. Table 30.1 shows a sample assertiveness log used to support this effort.

CONCLUDING THOUGHTS

Assertiveness training can be a useful therapeutic tool in cases like the one described, in which someone in our clients' social world does not respect their right to walk the path of grief in an appropriate fashion. Obviously the ideal would be that others show enough empathy to make such interventions unnecessary. However, when this is not possible, coaching the bereaved on assertiveness using straightforward procedures that enjoy extensive empirical support (Kelly, 2000) can help them reclaim their right to grieve, and with it, seek a less resentful or conflicted life with others.

References

Alberti, R. E., & Emmons, M. L. (1978). *Your perfect right: A guide to assertive behavior.* San Luis Obispo, CA: Impact.

Kelly, J. A. (2000). *Social-skills training.* New York: Springer.

Parsons, T. (1958). *The social system.* London: Routledge & Kegan Paul.

Wolpe, J. (1958). *Psychotherapy by reciprocal inhibition.* Stanford, CA: Stanford University Press.

31

A Finding Balance Writing Intervention

Lorraine Holtslander

CLIENTS FOR WHOM THE TECHNIQUE IS APPROPRIATE

Older adults who are bereaved after caregiving for a spouse. It may be insufficient as an intervention for complicated, intense grief, which may call for more focused psychotherapeutic interventions.

DESCRIPTION

The Finding Balance writing intervention is a self-administered tool, tailored specifically to focus on the needs of older adults who are bereaved after caregiving. Any professional who encounters older adults in their practice could offer this tool, including primary care physicians or nurses looking for ways to help a client with their grief. It would also be suitable in a support group setting or as part of a bereavement program. In follow-up phone calls or visits, or even group settings, an opportunity to share their writing could encourage a conversation on their unique journey through grief. The concept of "finding balance" initially emerged from a grounded theory study of the experience of hope for bereaved caregivers (Holtslander & Duggleby, 2009). Finding balance was an important first step to begin dealing with overwhelmingly difficult emotions and experiences after a frequently exhausting caregiving experience. It was a first step towards finding new perspectives and regaining of new meaning and purpose in their search for new hope. Some bereaved caregivers were able to move forward easily, while others had a great deal of difficulty; the initial step of not finding balance in their lives was holding them back. The participants kept a journal as part of this study and the effectiveness and impact of the writing itself were often of great benefit.

The specific contents of the Finding Balance writing intervention are based on the key processes that emerged from another grounded theory study with older adults who were bereaved after caregiving (Holtslander, Bally, & Steeves, 2011). Delphi processes with experts who work with bereaved older adults were used to develop the activities for each section. The three sections, "deep grieving," "walking a fine line," and "moving forward," are described and then specific writing exercises encourage reflection, expression of emotions, and the identification of personal and creative ways to find balance in their own unique journey through bereavement.

- *Deep grieving*: This section consists of activities that address the emotional aspects of grief, such as feelings of emptiness, sadness and loss. The grieving person is asked to write down "my emotions today," balanced with a planned "time out" activity that works for them (e.g., going for a walk, watching a movie, or calling someone). Another activity in this section is to create a support system, listing supportive people—family, friends, counselors, etc.—and alongside their name, their phone number and how they are most helpful. This list will act as a supportive directory for when clients need help with specific things (listening, fixing things, cheering me up) (see Chapter 80 by Doka and Neimeyer in this volume).
- *Walking a fine line*: This section consists of activities that address ways to combine two extremes and focus on balancing: activities that take clients back to grieving and activities that involve looking forward. These include maintaining a balance of daily life, such as using a weekly calendar to schedule three activities a week and three different ways clients can take time for themselves.
- *Moving forward*: This section addresses the processes of moving forward, including planning the day, reaching out to others, and taking the time for self-care. The main activity is to reflect on their caregiving story and how it has made them stronger, by considering which activities give them inner strength and to reflect on their experience of caregiving and loss and how this story might help others.

CASE EXAMPLE

Donna, a 65-year-old woman who lost her husband to cancer after a very difficult caregiving and illness journey, reflected on her experience in writing using this tool. In the "Deep grieving" section Donna wrote about her anger, sadness, numbness and exhaustion, "realizing one day at a time or even one hour at a time is all anyone can handle at this stage." Donna recognized that her tears were a natural part of the grieving process and that planning a "time out" from these emotions was necessary. Donna noted how she would "lose herself" in the form of reading, a movie, getting out in nature. She also noted that "identifying the support system was good, [as] people may need to be reminded to accept and appreciate the kindness of others." "The love shown by others increases our hope that things will be alright and that we are not alone." "Walking a fine line" and finding a middle ground described her experiences: "Life's challenges can be painful and upset the balance and normal rhythm of everyday. Thinking of one thing every day that was good and being thankful for it makes one have a more positive attitude." Donna identified that time for herself was key, including physical activity to clear her mind, spending time alone, and writing down her feelings. Donna described moving forward as taking one day at a time: "Don't get too hungry, too tired or too sad. Feed yourself physically and emotionally; rest when you have to; and focus on something positive. You are still on the journey of life. Your life has changed, not ended." Donna recognized through her writing that she was not dishonoring her loved one by being happy. Moving forward is accomplished by baby steps, acknowledging that backsliding is a part of grief, but concentrating on moving forward every day. For Donna, maintaining balance was achieved by focusing on what she was able to do and not what she could not do. When balance was challenged, she found that a concentrated effort was needed to maintain stability. It could often be a small adjustment, but one that made a huge difference. Donna wrote: "I don't think any of us are in perfect balance; life is a juggling act with our focus constantly changing." Donna emphasized how writing helped her to remember the good times but also to become more aware of the reality of her loss. "The relationship lost changes from one of a physical presence to a relationship of memory," a truly difficult challenge. With her practical reflective writing, Donna was better able to meet this challenge in a balanced way.

CONCLUDING THOUGHTS

This intervention is currently being tested with a sample of older adults bereaved after caregiving for a spouse with advanced cancer and is showing positive and practical benefit. The focus on the unique needs of this population, accompanied by tailored writing activities and written instructions to guide the writing activity, are important considerations when designing and testing this intervention (see Neimeyer, van Dyke, & Pennebaker, 2009). Each person's situation is unique and not everyone is able to participate in this type of activity. For those who are able and willing, following a structured writing guide can provide them with insight into what is triggering losses of balance and what might help them to become more balanced that day. Honoring the past while paying attention to their own unique journey gives them permission to both grieve a central person in their lives and identify ways to move forward into a new way of living, finding new meaning and purpose and creating activities that connect them to the person who has gone and to new sources of support. Grief can leave balance continually challenged; a concentrated effort is needed to maintain stability.

References

Holtslander, L. F., Bally, J., & Steeves, M. (2011). Walking a Fine Line: An exploration of the experience of finding balance for older persons bereaved after caregiving for a spouse with advanced cancer. *European Journal of Oncology Nursing, 15*(6). doi:10.1016/j.ejon.2010.12.004.

Holtslander, L. F., & Duggleby, W. D. (2009). The hope experience of older bereaved women who cared for a spouse with terminal cancer. *Qualitative Health Research, 19*(3), 388–400.

Neimeyer, R. A., van Dyke, J. G., & Pennebaker, J. W. (2009). Narrative medicine: Writing through bereavement. In H. Chochinov, & W. Breitbart (Eds.), *Handbook of psychiatry in palliative medicine*. New York: Oxford University Press.

Part VI
Restructuring Cognition

32

Changing Catastrophic Misinterpretations with Behavioral Experiments

Paul A. Boelen and Jan van den Bout

CLIENTS FOR WHOM THE TECHNIQUE IS APPROPRIATE

Bereaved adolescents and adults suffering from Prolonged Grief Disorder (PGD), that is, the experience of yearning, difficulties accepting the loss, disbelief, difficulties moving on without the lost person, and other symptoms of grief to a distressing and disabling degree, beyond the first half-year of bereavement. It may not be appropriate for the transitory distress commonly associated with adaptive grief in the early months of loss.

DESCRIPTION

People exposed to the death of a loved one and its inherent life disruptions confront severe challenges in managing painful emotions, thoughts, and memories associated with the irreversibility of the separation. *Experiential acceptance* of these psychological experiences is important in healthy adaptation. That is, willingness to confront these painful emotions, thoughts, and memories facilitates elaboration of the reality and implications of the loss, helps in adjusting views of the self and the relationship with the lost person, taking into account the irreversibility of the separation, and fosters engagement in rewarding activities that promote adjustment. On the other hand, *experiential avoidance* of emotions, thoughts, and memories associated with the loss is assumed to block recovery and to render mourners prone to an exacerbation of normal grief responses and the development of PGD. This experiential avoidance may take the form of cognitive avoidance (e.g., suppression of unwanted thoughts and memories; rumination about events surrounding the death as a means to refrain from painful realization that the lost person will never return) and situational avoidance (e.g., avoiding external stimuli—places, people, objects—that remind the mourner of the loss).

From the perspective of cognitive-behavioral theorizing, it has been proposed that catastrophic misinterpretation of one's responses to the loss is one important driving force behind this experiential avoidance (Boelen, Van den Hout, & Van den Bout, 2006). Specifically, when people fear the intensity of their own reactions and interpret these as indicative of an impending mental disaster, such as "going mad" or "losing control," they are more inclined to engage in experiential avoidance in the form of cognitive and situational avoidance behaviors. This in turn interferes with integration of the loss and blocks correction of the misinterpretations, adjustment of views of the self and the lost person, and constructive action, thus maintaining the pain (see Figure 32.1). Research has confirmed that such

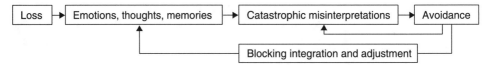

Figure 32.1 Schematic depiction of the role of catastrophic misinterpretations and avoidance in maintaining grief symptoms

catastrophic misinterpretations are indeed associated with avoidance behaviors which, together, contribute to PGD symptoms (Boelen, van den Bout, & van den Hout, 2006).

Behavioral experiments are of great importance in breaking the cycle of catastrophic misinterpretations and avoidance behavior in maintaining grief. Behavioral experiments are specified actions/assignments that patients undertake in order to test their catastrophic misinterpretations and reduce maladaptive avoidance behaviors. They can be applied in the following steps (cf. Mueller, Hackmann, & Croft, 2004):

> *Step 1: Problem formulation*: This step involves the identification of internal and external stimuli that the person avoids and the catastrophic misinterpretations that are behind this avoidance. Generally, "the reality of the loss" is the central avoided stimulus, and "going mad" the central catastrophe. Yet, in order to set up the experiment, therapist and patient identify specific avoided stimuli (*"Which particular internal stimuli— thoughts, memories, or external stimuli—places, people, objects, situations, do you avoid?"*) and specify the feared catastrophe (*"Exactly what anxiety-provoking things do you fear will happen on confrontation with these things?"*). Notably, specification of the avoided stimuli and catastrophe often already raises some initial doubts about the validity of the catastrophic prediction.
>
> *Step 2: Formulation of the target cognitions (or "catastrophic prediction")*: This step involves formulation of the problem in terms of a measurable (and falsifiable) catastrophic prediction, in an *"If . . ., then . . ."* form; with the "If . . ." referring to confrontation with the avoided stimulus and the "then . . ." referring to the feared consequence of this confrontation.
>
> *Step 3: Formulation of the alternative cognition (or "positive prediction")*: This step involves formulation of an alternative outcome of the confrontation with the "If . . . ." This outcome is not necessarily very positive, but more benign, realistic, and tolerable than the feared catastrophe. This alternative outcome is also formulated in measurable terms.
>
> *Step 4: Behavioral experiment*: This step involves setting up a concrete and specific behavioral assignment, in such a way that information is gathered that allows for an evaluation of the validity of the catastrophic prediction and the alternative cognition. This mostly involves confronting the avoided stimuli in a step-by-step and clearly defined manner. Sometimes this can be done in a treatment session, and sometimes the patient does the assignment at his or her own pace in-between sessions, possibly with the help of others.
>
> *Step 5: Evaluation*: After the experiment is completed, therapist and patient evaluate its results and compare the results with the patient's catastrophic and alternative prediction. Further assignments aimed at gathering additional information, strengthening the positive prediction, or testing other catastrophic cognitions can be planned.

CASE EXAMPLE

Mike lost his son in a car accident, two years before seeking treatment. He experienced a persistent desire to be close to his son, but also experienced protest and pain whenever he confronted the impossibility of attaining this desire, with great difficulties adjusting to his life, and other PGD symptoms, and suffering from distressing images of the car accident, pointing to comorbid posttraumatic stress disorder. Mike was convinced that he would "go insane" if he confronted the fact that his son was truly dead and gone forever (Problem). His catastrophic cognition was "If I allow myself to think about the circumstances and consequences of my son's death (and discuss the implications thereof with my therapist), I will turn into a wreck," defining this "wreck" as losing touch with reality and not being able to work and to socialize for several weeks (Catastrophic cognition). After some exploration, the alternative prediction was "If I allow myself to think about my son's death, I will feel sadness and distress but this will reduce to manageable levels by the end of the day and will not prevent me from engaging in work and social events over the next days" (Positive prediction). The experiment involved Mike describing the moment he heard about his son's death in detail, and reviewing the things he missed now that his son was dead, in a one-and-a-half hour session with his therapist (Behavioral experiment). Mike was sad and tearful when talking about the accident and horrified when thinking about the circumstances. Reviewing the accident helped him to see that there was no means by which he could have prevented it, and changed his feelings of guilt into anger toward his son for having been reckless. Although his feelings were intense, his story was coherent and his emotions did not run away with him. Articulating the things that he missed most confronted him with the enormity of this loss and elicited strong pangs of grief. Expressing the emotions that he thus far had suppressed exhausted Mike, but this was compensated by a sense of relief and liberty. His plans for work and social activities over the next week were briefly discussed and Mike felt confident that he could cope with his feelings in the days following the session. This was confirmed in the session one week later. The yearning and protest had been replaced by a saddening realization of the irreversibility of the loss; the fear of becoming a wreck had been replaced by confidence that he could cope. Further reviewing his activities over the preceding week, it was concluded that the experiment had falsified his catastrophic prediction and confirmed the positive alternative (Evaluation).

CONCLUDING THOUGHTS

Catastrophic cognitions about one's own grief reactions are associated with maladaptive avoidance behaviors that render bereaved individuals prone to persistent PGD symptoms (Boelen, van den Bout, & van den Hout, 2006). Behavioral experiments can be used to test the validity of these cognitions. Importantly, such experiments are not a therapy in themselves but a component of a more comprehensive cognitive behavioral therapy program. This program should include a safe working relationship between patient and therapist, room for telling the story of the loss, recognition of the patient's pain, and acceptance of his/her way of dealing with the loss.

Behavioral experiments should be applied in a congruent fashion, with the patient being aware of their rationale and being motivated to engage in them. Thus, it is only with patients who themselves feel that they are stuck and express a wish to move on, that behavioral experiments should be applied. Importantly, combined with other cognitive behavioral interventions, they have proved to be efficacious in reducing distressing and disabling symptoms of grief of patients suffering PGD (Boelen, de Keijser, van den Hout, & van den Bout, 2007).

References

Boelen, P. A., van den Bout, J., & van den Hout, M. A. (2006). Negative cognitions and avoidance in emotional problems after bereavement: A prospective study. *Behaviour Research and Therapy, 44,* 1657–1672.

Boelen, P. A., van den Hout, M. A., & van den Bout, J. (2006). A cognitive-behavioral conceptualization of complicated grief. *Clinical Psychology: Science and Practice, 13*, 109–128.

Boelen, P. A., de Keijser, J., van den Hout, M. A., & van den Bout, J. (2007). Treatment of Complicated Grief: A comparison between cognitive behavioral therapy and supportive counseling. *Journal of Consulting and Clinical Psychology, 75*, 277–284.

Mueller, M., Hackman, A., & Croft, A. (2004). Post-traumatic stress disorder. In J. Bennett-Levy, G. Butler, M. J. V. Fennell, A. Hackmann, M. Mueller, & D. Westbrook (Eds.), *Oxford guide to behavioural experiments in cognitive therapy*. Oxford: Oxford University Press.

33

The ABC of Rational Response to Loss

Ruth Malkinson

CLIENTS FOR WHOM THE TECHNIQUE IS APPROPRIATE

Bereaved individuals (adolescents and adults), couples and families, who during the acute phase or beyond, encounter difficulties in experiencing an adaptive "healthy" (rational) grief process. It should not be used in the immediate aftermath of loss, when supportive care is more appropriate.

DESCRIPTION

The ABC model used in Rational Emotive Behavior Therapy (REBT) refers to the cyclical interactions among the activating event (A), the beliefs about the event (B) and emotional and behavioral consequences (C). The terms *rational* and *irrational* highlight the difference between adaptive and maladaptive ways of experiencing and interpreting events. A number of assumptions underlie this model: (1) a loss through death is an irreversible adverse event that can be evaluated and interpreted in many different ways; (2) the distinctions between two types of thinking (rational and irrational) imply that the human tendency to irrationally evaluate life events (particularly adverse ones) can also be rationally interpreted and corrected. Evaluations and interpretations are a matter of choice; (3) the reciprocity between the event, the belief, and the emotion is related to the evaluations made about them. The model assumes significant interaction between cognitions and emotions, and refers to distorted thinking or irrational thinking as a major factor in emotional disturbance; and (4) the ABC of healthy grief distinguishes between the emotional consequences of sadness, concern and regret, and those of unhealthy grief of depression and anxiety.

Death, especially when sudden and unexpected, is a traumatic event (A) that affects the belief system (B) and consequently emotions and behaviors (C). Disputation (D) is the application of cognitive, emotional and behavioral interventions to change irrational responses to rational ones. Following death, the bereaved may respond with self-defeating (irrational) appraisals of the event, about themselves and others, and/or about their disturbed emotions (meta-cognition). Adaptive grief, from that perspective, is a healthy process of experiencing the pain of one's loss, which includes ways of thinking and emoting that help the bereaved person organize his or her disrupted belief system into a form of healthy acceptance. It distinguishes between healthy negative emotional (behavioral and body sensation) consequences (NHE) and unhealthy negative consequences ones (NUE) (see Table 33.1).

Table 33.1 Grief-related evaluations and emotional consequences

Adaptive grief	Maladaptive grief
Healthy (functional) evaluations and negative healthy emotional consequences (NHE)	Unhealthy (dysfunctional) evaluations and negative unhealthy emotional consequences (NUE)
Sadness: Life has changed forever	*Depression*: My life is worthless
Healthy anger: He didn't think about the outcomes	*Unhealthy anger (rage)*: How could he have done it to me?
High tolerance of frustration regarding pain: It's painful to think that I will never see her again	*Low tolerance of frustration regarding pain (anxiety)*: It's too painful, I don't want to think about it, I can't stand the pain.
Concern: I couldn't do much about the death. I will miss her/him greatly.	*Guilt*: It's my fault. I wish I were dead.

Rational grief responses minimize self-defeating feelings of depression, despair, horror and self-deprecation and increase self-acceptance and loss acceptance. The intervention aims to facilitate an adaptive process of grief where sadness, pain and frustration blend with positive feelings in a balanced way (Malkinson & Ellis, 2000). Interventions for the acute phase include five flexible modules as follows:

1. *Assessing the individual's cognitions, both rational and irrational.* This entails identifying dysfunctional irrational beliefs (demandingness directed to self, others and the world) and their maladaptive emotional (e.g. anxiety), behavioral (e.g. avoidance), and physiological (e.g. breathing difficulties, heart palpitations) consequences.
2. *Teaching the ABC of rational response*, explaining belief-consequence (B–C) connection and correcting irrational beliefs and their related maladaptive emotional responses by exploring alternative rational appraisals.
3. *Practicing rational responses* and their adaptive consequences, and strengthening them with between-sessions assignments.
4. *Identifying meta-cognitions* (also called secondary symptoms) that block emotional responses, such as "I must not think about it. It's too painful."
5. *Evaluating the changes* in the bereaved person's appraisals indicating healthier response to loss and practicing ways to maintain the changes. Preparing for relapses especially around anniversary days, birthdays, reminders of the deceased, etc.

CASE EXAMPLE

Molly requested therapy for her family a few months after the sudden loss of her oldest son during military service. Family members realized that their initial decision to be strong and carry on with life "as if nothing had happened" turned out to be impossible. They refrained from talking to each other about the dead son and brother so as to avoid the pain and the tears that followed the mention of his name.

There were six weekly sessions with the family. The goals of sessions included assessing each family member's grieving patterns, providing information about loss and grief with attention to individual differences (forms of expression, pace and intensity) and the ABC of rational and irrational responses to loss, and normal and legitimate coping styles. An additional goal focused on helping the family communicate more openly to support each other. At the end of the conjoint family sessions, the grief and pain of loss had become less overwhelming. Family members were sharing and talking more openly about the deceased. Molly asked to continue therapy individually as she felt she was having difficulties in "balancing and controlling her pain and tears." Therapy with her used the ABC model with the aim of facilitating a healthy process of grief.

A daughter of Holocaust survivors, Molly said she had suffered enough in her life, and following her son's sudden death, she decided to be strong and carry on. This turned out to be too difficult and painful for her. Molly described her distress, and downward arrow questioning (module 1) revealed her main irrational beliefs revolving around issues of control and self-depreciation: "I must be strong, and if I fail I am a weak person."

At this point Molly was reminded of the ABC of rational and irrational responses (module 2), which was introduced in the family sessions. Irrational beliefs and consequences expressed in her idiosyncratic way were explored and she could see the self-defeating connection between her saying, "I must be strong, this is my motto," and "If I cry, I am a weak person, I betray myself and I feel shameful." Molly was asked to think of an alternative rational belief that would moderate her emotion of shame (module 3), and after moments of exploration she said: "I guess I can be less harsh on myself when I cry. I wish I wouldn't cry." Molly was asked to monitor her emotions when saying this. She replied that she felt somewhat relieved. Therapist explained the differences between feelings of frustration (less distress) and feeling of shame. A new B–C connection was established: "I wish I would't cry, and it is frustrating if I do. I cry because I am sad, not because I am weak." Molly's between-session assignment was to practice the ABC of loss and grief worksheet (Malkinson, 2007, p. 85).

As therapy continued, Molly spoke of avoiding of reminders of her dead son (not mentioning his name, moving his photographs, and avoiding driving near the cemetery where he was buried). Irrational beliefs underlying avoidance (module 4) were discerned as: "This way, I don't have to confront the overly painful reality of my son's death. Also, it's my way of keeping my son alive. I don't want to think of him as dead." Her irrational belief over experiencing pain was associated with her appraisal of being weak. Cognitive restructuring with breathing exercises helped change it to a rational response of accepting the finality of the loss, reinforced with between session assignments.

Six months later, as therapy approached its end, Molly said: "I think the most painful thought to come to terms with is that my son will never realize his musical talent, which he was so much looking forward to doing." For Molly, the most transformative actions she undertook to overcome her avoidance of the loss were baking her son's favorite cake, discussing his love for music with family members, and publishing his letters in booklet form (module 5).

CONCLUDING THOUGHTS

In the case example discussed, avoidant behavior, a common response among bereaved during acute grief after the loss of a child, was understood as a potential block to the natural course of the grief response. Therefore, it was the focus of assessment and intervention. Sometimes the bereaved believe that avoidance will prevent the pain associated with memories of the deceased or will circumvent the need to accept the reality of loss. Molly's avoidance of reminders of her son as a strategy to bypass pain and crying (which she appraised as a sign of weakness) only increased her distress. A more rational and adaptive response may not circumvent the pain, but does increase the likelihood of less suffering.

In sum, the ABC of rational response to loss approaches grief as a normal and healthy reaction to loss. It is a structured integrated approach aimed at helping the bereaved reach a balanced approach to life without the deceased and to the ongoing relationship with the deceased (Rubin, Malkinson, & Witztum, 2012). It can be applied in cases of acute and prolonged grief with individuals, couples and families.

References

Malkinson, R. (2007). *Cognitive grief therapy: Constructing a rational meaning to life following loss.* New York: Norton.

Malkinson, R., & Ellis, A. (2000). The application of Rational Emotive Behavior Therapy (REBT). In R. Malkinson, S. S. Rubin, & E. Witztum (Eds.), *Traumatic and nontraumatic loss and bereavement: Clinical theory and practice* (pp. 173–195). Madison, CT: Psychosocial Press.

Rubin, S. S., Malkinson, R., & Witztum, E. (2012). *Working with the bereaved: Multiple lenses on loss and mourning.* New York: Routledge.

34

Acceptance and Commitment Therapy (ACT)

Bronna D. Romanoff

CLIENTS FOR WHOM THIS TECHNIQUE IS APPROPRIATE

Clients experiencing complicated or traumatic grief, as well as those in the early stages of emotional upheaval caused by the death. These techniques may be less relevant for those who are primarily focusing on the practical and social changes associated with post-loss adaptation.

DESCRIPTION

Acceptance and commitment therapy (ACT; Hayes, Strosahl, & Wilson, 1999) is one of the "third wave" of behavior therapies, sensitive to the context and functions of psychological phenomena. ACT "applies mindfulness and acceptance processes and commitment and behavior change processes to the creation of psychological flexibility" (Hayes et al., 1999, p. 10). A well-developed model of psychopathology and psychotherapy, ACT has been researched with a variety of clinical disorders. ACT utilizes therapeutic techniques such as mindfulness, guided imagery, story and metaphor to foster acceptance of thoughts and feelings, "de-fuse" language from its context and increase awareness of present experience, understand the self as an observer of thoughts, feelings, or experiences, define and clarify valued directions for living, and commit to taking action in the direction of one's value-determined goals.

Emphasizing acceptance of private events, including painful thoughts and feelings, as well as acting to create a rich and meaningful life, the ACT model is consistent with the dual process model of grief (Stroebe & Schut, 1999). According to the dual process model, mourners "oscillate" between loss-oriented coping processes such as grief work, experiencing surges of grief, yearning, etc., and restoration-oriented processes such as doing new things, denial or avoidance of grief, creating new roles and relationships.

Many bereaved individuals experience the pain of acute grief, a pain that gradually diminishes over time, and find a way to accept the permanence of the loss and go on living a life of meaning and purpose. However, approximately 10% of bereaved individuals develop complicated or prolonged grief reactions; continual rumination over the circumstances of the loss, prolonged yearning and searching, or avoidance of painful affect leave them unable to rebuild a "life worth living." They might be said to be utilizing one of the dual coping processes at the expense of the other. In cases of traumatic grief, intrusive and unwanted painful memories and affect derail the process of moving forward with one's life.

Psychotherapy is not indicated for most bereaved individuals. However, for those experiencing complicated grief, the core theoretical principles and therapeutic technology of ACT provide a useful framework for case conceptualization consistent with the dual process model of grieving. Clients who distance themselves from the pain of grieving by reliance on substances, clients who cannot accept the reality of their loss, or those who cannot escape the terrible sadness or anger or fear no matter how hard they try, can be helped to accept the experiences that they already have by learning and practicing mindfulness, a nonjudgmental attention to moment-by-moment experience and a core component of ACT.

Many clients will interpret their grief experience as, "I'm going crazy" or "I can't go on without him," and treat these thoughts and stories as literal truth rather than what they are—thoughts and stories. ACT techniques of defusion help clients see thoughts as thoughts or evaluative labels, and not as direct experiences. For example, a client can be asked to walk across the room while saying, "I can't walk across the room," or "I'm having the thought that no one will love me," rather than "I'm unlovable."

Clients experiencing traumatic grief will often experience their worlds as though devastated by a nuclear bomb, and themselves as irretrievably changed and broken. They move through an alien landscape with no familiar self-referents to guide the way. The ACT principle of self as context is used to help clients connect with a transcendent, compassionate sense of self that is bigger than our constructed identity or self-made concepts. Using guided imagery, clients are asked about memories from various time periods, and to "notice who is noticing"— an observing self that is continuous in time and is apart from the sensations, emotions, thoughts of experience. That self remains unbroken, despite a traumatic history and shattered assumptions.

Using principles and techniques of ACT, clients are helped to accept the reality of the loss and be willing to have the painful emotions of grief. Attention to values and commitments brings focus to restoration-oriented coping processes, asking clients what they want their lives to stand for and helping them achieve their goals. An ACT technique that can be particularly helpful with grieving clients is the epitaph (Hayes et al., 1999). After spending considerable time discussing an epitaph or desired epitaph for the deceased, clients can be asked to construct their own epitaph, should they die, say, five years from now. What would they like to be remembered for? What actions are consistent with those values? And when better to start moving in the direction of desired values than now? Barriers to movement are identified and worked through using behavioral activation and/or acceptance strategies.

CASE EXAMPLE

Mary is a middle-aged woman who was grievously injured in an attack in which her husband was killed. The trial and conviction of the alleged murderer led to fractured relationships among the remaining family members, resulting in multiple secondary losses for Mary. Because of the injuries she sustained, Mary had no memory of the attack and spent the initial subsequent years regaining physical health and function. Caught in restoration-focused coping, she had not plumbed the extent and depth of the changes in her life and her multiple losses. As therapy focused on loss-oriented coping processes, Mary practiced mindfulness and acceptance skills to create space to have the painful thoughts and feelings that emerged, and to acknowledge the reality of her changed world as it is, not as she wished it were. Her physical injuries resulted in a sense of a damaged self; by creating awareness of the observing self-as-context, Mary was able to see that though many aspects of her daily life were devastated by the tragedy, her core self was intact. Values clarification exercises consolidated the awareness that longstanding deeply held values of compassion and loving kindness remained. With this awareness, Mary was able to engage in actions of forgiveness toward all those who had damaged her cherished family. Because forgiveness is a process, and angry feelings come and go, Mary must repeatedly confront whether her actions are helping her move in the direction of a meaningful life.

CONCLUDING THOUGHTS

ACT is recognized by SAMHSA as an evidence-based practice for the treatment of depression and obsessive-compulsive disorder and there is extensive research support for its use in the treatment of multiple problems, including posttraumatic stress disorder. Complicated grief, while neither PTSD nor major depression, has similarities to both. Although ACT as a clinical theory is rooted in relational frame theory and functional contextualism, and ACT theorists caution that ACT is not a bag of techniques to be used without an understanding of the basic ACT model, the model is consistent with the dual process model of grieving. There is an extensive published literature on learning to use ACT that can be very helpful to the bereavement therapist.

References

Hayes, S. C., Strosahl, K., & Wilson, K. G. (1999). *Acceptance and commitment therapy: An experiential approach to behavior change.* New York: Guilford.

Luoma, J. B., Hayes, S. C., & Walser, R. D. (2007). *Learning ACT: An acceptance and commitment therapy skills-training manual for therapists.* Oakland, CA: New Harbinger.

Stroebe, M., & Schut, H. (1999). The Dual Process Model of coping with bereavement: Rationale and description. *Death Studies, 23,* 197–224.

35
Rational Emotive Body Imagery (REBI)

Ruth Malkinson

CLIENTS FOR WHOM THE TECHNIQUE IS APPROPRIATE

Bereaved adults who experienced traumatic loss and suffer from complications in the grief process. It is especially helpful in cases where clients use avoidance to try to circumvent the pain of the emotional experience. It is not suitable for bereaved in the early (acute) period of grief.

DESCRIPTION

Imagery, imaginary exposure and imagery re-scripting are forceful cognitive and emotive strategies. They are widely used in the service of recollection of painful memories or in the processing of feared emotional outcomes and introducing a new meaning to them. For those clients reliving the trauma, these procedures can be used to decrease the distress through repeated imaginings (Holmes, Arntz, & Smucker, 2007). Likewise, Rational Emotive Body Imagery (REBI) combines cognitive and emotive elements and enables the bereaved to recount and relive in the moment stressful events related to the loss and grief that follows. In its present version, this method incorporates elements of mindfulness with a special focus on awareness of body sensation. The emotional consequences of grief such as pain, anger, shame and depression are frequently intense and overwhelming. The flooding effect of emotions is followed by the mourner's subjective evaluation (a meta-cognition) that these are too painful and consequently may result in avoidant strategies as a self-protective mechanism. A more adaptive strategy, however, would include awareness and acknowledgment of these emotions, being attentive to them in a nonjudgmental way, and accepting them as part of grief.

A basic assumption underlying Rational Emotive Body Imagery within the ABC-REBT framework is that the client links his/her emotional distress as well as the accompanying body sensation (Consequence–C) to the loss event (Activating event–A), and not to his or her appraisal (Belief–B) of it. The aim of REBI is, through constructing a safe setting for the client, to reduce emotional distress by introducing the understanding that beliefs about the event act as mediators between the event and the consequences—a Belief–Consequence connection. In other words, the client is helped to understand that despite not having control over highly negative events, the right to choose one's belief and interpretive framework remains (Malkinson, 2007). The framework of applying REBI will be demonstrated through a case description.

The framework of treatment utilized in the case example with Neli included establishing a therapeutic alliance, joint evaluation of the problem, provision of social support, cognitive assessment of the B–C belief–emotional framework, and assessment of the potential for change and potential obstacles to it. There are three steps in applying this strategy:

1. *Explanation* of rational–emotive-body imagery and its usefulness in treatment along with an introduction to the SUDS (subjective units of distress) scale.
2. *Re-living the event* while the therapist guides the client's efforts and directs him or her, especially with regard to non-verbal expressions. Sub-steps in re-living include:
   (a) Constructing the image (A). In cases in which the client re-imagines, but does not relate the event, the therapist may encourage nonverbal communication such as nodding their head to signal progress.
   (b) Identifying the emotion and/or body sensation (C).
   (c) Measuring the intensity of the response (SUDS).
   (d) Reducing the intensity of the response that the client is experiencing in the moment (at his or her own pace) through reformulating associated beliefs.
   (e) Measuring change of intensity of the emotion and/or physical response (SUDS).
   (f) Evaluating the cognitive change (B).
3. *Follow-up* after completing the imagery exercise, discussing the cognitive change and its new emotional and body consequences (B–C connection) for the client. Typically, the client then practices further reliving and rational restructuring between sessions.

CASE EXAMPLE

We described REBI to Neli, an unmarried 29-year-old woman who requested therapy as the first anniversary of her brother's death was approaching. She was suffering from symptoms of prolonged grief such as profuse crying, and general unease (Rubin, Malkinson, & Witztum, 2012). Neli's brother committed suicide and she was preoccupied with her brother's final hours before his death. She saw images of the last moments when she heard the thud of her brother's fall, and she felt recurring feelings of intense anger at not having been able to save him. Neli was prepared to reconstruct the event after getting explanations on imagery, the SUDS and its application. The therapist emphasized that Neli would be the one doing the reconstruction of the event based on her recall of her experience. When she felt distress at any stage, she was to signal the therapist and would be helped.

Neli was instructed to recreate a sort of image or picture of the event of her brother's death and was given the choice to keep her eyes open or shut them. With her eyes closed she was asked to recall as closely as possible the feeling she experienced when it happened and signal when she had done so (Construction of the Imagery). Anger and tension in her chest were the consequences that Neli experienced. She was guided to attend to emotion and body sensation and be aware of them (Identifying the emotion and body sensation) and measure its intensity on a 1 (low) to 10 (high) scale. Concentrating, Neli answered 8 (Measuring the intensity of the response on the SUDS). Having measured the degree of the emotion, she was asked to concentrate on the intensity of the response and try to do something in any way she thought would help her reduce its intensity, taking her time to do so. With her eyes closed she was asked to make a sign when she had accomplished this. As Neli continued to hold her hand on the chest, she was supported by the therapist who encouraged her "to listen" to her body while doing something to reduce the intensity of her distress. This served as a way of empowering her and giving her a degree of control over her distress. Neli concentrated, and at a certain moment a look of relief appeared on her face, and her body relaxed somewhat (Reducing the intensity of the response).

The therapist told Neli that she could open her eyes and asked whether there was a change in the intensity of her anger and to report on its level. Neli answered 6 and opened her eyes (Measuring the change of intensity of the emotional and/or physical response). Neli was praised for her efforts to do the imagery and change the intensity and was asked what she did and what she said to herself to lower the intensity from 8 to 6, and also to assess their difference (Evaluating the cognitive change). Neli answered that she felt a relief in her body in the intensity of the anger, after she said to herself: "Don't be so angry with yourself; you know that he was sick." The therapist supported and reinforced the cognitive and emotional change. She encouraged Neli to repeat the statement and let herself re-experience the difference in the change in emotional intensity and body sensation, to give it validity, and suggested that it be reinforced by homework assignments.

The differences between adaptive (rational) and distressing (irrational) belief and the differences in emotional and body consequences were clarified. Neli's irrational belief, "I am insincere, bad, and irresponsible, I was involved with myself, and I didn't hear his cry for help," increased her anger as she continually condemned herself for not saving him, which further increased her anger. Being aware and mindful of her emotions and body sensation, and changing her beliefs and telling herself, "Don't be so angry with yourself; you know he was sick," decreased the intensity of her anger. She described how being aware of the tension in the chest and "listening to it" made her feel somewhat relieved. Focusing in a mindful way on the difference in the intensity of emotion and body sensation enabled a shift from unhealthy to healthy anger. The cognitive element followed the emotional and body sensations: By telling herself not to be so angry with herself, Neli became less judgmental of herself and more self-accepting.

Between-session homework and practice of the REBI were assigned to strengthen Neli's belief in her ability to regulate and control the level of her distress. She was told to repeat the imagery and write down her thoughts and accompanying emotions. In the following sessions, Neli reported practicing the imagery which she said helped her to clearly differentiate between the various responses (pain, fear, guilt, and sadness, mild versus intense anger), and identify the "bad" thoughts: "If I hadn't left the room . . . if I hadn't been preoccupied with myself . . ." and change them into more rational ones. The changes in Neli's emotional and physical body consequences were followed by cognitive changes and opened a path to her experiencing an adaptive grief process.

CONCLUDING THOUGHTS

Rational Emotive Imagery with added elements of awareness to physical sensation provide a mind–body experience in which the client is guided in a safe setting to choose a way to reduce the distress associated with the traumatic loss. Choosing to relive the event while experiencing mindfully observing emotions and body sensation to reduce their intensity and changing cognitions is a way to empower the client to be more self-accepting and thus increase inner control in the service of experiencing an adaptive grief process.

References

Holmes, E. A., Arntz, A., & Smucker, M. R. (2007). Imagery rescripting in CBT: Images, treatment techniques and outcomes. *Journal of Behavior Therapy and Experimental Psychiatry, 38,* 297–305.

Malkinson, R. (2007). *Cognitive grief therapy: Constructing a rational meaning to life following loss.* New York: Norton.

Rubin, S. S., Malkinson, R., & Witztum, E. (2012). *Working with the bereaved: Multiple lenses on loss and mourning.* New York: Routledge.

36

Schema Therapy for the Lost Relationship

Wendy G. Lichtenthal

CLIENTS FOR WHOM THE TECHNIQUE IS APPROPRIATE

Adults and adolescents who express guilt, prolonged grief reactions, or criticism about the lost relationship, the deceased, and/or themselves. However, schema therapy is probably inappropriate in the context of straightforward bereavement support for mourners with uncomplicated symptomatology.

DESCRIPTION

Much attention has been given in the grief literature to the important role of sense-making of the death in adjustment to loss (Neimeyer & Sands, 2011), but less has been written about strategies for making sense of the lost relationship. When clients present with distress about the lost relationship or about their grief responses (e.g., with feelings of guilt or criticism), I frequently employ the Schema Therapy model developed by Dr. Jeffrey Young and colleagues (Young, 1990; Young, Klosko, & Weishaar, 2003) to assist the client with developing a "compassionate conceptualization" of the relationship with the deceased. Young (Young et al., 2003) defines a schema as "any broad organizing principle for making sense of one's life experience" (p. 7). Many schemas develop early in life, but in order to maintain a stable view of oneself and the world, these schemas continue to be applied into adulthood even if they are dysfunctional. The Schema Therapy model highlights how individuals perpetuate their schemas through cognitive distortions, self-defeating life patterns, and schema coping styles; the goal of this approach, then, is to heal those schemas that are maladaptive through cognitive (e.g., thought restructuring), behavioral (e.g., gradual behavior change), and experiential techniques (e.g., imagery work to assist with reparenting and breaking unhealthy life patterns; see Young et al., 2003, for a description of techniques). Among the self-defeating life patterns one might engage in is becoming or remaining involved in relationships that reinforce one's maladaptive schemas.

There are several reasons why making sense of the relationship can be of therapeutic value. First, if the relationship was complicated by tension and conflict, then clients may find it helpful to understand what might have drawn them into the relationship; this can facilitate development of a compassionate view of this relationship "selection," despite its flaws. Second, as they move forward with life, it can be important to understand the role that the deceased served in reinforcing their cognitive schemas, and thus which tasks may lay ahead

139

in order to develop healthy, adaptive responses to the world without the physical presence of the deceased.

Use of this technique presumes some working knowledge of the client's dominant cognitive schemas and coping responses, particularly those that are most maladaptive (see Young & Klosko, 1993; Young et al., 2003 for details). This information can be gathered by providing a formal quantitative assessment and/or through a focused life history (Young et al., 2003). Application of this therapeutic technique is largely psychoeducational, first providing a definition of a cognitive schema, which I would characterize as a "lens" through with individuals view the world and relationships that is shaped by early experiences. I then offer illustrations of the maladaptive schemas that Young and his colleagues (2003, pp. 14–17) have described, selecting those frequently triggered after a significant loss. Examples include:

- *abandonment/instability* (perceive others who might be available for support and connection as unstable or unreliable);
- *defectiveness/shame* (feel that that one is defective, unwanted, bad, or unlovable);
- *mistrust/abuse* (expect that others will hurt, cheat, lie, abuse, humiliate, take advantage, or manipulate);
- *dependence/incompetence* (feel unable to handle everyday responsibilities without help from others);
- *unrelenting standards/hypercriticalness* (feel must meet very high internalized standards of behavior, often in response to feelings of defectiveness).

I also provide education about how individuals are often drawn to others who activate their schemas. This is followed by a discussion of the schemas that may have been triggered early on in the relationship, resulting in heightened attraction (both romantic and non-romantic) to and engagement with the deceased (this is often particularly relevant for relationships that were selected, such as spouses or close friends). If the deceased was a family member, then I might highlight the complex attachment to one of the very individuals who played a role in the development of the client's cognitive schemas and likely reinforced it over the years. Both the client's dominant schemas and the deceased's hypothesized schemas are discussed to make sense of how the relationship was maintained, or in some cases, severed. I often recommend that clients read Young and Klosko's (1993) *Reinventing Your Life* to help them with further conceptualization of their schema and its impact on their relationships and coping approaches. Over time, the client is encouraged to take a compassionate stance toward their respective cognitive schemas, as if to say, "*Of course*, you remained in the relationship . . . ."

CASE EXAMPLE

Christine is a 51-year-old widow who lost her husband, Aaron, to esophageal cancer over nine months ago. Christine's 29-year marriage to Aaron was a complex one, characterized by conflict and verbal abuse. Christine presented to grief therapy with confusion about why she was experiencing such sadness and grief over Aaron's death after so many years of harsh fighting and cruelty toward one another. She also criticized herself for remaining in the relationship for so many years despite the mistreatment. During our sessions, I provided psychoeducation about cognitive schemas and the chemistry that individuals may feel toward those who trigger their schemas. Christine provided a focused life history, including description of her highly critical, affluent family of origin, and details about Aaron's upbringing, which was characterized by emotional deprivation and criticism, as well. Through our discussions, we were able to identify the ways in which Christine's relationship with Aaron triggered her defectiveness schema, as

Aaron repeatedly chastised her over the course of their marriage, and her unrelenting standards schema, as he "underperformed" and could not financially provide for her and their three children in the way she had wanted. For Aaron, we hypothesized how Christine's high standards may have triggered his own defectiveness schema, highlighting his inadequacies and inferiority in social class, and drawing him closer to her. In addition, Christine's disappointment in Aaron led to her distancing herself from him, activating his emotional deprivation schema. We thus highlighted how the relationship "made sense." I encouraged Christine to view with compassion her decision to remain in the relationship, which was also influenced by the desire to keep the family intact for her children. Christine reported that this framework was helpful, and eventually began expressing forgiveness toward her husband and, perhaps more importantly, herself.

CONCLUDING THOUGHTS

Understanding bereaved clients' maladaptive schemas can be valuable for a variety of reasons: to help conceptualize their coping responses to the loss (e.g., high standards for grieving or "getting over it" because of an unrelenting standards schema), the ways in which they interact with potential sources of social support (e.g., isolation because of a mistrust schema), the way they view their future (e.g., reluctance to get involved in new relationships because of an abandonment schema), and, as is highlighted above, the way in which they view the lost relationship. Clients often present with harsh, critical assessments of the lost relationship or of their or the deceased's behavior within the context of the relationship. Such judgmental evaluation can lead to feelings of guilt, self-doubt, and anger. Applying the Schema Therapy model to help clients conceptualize why the relationship was selected, maintained, and/or severed can help them make sense of their choices. This, in turn, can enhance their feelings of compassion toward themselves, toward the deceased, and toward the relationship overall.

References

Neimeyer, R. A., & Sands, D. C. (2011). Meaning reconstruction in bereavement: From principles to practice. In R. A. Neimeyer, D. L. Harris, H. Winokuer, & G. Thornton (Eds.), *Grief and bereavement in contemporary society: Bridging research and practice.* New York: Routledge.

Young, J. E. (1990). *Cognitive therapy for personality disorders: A schema-focused approach.* Sarasota, FL: Professional Resource Exchange.

Young, J. E., & Klosko, J. S. (1993). *Reinventing your life: How to break free from negative life patterns.* New York: Dutton.

Young, J. E., Klosko, J. S., & Weishaar, M. E. (2003). *Schema therapy: A practitioner's guide.* New York: Guilford.

37

Cognitive Restructuring for Childhood Prolonged Grief

Mariken Spuij and Paul A. Boelen

CLIENTS FOR WHOM THE TECHNIQUE IS APPROPRIATE

Bereaved children and adolescents suffering from symptoms of Prolonged Grief Disorder (PGD)—a disorder of grief encompassing distressing and disabling symptoms of separation distress (e.g., yearning) and other debilitating grief-reactions, beyond the first half year of bereavement. It may be inappropriate for bereaved people simply requiring support in the recent aftermath of a loved one's death.

DESCRIPTION

In the past 15 years there has been recognition of a syndrome in adults referred to as Complicated Grief (CG) or Prolonged Grief Disorder (PGD). PGD has been described as a combination of grief-specific symptoms including separation distress, preoccupation with thoughts about the lost person, a sense of purposelessness about the future, numbness, bitterness, difficulties accepting the loss and difficulties moving on without the lost person (Prigerson et al., 2009). Children and adolescents can experience clinically significant PGD symptoms that are similar to those of adults (Spuij et al., 2011). To date, no effective treatments for childhood PGD yet exist (Currier, Holland, & Neimeyer, 2007). It is therefore important to develop and test such treatments.

As part of a larger research program, the present authors developed a cognitive behavioral treatment program for childhood PGD (Spuij et al., 2011). Cognitive restructuring is one of the central interventions of this program, apart from exposure and behavioral activation. The rationale behind cognitive restructuring is that emotional suffering (i.e., emotional distress and maladaptive coping behaviors) is not a direct consequence from particular situations and "activating events," but, instead, is the result of how these situations and events are appraised or perceived—that is, the *cognitions* that the person has about these situations or events. Accordingly, one important means to alleviate emotional suffering is by (1) identifying the (maladaptive) cognitions that underlie a person's suffering in particular situations and circumstances; (2) examining the validity and utility of these cognitions; and (3) reformulating these cognitions incorporating information gathered in step (2) into cognitions that are associated with less intense suffering and facilitate rather than block constructive action.

The usefulness of this intervention in the treatment of childhood PGD is supported by various observations. First, childhood PGD is associated with endorsement of negative cognitions about global themes including the self and one's own grief reactions (Boelen & Spuij, 2008). This implies that changing these cognitions is one important means to alleviate childhood PGD. Second, cognitive restructuring has proven efficacious in the treatment of adult PGD (Boelen et al., 2007). Third, cognitive restructuring have been found to be effective in the treatment of childhood anxiety and depression (David-Ferdon & Kaslow, 2008), phenomena that bear similarity with childhood PGD. In our treatment program, cognitive restructuring is applied in the following steps:

Step 1: Explanation of rationale: First, clinicians explain to children that the death of a loved one often shatters and violates positive thoughts about the self, life, and other themes that thus far have gone unquestioned. As a result, negative thinking patterns may occur. It is explained that, although these patterns understandably occur, they maintain negative feelings and block helpful coping behaviors. Thus, in order to adjust to loss, it is important to reestablish and maintain a more positive and helpful outlook on self, life, and other themes.

Step 2: Identifying central negative cognitions: In this step, children complete a brief Cognitions Questionnaire, tapping the degree to which they endorses negative cognitions related to nine themes: (i) the self ("I am no longer important to anyone since s/he died," "I am ashamed of myself since s/he died"); (ii) life ("Life is meaningless since s/he died"); (iii) other people ("Other people are not at all supportive," "I won't express my feelings, to avoid being treated differently by my friends"); (iv) the future, ("I don't expect to feel better in the future," "Things I had hoped for will never happen now s/he is dead"); (v) guilt ("It's my fault that s/he died," "I must know how this death could have been prevented to avoid other losses"); (vi) his/her own mourning ("My feelings are abnormal," "I am not grieving appropriately over this loss"); (vii) confronting the loss ("If I'd really thought over this loss, I would get so sad that I wouldn't be able to stop crying," "If I would allow my feelings to run loose, I would go crazy"); (viii) cherishing the grief ("I have to continue grieving, otherwise I would forget or betray him/her," "As long I grieve, I don't have to let him/her go"); and (ix) death anxiety ("Before I know it, other people I love will die as well," "I cannot bear the thought that my life can suddenly be over"). Together with information from other parts of treatment, completing this brief questionnaire offers important information about cognitions that play a role in the problems.

Step 3: Investigating the identified cognitions: Once important negative cognitions are identified, the validity and utility of each separate cognition are first examined using "verbal investigation." For every cognition, two questions about the validity ("How do I know that what I think it true?" and "What evidence is there in favor and against this thought?") and the utility of each cognition ("What will happen if I continue thinking this way?," "What is the worst thing that can happen if what I think it true?") are discussed. Then, "behavioral investigations" are set up (also termed "behavioral experiments" in adult cognitive behavioral treatment). These are introduced as activities the child can undertake to test the validity of specified cognitions—mostly predicted in the form of "If I would . . ., then . . . would happen" (see also Boelen & van den Bout, Chapter 32 in this volume).

Step 4: Changing negative thoughts into helpful thoughts: Based on the evidence gathered in Step 3, the final step includes reformulation of the initial negative cognition into a more positive, realistic thought that is associated with no, or less intense emotional suffering and facilitates constructive action. Central negative, maladaptive cognitions and their positive, adaptive counterparts are described on flash cards that the child carries along and reads whenever the negative cognitions come to mind.

CASE EXAMPLE

Twelve-year-old Eva lost her favorite aunt one year before coming for therapy and one of her grandfathers three months earlier. During the intake-interview, it became clear that the losses had shattered her positive view on life and fueled her death anxiety—leading her to avoid potentially rewarding activities and keeping people she loved at a distance. Completion of the brief Cognitions Questionnaire confirmed that negative thoughts in these areas were prominent. Completion of the questionnaire also brought to light that she was inclined to suppress feelings about these losses, because she didn't want her friends to think negatively about her. The three central negative cognitions were "My life will not bring me any joy anymore," "I'd better stay at a distance from other people, to prevent being hurt by a loss again," and "If friends knew how sad I feel, they would think I am pitiful." Recent moments when Eva felt sad and down and refrained from potentially nice activities were reviewed, to teach Eva how these cognitions likely contributed to her negative feelings and passivity in these moments. The therapist explained that investigation of these thoughts could help her to gain more realistic and even positive thoughts that would lessen these negative feelings and would help her to re-engage in potentially pleasant activities. A "behavioral investigation" was planned in which Eva arranged a meeting with a friend she had not seen in a while to test the prediction that this friend would respond negatively if s/he heard how sad Eva sometimes felt. The fact that this friend responded supportively to Eva's story and that they actually also had some fun together helped Eva to see that this prediction was not true. This experience also lessened the credibility of Eva's negative cognitions about life and death anxiety. After further "investigation" these cognitions were changed into "Although I feel sad sometimes, I am still able to experience fun and joy," and "Although I could be confronted with loss again, staying distant from others won't make me feel better," which Eva wrote down on flash cards she carried with her over the following weeks.

CONCLUDING THOUGHTS

Negative cognitions logically emerge when children are confronted with loss. Persistence of such cognitions may render children prone to emotional difficulties in recovery from their loss. Cognitive restructuring is an important intervention to target these cognitions. In doing so, it is important to search for the right cognitions. Not every negative cognition *can* be changed and *should* be changed—although it is a lively misconception that this is what cognitive behavioral therapists aim to do. Instead, the therapist looks for those cognitions that are central to the child's problems, that interfere with engagement in rewarding activities, and that are falsifiable.

Cognitive restructuring is not a therapy in itself but part of a more comprehensive cognitive behavioral therapy program (Spuij et al., 2011). This program emphasizes developing a safe working relationship with the child, and recognizing and accepting the child's pain. Moreover, tools are offered to adjust the interventions—cognitive restructuring as well as the other central interventions of exposure and behavioral activation—to the specific needs, age, and cognitive abilities of the child. Cognitive restructuring can appear to be a "rational" and even "cold" intervention. However, when applied in a caring and safe context, systematic investigation of negative cognitions (like a true Sherlock Holmes or Inspector Gadget), this is a useful means to alleviate acute pain following childhood bereavement and to prevent this pain from continuing into adulthood.

Acknowledgments

The work described in this chapter was supported by grant 15701.0002 (Project: Development and evaluation of a cognitive behavioral intervention for problematic grief in children:

A feasibility study, pilot study, and randomized controlled trial) from the Netherlands organization for health research and development (ZonMw).

References

Boelen, P.A., de Keijser, J., van den Hout, M., & van den Bout, J. (2007). Treatment of complicated grief: A comparison between cognitive-behavioral therapy and supportive counseling. *Journal of Clinical and Consulting Psychology, 75*, 277– 284.

Boelen, P. A., & Spuij, M. (2008). Negative cognitions in loss-related emotional distress in adolescent girls: A preliminary study. *Journal of Loss and Trauma, 13*, 441–449.

Currier, J. M., Holland, J. M., & Neimeyer, R. A. (2007). The effectiveness of bereavement interventions with children: A meta-analytic review of controlled outcome research. *Journal of Clinical Child and Adolescent Psychology, 36*, 253–259.

David-Ferdon, C., & Kaslow, N. J. (2008). Evidence-based psychosocial treatments for child and adolescent depression. *Journal of Clinical Child & Adolescent Psychology, 37*(1), 62–104.

Prigerson, H. G., Horowitz, M. J., Jacobs, S. C., Parkes, C. M., Aslan, M., Goodkin, K., et al. (2009). Prolonged Grief Disorder: Psychometric validation of criteria proposed for DSM-V and ICD-11. *PLoS Medicine, 6*(8): e1000121.

Spuij, M., Van Londen-Huibers, A., & Boelen, P. A. (2011). Cognitive-behavioral therapy for Prolonged Grief in children: A feasibility and multiple baseline study. Manuscript submitted for publication.

Part VII
Encountering Resistance

38

"Is It Okay for You to Be Okay?"

Therese A. Rando

CLIENTS FOR WHOM THE TECHNIQUE IS APPROPRIATE

Clients contending with the loss of a loved one, from a school-age child onward, who appear "stuck" in their mourning as manifested by refusal to relinquish pain and/or move forward adaptively in life. It is not appropriate for clients in acute grief following a loss, where significant distress is normal and to be expected.

DESCRIPTION

It is a fallacy that everyone coming for treatment in the wake of a loved one's death is willing to let go of their pain and move forward healthily in their life. Such actions can be enormously threatening to mourners. There are a variety of reasons, some conscious and some not, why a mourner may resist being "okay" after a loved one dies. If therapists fail to appreciate this, they might not grasp such crucial elements as reasons for a mourner's sabotage of treatment; obstacles to their improvement; or what fuels their guilt or keeps them immobilized, among other treatment concerns. While there are many potential impediments to a mourner's progress toward healthy accommodation of their loss, none is more fundamental than a judgment by that person that it is not acceptable for them to be without problems. If the mourner cannot permit herself to be healthy, no treatment in the world will make a difference until she decides it is permissible to let it do so (Rubin, Malkinson, & Witztum, 2012). Healthy mourning after loss, like healthy living in its wake, both mandate that a mourner implicitly or explicitly make the decision that it is all right to be unimpaired and experience well-being.

Taking into consideration the specific factors operating within an idiosyncratic situation, when it appears a mourner is stuck, it can be useful to identify their resistance and explore its functions. A simple, but effective, assessment technique to bring these to light is the timely posing of the query "*Is it okay for you to be okay?*" This can generate an enormous amount of information, while eliciting a minimum amount of defensiveness. First, the word "okay" is relatively neutral, non-specific, and lacks negative implications sometimes associated with pathology or medicalization. This permits the mourner to take the question in any direction she chooses, to determine what "okay" would mean for her, and to have the greatest leeway in identifying anyone or anything that could be making it unacceptable. Second, the phrasing of the question is such that it puts no limits on the type of information explaining the resistance. It can range from global beliefs or assumptive world elements (such as "No parent can ever be out of pain if they've buried a child") to specific personal data (for instance, "Because I broke up with him and he killed himself, I can't ever permit myself to have another relationship!"). Third, it is generic yet sensitive enough that it picks up even small senses of a mourner's discomfort.

If the mourner admits that it is not okay for her to be okay, the next step is to determine how this manifests and why. One primary way of not being okay is by not relinquishing pain. Many mourners erroneously think that if they do not remain in pain, this suggests it was acceptable their loved one died, they are unmoved by their loss, or they did not love the deceased enough. Others feel pain is a "testimonial" to their love of the deceased or construe it as a "betrayal" of their loved ones if they move beyond it. Some see pain as their "connection" to their loved one, while others perceive it as a way to atone for whatever guilt they feel. Another main way to not be okay is to not move forward adaptively in life. Reasons for this include feeling too guilty about "leaving" the deceased behind, trying to keep the world and the self the same as before to minimize the sense of loss, inaccurate expectations of what it means to mourn, and fear that one will forget the deceased.

If it is not okay for the mourner to be okay, useful questions for exploration include:

- *What would it mean if you were okay?*
- *What would it say about you? Your loved one? Your relationship?*
- *Why might you want to remain where you are?*
- *What do you get out of not being okay? What does it do for you?*
- *What ways could you have a connection to your loved one that don't involve pain?*
- *How can you deal with any guilt you have in healthier ways?*
- *What is your expectation of yourself as a mourner?*
- *How could you move forward adaptively in life and still maintain healthy connections with your loved one, if you so desire?*

Therapists can then take these answers and engage their preferred psychotherapeutic strategies to work through obstructions, mitigate their effects, or promote healthy new behaviors in the mourner.

CASE EXAMPLE

Steve had been divorced since his only child, a daughter, was 3 years old. Having joint custody with her mother, much of his life was taken up with Nia. He was an extremely involved father, who even kept his own social life minimal in order to focus on his daughter's upbringing. In the aftermath of her sudden death at 14 from a freak accident, Steve entered therapy where he did much good work identifying and expressing his painful feelings and finding ways to memorialize his daughter. As time went on, however, the therapist noticed that Steve always had an excuse for failing to follow through on actions designed to engage him more socially and to start to limit his constant expression of pain. When it became apparent that Steve was stuck in his acute grief, not making proper readjustments to accommodate his loss, his therapist wondered with him whether it was okay for him to be okay in light of his daughter's death. This simple question first stunned Steve, then brought forth a torrent of emotions and tears during which he cried, "I can't have a life if she can't have a life!" The query opened a most meaningful discussion into the parental guilt and expectations that had kept Steve holding on tenaciously to his distress, actively working to prevent himself from feeling better. Once identified, the therapist was able to productively intervene with Steve in ways to promote healthy mourning, accommodation of his loss, and desired appropriate connections to his deceased daughter, and it ultimately became okay for Steve to be okay in Nia's absence.

CONCLUDING THOUGHTS

Working with resistance has been a cornerstone of many types of therapies. When it comes to stalled or complicated mourning, the resistances are often the focus of intervention because they are what interferes with uncomplicated mourning taking place, essentially contributing to the development of complicated mourning (Rando, 1993, 2012). This technique offers a simple, "mourner-friendly" way of identifying such blocks for further address in treatment and increasing the mourner's awareness of self-imposed limitations.

References

Rando, T. A. (1993). *Treatment of complicated mourning.* Champaign, IL: Research Press.

Rando, T. A. (forthcoming in 2012). *Coping with the sudden death of a loved one: Self-help for traumatic bereavement.* Indianapolis, IN: Dog Ear Publishing.

Rubin, S. S., Malkinson, R., & Witztum, E. (2012). *Working with the bereaved: Multiple lenses on loss and mourning.* New York: Routledge.

39

Overt Statements for Deep Work in Grief Therapy

Bruce Ecker

CLIENTS FOR WHOM THE TECHNIQUE IS APPROPRIATE

Adults, adolescents and children older than about 5 years who have suppressed and avoided feeling their grieving of a loss, are stuck in interminable, complicated bereavement, or are in the natural process of revising their world of meaning in response to a loss. Overt statements can be used with a very wide range of clients in individual, couple and family therapy, but the therapist has to tailor or titrate it according to the client's emotional capacity, stability and developmental stage.

DESCRIPTION

The process of grieving usually involves unique, personal meanings and emotional themes and can become blocked or interminable if such material is outside of awareness. The unrecognized state of distressing emotional dilemmas maximizes their grip on mood, thought and behavior, and their negative effects seem mysterious and relentless. The overt statement technique is a simple way of "peeling the onion" and bringing implicit emotional material into direct, explicit experience. Identifying the individual's specific, loss-related emotional problems allows a constructive process of resolution to begin.

The purpose of an overt statement is to induce an emotional deepening in any specific area selected by the therapist. In an overt statement, the client, guided by the therapist, uses highly personal phrasing to express either key material that has already emerged in less personal or less direct form, or material that is strongly implied by what has already emerged. For example, it often happens that a client mentions something in an off-hand or dryly factual manner which the therapist recognizes as likely to be an intellectualization of some deep, important emotional material. If the client then is invited to say the same thing in a highly personalized way, emotional deepening and direct accessing of suppressed emotional themes can develop swiftly, as in the case example below.

Style of phrasing is critically important. In strong contrast to the intellectualized or socially polite styles, which mute elements that are most important to capture in an overt statement, the phrasing must be full of personal pronouns and, in present tense, give a completely candid, highly explicit, vivid and concrete expression of the client's living knowledge of vulnerability to a specific suffering and how to avoid it. I've named this style of verbalization *limbic language* because it is so helpful for retrieving the implicit emotional knowledge of the subcortical brain's limbic system. We rely on this style for overt statements and other experiential techniques used often in Coherence Therapy (Ecker & Hulley, 2007).

Overt statements may be designed to be spoken directly to the relevant person(s) (either visualized or in person) if doing so feels workable and safe to the client, or else to the therapist. The wording of an overt statement's one or two sentences can be crafted collaboratively by client and therapist or, alternatively, the therapist can assemble the words and offer them to the client to "try on." The therapist invites the client to make any alterations needed for a feeling of fit and accuracy, and, if needed, to say the statement a second and third time, which is usually enough for the client to drop into a feeling-level, subjective experience of inhabiting the verbalized meanings. The goal is not an intense experience of emotion, which may or may not happen, but rather the client's lucid, somatically felt recognition of his or her own emotional truth.

A variation is to offer an incomplete sentence which the client is to speak without prethinking, allowing the sentence to complete itself, over and over. This sentence completion technique can access underlying material very effectively, as the case example shows.

Important for success with these techniques is deference to the client's knowledge of what his or her emotional truth is. I therefore explain, "The idea is for you to 'try on' these words, even if saying them feels mechanical at first, and just see whether or not they fit and feel as if they capture an emotional truth for you, in your body. If any of the words feel off even a little, let's change them in any way to make them more accurate to what feels true for you."

Overt statements make use of this principle: Unrecognized, implicit emotional truths tend to emerge consciously in response to the utterance of words that are a close enough rendition of them. What the limbic system knows will flow into the cortical, conscious system if the latter's knowledge begins to align with and welcome the former's. Often, the immersive deepening induced by an overt statement does not stop at the content of the statement, but extends into other unconscious but linked, proximate material also coming into awareness. Another overt statement can be created for this material, and so on, in a bootstrapping process we call *serial accessing*.

CASE EXAMPLE

A woman in her early forties was still mired in heavy depression and anguish eight years after the death of her 5-year-old son, who was hit by a truck in front of their home and then died of his injuries one month later. My initial aim in addressing her complicated bereavement problem was to elicit the hidden, implicit emotional themes maintaining her debilitating mood state. For that purpose, I invited overt statements and sentence completions (with a softened, empathetic tone of voice throughout). The transcript below begins after she had referred, in a somewhat depersonalized style, to "the powerlessness over not being able to prevent his death. And since I could not do that, probably I'm unworthy."

> *Therapist: Would you be willing to picture Billy [not his real name] right now? Got him there? Good. And I'd like you to try out saying to him, "Billy, I feel so, so bad that I was powerless to prevent your death." Either silently or out loud—whatever feels best to you.*
> *Client: [Suddenly crying.] Billy, I'm just so, so sorry that I couldn't have prevented your death. It was so awful. And I'm sorry, little fella.*

The next several minutes focused on her self-blame. I raised the question of "whether you feel you deserve ever to be happy again," which led to this:

Therapist: Would you try to talk to me from the part of you that feels the guilt? I know there are these other parts, but from the place in you where you feel guilty, where you feel it was your fault that your dear little boy got hit by a truck, from that place what's the emotional truth for you about whether or not it's OK to feel happy again?

Client: [Silence.]

Therapist: Is something coming up?

Client: What's coming is it is OK. But the feeling's not there. I don't let myself be happy.

Therapist: How come? How come? Would you complete this sentence? "I don't allow myself to be happy because if I were happy—"

Client: I would have to forgive myself. [Pause.] And I've been unwilling to do that.

Therapist: Good. So keep going. "I'm unwilling to forgive myself because—"

Client: You know, there are parts of me that—I think it's about not wanting to go on myself, without him. And if I keep this going, then I don't have to deal with that.

Therapist: I see. So, would you see him again? Picture him and try saying to him, "I'm afraid that if I forgive myself, I'll lose connection with you and I'll go on without you."

Client: [Crying.] I am, Billy, I am afraid. Even though I can picture you as a little angel, I'm afraid to forgive myself—that you'll go away. And I don't want you to go away.

Therapist: And see if it's true to say to him, "It's so important for me to stay connected to you that I'm willing to not forgive myself forever. I'd rather be feeling guilty and miserable so I won't lose contact with you and move on without you."

Client: [Sighs.] Billy, I feel like I would do anything to keep this connection with you, including staying miserable and not forgiving myself for the rest of my life. And you know that's true.

CONCLUDING THOUGHTS

Overt statements can be put to many different uses in experiential therapy and are well supported by empirical findings (e.g., Watson, 1996). In the example above, they served to carry out the initial, discovery stage of Coherence Therapy (Ecker & Hulley, 2007), which is the accessing of implicit emotional knowledge or constructs according to which the presenting symptom is compellingly necessary to have. This bereaved mother had not been conscious that she was remaining in her anguished depression for the urgent, passionate purpose of maintaining connection with her son, tacitly expecting he would "go away" and she would have to "go on myself, without him" if her torment ended. (For a full transcript and video of the session, see Ecker & Hulley, 2008.) As a result of directly knowing, feeling and integrating her own purpose and agency, as well as her personal constructs or mental model that constituted the very existence of the problem, suitable avenues of change came into view—such as the possibility of actively fulfilling her now conscious purpose of maintaining connection in other rich, meaningful ways, ending the inner need for her state of distress to carry out that crucial function.

References

Ecker, B., & Hulley, L. (2007). *Coherence therapy practice manual and training guide.* Oakland, CA: Coherence Psychology Institute. Available at: www.coherencetherapy.org/resources/manual. htm.

Ecker, B., & Hulley, L. (2008). *Stuck in depression: A disabling bereavement.* (Video and viewer's manual.) Oakland, CA: Pacific Seminars. Available at: www.coherencetherapy.org/resources/ videos.htm.

Watson, J. C. (1996). The relationship between vivid description, emotional arousal, and in-session resolution of problematic reactions. *Journal of Consulting and Clinical Psychology, 64,* 459–464.

40

Controlled Avoidance in the Management of Grief

J. Shep Jeffreys

CLIENTS FOR WHOM THE TECHNIQUE IS APPROPRIATE

Adult clients who are intact and seeking a level of control over their grieving process in order to place limits on the extent of their emotional release. It may be less necessary when clients are farther into restoration after many months, when active and reflective exploration of their changed lives arouses less emotion.

DESCRIPTION

For many people the grieving process begins with emotional release in the form of crying, sighing, moaning, raging, dreading, screaming, sobbing, tearing and verbal expressions of fear, guilt and shame. The level of intensity of grieving behaviors may dominate most of the waking time of their early weeks post-loss. Some people find that they are able to compart-mentalize or push some or all of their active grieving aside, in order to meet the practical needs and responsibilities of daily life. Others need help in organizing a way to increase their focus on grocery shopping, taking the trash out, transporting children or paying bills; and want to know that it is okay to have "time outs" from grief.

This "side-by-side" approach to grieving (Jeffreys, 2011) is a custom-tailored design that permits and enables clients to place time limits on mourning by controlled avoidance of emotional release. This is accomplished by setting time limits on active grieving and engaging in an incompatible or non-grief activity following the interval of expressing emotional pain. There can still be some sadness, fatigue, sighing or some internal grief dialogue while cooking, scrubbing, jogging, praying, walking or talking, but the primary focus is on the distracting practical or non-grief activity.

The concept of a two-phase post-loss world comes directly from clients who do this natu-rally or verbalize a desire to do so. The work of Stroebe and Schut (1999) and Rubin (1999) supports the concept of duality of the griever's post-loss functioning. The well-known 23rd Psalm gives us a spiritual basis for "walking through the valley of the shadow of death." The griever can focus on the *shadow* or choose to look up at the *light* which casts the shadow. The person on this journey can determine how deeply and how long he or she will dwell on each focus and how the switch-over is to be managed. Here again the grieving person has available a choice and control over grief. For many, the reestablishment of a sense of control in a post-loss setting bathed in helplessness is the beginning of reclaiming a functional life.

The basic framework for creating this controlled avoidance of grieving is as follows:

1. First, on a sheet of paper jot down what you are hoping for from this exercise. Are there essential tasks or people that require attention, or do you simply need respite from the storm?
2. Set a time limit—perhaps 30 minutes to a couple of hours—for your active grieving period on a given day. Ask a loved one or trusted friend to do something with you at a specified time, or set a timer to let you know when the time has elapsed.
3. Know that you can extend the time for another interval, but make this intentional and time limited, rather than open-ended.
4. Set a time to re-enter an interval of active grieving. When your grieving interval is ended, change your physical position and location if possible and engage in the pre-planned non-grieving activity (see below for suggestions).
5. If you are able to do some writing, jot down the time and activity and how this worked to temporarily distract you from active grieving. Did it meet your expectations and if not, how would you change it?

Below are some suggestions for controlled avoidance activities that others have found useful:

- Social contact
- Prayer/meditation
- Relaxation exercise
- Nature walk
- Household chores—scrub a floor or clean a toilet, rearrange that messy drawer
- Grocery shopping—buy some favorite foods/treats
- Pay some bills
- Hobbies/crafts
- Physical exercise
- Reading favorite book
- Humorous videos/film
- Music—singing, playing, listening
- Helping another grieving person
- Retail therapy
- Other distracting activity of your choice
- Contact your counselor or spiritual advisor for other suggestions.

CASE EXAMPLE

Jenna, a PhD biochemist and senior supervisor in a large food processing firm, lost her husband to lymphoma after a short period of treatment. With two children in early elementary school, she was racked with horror and disbelief that her perfect life with the perfect man was over. She was overwhelmed with disbelief and that this was an irreversible change in her world. As a successful scientist and manager used to setting and accomplishing goals, she was traumatized by the wafts of reality that overtook her attempts at staving off the truth of the lost battle with cancer. After four months of straining to provide the level of child-care she felt was her requirement and maintaining intermittent contact with her work setting, she began to find ways to immerse herself in some of the practical demands of her life.

She was open to exploring a more controlled format for moving from intense grieving to non-grieving activities rather than allowing the grieving intervals to "run their course." She elected to use a timer and selected relaxation as the activity to be the initial alternate focus. We rehearsed the breathing, muscle relaxation and comforting imagery protocol in the office with recorded gentle music of her choice. She also selected lunch with a friend and a trip into work as additional post-grieving activities. After several weeks, she was able to set the timer and allow herself a period (30 minutes to an hour) of the free release of pain and then use the relaxation music to move to non-grieving. She followed this with seeing a friend or cooking a meal for her family and/or going to the gym for a workout. Shortly after this, she returned to work full-time. She commented that having and understanding the "side-by-side" structure for grieving and regaining control over her life fit her style.

CONCLUDING THOUGHTS

Grieving people who are racked with the overwhelming flood of continuous and intense emotional release and who request or are open to a way to soften this emotional outpouring, can benefit from the adage: "Don't do nothing! When you are able to, *do something* to take a break from grieving." Having a ready list of available distracting or incompatible activities smoothes the transition to the non-grieving activity. Regaining a sense of control of the journey *through* "the valley of the shadow" into the post-loss world provides a start-up to new meanings, new rituals, and new social locations—a new normal.

References

Jeffreys, J. S. (2011). *Helping grieving people—When tears are not enough: A handbook for care providers.* New York: Routledge.

Rubin, S. (1999). A two-track model of bereavement: Overview, retrospect and prospect. *Death Studies, 23,* 681–714.

Stroebe, M., & Schut, H. (1999). The Dual Process Model of coping with bereavement: Rationale and description. *Death Studies, 23,* 197–224.

Part VIII
Finding Meaning

41
Finding Meaning Through the Attitude One Takes

Wendy G. Lichtenthal and William Breitbart

CLIENTS FOR WHOM THE TECHNIQUE IS APPROPRIATE

Bereaved adults and adolescents attempting to restore a sense of meaning in their lives without their loved one's physical presence. This technique is contraindicated for clients exhibiting posttraumatic stress disorder symptoms (e.g., intrusive thoughts about a traumatic death) and for those whose spiritual worldview is incongruent with the concept of freedom of will.

DESCRIPTION

The death of a loved one reminds people that life is finite; a fact that many routinely work hard to ignore or deny. It also often takes from individuals the very relationship that filled them with a sense of purpose and connection. Thus, the bereft individual may be left with a sense that life has lost meaning or purpose without their loved one's physical presence. This technique addresses these existential issues, and is largely based on the work of Viktor Frankl (1959/1992), who described his experience in a Holocaust concentration camp and its influence on his development of logotherapy in *Man's Search for Meaning*. This approach has been further influenced by the development of a manualized meaning-centered psychotherapy for advanced cancer patients (Breitbart et al., 2010), which provides psychoeducation about Frankl's existential principles and encourages thoughtful contemplation of what is most meaningful through a series of provocative questions and experiential exercises.

In describing how people can transcend suffering, Frankl often applied Neitzche's philosophy, "'He who has a *why* to live for can bear with almost any *how*'" (1959/1992, p. 109). Each individual has his or her own sources of meaning, which Frankl categorized into three pathways: "(1) by creating a work or doing a deed; (2) by experiencing something or encountering someone; and (3) by the attitude we take toward unavoidable suffering" (1959/1992, p. 115). However, the death of a loved often robs the bereaved individual of core sources of meaning anchored in the relationship with the deceased, and disconnects them from previously meaningful roles, such as being caregivers to their loved one during a protracted illness. While we encourage clients to reconnect to these sources of meaning through creative endeavors (e.g., work, causes, deeds) and meaningful experiences (e.g., love, beauty, humor)—and to even identify new ones—this is rarely a quick fix to transcend suffering associated with a significant loss. Thus, in working with bereaved clients, we frequently highlight one of Frankl's central tenets, which is that individuals are free to choose the meaning they ascribe to a situation, including the most tragic.

Frankl once noted that ". . . everything can be taken from man but one thing: the last of human freedoms—the ability to choose one's attitude in any given set of circumstances" (Frankl, 1959/1992, p. 75). To illustrate this principle, Frankl recounted a consultation with an elderly physician who sought his guidance because he "could not overcome the loss of his wife who had died two years before and whom he loved above all else" (1959/1992, p. 117). Frankl asked the physician what his wife would have done if he had died first; the man responded, "'for her this would have been terrible; how she would have suffered!" Frankl then highlighted the *meaning* in the physician's suffering by pointing out how "such a suffering has been spared her, and it was you who have spared her this suffering—to be sure, at the price that now you have to survive and mourn her" (Frankl, 1959/1992, p. 117). Following this framework, the therapist's role is to assist clients with finding meaning in their grief. The therapist does this not by prescribing a specific point of view or way of looking at the situation, but rather by drawing attention to the choice and freedom that they have in the midst of their suffering.

Discussion of finding meaning in (or despite) tragic circumstances should first begin by validating the suffering; this is key, as introducing a reframing perspective when someone is in the midst of sharing profound grief can be viewed as non-empathic. Thus, the therapist should avoid simple cheerleading. After acknowledging the intense suffering the mourner is experiencing, an introduction of Frankl's work can begin with background about his experience as a concentration camp survivor. The therapist should be careful not to draw direct comparisons between the client's experience and being a Holocaust survivor, but rather simply highlight the commonality of suffering in painful situations that are beyond one's control. Providing psychoeducation about how individuals are free to choose their attitude can provide clients some semblance of control in a largely uncontrollable situation. Following Breitbart et al.'s (2010) approach with advanced cancer patients, we often suggest that our bereaved clients read *Man's Search for Meaning* and discuss any points that resonated in session.

In essence, the therapist can work with the client to transform the meaning of the grieving from one that focuses on an *outcome* (e.g., "relief") to one that focuses on the *process* (e.g., "How am I handling this pain?"). This may be construed as a distancing technique, but one that can foster a sense of self-efficacy. In cases in which the client is "keeping" the grief as a means of continuing the bond, highlighting the "choice" in surrendering to the suffering may be valuable. Discussion of the utility of maintaining this attitude can then follow, particularly when it is maintaining maladaptive thought patterns (e.g., rumination) and behaviors (e.g., avoidance of restorative activities).

The therapist can also explain how the attitude one chooses in facing suffering can become a source of meaning in and of itself; that in this way, as Frankl has commented, human beings have the unique capacity to transform "personal tragedy into triumph" (1959/1992, p. 116). It is important, however, to highlight that the suffering can persist, and that applying this type of cognitive reframing will not result in the pain dissipating. Instead, it removes the added layer of guilt and self-criticism that often arise when one is fighting against the suffering, judging it. The discussion can be stimulated by exploring how clients handled prior limitations or losses, highlighting any instances that they felt proud of the attitude they took or inviting contemplation of an attitude they might take looking back at the situation. Asking them to describe an attitude they would admire can stimulate thought about how they might face their current suffering and grief.

CASE EXAMPLE

Anne entered grief counseling shortly after her husband of over 30 years, Joe, died of prostate cancer. Anne, a retired teacher, described Joe as a wonderful partner and socially gifted man whom "everyone loved." She recalled stories of his impact on others with pride, and remarking on what a "presence" he was, noted how strongly and painfully his absence was felt in their home and in their social circles. She also noted how Joe in essence saved her from her lifelong struggle with depression and feelings of inadequacy; if Joe loved her this much, her life must have had meaning and worth. Now, without Joe's reassuring presence, she began to feel as if it did not and criticized herself for how she was "not doing enough." Anne busied herself with engagement in social activities, exercise, and volunteer work, but still reported feeling "lost." After validating the loss of what sounded like a loving and supportive marriage worthy of anyone's envy, Frankl's work was introduced, highlighting how, in the face of such a profound loss, one has the freedom to choose how he or she faces it. Anne's ability to still engage in life despite a loss of this magnitude was highlighted. The high expectations she had of herself in coping were also discussed, as these resulted in her criticizing and minimizing the ways in which she was acting responsibly, engaging in meaningful activities and experiences despite her pain. Anne was encouraged to examine the type of attitude she might admire in someone else, and her attention was called to the close resemblance between this idealized self and the very way she was living her life; the only snag was her difficulty acknowledging how she was turning her attention toward meaningful things. Over time, Anne, herself, began to highlight her ability to engage in life through valued activities and relationships despite her continued grief in sessions. In that way, the attitude she chose became a source of meaning and pride that ultimately seemed to enhance her appreciation of other meaningful aspects of her life.

CONCLUDING THOUGHTS

A meaning-centered therapeutic approach to managing grief and loss invites clients to turn their attention to various sources of meaning to help endure the pain of grief—through connecting with creative and experiential values, but also, importantly, through the attitude one chooses. Clients are viewed as the creators of the meaning in their lives. They may, for example, alter their meaning of their grief so that it is viewed as a reflection of the strength of the lost relationship or as a driving force to engage in a greater good, such as becoming active in a social cause. Highlighting this to bereaved clients can empower them; although their loss was beyond their control, what is within their control is how they face their suffering. How they face this pain may thus become a source of meaning—perhaps even a source of pride.

There are two assumptions woven into this approach that therapists should note:

1. *Suffering is inevitable and, thus, acceptable.* This means that the bereaved individual must incorporate this worldview into his or her existing cognitive schemas if it is not a pre-existing assumption. It also means that the individual must have the ability to tolerate experiencing the suffering. Individuals who are fighting tooth and nail to avoid distressing feelings and cognitions may find this assumption challenging to assimilate into their existing cognitive framework.
2. *Individuals have the ability to make choices, including the choice of the attitude they adopt.* Those who believe that a higher power determines our choices, behaviors and thoughts may find this perspective antithetical to their beliefs.

Again, it is important for the therapist to highlight that the client has a choice rather than directing the client to make a specific choice. The idea that the client can choose his or her attitude might be viewed as a cognitive reframing strategy. But this is not an explicit invitation to "just think about the situation differently . . ." Rather, and importantly, it is highlighting that whatever attitude they choose to take is their decision and their decision alone. This is a key point, as the therapist should not become the explicit "motivator." The existential principles are putting the responsibility into the hands of the client. It is the client's responsibility to respond to his or her individual life, and choose how to face its greatest challenges.

References

Breitbart, W., Rosenfeld, B., Gibson, C., Pessin, H., Poppito, S., Nelson, C., et al. (2010). Meaning-centered group psychotherapy for patients with advanced cancer: A pilot randomized controlled trial. *Psychooncology, 19*(1), 21–28.

Frankl, V. E. (1959/1992). *Man's search for meaning* (revised ed.). Boston: Beacon.

42

Directed Journaling to Facilitate Meaning-Making

Wendy G. Lichtenthal and Robert A. Neimeyer

CLIENTS FOR WHOM THE TECHNIQUE IS APPROPRIATE

Clients who are having difficulty making meaning of their loss, but who have expressed at various junctures aspects of their sense-making or benefit-finding processes in session. Benefit journaling is contraindicated for individuals who (1) are still experiencing intense acute grief symptoms for whom contemplation of positive consequences associated with the loss may appear offensive; and (2) have not revealed any consequences that could be construed as positive in the therapist's judgment.

DESCRIPTION

"Storying" our experiences allows us to incorporate and organize disruptive life events into our self-narratives, fostering a coherent sense of identity and shaping emotional reactions and goals for the future (Neimeyer, van Dyke, & Pennebaker, 2008). Such storytelling is a large component of the therapeutic encounter, after all. Likewise, a great deal of research has demonstrated the psychological and physical health benefits of expressive writing, which traditionally involves individuals expressing their thoughts and emotions about their most traumatic or stressful life event (Pennebaker & Beall, 1986; Smyth, 1998). However, studies of bereaved individuals writing about their loss do not always demonstrate the same benefits, which may be because the writing was *open-ended* rather than *directed* (Lichtenthal & Cruess, 2010; Stroebe, Schut, & Stroebe, 2006). Without guidance, grieving individuals may not write about topics that are helpful, or may, in fact, end up engaging in unhelpful coping behaviors, such as rumination (Nolen-Hoeksema, 2001). In contrast, when provided with direction and focus, grievers may profit from journaling. One recent randomized controlled trial showed, for example, that directing participants to engage in meaning-making processes through their writing resulted in lower levels of prolonged grief, depressive symptoms and posttraumatic stress symptoms, with the effects of benefit journaling being especially salutary. Moreover, these positive results actually *increased* over the months that followed (Lichtenenthal & Cruess, 2010).

When applying this technique in therapy, we commonly encourage clients to write freely and spontaneously, for at least 20–30 minutes, on several occasions, drawing on one or both of the following intentions.

Sense making entails addressing the client's own questions about how and why the loss occurred, specifically with respect to its circumstances and causes related to the loved one's health, their own or someone else's actions, or a higher force. This often involves focusing on how the loss fits into the client's core meanings, perhaps prompted by questions such as:

- How did you make sense of the death or loss at the time?
- How do you interpret the loss now?
- What philosophical or spiritual beliefs contributed to your adjustment to this loss? How were they affected by it, in turn?
- Are there ways in which this loss has influenced the direction of your life story? How, across time, have your dealt with this?
- How, in the long run, do you imagine that you will give this loss meaning in your life?

Benefit finding involves seeking the positive significance of the loss, the silver lining, if any, in the dark cloud of bereavement. This may be registered in any important domain, such as in terms of life goals, values, purpose or relationships with others. Questions that help prompt such reflections include:

- In your view, have you found any unsought gifts in grief? If so, what?
- How has this experience affected your sense of priorities? Your sense of yourself?
- What qualities in yourself have you drawn on that have contributed to your resilience? What qualities of a supportive kind have you discovered in others?
- What lessons about loving or living has this person or this loss taught you?
- Has this difficult transition deepened your gratitude for anything you have been given? Is there anyone to whom you would like to express heartfelt appreciation?

When we use this technique with clients, we often encourage them to journal on these themes outside of therapy, and to then bring their writing into sessions for processing and further reflection. Alternatively, we may capitalize on journaling that clients have spontaneously performed on their own, providing direction to expand upon this writing and further craft the meaning they have begun to make (Neimeyer et al., 2008). The therapist may highlight various facets of the writing, such as cognitive schemas underlying the client's belief system, related assimilation of the loss, conflicting ideas and the potential for their reconciliation, and other shifts in thinking that may have taken place across the writing sessions. When changes in how the client has made sense of the loss are less pronounced or a struggle to make sense of the loss remains apparent, the therapist may discuss the potential threat to the client's belief system that this loss may be causing. Given that writing frequently prompts the type of emotional expression believed to be an important part of adaptive grieving (Stroebe et al., 2006), the therapist may capitalize on clients' engagement in this process and highlight their ability to experience and tolerate distressing feelings as they struggle to find meaning in their pain.

CASE EXAMPLE

Gayle Rose sought therapy with me (RAN) a few months after the death of her middle son, Max, at age 19 in a vehicular accident. * Among the narrative methods she found helpful in exploring*

---

* Gayle requested that I use her son's actual name, rather than the conventional pseudonym to disguise his identity, as a way of honoring him and drawing on the tragedy of his death to offer something of value to the grief therapy community and the clients we serve. I am only too happy to do so, as I take inspiration from Gayle's integration of this traumatic loss in a way that affirms her core life meanings. Those readers interested in further expressions of benefit finding in the wake of Max's life may wish to learn more about Team Max, the remarkable virtual social network pursuing "vigilante philanthropy" in the form of dozens of humanitarian projects, from feeding the hungry to delivering medical aid to earthquake-stricken communities. For more, visit Team Max on Facebook at: http://www.facebook.com/groups/42807539787/.

and ultimately transforming her grief was directed journaling, which she used not only to vent her anguish over Max's death, but also to seek affirmative meaning in it. One outgrowth of her meaning-oriented journaling was the following letter, sent four months after her son's funeral to the many supporters who had rallied around her family in the aftermath of the shared tragedy.

My dearest friends and family:

I want to personally thank you for the beautiful cards, letters, food, flowers, and donations to Street's Ministries and other worthy charities in memory of our beloved son, Max. I am so moved by the outpouring of love and support for our family and I vowed to write everyone a personal note. However, what I hope to express requires more space than the note card allows, so please forgive this letter.

Grace has surrounded me. The sharp blade of grief that threatens my heart has been blunted by the beauty of the love and prayers from each of you. It has become evident that pain and grace are of one piece. They are separate, but one; each the bearer of the other.

Since January 3, I have begun to see my life in a larger context. I am able to abandon my self-image as an independent person and see myself as interdependent; my grief shared among each of you through grace. There were divine moments of grace in the hospital in Wichita; grace in the loving arms of family and friends in the immediate days before the funeral; communal grace of shared pain on January 8th, when the church overflowed with love for us and for the witness of Max's life; and steadfast grace as Max's friends continue to show up on Friday nights to 'hang out' as they always have, and as notes and gifts are left in my mailbox along with letters of such poetic beauty that I'm left breathless and profoundly blessed.

As I conscientiously walk the path of parental grief, I have discovered that time does not heal all wounds. Healing is an active process, not a passive one. It doesn't happen to us, we must participate in our own healing. It is a gift we give to ourselves the moment we decide to "open" to that which has broken us. So I am taking the time to grieve; to face the sadness and loss and not attempt to step out of its way; to savor each card and letter, to meditate, to walk in the woods, to be present for Morgan and Mikey, and to ponder the story of Max's life and legacy.

This loss has thrown me into a heightened state of awareness. I will never be the same. Through a new lens, the world looks different and yet grace is the gift of seeing that which was there all along. I find new strength in family and friends and understand that the only vitally important purpose in life is the giving and receiving of love. I have looked into the face of impermanence and am mustering the courage to live a life of meaning that reflects the profound importance of Max's life.

Thank you for being bearers of grace; for it is grace that will wrench something beautiful out of the jaws of this tragedy, and it is grace that binds us to each other and to Max now and forever. My gratitude knows no bounds. Thank you.

CONCLUDING THOUGHTS

Many clients naturally use journaling as an expressive outlet, but it is unclear whether all such forms of writing are beneficial. However, controlled research has demonstrated the utility of guiding the writing process with clients who are struggling to find meaning in their loss or in their lives in its aftermath (Lichtenthal & Cruess, 2010). Writing can facilitate creation of an adaptive, coherent narrative about how the loss of a loved one fits into the larger scheme of the writer's life and worldview. The written piece can then become a resource for reflection that reinforces the meaning made at the time of writing and further stimulates the ever-dynamic meaning-making process. In a phrase, reflective writing can help us make sense of a world that doesn't. While no panacea for the pain of separation, it can help grievers find significance and reorientation in a life that has been challenged by loss.

References

Lichtenthal, W. G., & Cruess, D. G. (2010). Effects of directed written disclosure on grief and distress symptoms among bereaved individuals. *Death Studies, 34*(6), 475–499.

Neimeyer, R. A., van Dyke, J. G., & Pennebaker, J. W. (2008). Narrative medicine: Writing through bereavement. In H. Chochinov, & W. Breitbart (Eds.), *Handbook of psychiatry in palliative medicine* (pp. 454–469). New York: Oxford University Press.

Nolen-Hoeksema, S. (2001). Ruminative coping and adjustment to bereavement. In M. S. Stroebe, R. O. Hansson, W. Stroebe, & H. Schut (Eds.), *Handbook of bereavement research* (pp. 545–562). Washington, DC: American Psychological Association.

Pennebaker, J. W., & Beall, S. K. (1986). Confronting a traumatic event: Toward an understanding of inhibition and disease. *Journal of Abnormal Psychology, 95*(3), 274–281.

Smyth, J. M. (1998). Written emotional expression: Effect sizes, outcome types, and moderating variables. *Journal of Consulting and Clinical Psychology, 66*(1), 174–184.

Stroebe, M., Schut, H., & Stroebe, W. (2006). Who benefits from disclosure? Exploration of attachment style differences in the effects of expressing emotions. *Clinical Psychology Review, 26*(1), 66–85.

43

Using the Loss Characterization
with Bereaved Parents

Nick J. Gerrish

CLIENTS FOR WHOM THE TECHNIQUE IS APPROPRIATE

Parents who have lost children, especially several months after the death. Earlier application can be difficult when parents are wrestling with overwhelming emotional demands in the present, when supportive and directive assistance are most beneficial.

DESCRIPTION

For many parents, the death of a child represents a loss of profound and traumatic proportions with a grief trajectory that may be lifelong. Complications in grieving that can occur following this type of loss are well documented. However, at the same time, emerging from their struggle with grief, some parents report adaptive changes in their sense of identity, or what has been termed 'post-traumatic growth' (PTG). Within the therapeutic setting, while it is encouraging to witness and (where possible) to facilitate PTG, how adaptive responses to loss are assessed and then discussed with bereaved parents should proceed with caution. In particular, direct questioning about such responses using terms such as "positive changes," "benefits" or any other language that might be perceived to imply something "positive" has emerged from a child's death can be experienced as offensive to some parents and may even lead to a denial of such experiences (i.e., based on the sense of guilt this evokes). In light of these concerns, one technique that holds promise for sensitively exploring PTG in the wake of a child's death is the Loss Characterization (Neimeyer, 2002). Consistent with other constructivist and narrative-based techniques used to explore parental grief (Gerrish, Steed, & Neimeyer, 2010), one advantage of using the Loss Characterization is that it invites the bereaved parent to use his or her own formulations, definitions, and language to explore PTG (as well as possible complications) within their grieving experience. In particular, through using indirect and open-ended instructional prompts, the bereaved parent is simply asked to reflect on how the death of their child has impacted on who they are as a person. In more specific terms, the bereaved parent is provided with an instructional set at the top of a blank page that reads as follows (adapted version):

> In the space that follows, please write in your own words a description of the kind of person you are following your child's death. Alternatively, if you would prefer, you could dictate an audio recording of the same description of yourself. Please be aware

that spelling and grammar do not matter, or even the way you write it. For example, you may just want to just jot down some notes, or even use some points to describe how you feel. How much you write is also up to you – please write as much or as little as you wish.

This exercise is one that I would like you to complete at home to allow you whatever time you need to "speak for yourself" about the loss of your child and how this has affected you. You may wish to begin as follows: "Since [child's name] died, I . . ."

The above instructions are designed to be simple and to minimize the parent's defensiveness and to allow him or her to focus on the *experience of bereavement* without implying any particular outcomes from the loss. The Loss Characterization can also be completed by asking parents to write their self-description as it might be written by a friend (or other significant person) who knew them very intimately and very sympathetically (i.e., they are asked to write it in the third person). In adopting the perspective of a friend or other significant person, the potential for self-criticism and other condemnation that may occur with this exercise can be reduced (Neimeyer, 2002).

However, based on my own research with bereaved mothers, the modified format as outlined above was one that mothers found more understandable and therefore manageable. Bereaved mothers wrote varying amounts in accordance with their own capabilities, with some mothers writing as little as two paragraphs. Despite this, the content of many of their accounts highlighted clearly how their loss had impacted their identity. Furthermore, adaptive (and complicating) aspects to mother's grief experiences were revealed in their writings—thereby bypassing the need for direct (and potentially distressing) questioning about such responses. This did not mean that exploration of the quality and meaning of mother's responses to their loss was not required. However, importantly, these discussions were able to proceed in a more sensitive manner by adopting the language, wording and examples of identity change of the bereaved mother (not the therapist) as a reference point.

CASE EXAMPLE

A mother who had lost her child to cancer five years earlier provided the following Loss Characterization; pseudonyms have been used to respect her confidentiality.

> *It's difficult to write about "me" but I will attempt to do so. Firstly, losing Jess is the worst event that has ever occurred in my life. Losing a daughter is losing someone much, much more than a best friend, it is like losing a part of myself. In response to describing what kind of person I am now following Jess's death . . . sad, but also grateful to have known and loved Jess.*
>
> *There is a lot of regret for everything that led Jess to endure any suffering. To watch an innocent child be subjected to chemotherapy treatment that her parents had consented to was mental torture for us, physical torture for her. It is a choice we made and the consequences we will have to live with forever. There is nothing that can take away that horrific event. So yes, I live with sorrow for the suffering; regret that I wasn't stronger to give of myself more and live with many thoughts of how it may have been if other decisions had been made. I remember often whispering in her ear that we loved her and were there beside her, but I will always wish that I'd had the words to be more insistent, stronger and more determined to somehow keep her alive. However, this was not the outcome and acceptance is all that is left.*
>
> *When Jess first passed, the pain of losing someone so dear to me was so extreme that any previous experiences or conclusions that I had come to about life being beautiful or about*

a creator being kind, were impossible to believe any more. They were a concept only, a memory that I knew I had believed all my life, but it was one I thought I'd never be able to believe again. The experience of grief is so powerful, so overwhelming, so all encompassing, it was hard to comprehend that a "kind" creator could also create the ability for a human being to experience such depths of sorrow. Through that grief, needs to understand where my daughter now was and whether she was still suffering, were crucial to me. Over time, in many unexpected ways, incidences occurred that helped me to see certain resolutions to my needs. Be it through words in a song, people who came into my life and spoke about their experiences, dates and places that were significantly related to my own life, kindnesses shown to me from other people's actions . . . all of these things over time helped to heal the grief.

Fortunately, I am alive. To appreciate this unique opportunity is important and feels good. Perhaps now I'm more focussed on valuing the moment, more aware of how fragile this life is, more appreciative of this limited time I have to be alive and recognise the need to live more from my heart. Learning to live with an "invisible" Jess is what I do now. I will always love and admire her for everything that she was during her lifetime and that bond we have will never die.

In examining this mother's Loss Characterization, the devastating impact of her child's death on her identity and assumptions about the world were clearly evident. Her inability to erase the memories of her daughter's suffering left her with pain and regret that she had come to accept would be with her for life. At the same time, through grieving her loss, she felt she had been transformed in profound ways. She described a greater appreciation for her own life, an increased valuing of the moment, a desire to live closer to her feelings and the creation of an ongoing and meaningful symbolic bond with her daughter.

CONCLUDING THOUGHTS

Exploring bereaved parents' experiences of PTG and other adaptive responses that can potentially follow the death of a child can have important therapeutic benefits for parents' overall adaptation to their loss. With appropriate precautions against directly asking the bereaved if they have "changed in any positive ways," the Loss Characterization exercise allows survivors (of many types of losses) to write about "who they are in light of their loss" and to report of their own accord, using their own words and examples, changes to their identity that may reflect PTG.

References

Gerrish, N. J., Steed, L., & Neimeyer, R. A. (2010). Meaning reconstruction in bereaved mothers: A pilot study using the biographical grid. *Journal of Constructivist Psychology, 23*, 118–142.

Neimeyer, R. A. (2002). *Lessons of loss: A guide to coping*. Memphis, TN: Center for the Study of Loss and Transition.

44
Metaphorical Reframing

Eliezer Witztum

CLIENTS FOR WHOM THE TECHNIQUE IS APPROPRIATE

Adolescents and adults reorganizing a continuing bond with the deceased and those who experience traumatic grief or complicated grief. Metaphors may be less appropriate for young children and highly concrete clients, who may be more responsive to more directive interventions.

DESCRIPTION

Using metaphor and metaphoric reframing is a therapeutic approach by which the therapist uses broad approaches to intervene, in this case, following bereavement. Complicated grief is one of the conditions for which grief intervention is efficacious. Grief and mourning can be facilitated by a variety of therapeutic methods that can ease suffering and assist the bereaved who is experiencing complicated grief and associated depressive syndromes.

The main purpose of this intervention is to facilitate an adaptive process of meaning construction. The application of this approach within the continuing bonds framework helps the bereaved express thoughts and feelings through symbolizing meaning. Metaphorical reframing addresses multiple strands in the construction of meaning in life and the reorganization of the continuous bond with the deceased.

Metaphors are seen as ideal meaning-making symbols in treating trauma and grief. In such cases, working through the problem directly can be too anxiety provoking or complicated. Using the understandings gained from the interchange in the metaphoric field can help the client reframe the situation (Witztum, van der Hart, & Friedman, 1988).

Grieving people use metaphors to talk about their experiences of loss. Metaphors used in therapy may be constructed by clients or therapists, or they may co-evolve in the process of therapy. Alternatively, metaphors can be developed through the telling of stories. The use of story allows us to communicate with the non-verbalized domain beyond the customary limitations of familiar language. Metaphors can be useful in grief therapy because: (1) they can reveal how the loss is perceived by the grieving person: (2) they provide a potentially less threatening way of talking about the loss; and (3) they can suggest alternative ways of responding to it.

Strategy 1: Transforming the client's metaphoric kernel statement

Patients often describe their complaints in metaphoric expressions: "*I'm up against the wall, I'm down in the dumps, I'm falling apart, I'm trapped, People look down on me.*" One way of bringing patient metaphors back to life is by creating an image of the client's words of the metaphoric domain. Therapists may use their own imagery, but helping patients to create images is usually more effective. These images become the starting point of guided metaphoric imagery work, essentially consisting of a series of emotional-perceptual transformations of the original statement.

CASE EXAMPLE 1

Ruth, a 43-year-old woman, sought help for numerous complaints: chest and lumbar pain, general anxiety, emotional instability, and social isolation (Witztum et al., 1988). She felt desperate, as her state was deteriorating rapidly and previous therapies had been of no help. Initially, in the first session she broke down saying, "My problem is that I have no backbone." The therapist directed Ruth to explore this metaphor further. She discovered that in her imagination, her backbone was normally developed up to the middle lumbar vertebrae; from there on it was very weak and completely underdeveloped, unable to support her at all. When asked how she could maintain an upright posture and give the impression of being a strong person, Ruth replied that she was (figuratively) wearing a stiff iron corset for support. Although it hurt terribly, she could not live without it. She readily accepted the therapist's remark that, while the corset provided support, her body might be so constricted and immobilized by it that her backbone had no opportunity to grow and become strong. Ruth then related dramatic events of her childhood. Her mother, a single parent, had become seriously ill and died when she was 11. Ruth and her younger sister were sent to an orphanage, a cruel place that separated the children from one another and provided no emotional support. There Ruth had to make herself artificially strong in order to endure the ordeal and support her sister. Therapy consisted of alternately working in the metaphoric and literal domains. In the metaphoric domain she imagined loosening the corset, taking it off for a while, feeling her backbone gradually become stronger. Then she returned, often spontaneously, to subjects in the literal domain of her grief where she continued to work through her traumatic past.

Strategy 2: Metaphoric reframing

Clients' symptomology can also constitute the "vehicle" part of incomplete metaphoric expressions. The therapist can reconnect the symptomatic domain with the domain of the more basic problem by using metaphoric reframing.

CASE EXAMPLE 2

An example of a metaphoric reframing and its use in linking client's symptoms or conflicts to a problematic relationship arose with Sarah, a woman in her twenties who suffered a severe skin condition and also a problematic relationship with her ill but demanding mother. The therapist used the metaphoric reframing, "She really gets under your skin." The results were striking: The precision of the reframing enabled Sarah to concentrate in the therapy on the loaded relationship with her mother which involved both her acting out aggression towards her mother and a worsening of her symptoms. With the metaphor as a linchpin of therapy, treatment subsequently brought about significant relief of her skin condition.

Strategy 3: The metaphor as a bridge to the patient

This kind of metaphoric reframing technique is a less comprehensive strategy than the previous approaches. In the beginning of treatment, the primary task of the therapist is to establish rapport, conveying to the patient that he or she is understood. For example, one described herself as being on an island, to which the therapist offered to build a bridge to her. Metaphoric stories with different images enable therapists to connect empathically with their clients.

CASE EXAMPLE 3

In this case, a therapist's images of a client led to a series of metaphoric reframes, which became the cornerstone of the therapy (Witztum & Roman, 2000). Einat, a 53-year-old married mother of four, became depressed after her father's sudden death in the hospital where she sent him for a check-up. In her opinion, the doctors to whom she referred him were mistaken in their diagnosis and treatment, resulting in his demise. After his death, she longed for him. Despite her age, she became severely depressed and she felt guilty and angry. Antidepressant medication brought no improvement. During the ninth month after her father's death Einat was diagnosed as suffering from depression and complicated grief. She began therapy by writing a long "unsent letter" to her father on which she made slow progress. Three months into this an impasse occurred, however, related to the anniversary of her father's death, though recognizing this intellectually did not lead to any change and Einat ultimately became suicidal. The therapist related an image he had of the patient: He saw her standing motionless on a narrow bridge connecting two huge mountains, one of them bright and the other dark. Each side has something attractive and seductive and she didn't want to be pushed in one direction or the other. Einat's emotional response to the metaphor was dramatic and powerful. She began to shake and said that she saw an identical picture. From that point onward Einat and her therapist began to speak in the language of the metaphor. She observed, "I feel that I've moved several steps to the bright side but my face remains turned to the dark side." In the next session she referred to the aptness of the image and its enactment, completed her writing to her father, and reported sharply reduced suicidal ideation. Therapy continued until Einat securely crossed the bridge to the bright side (Rubin, Malkinson, & Witztum, 2012).

CONCLUDING THOUGHTS

This model employs a combination of interventions using metaphorical reframing to help clients who suffer from complications of grief. This approach can support meaning making and self-change of the client and/or concentrate on reworking the relationship with the deceased. Metaphors used in therapy may be constructed by clients or therapists, or may co-evolve over treatment, making a contribution to the process and outcome of therapy for the bereaved.

References

Rubin, S.S., Malkinson, R., & Witztum, E. (2012). *Working with the bereaved: Multiple lenses on loss and mourning.* New York: Routledge.

Witztum, E., & Roman, I. (2000). Psychotherapeutic intervention in complicated grief: Metaphor and leave-taking ritual with the bereaved. In R. Malkinson, S. S. Rubin, & E. Witztum (Eds.), *Traumatic and nontraumatic loss and bereavement: Clinical theory and practice* (pp. 143–171). Madison, CT: Psychosocial Press.

Witztum, E., Van der Hart, O., & Friedman, B. (1988). The use of metaphors in psychotherapy. *Journal of Contemporary Psychotherapy, 16,* 270–290.

45

Spiritual Devotionals

Laurie A. Burke and Tina C. Elacqua

CLIENTS FOR WHOM THE TECHNIQUE IS APPROPRIATE

Homicidally bereaved individuals, although modifications of the materials could easily enable its use with other violently-bereaved (e.g., suicide, war crime, or fatal accident) or non-violently bereaved individuals. Spiritually inclined grievers will glean the most from this technique; however, its basis in the Christian sacred text may make it less suitable for those of other faith traditions or grievers who do not espouse faith.

DESCRIPTION

Human beings frequently strive to make sense of loss and subsequent grief through spirituality or religion. For many believers, faith sustains them through what can be one of life's darkest moments—the loss of a loved one. Faith can facilitate an ordering and re-ordering of emotional experiences that initially feel random and cruel, transforming them into something that, at least from God's vantage point, has divine purpose and eternal meaning.

Conversely, although God and the spiritual community might seem closer and more tangible than ever during the mourning period, some survivors struggle severely in existential terms, finding it to be a doubt-filled time of spiritual unrest. When spiritually inclined individuals are unable to accept the death, struggle to make sense of their loss, or lack reassurance for either the immediate future or the hereafter, questions abound, and faith swings on a pendulum between belief and doubt. When experienced within the context of bereavement, Shear and her associates (2006) refer to this as *complicated spiritual grief* (CSG)—a spiritual crisis in mourners' relationship with God such that they struggle with disruption of spiritual/religious activities and experiences, a sense of discord, conflict, and distance from God and at times from members of one's spiritual community. Burke and her colleagues (2011) found that homicidally bereaved individuals who struggled the most with their grief were also the ones who struggled the most in terms of their relationship with God. Specifically, such grievers wondered what they did to receive God's punishment, questioned God's love and power, and felt abandoned by the church. Unfortunately, little exists in the way of specialized interventions available to target bereavement-induced spiritual crisis.

One exception to this neglect is Elacqua and Hetzel's (2010) book of *remembrance devotionals,* originally designed for survivors of homicide loss, but easily adaptable for the treatment of many types of losses. Whether the mourner's faith has been strengthened or challenged as a result of the loss, the purpose of this biblically based collection is to invite the reader to explore the depths of the Christian scriptures, on an intentional quest for increased closeness to God through specific Bible verses, and the personal testimonies and prayers offered by like-minded others who have suffered similarly.

Each weekly devotional consists of two pages, where on one side a photo with a short inspirational message, often featuring scriptural verses, is offered, below which is a weekly calendar with room to write notes, and a scripture that reinforces the main point of the devotional. On the adjacent page is the reflective account of an author who has felt the pang of irreplaceable loss, and yet has managed to find some comfort in his or her faith. Fully God-centered, without exception, all entries point to the "only Hope . . . there is" (Elacqua & Hetzel, 2010, p. 3). As a graphically pleasing manual, this devotional set can be used as an in-session exercise, with the clinician (or the client) reading aloud the current week's entry regarding a relevant aspect of loss (e.g., forgiving the perpetrator, overcoming sleeplessness, rebuilding a new life), with prompts for discussion. Equally, the devotionals lend themselves to homework over the course of a week, especially when utilizing the calendar portion that allows for jotting down important events, specific struggles, or names of supportive others. In both cases, use of the devotionals helps clients become aware of the emotions that arise during the process of meditating on loss and grief and on the comfort that comes through scripture. Practical assignments focus on trauma symptoms and how to deal with them, questioning and doubting, the rippling effects of loss, forgiveness, emotional anguish, and more, which collectively promote spiritual sense making in the wake of horrendous loss.

CASE EXAMPLE

Michael, age 56, recalls all too clearly the day some ten years earlier when he first got the news that his son, Cedric, had been shot and killed. "It was," he recalled, "like a furious storm or tornado appearing out of nowhere." Drawing on one of the devotionals, he wrote,

> *My experience was quite like that of Jesus' disciples when one day, they were in their boat, and "[w]ithout warning, a furious storm came up on the lake, so that the waves swept over the boat" (Matthew 8:24). Jesus was sleeping in the boat. The disciples woke Jesus up saying, "Lord, save us! We're going to drown!" Jesus' reply to the disciples was also His Words to me, "You of little faith . . ." (Matthew 8:26). Indeed, my faith had weakened. Cedric's death was a dark, dreary, stormy time in my life for a very long time.*
>
> *I could not let other people know or see that my faith was deteriorating because I thought I had to be strong and carry this burden for my family. I was wrong in my thinking. I learned that this was not something that I was to carry nor should I try to carry it. God's Word tells us to "Cast your cares on the LORD . . ." (Psalm 55:22). Jesus calls us to come to Him when we are weary and burdened (Matthew 11:28–30).*
>
> *Though the sun was shining outside, it was still so dark in my heart because of the hurt, the trauma, the grief, and the pain of losing a child to homicide. I stayed in the church, trying to see or hear if I would ever see the sun shine in my heart again. I even became involved in Victims to Victory, a Memphis, Tennessee, organization and support group that enables survivors of homicide to find comfort through Christ Jesus. As time passed, I saw the dark clouds slowly moving and drifting away day-by-day.*
>
> *I had read and heard the story of Jesus and His disciples being in the storm, many times. However, it never dawned on me that the disciples had forgotten that Jesus was right there in the storm with them. The same thing happened to me; I forgot that Jesus, through the power of the Holy Spirit, was right there with me in the middle of my storm. Now, I know, and I have been assured by Jesus Christ himself, that no matter what storms come my way,*

He is right there with me. John 14:16 reads, ". . . I will ask the Father, and he will give you another Counselor to be with you forever." Jesus is my life in the storm.

Father God in heaven, I thank You for being there in my storm, even when I forgot You were there. I thank You for moving the dark clouds and allowing the sun to shine in my heart again. Thank You for allowing me to be a father. Thank You for always being there no matter how dark or stormy it gets. Continue to bless and guide me, that I may be a blessing to someone else.

Michael concluded by meditating on the Inspirational Message: "During a storm, if Jesus asked you to get out of this boat and walk (on water) to Him, would you?" as well as the Reflection Questions: "What specific burdens do you need to cast unto the Lord? Do you believe Jesus is in the midst of the storm with you? Tell Him how you feel."

CONCLUDING THOUGHTS

Death can give rise to a myriad of spiritual questions. Grievers who turn to God, their faith community, and/or aspects of their religion to cope often find comfort and strength. Other believers—those who cannot find their way out of the dark pit of grief, who feel God's absence more acutely than His presence, whose questions for God are seemingly left unanswered or are answered insufficiently, who view God as the neglectful parent, powerless or uninterested, who are left feeling alone even while surrounded by a community of fellow believers—experience a crisis of faith. Despite their pre-loss level of religious engagement or faith in God, when tragedy strikes in the form of loss, many religious mourners take comfort in the kind of spiritual assistance found in remembrance devotionals.

References

Burke, L. A., Neimeyer, R. A., McDevitt-Murphy, M. E., Ippolito, M. R., & Roberts, J. M. (2011). In the wake of homicide: Spiritual crisis and bereavement distress in an African American sample. *International Journal of Psychology of Religion*, *21*, 289–307.

Elacqua, T. C., & Hetzel, J. (Eds.). (2010). *Hope beyond homicide: Remembrance devotionals* (2nd ed.). Jackson, TN: Elacqua & Hetzel [available from TinaElacqua@letu.edu].

Shear, M. K., Dennard, S., Crawford, M., Cruz, M., Gorscak, B., & Oliver, L. (2006). Developing a two-session intervention for church-based bereavement support: A pilot project. Paper presented at the meeting of International Society for Traumatic Stress Studies, Hollywood, CA, November.

Part IX
Rewriting Life Narratives

46
Life Review

Mimi Jenko

CLIENTS FOR WHOM THE TECHNIQUE IS APPROPRIATE

People who are grieving their own impending death, or that of a loved one. It is contraindicated for those who have no desire to recall the past, or are emotionally unable to tolerate the process.

DESCRIPTION

Beardsley notes, "at some point in life, there are suddenly more yesterdays than tomorrows" (Beardsley & Vaillant, 2003, p. 171). This is certainly the case for many patients in critical care units, whose life is often "hanging by a thread." In this context, loved ones are asked to make care decisions. Even for the psychologically healthy families, confronting possible death and all of its associated losses is an anguished task.

It is easy for the personhood of the patient to be lost amid the array of life-prolonging technology. Yet, caring for the patient with a life-threatening illness invites an opportunity to extend clinical practice beyond a solely physiological approach. Recognizing the time limitations of critical care staff, many hospitals utilize palliative care consultation teams to guide grief-stricken families by supporting fragile emotions and clarifying goals of care. Conceptually, a palliative approach uses goal setting as an organizing principle. The focus broadens: taking time to incorporate realistic assessments of patient prognosis and treatment preferences of the family system (Fins, 2006). It is within this setting that profound listening work can recapture the patient's personhood.

Referring to a progressive return of the memories of past experience in search of meaning and emotional resolution, life review is a formal concept with roots in lifespan developmental psychology. By recasting the past in the context of the present, one has the chance to re-examine life and solve old problems, to make amends and restore harmony (Garland & Garland, 2001).

Before initiating life review, pain and symptom management issues must be addressed. Always consider the family's cultural, religious, or spiritual beliefs, for life review is grounded in the therapeutic relationship. Use open-ended questions, minimizing the feeling of interrogation and maximizing respect for the narrator. Learn when not to speak, taking care not to interrupt a thought or discourage the narrator from continued review. For those new to the process, prompts can make a useful beginning. Balancing both the positive and negative aspects of life, it can be used with either cognitively intact patients or families of incapacitated patients. Practitioners can use any prompt to begin; there is not one "right" way to initiate a life review. Examples include:

- Tell me about an obstacle you overcame in life and about the skills you used in overcoming it.
- What have been the most important things in your life?
- What is important to you today?
- What would you like to leave your family?

Although there is no definitive end to a life review, a practitioner stops when the family either feels emotionally satisfied or emotionally unable to tolerate the process. Some patients/families have no desire to recall the past; they should never feel compelled to participate. Be attentive to overt verbal responses (such as "I just don't feel like talking now," "Why are you asking me this?" or "That's a personal question!") or subtle nonverbal reactions (such as looking uninterested, distressed or annoyed). Practitioners should guard against pushing for a more intimate or emotionally laden relationship than the family can tolerate or desires (Garland & Garland, 2001).

Within the framework of the therapeutic relationship, documentation is completed with responsibility. Guided by a code of ethics, entries in the medical record must have respect for human dignity, honoring confidentiality. While it is vital for the health care team to be informed on the patient's condition, facilitation of life review often brings forth painful, private and often delicate topics that do not need to be broadcasted in a "tabloid" format. One should keep the therapeutic intent of life review in the forefront, always honoring the practitioner–patient relationship.

CASE EXAMPLE

Health care professionals have a definitive opportunity to foster a "good death" by promoting the completion of final developmental tasks. As part of a palliative care service, I responded to a consult that actually read "PEG and trach?" The patient, an intubated and unresponsive 79-year-old man named Roger, had suffered from years of progressive cognitive decline. Recent aspiration issues resulted in pneumonia and respiratory failure, with a subsequent two-week critical care admission. Treatment was halted at the proverbial fork-in-the-road: transfer to a long-term ventilator facility on artificial life support or allow a natural death. Hovering at the bedside was Sally, Roger's fretful wife of 62 years, a child bride whose husband had "finished raising" her. The couple never had any children, and no other family members were present. After providing for as much privacy as possible, I settled Sally comfortably in a chair by the bedside. I acknowledged her fatigue from the two-week battle, and created a sacred space with quiet and gentle interactions.

"Roger is a very treasured person to you. Can you share with me a bit of his story?" Sally shared many memories and insights, as I asked key questions that guided her chronologically through her husband's life. She recounted his passion for woodworking, and how his worsening memory had become a significant safety issue for the beloved hobby. We honored Roger's careful nature that had sustained the family for so many years, and how that was lost amid the progressive decline of dementia.

After nearly an hour of sharing, Sally suddenly became quiet for a long time. "I really lost him a long time ago, didn't I?" Another long silence preceded my softly spoken response: "Yes, ma'am, you did." Later that day, Sally made the painful, yet peaceful, decision to withdraw artificial life support, and her husband died within 5 hours of a respiratory failure.

CONCLUDING THOUGHTS

Life review with Sally and Roger honored the patient's "psychological and spiritual land-scape that influenced their sense of dignity" (Chochinov 2002), without a single mention of a "trach or PEG." The facilitated session prompted Sally to accept the reality of her husband's terminal condition—an unconscious truth known to her, yet never verbalized. By acknowl-edging a life well lived and grieving the loss, she was able to make health care decisions based on the patient's values of life. Supporting the psychosocial and spiritual dimensions of life review is an evidence-based approach (Chochinov et al., 2011), enriching goal-of-care conversations that often form the backbone of palliative care. Such is the essence of life review.

References

Beardsley, W. R., & Vaillant, G. (2003). Adult development. In A. Tasman, J. Kay, & J. A. Lieberman (Eds.), *Psychiatry* (2nd ed.). Chichester: John Wiley & Sons, Ltd.

Chochinov, H. M. (2002). Dignity-conserving care—a new model for palliative care: helping the patient feel valued. *Journal of the American Medical Association, 287*(17): 2253–2260.

Chochinov, H. M., Kristjanson, L. J., Breitbart, W., McClement, S., Hack, T. F., Hassard, T. et al. (2011). Effect of dignity therapy on distress and end-of-life experience in terminally ill patients: A randomised controlled trial. *The Lancet Oncology, 12*(8): 753–762.

Fins, J. J. (2006). *A palliative ethic of care: Clinical wisdom at life's end.* Boston: Jones & Bartlett.

Garland, J. & Garland, C. (2001). *Life review in health and social care.* Philadelphia, PA: Taylor & Francis.

47

Loss Timelines

Alison J. Dunton

CLIENTS FOR WHOM THE TECHNIQUE IS APPROPRIATE

Children, adolescents, adults, and families may benefit from the development of loss time-lines. Additionally, it is crucial that all grief care providers review their own personal loss histories in search of unresolved grief or "unfinished business" that may enter the therapy room and shift attention away from grieving clients (Jeffreys, 2011). Loss timelines might be less appropriate in the immediate aftermath of a death when an agenda of support rather than exploration is called for.

DESCRIPTION

We all experience loss. Rarely do we pause to consider the many ways in which our personal loss histories contribute to the shaping of our lives. Timelines have long been used to iden-tify or connect points in time to create well-integrated histories. They assist us in under-standing events and trends. The development of a loss timeline is a concrete means of assisting clients in raising insight and obtaining clarity and organization regarding the impact that their losses have had on personal development.

A loss timeline is developed by identifying all the losses one has experienced by noting them on paper in a linear, chronological order. While many prefer the traditional method of creating timelines using paper and pencil, technology allows for greater variety of artistic approaches, using digital and computer software, which often removes barriers related to space and functional limitations. Developing a loss timeline using a roll of register tape rather than a sheet of paper is an example of a unique means that allows for documentation of extensive loss. Dates of significant events are typically used to sequence losses; however, children and adolescents may prefer to identify their ages at the time of each loss rather than noting dates.

It is important when facilitating the development of a loss timeline that losses of all nature are explored, including any significant life changes that the client perceives to have been a loss. Examples include death, separation or divorce, loss of employment, geographic reloca-tion, trauma, and other life-altering events. For children, the moving away of close friends, peer rejection, failing to make tryouts for a sports team or membership in a group, the birth of a new baby in the family system, the deterioration of a grandparent due to Alzheimer's Disease, and family financial difficulties are losses that are experienced by many. At times, the mere threat of a loss may initiate the grieving process and significantly impact one's functioning. Such threats should also be included when constructing a timeline. Furthermore, loss timelines may depict various stages of a single loss, such as a family member's diagnosis followed by physical and cognitive decline and finally death.

Once a loss timeline has been created, it serves as a valuable tool that can be used to facilitate numerous therapeutic discussions, creative therapy expressions (e.g., art therapy activities, letter writing, etc.), and play therapy opportunities (e.g., sand tray depictions, therapeutic games, etc.) related to the client's past experiences of grieving, resilience, the ways in which others around the client responded to each loss, whether the losses were discussed, processed, and provided attention, whether grieving was encouraged or discouraged by others, and any secondary losses that may have occurred as a result of each loss. Loss timelines open the door for examination of attachment styles, family of origin issues, unspoken family rules, cultural and societal expectations, and religious and spiritual beliefs, all important subject areas worthy of exploration in the therapeutic context (Balk, 2007). Ultimately, relationships, patterns, and memories are identified as well as losses in need of further processing.

Timelines convey a sense of change over time. Noting the significant losses one has experienced and processing the effects that each loss has had on personal development brings a sense of concreteness to the past. Loss timelines also bring to light the fact that life continues beyond the present, allowing opportunity for movement and growth in one's future. The highlighting of one's past, present, and future fosters discussion related to the cognitive restructuring within one's self that takes place after a loss. "Who am I now that I have experienced this loss?" Loss timelines are therapeutic tools that allow for immeasurable insight raising, meaning making, and personal growth.

CASE EXAMPLE

Tracy is a 14-year-old girl whose stepfather initiated individual psychotherapy services for her after learning that Tracy had engaged in self-injurious behaviors as she attempted to cope with the stress of a recent break-up with her boyfriend. After gathering additional information from both Tracy and her stepfather and learning that Tracy had experienced several significant losses in the past, I engaged Tracy in the development of a loss timeline (Figure 47.1). Tracy's timeline highlighted the numerous significant losses that she had endured in her 14 years of life, including the abandonment by her father, several shifts in caregivers, the death of her mother, and the death of several extended family members. Tracy's loss history, along with information obtained through clinical observation and interview, shed light on the fact that Tracy was struggling with issues related to attachment and personal identity. She was now being raised by her stepfather, a man who entered her life as a caregiver just one month prior to her mother's death. Having lost both of her biological parents, Tracy was being raised by a man to whom she did not feel emotionally connected, and she lacked a stable sense of self. The loss timeline proved to be an insight-raising experience for Tracy, highlighting the ways in which her losses have shaped her attachment style and her approach to relationships with others. Tracy came to the conclusion that she tended to allow herself to be controlled in relationships for fear that she would lose them if she asserted herself. Having gained such insight, Tracy was now in a position to better assess her current relationships and was available to engage in the therapeutic process of developing a positive and secure sense of self.

CONCLUDING THOUGHTS

The incorporation of loss timelines in work with grieving clients is congruent with evidence supporting the importance of obtaining comprehensive personal loss histories (Jeffreys,

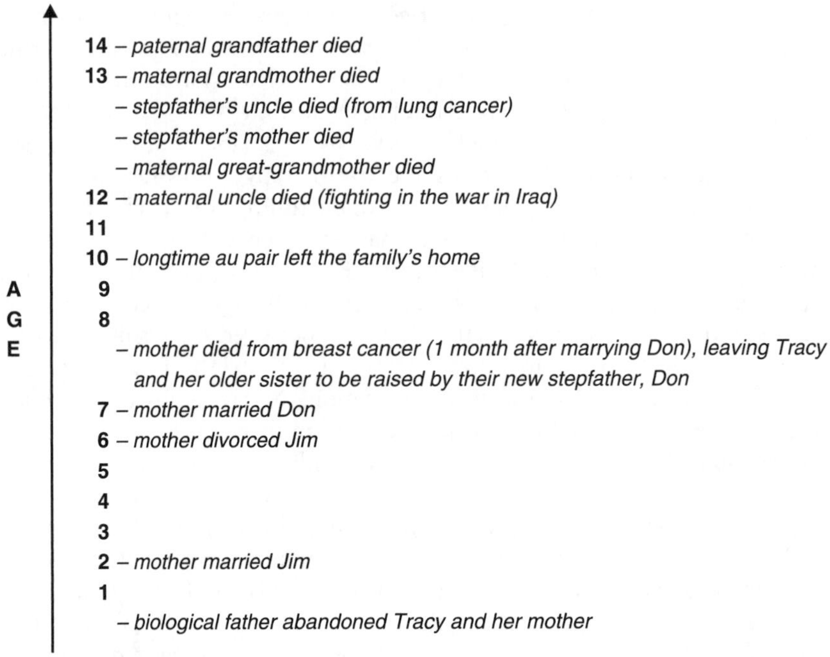

```
          ↑
          14 – paternal grandfather died
          13 – maternal grandmother died
              – stepfather's uncle died (from lung cancer)
              – stepfather's mother died
              – maternal great-grandmother died
          12 – maternal uncle died (fighting in the war in Iraq)
          11
          10 – longtime au pair left the family's home
    A      9
    G      8
    E
              – mother died from breast cancer (1 month after marrying Don), leaving Tracy
                 and her older sister to be raised by their new stepfather, Don
           7 – mother married Don
           6 – mother divorced Jim
           5
           4
           3
           2 – mother married Jim
           1
              – biological father abandoned Tracy and her mother
```

Figure 47.1 Tracy's loss timeline

2011) and is appropriate for clients of all ages. However, one should consider each client's unique needs, strengths, and weaknesses when developing loss timelines and be aware of possible re-traumatization. Young children may require assistance in creating timelines and may need help from family members. The development of loss timelines within the context of family therapy allows for rich discussions and opportunities for systemic growth. Drawings or photographs may be used in place of written descriptions for children who have special needs or for those unable to read. Care should be taken to allow clients to choose their methods and set the pace when developing timelines, as the process may provoke symptoms of anxiety or depression for those who have experienced traumatic loss, complicated grief, or for those who have preexisting mental health conditions. Throughout the process, clients' mood and anxiety levels should be continually monitored, and relaxation strategies introduced and utilized as needed. Individual differences, unique circumstances, and personal strengths allow for infinite variations of loss timeline development. No matter the approach, the review of one's personal loss history provides insight, organization, and clarity into the many ways past losses shape the present self.

References

Balk, D. (Ed.). (2007). *Handbook of thanatology*. New York: Routledge.

Jeffreys, J. S. (2011). *Helping grieving people—When tears are not enough: A handbook for care providers* (2nd ed.). New York: Routledge.

48
Virtual Dream Stories

Robert A. Neimeyer

CLIENTS FOR WHOM THE TECHNIQUE IS APPROPRIATE

Adolescents and adults who are processing an experience of loss or transition, and particularly the bereaved, tend to respond well to the virtual dream method. As an exploratory technique, it may be less appropriate for use in the immediate aftermath of a traumatic loss, when direct support and coping interventions may be indicated.

DESCRIPTION

Many people do not remember their dreams, but virtually everyone is able to write a brief, dreamlike story that imaginatively addresses themes of loss, often with surprisingly therapeutic effects. In keeping with the work of Douglas Smith, my colleague and the originator of the method, my usual practice in bereavement support groups or workshop settings is to request that participants take out a sheet of paper and without forethought or planning, spend between 8 and 10 minutes writing a story that includes, in whatever way they choose, an assigned list of 6 elements, two of which typically refer to the setting of the narrative (e.g., a dark forest, a sudden death), two of which are characters with "voice" or intention (e.g., a weeping woman, a mysterious stranger) and two of which represent potentially symbolic objects or events (e.g., a torn photograph, an ancient chest). Elements can be selected to correspond to a loss experienced by a specific client or group of clients, but should be left sufficiently general to invite many interpretations. For example, each participant in a widows' support group might be invited to write a virtual dream story that contains the following elements: (1) a violent storm; (2) a partner's death; (3) a lonely wanderer; (4) an empty bed; (5) a whispering wind; and (6) a full moon. The resulting story can then be shared with the therapist or with other members of the group, being read aloud by the author or by another person at the author's discretion. Such stories nearly always reflect important themes in how the authors have dealt with loss, even if the literal plot of the story differs greatly from their own. It is commonly an emotional experience writing and especially reading the dream-like stories, during which authors commonly associate to losses they themselves have suffered. The respectful listening of others then provides a sense of affirmation, and insights and steps in healing can be further taken through any of a number of additional optional components, as noted below.

CASE EXAMPLE

In a 10-person grief workshop Emily penned the following virtual dream story in response to the following six prompting elements: (1) a tragic loss; (2) a crying child; (3) an empty house; (4) a talking animal; (5) a mountain; and (6) a sunrise.

Raven Rising

The empty house, abandoned long ago by unknown occupants, looked skeletal and hollow in the last gray of the fading night. A child, innocent and alive and afraid, cried and rocked alone in the corner. Where were her protectors? Her only shelter, a cold and dark frame of forgotten wood and stone—crumbling and rotting around her.

She was lost . . . or had lost something—her way, maybe. She gripped her knees tight in front of her, shielding herself from the ghostly, oppressive, lingering shadows. Would she be swallowed and forgotten, too—like the house that provided her only vestige of protection?

A bird, big and black, landed in the pane-less window. He looked at her and said, "Fly."

She took her hands from her face and rose slowly. The first rays of a new day's sun cut the horizon. For the first time she could see more than three corners from her corner.

The light, golden and new and alive, fell upon the bird and emblazoned his feathers in gold and scarlet—fire and heat and light. The Phoenix said again, "Fly."

The girl climbed through the hollow window—her empty confinement—into the wide-open space of a mountainside . . . big and new—open, yet full.

She raised her pale arms, so accustomed to the dark, glowing gold and scarlet now . . . and flew . . . letting go of a shelter that was not home.

To her own surprise, the act of formulating the virtual dream allowed Emily to tearfully acknowledged the emotional truth of the story, which she grasped only after it was written, but also to affirm a sense of hope and growth in the aftermath of devastating loss. But even when clients conclude the story on a tragic or somber note, the virtual dream helps focus the client, the therapist, and, in the case of group work, other members on the emotional problem or impasse the client is confronting, in a productive way.

CONCLUDING THOUGHTS

Beyond intuitive processing of the virtual dream (asking Emily, for example, "What experiences did the little girl feel cornered by?" or "What qualities were ignited in her by the Phoenix that allowed her to rise above her circumstances?"), there are several specific procedures that can extend the use of this method. For example, clients can be encouraged to write "feeling words" they associate with particular elements and then use these to formulate personal goals. In Emily's case, she might reflect on the Raven/Phoenix figure, and associate with it a sense of "hope for transformation." She could then be asked to formulate a personal goal relevant to that feeling, such as, "I will foster a sense of hope for transformation by reading inspirational stories of people who rise above tragedy to live rich and full lives," and then pursue this goal as part of her therapy homework. Other ways of processing the virtual dream can involve re-writing the story as one of the other dream elements (e.g., the Phoenix, the empty house) might experience it, or interviewing a specific figure, asking the client to answer for it (e.g., asking the house, "Was there a time before you crumbled and fell to ruin? What sort of life did you hold at that time?"), or fostering a dialogue between two figures, with the client alternately taking the part of each in an "empty chair" enactment in therapy or in a series of journal entries as homework, alternating between the two voices.

Research on large numbers of virtual dreams offers an impression of how they are commonly formulated by their authors. For example, Neimeyer, Torres and Smith (2011) found that over half of writers identify themselves as the protagonist of the story, and nearly 60% cast the helping animal (in the case of the elements used above) in a benevolent supportive role, while less than 10% cast it as malevolent or neutral, respectively. Virtual dreams evoke stories covering a wide range of losses, both death-related and non-finite (Harris, 2011), and are more likely to conclude on a note of hope (over 40%) than despair (under 30%). Nearly 60% of stories are progressive, in the sense that the action moves toward preferred outcomes, with less than a quarter and a fifth of accounts representing regressive or ambivalent narratives, respectively. Neimeyer and his colleagues (2011) provide more extensive discussion of virtual dream stories including numerous examples, and further discuss data on their structure and content as well as optional extensions that enhance their therapeutic use. As part of a broad repertory of methods based on the "writing cure" for issues arising from loss (Neimeyer, van Dyke, & Pennebaker, 2009), the virtual dream can make a novel and creative contribution to grief therapy.

References

Harris, D. (Ed.). (2011). *Counting our losses*. New York: Routledge.

Neimeyer, R. A., Torres, C., & Smith, D. C. (2011). The virtual dream: Rewriting stories of loss and grief. *Death Studies, 35*, 646–672.

Neimeyer, R. A., van Dyke, J. G., & Pennebaker, J. W. (2009). Narrative medicine: Writing through bereavement. In H. Chochinov, & W. Breitbart (Eds.), *Handbook of psychiatry in palliative medicine*. New York: Oxford University Press.

49

Find Your Voice
Creating Healing Dialogues

Gail Noppe-Brandon

CLIENTS FOR WHOM THE TECHNIQUE IS APPROPRIATE

People across the lifespan who have lost their sense of self, including those in the wake of losing a significant other. However, this group methodology might be inappropriate for clients who are in the immediate aftermath of a profound loss. These clients might be better served with one-on-one narrative articulation, while being helped to focus on self-care, affirming bonds of support, and caring for others prior to major narrative reconstruction.

DESCRIPTION

As a clinician with a background in theater, twenty years ago I developed 'Find Your Voice' (FYV) (Noppe-Brandon, 2004), a practice that uses playwriting (and often acting as well) in order to help people of all ages articulate and revise their stories. As in more traditional forms of Narrative Therapy (White & Epston, 1990), it allows the clinician to collaborate with client participants in a creative meaning-making exercise that is designed to help them give voice to that which needs to be more fully externalized and understood.

Based on the premise that our identities are reflected in our stories, and the notion that it is almost always difficult to start the process of telling, the FYV practice begins with an evocative photograph. In response to this Rorschach-like stimulus clients are asked to do a two-minute free write about what just happened—or is about to happen—in the chosen picture (my favorite is that of a Gestalt-like empty chair sitting beside a closed door). After sharing this free-write aloud, clients enter a dialogue, or inter-play, about who could enter the scene and what conflict might arise. This interplay is designed to lead them to two characters and one conflict, the basis of a play.

Because we all write through our own experience, and because of the further suggestion to include a conflict—the crux of all drama—it is inevitable that the participants write about some loss or difficulty that is pressing on their minds, or in their hearts. Over the course of guided re-writes—in response to deep questioning—and with the intent to re-story the event into one in which both characters have valid wants as well as a desire to achieve some kind of resolution to their conflict, alternative narratives emerge. A final, polished, five-page play is written, and five times re-written, over the sessions. After the piece is completed, it is then shared (by professional actors, or by fellow group members if they have been studying acting as well) as a presentation for key outsider witnesses. After the reading, these witnesses are asked to mirror those things with which they felt an affinity in the story, providing both mirroring and empathy. The healing power of this intervention is manifold:

- The trigger image gets clients writing from an unconscious, and un-self-conscious, place.
- The imposed limitations of character and length afford a manageable task that offers the benefit of completion of task as well as closure of experience.
- The art and craft of re-vision experientially models the possibility of change.
- The assignment of character names and heightened plot points, lead group partici- pants safely beyond the potentially over-exposing construct of memoir writing and toward some externalization with objectivity.
- The task of balancing the characters, so as not to create a good guy/bad guy scenario, discourages splitting and advances self-and-other-forgiveness.
- The necessity for conflict engenders the ability to fight for, rather than fighting with or simple surrender.
- The need for a resolution, happy or otherwise, helps to enable one. For those who will never be able to actually have a conversation with the character who has left the scene, this is particularly good medicine.
- The ability to see the story come to life at the final reading embodies the possibility of change, thus unfreezing trauma into action.
- The exchange with the invited witnesses offers participants the opportunity to be seen, heard and understood which, particularly for those experiencing grief in a death- phobic society, is both freeing and containing.

CASE EXAMPLE

I began working with Sasha when she was 13 years old. Her parents had divorced when she was a small child, and her mother moved quite a distance geographically from the father; Sasha rarely saw him. She and her sister lived alone with her alcoholic mother who, over time, became involved with a man who eventually moved in, and to whom Sasha developed a strong attach- ment. After several years the relationship between him and her mother began to fail, and he decided to take a job at some distance away. It becomes easy to imagine how the initial traumatic loss got repeated and how, with a self-absorbed and alcoholic mother, neither loss was ever contained, addressed or healed. Though Sasha was extremely gifted, when I met her, she was failing most of her high school subjects. She was also spending a good deal of time alone, and covering up for her mother's drunkenness and her own pain. To the world, they were all doing "just fine." Working within a group of other teenaged clients, Sasha wrote a play in response to the Van Gogh painting, "Starry Night." Her free write gave expression to "the wish" she would have made upon that star: that the male caretaker in her life might decide to stay. The piece, which took place in one scene between a father and daughter, enacted the moment when the girl learns that her "weekend father' is going to be accepting a job on the other coast, rendering their visits a sometime thing, at best.

In this piece, Sasha gave virgin expression not only to her longing, but also to her loss. And, unlike in her real life, the girl in her play got to voice the anger she'd been holding about the abandonment. Sasha felt safe to do this, because all of the other participants were also telling stories that revealed their experiences and vulnerabilities, however disguised. Autobiographical accuracy was never the goal, as the discussions in this task-oriented group dealt only with the arc of the characters at hand, and the development of playwriting (and acting) craft.

CONCLUDING THOUGHTS

As with hundreds of other participants, the most reparative moment for Sasha came not during the presentation of her piece by two teens who had developed a lovely craft—and portrayed the scene tenderly and vividly—but during the discussion with the invited witnesses afterwards. Sasha not only got affirmation for the hurt that "this character" had endured, she heard empathetic feedback from others who had experienced the divorce or loss of their own parents. Such affirmation rendered this first-ever public sharing and airing of what was really her own situation a surprisingly healing one, and one during which she was never forced to reveal that the girl in the story . . . was herself. When she voluntarily chose to do so during the Q & A, she did so at great risk to her internalized system of loyalty and taboos, though her drunken [external] mother had neglected to show up for the event anyway. This voicing was so healing for Sasha that she still vividly recalls the experience . . . some twenty years later. When used as a bereavement tool, the emerging story just as often usefully focuses on the conflictual relationships that the survivor is left to negotiate, as it does on the one with the key figure who has exited the scene. Extensive empirical documentation of this method is amply compiled in the anthology and method books cited below (Noppe-Brandon, 2011), as well as in the documentary film *Listening with Their Eyes* (available through Amazon), 28 minutes of which airs regularly on PBS.

References

Noppe-Brandon, G. (2004). *Find your voice*. Portsmouth, NH: Heinemann Press.
Noppe-Brandon, G. (Ed.). (2011). *One vision, many voices*. Bloomington, IN: iUniverse.
White, M., & Epston, D. (1990). *Narrative means to therapeutic ends*. New York: Norton.

50

Documenting Children's Life Stories

Mieke De Preter and An Hooghe

CLIENTS FOR WHOM THE TECHNIQUE IS APPROPRIATE

Writing is a playful, creative and accessible method for children with recent or old grief. It highlights their connection with important people, animals and things around them. Many small stories can be collected and cherished in a Life Story. This method is low-threshold, with therapeutic effects even for "difficult" children and youth. However, it is labor-intensive, for children and therapists, and should be used only in contexts that permit ample time for listening.

DESCRIPTION

Connecting and reconnecting the bereaved with their natural support network enables the ongoing human adjustment needed for resiliency in the wake of loss. New meanings, stories and support resources can be evoked. Kissane and Hooghe (2011) describe how therapists can facilitate this family connection through the sharing of stories of loss, grief and ways of coping. In this contribution we describe how "small talks" about many contexts and less loaded themes help bereaved children construct "big stories" that capture their experience of loss and connection.

Children enjoy playing and telling stories about the people, animals and things they like. Connection can be found in countless small and big stories. A therapist can focus on experiences in the present, the past or the future; themes corresponding with loss and non-loss events; real people in the support network and unknown or magical figures. Stories are told about the many people in the farewell service, a memorial page on Facebook, text messages from friends, having the same eyes as dad, his picture above your bed, a friend who also has no father, sitting together with mom in silent tears, or about caring people who interact with no words, comforting words or tricky words. Equally stories are shared about Mowgli, Simba and the *Sound of Music*, about a wink or kiss from the teacher, a candy given by a friend, going to a soccer game with grandpa or shopping for clothes with grandma, the cat snuggling up to the child, an invitation for a birthday party, arguing with your brother or stealing your sister's favorite dress. These stories arise naturally in playing and talking with children. They seem small and evident, but so special and unique when they come to the foreground. They are worth documenting and collecting in a booklet: a Life Story, about the child's life so far. Children can be invited to illustrate the story and supplement it with other treasures:

memories of the deceased, pictures, drawings, poems, music, feathers and stickers, finger-prints, or addresses and phone numbers, and other media. Through creating this Life Story together, a richness of stories grows about the person the child is and what he or she has experienced. Connections can be felt again, and resources, competencies and resiliency surface. They also color the world outside the therapy room in a new way.

CASE EXAMPLE

Anna was 6 when her dad died by suicide. Raising three kids proved to be too difficult for her bereaved mother, and as a consequence the care for the children was assigned to different foster families. I (MDP) met Anna two years later, when she was 8. She wanted to talk about the past and the present. Together we created a booklet in which many of the ordinary, the good and the difficult stories of her challenging life found a place. Some excerpts of this evolving story, which I dutifully recorded for her, follow:

> *My mom and dad loved each other. They got married and wanted three children: Thomas, Seth and me. . . . We had a lot of animals: rabbits, chicken, geese, turkeys, birds, fish, a cat and a dog. In the garden there was a hut and a climbing house. We drove with a tractor, we rode through the fields with our bikes, and I played with Elena, Ruth and Bas. I had a golden bed, which my daddy had made for me.*
>
> *One night Daddy gave me a kiss and put me to bed with Mummy. He went outside, took a rope and went to the swing. Daddy is dead. Mummy, Thomas, Seth and I are very sad. We miss Daddy. At night I often think about Daddy. I've put a flower on his grave.*
>
> *The grown-ups had a meeting: Mummy, Grandpa and Grandma, my aunts and uncles, Liza from foster care and the Judge from juvenile court. They talked about the children and made some agreements. There still are discussions, fights and sorrows in our family. A lot of people are worried. That's the way it is when terrible things happen. Complicated things need time. Now I live with my aunt Marie and uncle Leo, Tim and Isabel and our dog Bo. I go to a new school and take part in athletics and drawing classes. Elise is my first new friend. My teacher from my previous school has sent me a card. She said she was glad that I was in her class. I miss my brothers. Every Sunday my mother makes spaghetti for us. Seth is the star in his soccer team and Thomas wants to be a police officer.*
>
> *I miss my friends and they miss me. They send me letters and we chat. I miss my home like it used to be. Then I'm sad, sick or angry. It's good to be in my new family. I try to do my best at school and I make some new friends. I have Mummy, Thomas and Seth and the memories of Daddy. One day I want to marry and have children.*

Anna told, drew and played. I wrote and re-wrote, proposed and weighed. Anna corrected the texts, careful and critical, time after time, part after part. She ended tired, relieved and proud and shared her booklet with her two families. She became comprehensible, to herself and to others, and her sickness and anger diminished.

CONCLUDING THOUGHTS

Children's stories about grief and loss frequently evoke pity and powerlessness in the adults around them. For adults and well as children, Life Stories create a broadened context in which a difficult narrative can be less confining (De Preter, 2009). Writing together with the child can also overcome the powerlessness often felt by the therapist. This technique is a natural way to connect the common, the pleasant and the difficult stories. It preserves the good things and the good people. It counters the loneliness of bereaved children and the inevitable fractures in relations that arise in the aftermath of tragic loss (Breen & O'Connor, 2011. It is also helpful when the loss is dramatic and the search for meaning is difficult. It makes the children and their supportive network feel that big and little things matter, and influence their world. Children love the playfulness of this technique and cherish the booklet that results, as it captures and validates their experience.

References

Breen, L., & O'Connor, M. (2011). Family and social networks after bereavement: Experiences of support, change and isolation. *Journal of Family Therapy, 33*(1), 98–120.

De Preter, M. (2009). Levensverhalen schrijven met kinderen en jongeren. [Writing Life Stories with children and youngsters]. *Systeemtheoretisch Bulletin, 27*(3), 245–271.

Kissane, D., & Hooghe, A. (2011). Family therapy for the bereaved. In R. A. Neimeyer, D. L. Harris, H. Winokuer, & G. Thornton (Eds.), *Grief and bereavement in contemporary society: Bridging research and practice.* New York: Routledge.

51

The Story Mountain

Patsy Way

CLIENTS FOR WHOM THIS TECHNIQUE IS APPROPRIATE

Bereaved children aged 4 to 11 years who are developing strategies in school for planning and writing stories. It would not be suitable for a minority of children who are reluctant to write, though adults can act as scribes.

DESCRIPTION

Family storytelling in the wake of bereavement can be powerful (Way, 2009), but adults sometimes find it difficult to include young children in conversations that support a coherent story that includes people, events and experiences. And yet engaging children in such story-telling can help them define how they view themselves in a changing context, helping make sense of past, present and future. To facilitate this, I enquire about the writing frame used by the child in school. These vary, of course, but children have readily explained them to me. As the framework is more familiar to children than adults, it offers them more possibilities for a sense of expertise, often giving them confidence to take the lead. I have sometimes used the large whiteboard (as described below) as this is closer to the school experience and puts children in the role of "teacher," taking a photograph of the board afterwards as a record for the family. Alternatively we have simply used a large piece of paper.

Ground rules of story construction are established giving final decision-making authority to the children but also clarifying the role of adults. I initiate a discussion around the nature of stories, exploring ideas around who may be a storyteller or writer and what forms stories can take. This may range from the oral narratives of the bards of old to medical and social work reports, emphasizing the importance of an awareness of the intended audience. This in turn may lead to discussions about genres of telling and writing and the nature and value of "truth" in a story. It can lead to talk about rights of authors and editors to choose who may hear or read the story.

As this is a joint conversation, different family members may have different and alterna-tive perspectives to contribute but the children will have final editorial authority. We will shape the plan for a story which can be written up if it is desired. As this telling is located in a particular place and time, it will change and the editors may include or leave out parts of the story in the future if they care to put out a "new edition." This process appears to help children and families in making meaning of what has happened as telling the story involves sequencing and bringing order and shape to what is often a jumble of memories, ideas, and partially understood events. Stories require coherence in narrative, though temporary and subject to change in different times and contexts.

CASE EXAMPLE

I found myself discussing genre with Joe, a very bright 5-year-old. We were not using the term but I was explaining that there are many ways of telling the story of what had happened in his family. Doctors and nurses made notes in what we call a file about how ill their mother was when she had cancer and the notes told the story of how they had tried hard to make her better but, unfortunately were not able to do so. Social workers had written in a file telling the story of the different people the children had lived with in the period of their mother's illness and afterwards. School teachers had written to me about Joe and his sister Abigail in what is called a referral form, to tell me what they had noticed in school and why they thought it might be a good idea for me to meet Joe and Abigail and the grandparents they now lived with. All these were different kinds of stories.

Just as they told, planned and wrote stories in school, we could tell the story of what had happened to them and they could decide what was important to put in or eliminate, as an editor does with books. We had the great advantage of having grandpa and grandma here who might remember useful things, but Joe and Abigail retained editorial rights.

Seven-year-old Abigail announced that she used the "Story Mountain" in school and she drew this on the large whiteboard. The "Story Mountain" writing frame is a bell-shaped curve requiring "a beginning" in the lower left-hand side, a "problem" at the "mountain peak" and a "solution" or "ending" in the lower right-hand corner. She then started musing as to where the story began. Joe said that "the problem" had been the need to move in with other people when their mother became ill and losing contact with school and other friends and family. They described a very unsettled time of not knowing what would happen to their mother or to them or who would care for them. There was a series of moves and changes of school following their mother's death until they went to live with the grandparents, where they were now very settled. Included in this was an account of the death, funeral and cremation. Decisions were taken as to what was most important to this story and where it fitted in the story plan.

They returned to the question of "the beginning" and the grandparents offered descriptions of memories of their mother's joy when they were born. They offered short anecdotes of episodes in their early years. Some memories had been recounted many times before but some were "new memories" (Way, 2010) that we were co-constructing. Some memories triggered others and a new energy came into the room.

The family turned next to the period after the death and this brought up the question of an ending to the story. This felt quite puzzling until Abigail suggested that "now" was the end because we don't know what will happen in future. There followed a debate about the future and whether this could be part of a "true" story if it hadn't happened yet. The consensus was that we could imagine the future and maybe this would even help it to "come true." The grandparents supported this by feeding in hopes for the children's futures that they had heard expressed by their mother and in this sense she too entered the conversation. Abigail wants to be a teacher and have children of her own. Joe wants to be a footballer. The imagined future included fun and interest in their new school and a much more settled time with the grandparents.

CONCLUDING THOUGHTS

Not all children will be keen to use their school experience when talking in another environment. However, I have found most to be very pleased to bring skills from the familiar school setting to a session in which they can take on a role as "expert." This allows for a broadening and thickening of their experience, valuing their knowledge from school and expanding it in a family context, surely an important part of education when learned skills transfer to life experience.

Negotiating relationships of power between children and adults needs constant attention in a family session and I have found this technique helpful in giving the voice to the child.

References

Way, P (2009). Bereavement, children and families. In Y. Gunaratnam, & D. Oliviere (Eds.) *Narrative and stories in healthcare*. Oxford: Oxford University Press.

Way, P. (2010). Co-creating memory: Supporting very young children. In B. Monroe, & F. Kraus (Eds.) *Brief interventions with bereaved children*. Oxford: Oxford University Press.

Part X
Integrating the Arts

52
Intermodal Expressive Arts

Rebekah Near

CLIENTS FOR WHOM THE TECHNIQUE IS APPROPRIATE

Children, adolescents and adults who are experiencing anticipatory grief, or grief itself due to a loss. This intervention will need to be adapted for use with young children or developmentally delayed individuals.

DESCRIPTION

What experiences lie beneath the words we use to describe grief, and how can we access them? One answer is through the intermodal expressive arts. In my career as an expressive arts therapist who specializes in grief work, I have found that bringing the arts to grief counseling has been beneficial for children and adults alike. Intermodal expressive arts therapy invites people to move fluidly among media following their creative instincts (Wood & Near, 2010). Within the media of visual art, music, movement, drama, poetry, and play, clients/artists are brought to an encounter with their grief. Expressive arts therapy directly engages auditory, visual and kinesthetic senses as well as emotions (Knill, Levine, & Levine, 2005; Wood & Near, 2010). Through the *intermodal shift*—moving from one art modality to the next—we can experience and hold both ends of the grief spectrum: pain and joy. The shaping of experiences through the imagination allows the client/artist to receive gifts from the emerging creations. The act of creating crystallizes a client's grief and allows him or her to see it in a new light. The following are useful in creating intermodal expressive arts:

- *Materials*: Large painting paper, painter's tape, tempera paint, large paintbrushes, variety of non-traditional painting utensils (hair brush, feather duster, comb), pen/ pencil, writing paper, variety of musical instruments, paper towels.
- *Set-up*: Have a large piece of painting paper taped fully on all four sides to the studio wall. Allow the client to choose two paint colors to begin. Pour them out into containers before starting the movement warm-up. Next to the paint have paintbrushes along with the utensils, cup of water, paper towels. Also available should be lined writing paper and a pen or pencil. Have a variety of musical instruments close by.

Facilitation of the intermodal shift

- *Movement*: While standing, starting with the feet, have the client begin to awaken each body part. A helpful prompt might be, *"Now let's wake up our ankles by slowly rotating them to the right, and now to the left."* After the body is warmed up, encourage the client to explore a small movement such as wrist rotation. These small movements can help clients center themselves and feel more comfortable in their bodies. Gradually engage the body in a full range of movements. The facilitator should mirror the movement and come up with others as a way of "dialoguing" nonverbally with clients.

- *Intermodal shift*: Have the client choose an already explored movement from the warm-up to perform repetitively. Now invite the client to pick up two large dry paint-brushes and repeat this chosen movement. For example: *"How would this movement shift if we made it really small? What would it look like if we exaggerated it? Can this movement move from top to bottom in your body?"* Once clients have examined multiple progressions of this movement, invite them to bring their dry brushes to the paper and move them on the page. Then have them put one of their chosen paint colors on each brush. With their eyes closed guide them to the paper and ask them to begin the repetitive motion again. Instruct them to repeat the movement over and over. Advise them to open their eyes once they have become relaxed. During this intermodal shift the client goes deeper into decentering—moving from everyday reality into art making.

- *Moving the paint*: Continue to encourage clients to stay connected with their body while they respond to the colors and shapes of the painting. Introduce the other painting utensils. If at any time you see clients getting stuck or rigid within their bodies, encourage them to close their eyes and move as they did in the beginning. Give time for clients to engage in and with the paint. When finished, ask them what they notice about their images. This should be done in a phenomenological way, setting aside all assumptions in understanding of the image. This is not an interpretation of the art by the facilitator or client. Moving the paint can act as a physical release for individuals who are grieving. Both physical and emotional aspects of grief can emerge.

- *Intermodal shift*: As clients witness their image and feel their creation is complete, ask them to do a free write. The facilitator might encourage writing by offering a prompt such as, *"If this image could speak, what would it say?"* For individuals or children who do not feel comfortable with writing, the facilitator can act as a scribe. Have them write for 10 minutes without stopping. In this second intermodal shift clients have the opportunity to formulate an unseen understanding of their current situation.

- *Playing with words*: From their writing ask clients to circle from 5 to 10 words that attract their attention. Have them construct a poem from these words. The poem can be written as an arrangement of the words or a list. Have clients share their poem. The poem clarifies and gives voice to the client's lived experience.

- *Intermodal shift*: From their words ask the client to play with the sounds of the words through voice or instruments. The third intermodal shift provides the opportunity for clients to take their understanding of their experiences to another level.

- *Sounding the image/poetry*: Allow the image and poetry to inspire the client's exploration through music. Prompts may include, *"What does this image sound like? Do the words elicit the sound or does the sound elicit the words?"* In sounding, the client is given yet another opportunity to relate to "what is" through the creation.

- *Harvesting the decentering*: It is crucial to bring clients out of the decentering and thus harvest the arts. This means bridging the connection between what was created and clients' lived reality. It is an exploration of what they noticed for themselves as they created. This is not an analysis or interpretation of the arts. Harvesting is a reflection on the material that has emerged. Clients reflect back on the situation that brought them to counseling (Knill, Levine, & Levine, 2005). The facilitator's role is to guide clients through the arts, witness their lives, and empower them to find restoration in adversity.

CASE EXAMPLE

Alley was an 11-year-old girl dealing with the stark reality that her mother Rene was dying. An expressive arts therapy session with Alley allowed her to explore her fears and hopes relating to her uncertain future. I guided her through the intermodal expressive arts intervention as described above. Alley began to connect with her body through the movement warm-up. She easily found a gesture that resonated within her. As Alley moved she put this motion to paper with paint. After painting one image for a while, Alley found a movement that carried her onto another sheet of paper. Then she began to paint simultaneously on the two paintings. When completed, I prompted Alley to title her images and to do a free write. The first painting she called "Terror." The second painting she called "Freedom." From her free write Alley constructed the following poetic verses.

TERROR
Do not feel abandoned
Do not feel forgotten as this terror seeps in
You are beautiful
You are extraordinary
Explore the meaning of life and this world
Know that You are loved not left out

FREEDOM
Nothing can hold you back
Together wrapped in love
We are the heroes of everyday life
You are the healing hope of freedom
The voice of peace and harmony

In the intermodal shift to music Alley gave sound to each image separately. She played with an array of percussion instruments when sounding "Terror." She explored "Freedom" by playing the piano and wind chimes. Alley expressed that she was feeling stuck in terror and longed to live in freedom. When prompted, Alley was able to transition from the musical score of one to the other by graduating the intensity of the musical tones. Using her created images, music, and props Alley constructed a musical story that took her on a journey from "Terror" to "Freedom." During harvesting the session Alley was able to identify and open up about her fears (Figure 52.1). This

Figure 52.1 Bridging from "Terror" to "Freedom"

allowed her to reflect on what had emerged during the session. Through the arts, Alley learned that she had the power to create a different story line in her life.

CONCLUDING THOUGHTS

To fully engage in expressive arts therapy, facilitators should be trained in the different media and the use of intermodal shifting. The arts allow us to enter our grief, building a bridge between our emotions and intellect. Through the arts, our emotions and thoughts play together to discover the mutual comprehension of one another's nature. Transformation cannot happen, personal or communal, unless we are in contact with "what is." Using the arts to dialogue with grief releases the vitality individuals need to carry on living. The process of art making provides a venue for us to value our grief. The expressive arts allow individuals to access their grief, connecting with their deepest reservoir of pain. The best way out of grief is to go through grief. The expressive arts offer a porthole into grief by engaging in *poiesis*— learning through making. This chapter gives a glimpse into how the intermodal shift, which is found in the expressive arts, can access the client/artist's grief. The arts as well as the facilitator act as a witness to the grief process. The expressive arts are a concrete reminder of where clients have been and where they are going (Wood & Near, 2010).

References

Knill, J., Levine, E. G, & Levine, S. K. (2005). *Principles and practice of expressive arts therapy.* Philadelphia: Jessica Kingsley.

Thompson, B. E., & Berger, J. S. (2011). Grief and expressive arts therapy. In R. A. Neimeyer, D. L. Harris, H. R. Winokuer, & G. F. Thornton (Eds.) *Grief and bereavement in contemporary society: Bridging research and practice.* New York: Routledge.

Wood, D. D., & Near Lancto, R. (2010). Using expressive arts when counseling bereaved children. In C. A. Corr, & D. E. Balk (Eds.) *Children's encounters with death, bereavement, and coping.* New York: Springer.

53
Prescriptive Photomontage

Nancy Gershman

CLIENTS FOR WHOM THE TECHNIQUE IS APPROPRIATE

Grievers who seek but who have not yet found hope or meaning from individual or group therapy and who have opted out of expressive arts therapy and life in general. Prescriptive photomontage may be less impactful for less visually oriented mourners, as well as those in the early weeks of loss.

DESCRIPTION

Grief not only follows the loss of a beloved person. It also poses a fundamental challenge to one's identity, goals, plans and dreams (Neimeyer, 2000). Inside a negative filter, reclaiming hope or envisioning the future dies with the deceased. Fortunately, a new generation of narrative methods has evolved to help individuals get unstuck from loss and regrets. For those who seek but do not find meaning outside of therapy or support groups and who have yet to experience a marked shift in perspective and feeling, narrative and play-based methods can be greatly enhanced by prescriptive art.* Cognitive neuroscience has shown that while trauma is still fresh (or refreshed by memory), Broca's area (the language center of the brain) becomes suppressed. This leaves the amygdala in large part unreachable—a location believed to be critically involved with memory and where our attachment symbols reside.

However, the preferred mode of communication for the emotional brain is the language of sensory images, metaphors and symbols. This is the level at which prescriptive photomontage operates. Capitalizing on advances in technology (namely digital photo manipulation), my methodology involves digitally repurposing the positive fragments of an individual's memory into a *Preferred Story*. All available photographic imagery that can stand in for my client's stories, anecdotes and epiphanies from therapy is utilized so that I can craft a film still of a time and place where my client is no longer stuck. This *Healing Dreamscape*, as I call these fine art photomontages, can then become a starting point for beginning the re-identification process in an individual rudderless from loss.

A typical *Dreamscape* is an iconic scene populated with people, objects and landscapes from the griever's life that hold positive connotations, with imagery extracted from personal

---

* *Prescriptive art* is a term I coined for meaning-laden artwork custom-created by trained artists with and for individuals through empathic listening, brainstorming and consensus-building.

photos, and if no photos exist, researched and fabricated from any means available. Indeed, the very reason these visualizations are called *Dreamscapes* is because dreams have their own set of rules. They give us a freer rein to interpret and make free associations. So by meshing together fantasy, reality, past, present and future, *Dreamscapes* allow us to view emotionally-wrought photos from a different cognitive place as symbols, metaphors, and sensory images, and on a purely artistic plane, as players, props and plots.

The injection of play, humor and irony into both the process and product is also key—helping individuals view their tragedies more universally and thus philosophically. Responding with laughter or even the laughing cry further stimulates their brains to deliver encouraging bursts of dopamine, moving the individual one more baby step towards recovery and resolution.

Shared with family and friends, the *Dreamscape* launches a second round of healing—a process of joint reminiscing—and then a third as the individual's own words are read back to him or her from transcripts made throughout the *Healing Dreamscape* process. The reaction to their own grace and wisdom is commonly, "No! Did I really say that?"

CASE EXAMPLE

Hope (a pseudonym), age 62, is exhibiting complicated grief and suicidal ideation after her youngest son, Ishmael, is murdered. Concerned about Hope's lack of progress in support group after 15 months, her social worker suggests expressive arts therapy. "Using brush and paint, I couldn't deal with it," says Hope. "I was completely numb. I wanted to do nothin', know nothin'. Nothin' to do with nothin'." When Becky suggests the playful process of Dreamscaping, Hope agrees. During the photo review, anger surfaces over the botched murder investigation and Ishmael's murky involvement with his murderers. With legacy in jeopardy, I point out photos that capture Ishmael's upbeat and loving nature and exemplary work ethic. Given Hope's expressions of faith and spirituality, I curate photos that are a fitting metaphor for "being in the light" and that represent her Safe Place (i.e. cruise ship memories). Hope delights at resolving photo challenges (e.g. seeking an Afro for baby Ishmael from Ishmael's own son, Aquil, Figure 53.1), as it feels like a posthumous gift from father to

Figure 53.1 Baby Ishmael
Source: Courtesy of the family.

son. Hybrid memories, like those occurring across two time periods (e.g. Baby Ishmael's footed pajamas, warmed by the adult Ishmael's grill in the snow, or at bathtime, Figure 53.2), allow for memory reconsolidation and mobilize her positive thinking. "When I used to close my eyes I'd see my baby in his casket. The hot dogs take my mind off trying to take revenge and getting even. In the night I get up and go to the computer and put up the little baby part and hey, I can go right to sleep." *Presented with her Dreamscape (Figure 53.3), Hope makes a discovery. Her left arm branches*

Figure 53.2 Ishmael's sons in the bath
Source: Courtesy of the family.

Figure 53.3 Hope's Healing *Dreamscape*
Source: Prescriptive photomontage by Nancy Gershman, copyright 2008.

Escher-like from Ishmael's left arm, a reversal of Finkbeiner's amputation effect, reaffirming the bond between mother, son, and the future. Hope is now Ishmael's "memory-keeper." Her gifting of Ishmael's Dreamscape to others initiates a ritual of healthy reminiscing. Receiving an artist's portrait made for Hope's recovery is perceived as a special honor. In turn, Hope is rewarded with loving memories of her baby boy.

THE METHOD

The *Healing Dreamscape* method—both product and process—has two aims: (1) to shift the griever's perspective of the deceased from absent supporter to supportive presence; and (2) to provide the griever with a tangible object that reinforces this shift. Made in consultation with a grieving client to augment traditional bereavement support, the *process* entails an interview and photo review, culminating in a brainstorming session where the Preferred Story is defined. Up until this point, it has been a co-creation. Now in the final phase, the *product* is executed solely by the prescriptive artist, in studio.

The *Dreamscape* visualizes how the griever might draw strength from a continuing bond with the deceased, without the co-dependency. For example, a choral singer appears on a grand stage with his deceased partner—a choir master—because this was a shared dream. Upon closer inspection, we see the deceased is conducting from *behind* his partner so that his widely spread arms can be read either as an embrace or a musical cue. Or, a new baby is slipped into the arms of her [deceased] great grandfather as he enjoys his favorite treat, a turkey leg, because the family always shared in his adventures (and vice versa). In this respect, the *Dreamscape* gently reminds grievers to do active work on their Preferred Legacy (to see the deceased as a role model), or with their Preferred Future (by consummating a dream or goal shared with the deceased). The more it activates the imagination, the more invested grievers become in their own healing.

Tracing the steps of prescriptive photomontage, a recursive process, you will notice movement back and forth between any two steps:

> *Step 1: Intake phase*: A major premise of prescriptive photomontage is that *the problem is not all there is*. As my client flips through personal photos introducing the loved one and the circumstances of the loss, I probe for nearly forgotten events once associated with great joy. I ask them to elaborate on their sense-impressions (as this rich visual detail later becomes sustenance for the emotional brain). I identify any positive recurrent themes that translate well into visual terms. For example, holistically viewing the "bright" elements in her *Dreamscape*, Hope will finally be able to see herself as an epic character persevering against evil (White & Epston, 1990).
>
> *Step 2: Brainstorming phase*: Determining whether the *Dreamscape* should represent a Preferred Future or Preferred Legacy leads to a set of questions that take on more of a provocative quality. Each is designed to stretch clients creatively as they think about their loss and continuing bond with the deceased:
>
> * *What would [the deceased] say about the current state of affairs (i.e., his/her death)?*
> * *What do you think [the deceased] would want you to do now in terms of changes/goals?*
> * *Where do you think [the deceased] lives now? What do you think it looks like?*
> * *Where might you and your loved one meet again? What props would be there?*
> * *Other than you and [the deceased], who else would be there?*
> * *What is the deceased wearing? What are the others wearing?*
> * *Who gets to keep the Dreamscape? Where do you think it will be displayed?*

Step 2 ends with a final selection of photos, an inventory of missing imagery and a more defined Preferred Story. At this stage clients may change direction as they become aware of implied meanings in the final composition. (Example: Hope's second husband is the true father figure. Later Hope feels obligated to include the biological father as well.)

Step 3: Photo Search phase: Wolfelt (2006) emphasizes "doing" in play therapy, so the goal-oriented activity now is the hunt for missing elements. It is not at all unusual to find a person otherwise limited in his or her social interactions due to grief now finding this activity intriguing and even fun. A hunt might be for preferred body parts—as heads and bodies can be swapped at any time due to the digital medium. (Example: Because Baby Ishmael's precious Afro disappears into the background, Hope locates a similar Afro among Ishmael's own sons.)

Step 4: Creation phase: Back in the studio, I survey the final photos and review the key memories for which there are no photographs. The final assemblage is informed by my intuition and experimentation, with input from my client limited now to feedback about the mock-up. Now with a deep understanding of my client's motivations, goals and the important themes in her life, I will need to stimulate my client to engage in imaginative and interpretive processes of her own. I may embed a piece with visual cues about the deceased known only to the griever; pose the players so that they are literally and/or metaphorically linked together; create a Safe Place enhanced by favorite colors, objects and locations; and/or fuse together past, present and future to demonstrate that souls across time lay witness to our traumatic events so that we never feel alone.

Step 5: Sharing phase: My client now has ownership of the *Dreamscape* (and a transcript of all recorded conversations taking place during the *Healing Dreamscape* process). Sharing is bi-directional, although I disclose my own interpretations or intentions if my client desires it. Tentatively or with great enthusiasm, a client will share the piece with all who loved the deceased. Gradually the sharing tends to open dialogue about the human being who was lost rather than on the loss itself.

Today, Hope's *Dreamscape* has given her the courage to reprocess, recover and reclaim the shattered pieces of her life. The living Ishmael is gone, but through his redemption, Hope has never felt more alive. "We really should not grieve ourself to death; our loved ones will not like that," says Hope. "They are at peace and they want us to be happy with the time that we have here."

CONCLUDING THOUGHTS

To date, there is no formal association or discipline of prescriptive artists. Until a formal discipline is established, as it was for the field of expressive arts therapy, the mental health community will need to rely upon articles, posters, presentations and panel discussions to recognize existing and emerging prescriptive artists. As for identifying whether prescriptive art is even appropriate for a client, this is dependent upon what the prescriptive art method needs to accomplish for the individual rather than what medium is best. The question to ask is: would my client benefit from healing artwork that feasibly: (1) re-contextualizes a distressing event in order to open dialogue?; (2) documents legacy to make meaning out of loss?; and/or (3) reinforces goals and purpose that surface during therapy, spurring them on to positive action?

As for selecting a prescriptive artist who would best fit a client, allow me to make this suggestion. As you familiarize yourself with a prescriptive artist's body of work, try also to get a firsthand opportunity to speak with the artist to assess their range of experience. A precedent has been set in my work to document the *Healing Dreamscape* process from intake period forward, providing real-time conversations in transcript form. Clinicians should be able to get a good sense of the interpersonal sensitivity and interviewing skills of a prescriptive artist from these entities.

References

Neimeyer, R. A. (2000). Searching for the meaning of meaning: Grief therapy and the process of reconstruction. *Death Studies, 24*, 541–558.

White, M., & Epston, D. (1990). *Narrative means to therapeutic ends*. New York: W. W. Norton.

Wolfelt, A. (2006). The grief gardener's tools: Techniques for counseling bereaved children – play therapy. *Living with Loss Magazine, 20*(26–27), 44.

54
Playing with Playlists

Joy S. Berger

CLIENTS FOR WHOM THE TECHNIQUE IS APPROPRIATE

Bereaved persons familiar with today's technologies for using and creating playlists on a computer, iPod, iPhone, iPad, or other device. This technique is not appropriate for persons whose concern with technical or social media aspects of this technology interferes with their need to explore or express their grieving.

DESCRIPTION

Simply put, a playlist is a list of music that has been grouped together for a purpose and is ready to play when the right time arrives. Originally compiled for broadcast on a radio show, a "playlist" functioned as an audio accompaniment to interpret the radio show's storyline with significance to certain sounds, associations, durations, intensities, recurring themes, and emotional reactions. Similarly, today's playlists found on bereaved persons' iPods, cell phones, laptop computers, iPads, and other electronic devices can be designed to "accompany" the person through various daily moments of mourning, while in the car, on the computer, walking, working, traveling, and engaging the daily tasks of living in a stark world of loss. Playing with these playlists can include creating personalized mp3 music (i.e., iTunes, Mixpod), YouTube videos, photo/music slideshows; composing, arranging, or recording one's own music (e.g., Finale, GarageBand software); and sharing one's music with others in person (McFerran et al., 2010) or through appropriate social media (i.e., Ping, Facebook).

Reframing the phrase "grief work," this technique of "playing with playlists" creatively suggests ways for bereaved persons to tell and retell their story both as orators and listeners; to reconstruct its meanings in ever changing life-contexts; to create a social container for expression, interpretation, and shared connection; to continue bonds through music associated with the deceased; and to do so in dual processes orientating to both loss and restoration. Consider the following repertoire of playlist questions to incorporate into one's professional practice, to be sensitively matched with the client's "right times."

Narrative storytelling

What were _____ [your loved one's] favorite pieces of music?
When did you experience these together?

What do you miss about those times?

If you were to create a movie about your loss, what music would you use on its soundtrack?

Which pieces of music, where?

What music best describes your experience of loss?

- In the immediate moment, hum or sing with the person phrases from what s/he identifies.
- Invite the client to play the music from an iPhone, iPod, or iPad. Have portable speakers available, so that the person can hold the phone in hand (for a sense of ownership) while sharing his or her personal music with the clinician or grief group.
- Invite the person to find several pieces of music that tell different facets of his or her story, and to create personal playlists for easy access, updating, listening, and reflecting.
- Encourage the client to order the songs in a sequence that holds personal meaning, i.e., chronological time; from love to despair to hope, from attachment to loss to continuing the bond; a connection with a past loss; or something else of personal meaning.
- For clients comfortable with graphics, encourage them to make a photo/music slideshow that tells the story. (Adhere to copyright laws where applicable.) Add video. Doing this can provide an active "instrumental" outlet for expressing more "intuitive" grief.
- Suggest this as an intergenerational activity between older storytellers and younger family or friends with technological skill and relational empathy. Establish guidelines to ensure accurate grasping and conveying of the older person's story, music, and meanings.

Reconstructing meanings

What does hearing your music from the past mean to you today, now?

What lyrics no longer fit for you?

What word(s) or sounds would you change?

- The same music from earlier bonds may confront a painful realization of absence. It may no longer fit, especially music of a naïve love or of a shaming, judgmental faith system.
- Use similar steps as in "Storytelling," this time focusing on changed meanings.
- Explore different musical settings of the same songs. "Which fits you better? Why?"

Social connection

What would you want someone else to grasp about _____'s life?

Who do you trust with your story, your music?

- Sharing one's personal stories through social media can be either beneficial or harmful (Dominick et al., 2009). Guide appropriately. Honor copyright laws where applicable.
- Post a "Like/Dislike" to a musical piece and describe how it connects to one's loss.

Continuing the bond

If you could sing a song or play music for _____ right now, what would it be?

If s/he could, what would _____ sing to or play for you right now?

- Choose music that was shared with the deceased (like a lullaby between parent/child or a love song between spouses), or may be brand new to the bereaved.

- Consider that songs sung to a lost love abound in virtually all popular genres of music, especially the blues, country, and folk styles. Simple keyword searches on lyric-based websites can open floodgates of compositions. Individual songs (versus entire albums) can be easily previewed, purchased, downloaded, and readied for personal use.
- Encourage clients to create times and spaces for musical exploration between now and the next session, and to journal their thoughts about the experiences.

Dual processes

When do you feel a need to be with the pains of your loss?
When do you feel a readiness to move forward with hope?

- Encourage the client to put together a playlist that provides a safe container to simply be in mourning, to be with the loss. Each piece of music provides a safe start, middle, and anticipated end. The listener can start and stop and replay the music again and again. Note: it's not about the music, but rather about the person's experience of grief.
- Similarly, create a playlist for facing the future, recreating life, and transforming oneself.
- Before significant anniversaries or other trigger events, prepare a playlist with music associated with the event. Go ahead and experience, practice, and play-through responses to the event ahead of time with empowered preparation, versus anxious anticipation.
- For the more musically and technologically advanced, create a "mash-up" in which two songs overlap and blend into one another for a transformative new rendition.

CASE EXAMPLE

Sue lived long-distance from her parents, and the time arrived to move her Dad into a Memory Care Center, and her Mom into Assisted Living. In cleaning out their home, Sue saved her parents' favorite CDs and photos. She imported their favorite songs from numerous CDs onto her computer, created playlists and burned CD compilations for both Dad and Mom. She took a simple CD player to her Dad's room, with green and red stickers marked "Play" and "Stop." She'd burned four CDs for Dad, and coached staff caregivers on ways to use them with him: When waking him up (music increasing in movement), in the evening (decreasing into calm), a cassette recording of her Mom singing years earlier (transferred to mp3), and her Dad's rich hymns of faith. Sue recorded in her own voice, "Wherever you are Dad, I'm right there with you. And wherever I am, I know you're here with me, too."

Months passed. As her Dad was dying, Sue played those CDs on her long car drive to be with them. For the wake, she created a photo/music slideshow. Weeks later, she added track settings to a CD recording of his funeral, and sent it to many long-distance family and friends. For months, Sue's Mom found great comfort going to sleep with the CD playing, hearing and memorizing voices of family and friends with their loving stories of her beloved husband and their life together. New playlists were created about Mom for her 85th birthday, incorporating 78 speed LPs of her college choir in the late 1940s (while she was an independent single woman), which Sue transferred to mp3s. Two years later, when Sue's nephew (Dad's namesake) graduated from high school and was headed to college, Sue gave her nephew an iTunes gift card to create his own personalized playlist about home, and another playlist for his future dreams. This was accompanied with a last, proud photo taken of Granddad (Sue's Dad) and namesake Grandson, together. Life-long legacies and new life-dreams play on.

CONCLUDING THOUGHTS

These examples can transform today's common playlists into meaningful interventions. More technological innovations are sure to provide new techniques and to become new norms during the shelf-life of this book.

References

Dominick, S. A., Irvine, A. B., Beauchamp, N., Seeley, J. R., Nolen-Hoeksema, S., Doka, K. J., & Bonnano, G. A. (2009). An Internet tool to normalize grief. *Omega*, 60(1), 71–87.

McFerran, K., Roberts, M., & O'Grady, L. (2010). Music therapy with bereaved teenagers: A mixed methods perspective. *Death Studies*, 34(6), 541–565.

Thompson, B. E., & Berger, J. S. (2011). Grief and expressive arts therapy. In R. A. Neimeyer, D. L. Harris, H. R. Winokuer, & G. Thornton (Eds.), *Grief and bereavement in contemporary society: Bridging research and practice* (pp. 303–313). New York: Routledge.

55

Figurative Sand Tray Therapy

Heidi Bardot

CLIENTS FOR WHOM THE TECHNIQUE IS APPROPRIATE

This technique is applicable for all ages and can be used to process an impending loss, after the death to deal with the grief, and as self-care for the therapist. As this technique can be quite powerful in accessing the unconscious, it should not be utilized casually or as a brief intervention.

DESCRIPTION

Sand tray therapy utilizes a flat tray with sand and a variety of figures to allow a client to create their own personal story in the tray. Clients express themselves symbolically through their arrangement of figures in the sand tray to reflect their inner worlds. This nonverbal process is extremely personal, can usually bypass the client's defenses and directly access the unconscious and can do so in a safe and nonthreatening manner. Through the creation by the client and exploration with the therapist, growth, awareness, and healing can take place.

Materials needed include a sand tray (traditionally 19.5″ x 28.5″ x 3″, painted blue on the bottom), fine white sand, and various figures and symbolic objects, described below. Though these are the formal requirements for sand tray therapy, I work with clients in a variety of locations and therefore have a travel tray and figurine set (as seen in case example) that is a blue plastic container (14″ x 11″ x 6″) with a lid and a drop cloth large enough to place under the tray and figures (this will aid in clean up as well).

Categories of figures

These are the "ideal" categories and may take a while to collect and may change over time as you work with clients. Keep in mind that you need to have enough variety for your client to have options that fit their own story; however, a smaller sampling is possible for a travel set.

- *Human figures*—families (multicultural, elderly, adult, adolescent, children, babies); fantasy figures (witches, kings/queens, fairytale); action figures; fighting figures; gods; occupations; stereotypically good and evil characters
- *Creatures*—large, small, domestic, wild, prehistoric, fantasy; animals, birds; insects; reptiles; sea creatures, monsters

- *Plant life*—trees, flowers, full or bare
- *Nature*—rocks, shells, fossils, pine cones, feathers, found objects
- *Environments*—mountain, cave, volcano, fire, sun, moon, stars
- *Barriers*—road, fence, signs, bridge
- *Buildings*—castle, houses (different cultures)
- *Transportation*—variety of types of sizes, rescue vehicles
- *Grief and loss items*—tombstones, spiritual items, coffin, skeleton, ghosts, angels
- *Miscellaneous*—furniture, computer, phone, food/drinks.

To introduce sand tray therapy with a client, allow your clients to play with the sand and get used to the feel. Show them the blue of the bottom (this can be used to depict water or sky). While they are moving the sand around, put out the figurines in groupings. Let them know the only "rule" of sand tray—that the sand must stay in the tray. Then invite them to explore the figures and "using as few or as many figures as you want, create a story in the sand." The idea is that they will be drawn to symbols or metaphors for their inner, unconscious world and so create a tangible image of that world to be explored and discovered by themselves and the therapist. During this time, the therapist should note the process of the creation (i.e., items chosen first, items moved around, etc.).

When they have completed their story, wait for them to begin talking or simply ask them to "*tell me about your story.*" During this process you can ask questions about various areas of the tray ("*Can you say more about this area?*") or make comments about their process ("*I noticed that you placed this figure in the tray, but then removed it. Can you tell me more about that?*"); however, the therapist should *never* touch or move items in the tray and when pointing to a certain area, remain above the tray, never allow your hand to break into the world of your client—remember this is a sacred space.

During the discussion, the client may want to move items in order to resolve an issue (i.e., moving a scary figure away from a vulnerable figure). Just make sure that photographs are taken before each move (permission to photograph is usually asked for in advance) so that you and the client have a visual record of each part of the story.

This technique, particularly in the grieving process, allows clients to explore conflict regarding the burial or cremation (i.e., what happens to the body), issues of spirituality, magical thinking, changing the past, and exploring the future. I have seen grieving children repeatedly return to the tray to bury and rebury a loved one who has died, as if they need to repeat the scenario in order to process, integrate and accept the loss. This technique also allows magical control over the world they have created, when death has made them feel so out of control. The client can create the death as they would have wished it or, quite frequently, imagine the world where the deceased has gone. This process allows them a measure of healing as well as an opportunity to explore feelings.

CASE EXAMPLE

Kevin, a 9-year-old boy diagnosed with terminal cancer, and Christy, his 7-year-old sister, were referred to me for art therapy to help them deal with his impending death. I frequently used sand tray as often he was unable to express in other modalities the physical and emotional pain he was experiencing. The sand tray allowed him to quickly create an image for us to explore before he was too tired. Figure 55.1 was one of his first sand tray images, and he chose a little red monkey figurine to represent his more playful former self. He almost completely buried the monkey and surrounded himself with red glass stones which he described as the pain that overwhelms him at times. Around all of this he wrapped a white fence that kept him trapped in this pain. However, a bit of hope remained as he left an opening in the fence.

Figure 55.1 Trapped in Pain

Source: Photo by Heidi Bardot.

I continued to work with him and as he declined he requested working with the sand tray more, often choosing figures and instructing me where and how to place them in the tray. Figure 55.2 was one of his final stories before his death. He chose the little monkey again to represent himself and placed himself on a chair in the water with a brick wall behind him. He was backed into a corner and surrounding him was his pain. Coming at him from all directions are a variety of dangerous figures—a shark, an octopus, a spider, a bat, a dinosaur, a raven, and a man with hands reaching out and a snarl on his face. Amongst these are four tombstones.

When he finished, he sat and stared at the image for a long time and then said, "I am going to die soon." He talked about how these "evil" creatures that represented cancer were all coming for him. He knew the treatment wasn't working anymore, but his pain was becoming manageable due to medication and after making this image he stated that he wasn't as scared anymore. Once he died, he said, the cancer would die as well. The sand tray allowed him to express his greatest fears, face them, and realize that he was still stronger than all of them. He was able to recognize that though he would die, he would ultimately beat cancer.

A week later he died and I met with his younger sister, Christy. She created Figure 55.3 in response to her brother's death. She divided the tray into two sides. On one side was her, her parents and their dog circled around her brother's gravesite. On the other side was her brother, the little monkey, in heaven with their grandparents and dog who had died previously. She added that they met him when he arrived and she filled heaven with "beautiful things that will make him happy" (i.e., doves, angels, snowflakes, blue glass stones, a lit candle). The tray gave her a safe space to process her grief and to imagine a different world, one where her brother was

Figure 55.2 Death Approaching
Source: Photo by Heidi Bardot.

Figure 55.3 Heaven and Earth
Source: Photo by Heidi Bardot.

safe, happy, and no longer in pain. Through the tray she was able to recognize that he was gone, but also to magically create a connection between his world and hers.

Both of these children were able to process the loss at a deeper level than just verbal therapy might allow, as they could work through the metaphor and confront in a nonthreatening manner the fear and loss in their current life.

CONCLUDING THOUGHTS

Created by Dora Kalff and based on Jungian and humanistic ideas of symbolism, metaphor, and the present moment, sand tray therapy provides a unique and safe environment to allow a client to recreate and tell their story (Gil, 2006). However, Homeyer and Sweeney (1998) noted that sand tray "should be used purposefully and intentionally" (p. 53). As is seen in the case example, it can be a powerful and effective process.

References

Bardot, H. (2008). Expressing the inexpressible: The resilient healing of client and art therapist. *Art Therapy*, 25(4), 183–186.

Gil, E. (2006). *Helping abused and traumatized children: Integrating directive and nondirective approaches.* New York: Guilford.

Homeyer, L. E., & Sweeney, D. S. (2011). *Sandtray therapy: A practical manual* (2nd ed.). New York: Routledge.

56
What's in a Name?

Jane Moss

CLIENTS FOR WHOM THE TECHNIQUE IS APPROPRIATE

Adolescents and adults at any stage of grief work, for the expression and containment of current thoughts and feelings. The technique may be used with individuals and in the context of group work. Those experiencing blocked or stuck grieving may find the technique challenging to begin with (faced with the blank page), but the structure it offers can provide a creative and liberating alternative to verbal expression.

DESCRIPTION

There is so much to be said in answer to the questions "How am I?" and "Who am I now?" after a loss; yet the confusion that sets in before acceptance of or adjustment to a bereavement can render the most articulate client speechless. When a life narrative is interrupted by bereavement, chaos may ensue (Walter, 1996). Answers to these questions may not be as clear to the speaker as they once were. The process of meaning reconstruction (Neimeyer, 2001) takes time. When asked *"Tell me (or us) about yourself,"* in group work or in one-to-one bereavement support, the answer can seem both enormous and ungraspable.

This accessible technique uses the literary form of the *acrostic*: a short poem or prose piece which is thematically structured around a name, word or phrase, the letters of which are arranged down the left-hand column of the page. I offer three applications:

1. *As an ice breaker in group work,* to enable people to introduce themselves to others who may be at different stages of their grief work and with different loss experiences.
2. *To enable individuals to check in with themselves* and answer the question "How am I today?" or "Who am I?" within a framework of containment.
3. *As a creative prelude* to further written or verbal exploration of the material expressed in the acrostic, either individually or as part of facilitated support in the group. In other words, what arises from the acrostic may surprise or provide unexpected insight. This can give rise to further self-exploration verbally or on the page.

The beauty of the acrostic for people writing about themselves in bereavement is that it provides a place to start. The fear of the blank page and the invitation to write are eased by the safety of containment (Bolton et al., 2004, p. 110). The writer knows how to begin each line and knows when the piece has finished.

The name-based acrostic offers a sense of control over chaotic thoughts. The panic of 'How do I even begin to describe myself?' is tempered by knowing the first letter of the first line. The exercise becomes like a puzzle in which the writer makes the letters and words fit the pattern on the page. In group work, the acrostic removes the awkwardness of hesitant introductions around the table. The invitation to introduce oneself acrostically immediately enables people to focus on the creative act.

I invite participants to write the letters of their names down the left-hand side of a clean page. I invite them to use their first name, surname, a nickname, or their preferred style of address. If encouragement is needed, I offer my own:

Jane is
About to invite you to try a
New writing
Exercise.

The simplicity provides reassurance to the most hesitant. I suggest three minutes and offer a one-minute reminder before calling time. Rather than adding pressure, the tight timing engenders spontaneity in the writing and a sense of safety (Thompson, 2010, p. 45), in which permission is granted to stop writing when time is up. I encourage participants to use the first thoughts that enter their heads rather than to over-think their response.

When time has been called and pens have been set down, I invite people to share what they have written. It is a common ground rule in group work that people can choose to keep their writing private. I would always reiterate this, but in my experience in this exercise everyone is willing to share as part of group bonding. This is to be encouraged. In the context of individual bereavement support or as a technique for journal writing, people may be similarly invited to share what is written and to reflect, with the therapist, on the insights gained.

Participants usually find this an enjoyable, engaging exercise. It offers scope to be playful and funny as well as serious and truthful. People experiencing chaotic thoughts and feelings, or who are feeling stressed and blocked, may find it helps them to settle and pinpoint feelings of significance. As a technique it offers the twin benefits of flexibility and structure; an example of the use of a simple form that can both hold and liberate expression.

CASE EXAMPLE

Linda, a participant in a writing group (Moss, 2010), used the acrostic to introduce herself to the rest of the group. She had earlier expressed her feelings of tiredness and stress and had spoken about the loss of her husband as well as her mother, whom she had nursed while working full-time. She spoke about her mother's illness and explained that she felt regret at having been unable to do more for her, amidst her other commitments. Linda was someone who enjoyed the social aspects of meeting as a bereavement writing group. She often hesitated before writing and preferred to talk more than write; nonetheless the writing she produced was often deeply insightful and strongly felt. Her acrostic, based upon her first name, exemplifies this.

Love
Is
Never
Dying
Alone

With some tears, she read her acrostic and reflected that it enabled her to recognize that she had done all she could for her mother. She had offered her the greatest gift she could, by being with her when she died. Others in the group affirmed this with her and she commented that she felt a sense of relief in having realized that she had not let her mother down at the end.

CONCLUDING THOUGHTS

The containment offered by this form of expression has the power to enable people to gain insights into their current mood and situation, and to explore experiences and emotions. The response is always personal and, I would suggest, should not be overly guided by a facilitator. In a case example such as the one quoted, the technique provided a means to balance feelings of guilt (at not having done enough), with the recognition that the most important thing that could be done was achieved (support for the mother in her dying moments). Everyone will respond differently, but the value of the technique lies in its ability to contain what needs to be expressed or explained, in a focused and manageable way.

References

Bolton, G., Howlett, S., Lago, C., & Wright, J. K. (Eds.). (2004). *Writing cures.* London: Routledge.
Moss, J. (2010). Sunflowers on the road to NASA. *Bereavement Care*, Summer, p. 24.
Neimeyer, R. A. (2001). *Meaning reconstruction and the experience of loss.* Washington, DC: American Psychological Association.
Thompson, K. (2010). *Therapeutic journal writing.* London: Jessica Kingsley.
Walter, T. (1996). A new model of grief: Bereavement and biography. *Mortality*, 1(1), 7–25.

57

Secrets of the Heart

Maria M. Entenman

CLIENTS FOR WHOM THE TECHNIQUE IS APPROPRIATE

Adults involved in a bereavement support group. These two techniques are especially meaningful to those involved in a widow/widower group. Those who have limitations due to poor eyesight or manual dexterity may find these techniques to be difficult. These activities are also appropriate for ages approximately 8 to adult.

DESCRIPTION

When someone we love dies, it seems that our interaction with him or her dies as well. Because of the physical void their death has left in our lives, there is nothing tangible to prompt observable forms of communication. And so, we lose a valuable connection, one established over years of shared emotions, memories, events—life. We no longer think of writing notes to them or sending them cards on significant holidays or family dates. That sense of those Hallmark™ moments is gone.

When facilitating support groups, I have found it beneficial to draw on my previous work in teaching elementary school children. To have someone acknowledge and internalize information, using as many sensory modalities as possible to process information gives the best results for success. Young or old, when a person's hands are actively engaged with something focused on a topic, I've found they are much more willing to share their thoughts, feelings, emotions, and concerns. Bringing craft ideas into a support group environment often elicits a number of reactions, from almost childlike excitement to guarded reservations about production of a respectable result. Yet, it is rare that I have found anyone who was totally resistant to trying, although each person is given the option to watch while others "play" (Webb, 2007).

The holidays are an especially challenging time to be working through grief. Others celebrating around you—laughing happily, talking lovingly—are some of the most difficult moments a grieving person can endure. It's during these times that the griever feels most disconnected from their loved one. No card is sent; no loving words are written. Decorating seems irrelevant and unnecessary when the one who has died is not physically there to enjoy the festive view. Finding a way to bring the deceased into the holiday celebration or observation is essential to maintaining a connection to their impact on our own life, even if it's in a secret way known only to the griever.

Valentine's Day—the holiday of love. When a precious loved one has died, where do you send the card? Writing our thoughts, our feelings of love, can be a soul-deep bond that cries out for validation. One activity I've found useful is the constructing of a "secret pocket heart." Although the exactness in folding is particularly important when doing origami, once people grasp the basic folds, they then move as slow or as fast as they can to complete the construction of the heart itself. It is important that the therapist or facilitator knows and understands the intricacies of origami folding in order to help the clients and keep frustration to a minimum. Practicing this heart construction ahead of time is recommended, as is the use of the special origami paper. Once the heart is completed, each participant is given a small piece of paper on which to write his or her loved one a love note. When this is written, they tuck it inside the secret pocket in the heart so only they know it is there. They are also given the written/drawn instructions to take with them should they decide to make more, or have others make them to commemorate the life and love of the deceased.

Another idea for secret thoughts can be used during the winter holiday season in the form of a "Remembrance Ball." Materials needed are: clear glass ball ornaments, polyester filling, paint pens in various colors, thin ribbon, small strips of white paper, pens/pencils. After taking off the top loop assembly, decorate the outside with paint pens. Participants may draw, write words that remind them of their loved one, the holiday and year (e.g. *Christmas 2012*)—however they want to decorate it. Then, taking a thin pencil or pen (or anything that will fit through the opening in the top of the ball), stuff it about half full with polyester filling. Take a small piece of paper, write the loved one a short note, and roll up tightly. Insert it into the middle of the ball in the filling, then finish stuffing ball with filling—around and over the note—so that the ball is completely filled and the note is invisible to the eye. Replace the top loop assembly. Attach a length of ribbon for hanging.

CASE EXAMPLE

Needing to feel a connection to their spouses on the "holiday of love," the group began with a short imagery exercise in which they pictured their loved ones with them. They were given the suggestion that they tell them how they were feeling with Valentine's Day coming, yet having no place to send their card, and to "speak from their heart." Next, origami paper was handed out and a sample of the heart they were going to make was shown. With verbal and visual instruction (Smolinski, 1999), they slowly folded and constructed their hearts. When they had finished this, each was handed a small piece of paper, asked to recall their recent imagery of the spouse, and write a short note to him or her. They folded the paper and placed it inside the secret pocket created in the heart. With little prompting, they shared their thoughts in being able to write a Valentine's note to their spouse, and all ended with placing their hearts in their wallets or handbags, some to carry them with them, some to place them in a special place in their homes. All said they felt more connected because of their perception of a Valentine validating a deep and abiding love in their life.

CONCLUDING THOUGHTS

The activities explained previously have the potential to be extended in various ways. For the glass ball activity, participants are given suggestions on how to expand on this basic activity. Possible extensions include:

1. Setting up a small "Memorial Tree" where each member of the family and any other special/significant people are encouraged to make a remembrance ball of their own and hang it on the tree.

2. Make another new ball each year, with date, to include in holiday remembrances either during winter holiday season only, or at each celebrated holiday throughout the year.

3. Depending on the size of the origami paper used, the secret pocket heart may be tucked into a wallet and carried daily, tucked away somewhere special in the home, or burned while playing a special song, saying a special prayer or observing moments of silence as it burns, the smoke rising as a silent offering.

References

Smolinski, J. (1999). *Holiday origami* (1st ed.). New York: McGraw-Hill.

Webb, N. B. (Ed.). (2007). *Play therapy with children in crisis: Individual, group, and family treatment* (3rd ed.). New York: Guilford.

58

The Art Studio Process

Sharon Strouse and Jill Harrington LaMorie

CLIENTS FOR WHOM THE TECHNIQUE IS APPROPRIATE

Art therapy is helpful to those who have trouble putting feelings into words. It is especially effective with those suffering the ravages of severe trauma, such as suicide loss survivors. However, it may be premature in the early weeks of tragic bereavement, when clients are often focused on absorbing the reality of the loss and managing practical and emotional tasks that attend it.

DESCRIPTION

A traumatic event often sends one into a state of shock, whereas the process of creating helps people integrate their experience and understand themselves. Suicide loss, in particular, may be accompanied by feelings of guilt, shame, stigma, rejection, anger, relief—all contributing to a survivor's increased vulnerability to complicated grief and distress (Jordan & McIntosh, 2010). Thus survivors of suicide and other traumatic losses may benefit greatly from The Art Studio, which provides a safe, judgment-free place of healing and the universality of a community of similar others who can help provide support.

The art studio is an alchemical vessel that nurtures a community of facilitator/artists and client/artists through a process, grounded in the intention to increase self-awareness and foster compassion for personal growth and transformation (McNiff, 2004). Our studio is spacious, safe, inviting, and filled with a variety of art materials that include paint, brushes, oil pastels, markers, watercolors, tissue and construction paper, magazines, fabrics and found objects. Its philosophy is rooted in the works of Shaun McNiff and Pat B. Allen, who pioneered the studio concept within the field of art therapy.

In our art studio, the facilitators function as fellow artists. We are the keepers of the space and serve as guides by example. We are fully engaged in our own creative process and do not interfere in the creative process of our client/artists. We create side by side. We model risk-taking and problem-solving and demonstrate our trust in the healing qualities of art making. We are non-judgmental, have no personal agendas, and no attachments to the product. We are grounded in our bodies, present to the moment and willing to journey with our client/artists. We serve as mirrors and silent witnesses. We surrender to both joy and sorrow. We listen to our intuitive voice and hold the space for others to listen too.

The three essential components of our creative practice are: (1) Consciousness/Intention/ Experience; (2) Art Making; and (3) Witnessing/Sharing.

1. *Consciousness/intention/experience*: Each session begins with an opening meditation. Awareness is directed into our bodies as we focus on our breath and relax. In this altered state of consciousness we let go into what we are thinking and feeling and align with our deepest purpose and ultimately with self. Intentions and experiences arise out of quiet mind as we open to the moment fully. We embrace what is and in so doing assume responsibility for the creative process which allows formlessness to come into form. This opening guides us and serves as a foundation. We do not require client/ artists to write their intentions or experiences down; however, most do and refer to them during the art making, sharing and witnessing. Intentions are often single words such as "perspective," or "forgiveness," or short statements such as, "I release, I manifest." Experiences are varied and arise out of the *temenos* or sacred space that has been invoked by the group. Its vitality is informed by the presence of the people who populate it and with the images that emerge from our consciousness.

2. *Art making*: This time is devoted to the personal spontaneous making of art by each facilitator/artist and client/artist. One's process cannot be predicted; it flows from the heart. One simply arrives open and willing, allowing the soul to find its purpose. We create as singular human beings at the same time we create together, around several tables, in an intimate communal environment where the creative energy is healing in and of itself.

3. *Witnessing/sharing*: The witnessing process begins with a few moments of silence as the community gathers with their artwork. It is a time for contemplation. We quiet our minds and open our hearts. We are aware, conscious and present. During this time we sit with our images quietly and/or write using a variety of journaling practices which include a title and date, a description of the piece, writing about process, feelings, and dialoguing with images. Writing should be free-flowing and uncensored. Participants then share what they are comfortable with and listen to what the community offers in terms of insights and impressions. It is intended as a non-threatening exploration and healing opportunity. Once this process is over the session formally ends.

CASE EXAMPLE

Susan, a 24-year-old social worker, mixed media artist, and surviving daughter of a Marine Corps gunnery sergeant, came to the art studio two years ago with the intention of addressing a longstanding grief reaction to her father's suicide. She was 16 years old when he shot himself in the head just months after returning home from Afghanistan. Over the years she participated in traditional talk therapy, which for her "was not enough." She had a pervasive sense she was different and experienced her body as "tight and rigid." In her first session, Susan created a collage entitled, "Healing?" This black, white and gray fragmented assortment of shapes was constructed on a 5 x 8-inch piece of cardboard. Four sets of eyes look off in different directions, while a disembodied hand holds the words, "The end of life."

Susan continued using collage monthly as a modality to investigate her fragmented self. In the fall of the following year, Susan created another small 5 × 8 collage entitled, "The Lineup." She wrote, "I am in the lineup. I am holding the phone. My line of communication is clear. My heart is light but wounded. I am supported by ancestors and angels. I look out to the world with open eyes." A month later Susan created "Progression" on an 8 × 10-inch piece of white paper. Her intention was, "I emerge from the darkness." This black, white and gray collage image is punctuated by red shards that explode out of the top of a man's head. A single open eye rests in the middle of the explosion. The other client/artists noted, "This piece feels different from your other work. It feels more cohesive and more informed. The trauma is more evident and reality is less obscured." Susan noted her "progression" over time, "getting more and more comfortable with the story." She admitted, "That's the face that has been cut up into many pieces, his and mine. He blew his brains out. I (eye) am emerging out of that dark place." Susan dialogued with the images in this simple collage and wrote, "I am the one who whispers in your ear. I impinge on your vision. I am the one who never understood the flame of your being. I am the one who wishes I could have said, 'Don't do it.' I let go of my attachments to suffering."

One month later, Susan created an 11 × 14 inch collage entitled, "The Goddess Has Arrived." It is more organized and cohesive. A field of black, white and red words forms a base out of which two distinct images emerge. A young woman with her eyes closed appears to be in ecstatic contemplation. The top of her head is open, like a box that is crowned by a heavy silver ornament. The other side of the page holds a set of bare arms in a prayerful pose. The arms are chained and rest against a back background through which a slice of a single eye can be seen, as well as the face of a smiling woman. The single collage holds both the light and the darkness; both rest comfortably side by side. Susan wrote, "I am the new seamless emergence. I am breaking away from the chains. I am in ecstasy of my awakening. I celebrate my unique individuality."

Susan continued to explore herself and her relationship with her father. Recently she created a small 5 x 8 collage entitled, "Seeing What Is." It is a collage of a woman's face: She gazes at the observer, eyes wide open. A red jewel adorns the area of her third eye, the place where her father shot himself. She seductively touches her parted lips as a single silver chain hangs from her mouth. Susan shared that her father physically abused her. She wrote, "I am the one who feels the piercing bullet which destroyed my innocence." This extensive creative process freed Susan from the symptoms of physical trauma, held in her body for nearly eight years. Her willingness to let go into the trauma and to create from her broken places supports her journey toward wholeness. She continues to embrace this process for further awakening.

CONCLUDING THOUGHTS

Although loss is universal and a part of our shared experience as human beings, each of us moves through it in individual ways. Clients drawn to a creative process for healing may find their needs met in diverse settings such as military bases/posts, schools, mental health and rehabilitation centers, self-help groups, shelters, hospitals, social service agencies and private offices. The physical structure is less important than the caretakers of the space who create a conscious environment that welcomes facilitator/artists and clients/artists and the images that pour from combined souls. "Art and creativity are the soul's medicine—what the soul uses to minister to itself, cure its maladies, and restore its vitality" (McNiff, 2004). We hope this chapter has encouraged clinicians and caregivers to become more aware and utilize complementary therapies in partnership with traditional approaches to grief and trauma as a holistic and comprehensive model of care.

References

Jordan, J. R., & McIntosh, J. L. (2010). Is suicide bereavement different? In J. R. Jordan, & J. L. McIntosh (Eds.), *Grief after suicide* (pp. 403–411). New York: Routledge.

McNiff, S. (2004). *Art heals.* Boston: Shambhala.

Part XI
Consolidating Memories

59
Opening the Family Photo Album

Louis A. Gamino

CLIENTS FOR WHOM THE TECHNIQUE IS APPROPRIATE

Use of family photographs in grief therapy is a broadly applicable technique that may be employed with bereaved adults, adolescents and children. Photographs can be a powerful tool for memory consolidation and building an internalized representation of the deceased person that facilitates adaptive grieving and a healthy continuing connection. Caution is encouraged when working with individuals who have sustained a traumatic or horrendous death wherein images of the deceased may be psychologically fused with trauma material, making such a technique less predictable.

DESCRIPTION

The initial encounter between provider and client in grief counseling naturally involves a detailed recounting of the "grief story" including some staple elements: what happened to the deceased; the experience and outcome of funeral/memorial arrangements (if any); whether a fitting "goodbye" occurred; the nature of the relationship between client and decedent; presence of complicating risk factors; issues of legacy; and, current functioning within the trajectory of grief. At the same time, as with other forms of psychotherapy, a broad spectrum assessment of the grieving person's "life story" is also important for grasping a more complete context of how the loss impacts this grieving individual at this particular time in the life cycle.

The technique of opening the family photo album is disarmingly simple. Typically, this maneuver is deployed toward the end of the initial session of grief therapy and carries over to the subsequent meeting. After hearing both the grief story and the life story of the client, the therapist is already in the process of becoming acquainted with the decedent and other salient members of the client's interpersonal network. The provider then suggests that the client could facilitate the counseling process by completing a brief "homework" assignment. While such a suggestion sometimes elicits unpleasant associations to school work, the therapist quickly explains how homework is often part of psychotherapy but that this assignment should be easy to complete—*bring to the follow-up session some family photographs that would allow the therapist to see the deceased as well as other important individuals in the client's life*. Generally, the therapist will ask for a sampling of photographs: some more recent snapshots of the deceased; pictures from earlier in life, such as graduation or wedding portraits;

photographs that show all the members of the family together; and, pictures of childhood and family of origin, if accessible.

The intentionality behind opening the family photo album borrows from the concept of "joining" that is championed by the structural model of family therapy (Goldenberg & Goldenberg, 2008). The notion of joining means that the therapist strives to gain the confidence of the family to the point that they accept the therapist enough to share the more intimate aspects of their history, including any "family secrets." By developing a sense of connectedness with the family, the therapist in essence "joins" the family as an honorary or quasi-member for purposes of the therapeutic endeavor. One of the crucial factors in fostering this connection is the genuineness with which the therapist relates to the family members who, in turn, can sense the earnestness and authenticity of the provider's empathy and concern. That genuineness can help the therapist move from the position of "outsider" to "insider" within the family structure.

When the client returns for follow-up, the photographs can be viewed and discussed in a relaxed, unhurried manner. Often, such a process enhances empathy by enabling the therapist to actually "see" the relationship between the client and the decedent with an appreciation and insightfulness that mere verbal descriptions may not convey. Giving language to such nuance (e.g., "*What a kind face she has*" or "*You look so radiant next to him*") can reflect to a grieving client the special nature of their relationship. Sometimes photographs of the decedent in robust health contrast sharply with pictures taken during a progressive illness or terminal decline so that the therapist can better comprehend the devastation wrought by disease and death (e.g., "*This helps me see just how much she wasted away and how hard that must have been for you to watch*"). In some cases, negative personality characteristics or troublesome aspects to the relationship can be detected in family photos (e.g., "*It looks like it might be difficult to get along with her*" or "*I notice your body arching away from him*"). Such comments from the therapist can range from merely observational to clearly interpretive but they are intended to deepen the connection to the client's phenomenological experience with bereavement and sharpen "empathic accuracy" (Roos, 2002).

CASE EXAMPLE

Lynn was a bereaved mother whose adult son, Liam, died from a self-inflicted gunshot wound to the head. Tragically, Liam's suicide occurred in a motor vehicle while he was attempting to flee from law enforcement personnel pursuing him for possible illicit drug violations. Liam's wife was in the escape car with him and was the only one present during his final moments before death.

Liam had cancer of the bone—osteosarcoma—but hid the disease from Lynn. At the same time, he became addicted to pain-killing opiates and the daughter-in-law exploited his prescription privileges to supply her own drug habit. To conceal her addiction, the daughter-in-law fostered secrecy and alienated the young couple from Lynn and the rest of the family. After Liam's death and burial, the daughter-in-law consistently refused to discuss the events surrounding his suicide or her role in it and eventually disappeared from contact. Lynn abhorred the fact that the daughter-in-law had failed to intervene and stop Liam's suicidal behavior. However, she regarded the withholding of crucial information about her son's last moments of life to be the greatest cruelty of all.

The intake interview with Lynn was emotionally intense as she poured out her story and lamented the loss of her treasured son. When invited to open the family album and bring some photographs to the follow-up meeting, she readily complied. The pictures she brought showed a once athletic, handsome young man who performed rodeo and cut a dashing figure. Later images of Liam revealed a still smiling persona but a gaunt, thin man ravaged by a merciless disease.

Lynn's lingering questions about just when her son's condition was diagnosed and how it progressed could be answered speculatively by looking at the photographs and tracing his emaciation.

Included in the array of photographs was a family portrait: Lynn and her husband; their daughter and son-in-law together with grandchildren; and Liam with the querulous daughter-in-law. The therapist commented on how the daughter-in-law was positioned in the center of the portrait and seemed to dominate the space with her very presence and demeanor. This observation struck a chord with Lydia whose revulsion for the daughter-in-law comprised a great deal of her anger over Liam's death. She returned to the next therapy session carrying a "photo-shopped" remake of that same family portrait with the daughter-in-law removed and Liam re-positioned to occupy the limelight in the center! This revised image fit better with Lynn's psychological reality of who are her family and the degree of closeness she felt to each loved one. In this instance, the process of opening the family album produced a salutary shift in how Lynn remembered her son, Liam, and took comfort from that image.

CONCLUDING THOUGHTS

Although the technique of opening the family photo album in grief therapy is not usually a complex assignment for the client, the handling of the photographs by the therapist obviously requires some level of clinical acumen and sophistication in order to make observations or venture interpretations that deepen the empathic understanding of the client's plight as well as advance the connection between provider and client. As with all new techniques, the therapist must develop and demonstrate competence with the method in order to employ it in a clinically effective and ethically conscientious manner in the everyday practice of grief counseling (Gamino & Ritter, 2009).

References

Gamino, L.A., & Ritter, R. H., Jr. (2009). *Ethical practice in grief counseling*. New York: Springer.

Goldenberg, H., & Goldenberg, I. (2008). *Family therapy: An overview* (7th ed.). Belmont, CA: Brooks/Cole.

Roos, S. (2002). *Chronic sorrow: A living loss*. New York: Brunner-Routledge.

60

The Commemorative Flag

Barbara E. Thompson

CLIENTS FOR WHOM THE TECHNIQUE IS APPROPRIATE

Individuals, families and small groups such as peer support groups for bereaved military mothers or veterans, may benefit from making commemorative flags, as a way to remember and memorialize a deceased loved one who served in the military. This technique might feel less appropriate in other contexts, and especially for mourners resentful of the circumstances under which their loved ones died in the service.

DESCRIPTION

Memory provides a sense of continuity, meaning and identity for individuals, families, communities and nations. The construction of personal and collective memory involves the interaction of individuals in a social field where memories are shared, created, and given meaning. The arts provide tangible ways to embody, explore, recast, reappraise and create memories through representation in images, such as photographs, objects of symbolic significance, or poetic renderings. Sympathetic interaction with an image can engage the imagination in a remaking of one's story about self and other, and the art object itself can invite interaction with others in the social field where meanings and memories are generated (Thompson & Berger, 2011). In the example to follow, community members were invited to make a commemorative flag honoring someone who served in the Armed Forces, as part of a weeklong series of events dedicated to veterans and their families. Participants were provided with khaki colored fabric in 11 × 14" seamed rectangular blanks with 1" pockets at the top for hanging. Various materials were used for construction of the flags, from pieces of old uniform to photo transfers, appliqué, paint, and markers. Symbols and text suggested a wide range of stories, in some instances, spanning multiple generations. Encouragement was sometimes needed to overcome concerns about "not being creative." While therapists using this approach need no prior artistic training, personal experience in making a flag is recommended. Sensitivity to the art making process and a non-judgmental, inquisitive approach to the art object are essential (Thompson & Berger, 2011).

Ritualized ceremonies for dedication of commemorative flags can be used as a way to promote community awareness of war-related grief and loss as well as the contributions of people in military service across time, while providing a sacred container supportive of the mourning and meaning-making process for survivors. Smaller-scale, private rituals of dedication and remembrance can also be developed. Well-designed rituals incorporate images, objects of symbolic significance and forms of enactment that convey meaning and can contain complex emotions (Romanoff & Thompson, 2006). For instance, a commemorative flag dedication ceremony was held on Veterans Day 2010 at The Sage Colleges and close to three hundred flags were displayed in a 19th-Century Greek Revival Church turned memorial auditorium. Viewing one's flag in a public context such as this and participating in community-based commemorations can complement and expand dialogue and discovery occurring within the therapy room with veterans and their family members.

CASE EXAMPLE

Ardelle is a middle-aged African American woman born and raised on the Mississippi River to a family with a history of military service. Her grandfather served in the U.S. Army during WWII and her father served in the U.S. Army during the 1950s. According to Ardelle, her father had few options as a young black man in Memphis before the civil rights movement so, like many of his childhood friends, he enlisted in the Army after high school. Most of his friends never made it back from Korea. Her father's youngest brother served in Vietnam. When she was a teenager, he died from complications related to Agent Orange exposure.

After his military service, Ardelle's father worked three decades for an Army foundry. Ardelle and her family were active in their church and community. She also accompanied her father, mother, and brothers on visits to a Veterans Hospital where they volunteered. Once retired, Ardelle's parents founded a progressive church with others in their community. Her father was affectionately known as the "chicken man," because he could always be counted on to bring a plate of fried chicken to grieving families after a funeral or during times of need.

Growing up, Ardelle remembers herself as shy and lacking in self-esteem, which she attributes to being overweight and being black. After high school, she moved away for college and worked for a few years thereafter as a seamstress. Later, she experienced episodes of recurrent depression that interfered with her employment and resulted in a period of homelessness.

Currently, Ardelle is working with a community group serving veterans and is living alone. She attributes her recovery from depression to having safe and stable living conditions, meaningful work where she is able to be of service to others, therapy, the example of her father, and the spiritual support she receives from her ancestors.

Ardelle's father developed cancer ten years ago. Despite geographical distance, she visited him regularly and learned much about her family history through conversation while reviewing old photographs. She and her brothers provided their parents with emotional and material support as unfunded medical expenses burdened their parents financially. Her father died a year ago and was given a military funeral and burial.

Last autumn Ardelle contacted extended family to gather stories related to her family's military service, and made commemorative flags for her grandfather, father, and two uncles. This process strengthened her bonds with family members, both living and deceased, and her appreciation for her heritage. Ardelle also made flags for several veterans she knew through her work. For instance, one flag was adorned with the image of an unraveling scroll, representing the evolving story she was hearing from a young Iraqi veteran. He subsequently attended the dedication ceremony on Veterans Day. Yet another flag, with images of multi-colored autumn leaves and text related to suicide numbers, honored the many service men and women who have committed suicide before, during, or after deployment. In making this flag, Ardelle wanted to recognize the service of veterans who are sometimes forgotten and the difficulties that can be associated with coming home.

On Veterans Day, Ardelle participated in a ceremony called the Reading of Names that memorialized service men and women who had died in Afghanistan and Iraq. Then, she visited the auditorium where the commemorative flags were hung and circumnavigated its interior several times. Seeing her family members' names and photo images on display reconnected Ardelle with life-affirming values and relationships.

Ardelle believes that the "warrior's way is not just about war," but about "bringing home those noble ideals." Her father did so in his church work, by "creating a place to learn and to serve others." Ardelle feels she is embodying her family's values by serving veterans and "doing the work that needs to be done." She is "inspired to do more" next year and wants to extend her involvement with the commemorative flag project to include military spouses and children. In addition, she plans to continue research on her own family as little is known beyond her grandfather's generation. She has benefited from discovering and reclaiming her historical roots.

Making commemorative flags and participating in rituals of remembrance provided tangible opportunities to mourn multiple types of loss, nourish continuing bonds with deceased loved ones, build relationship within a community, and contribute to the meaning-making process in the aftermath of loss.

CONCLUDING THOUGHTS

Many of us have family members who served in the Armed Forces, yet these stories may be difficult to share within the family context, especially those related to war. Notwithstanding, both told and untold stories leave intergenerational traces that influence the ongoing construction of individual, family, community and national narratives and identities. Whether or not a service member is able to reintegrate successfully into family and community life or how war-related losses and service are understood on both personal and collective levels may depend on whether or not there are opportunities to revisit and reconfigure the past in communion with empathetic and interested others (Tick, 2005).

References

Romanoff, B. D., & Thompson, B. E. (2006). Meaning construction in palliative care: The use of narrative, ritual, and the expressive arts. *American Journal of Hospice and Palliative Medicine, 23,* 309–319.

Thompson, B., & Berger, J. (2011). Grief and expressive arts therapy. In R.A. Neimeyer, D. L. Harris, H. D. Winokeur, & G. Thornton (Eds.), *Grief and bereavement in contemporary society: Bridging research and practice* (pp. 303–313). New York: Routledge.

Tick, E. (2005). *War and the soul: Healing our nation's veterans from post-traumatic stress disorder.* Wheaton, IL: Quest Books.

61

En-Training Memoir Slices

Harold Ivan Smith

CLIENTS FOR WHOM THE TECHNIQUE IS APPROPRIATE

Adolescents and adults grieving the death of a significant person. Memoir may not be the therapeutic technique of choice in the immediate aftermath of death, when emotion regulation may take precedence, or when a traumatic loss requires greater processing before the attachment-related focus of memoir is feasible to pursue.

DESCRIPTION

In a nation of memoir readers, growing numbers of individuals are interested in capturing portions of a loved one's life through memoirs of selected memories, rather than a biography or autobiography focusing on the entire life. Memoir gives an individual a means to deliberately remember.

Thomas (2008) contends that, "Writing memoir is a way to figure out who you used to be and how you got to be who you are" (p. 2). Grievers often say, "I ought to write a book about what I've been through." That, unfortunately, remains only a dream for many because of the challenge of organizing a life on paper. The memoir-writer, however, focuses on a particular season or experience in a deceased individual's life to answer the question: How did the loved one get to be who they were?

"En-training" offers a way to focus on aspects of an individual's life or relationship in three-page writing assignments. The particular death is the engine and the individual writing segments are "boxcars" that compose a memoir train.

I developed this technique for use in Grief Gatherings at Saint Luke's Hospital, in Kansas City, in response to the scene in *Sleepless in Seattle*, when Dr. Marsha Fieldstone asks Tom Hanks' character, "What was so special about your wife?" Hanks responded, "How long is your show?" Writing a memoir slice offers an opportunity to identify elements that made the individual loved, admired or special.

As homework for the fifth session (in a six-session group) participants are asked to write a three-page, double-spaced memoir slice. Individuals are encouraged to avoid writing a rehash of the obituary.

The basic organizing guidance is: Highlight something that made your loved one unique, beloved, or irascible. The facilitator offers several "jump start" questions for participants' consideration:

- *What was your loved one's favorite flavor of ice cream?*
- *What public figure could your loved one imitate?*
- *What is something your loved one said 1000 times that drove you nuts?*
- *What was your best birthday surprise for your loved one?*
- *What was your loved one's favorite holiday?*
- *What piece of wisdom did your loved one give you?*
- *What did your loved one's laugh sound like?*

At the start of the fifth session, the facilitator explains simple guidelines to make reading aloud to the group easier: (1) sharing is optional—no one has to read; (2) feedback is to be positive and supportive; (3) other participants can offer affirmation or ask for more information. At the end of the session, the facilitator asks participants to think of a freight train. "*Imagine the engine. That is your loved one. What you have created tonight is one boxcar. I hope you will continue writing 'boxcars' to add to your memoir train.*"

In closing, the facilitator asks participants:

- *When did you write your memoir slice?*
- *Did you share your assignment with a family member, worker, or colleague? With whom might you share your writing?*

This closing allows clients to encourage one another to consider wider sharing of the loved one's life story in manageable segments with others outside the group.

CASE EXAMPLE

Frank, a widower, grieved for Marcia, his wife of 30 years. He attended the group faithfully, listened attentively, but rarely spoke. He volunteered to read his memoir slice. It became evident that he had written far more than three double-spaced pages. Among the string of segments, one particularly resonated with the group: Frank described a moment when he overheard his wife trying to teach a cat tricks, specifically shaking hands and sitting on command. "Honey," he laughed, "Cats have minds of their own. You are trying to teach him a dog trick. He will never learn to do that!" Nevertheless, she kept trying. One day she asked him to come into the utility room.

"Remember when you said cats have a mind of their own?" she asked him. "Well, watch this." His wife said "Sit" and the cat sat. She said "Shake hands" and the cat lifted his paw. Frank grinned, "She loved to tease me when we had guests, by showing off her cat's 'never' tricks." When someone pointed out how special his wife was, Frank responded, "She always did things that people said could not be done. I see the cat and I think of her." As facilitator I let him read his full document. Clearly, he had given a great deal of thought to capturing multiple slices of his wife's life.

CONCLUDING THOUGHTS

Although a mourner's memoir of a loved one may never be published, it could easily become a document that is shared with other family members and friends. Reading through the boxcars might entice a reader who also knew and appreciated the deceased to contribute a memoir slice or to en-train a memoir of their own.

I suggest to Grief Gathering participants that people are not "gone" until two things happen: We stop saying their names and we stop telling stories about them. The facts of a memoir slice might lead someone to say, *"Well, let me tell you a story about the time she . . ."*

Reference

Thomas, A. (2008). *Thinking about memoir*. New York: AARP/Sterling.

62
Memory Work with Children

Linda Goldman

CLIENTS FOR WHOM THE TECHNIQUE IS APPROPRIATE

Nearly all bereaved children can benefit from memory work, but more intensive interventions may need to precede those described in this chapter when children have witnessed the traumatic death of a loved one or experienced the death of a significant other who also abused or mistreated them.

DESCRIPTION

Memory work serves as an appropriate grief intervention for children that allows for sharing stories, recalling special moments, creating rituals, and making memories into projects and books that facilitate remembering a special person. The bereaved child constructs the deceased through an ongoing cognitive process of establishing memories, feelings, and actions appropriate to the child's development level. This inner representation reinforces a continuing bond to the deceased, supporting a relationship that changes as the child matures and his or her grief diminishes. Silverman, Nickman and Worden (1992) found that it was normal for children "to maintain a presence and connection with the deceased and that this presence is not static" (p. 495). This ongoing relationship is supported through memory work.

Memory work is an important part of the therapeutic process, providing a helpful tool to safely process grief and trauma. Bereaved children often ask the question, "Will I forget my _____?" Memory work helps them remember. Memory books store pictures and writings about loved ones; memory boxes (discussed in Chapter 63 in this volume) hold cherished objects belonging to a special person; and memory picture albums hold favorite photographs. Caring adults can ask children the following questions as a foundation for discussion and processing memories: "Where were you when your _____ died? What was your first thought? What are the facts about how your _____ died? What makes you sad, happy, angry, and frustrated? What sticks with you now? Do you feel like you did anything wrong? What is it you still want to know? What scares you the most? What makes you feel peaceful? What can you do to feel better?" (Goldman, 2005, p. 125).

Memory books are useful tools to allow children to express feelings and thoughts, some of which they might not have been able to communicate at the time of their person's death. Children can use stars, stickers, photographs, and other decorations inside a memory book to expand their own writings and drawings about their person. The following are themes for memory book pages: "The most important thing I learned from my person is . . ., What was life like before my person died?, What is life like now?, My funniest memory is . . ., My most special memory is . . ., If I could tell my loved one just one more thing, I would say . . ., If I could say one thing I was sorry for it would be . . ." (Goldman, 2000, p. 85). Tyler, age 9, tried to make sense of the terrorist attack by making a memory book page illustrating the events of September 11, 2001. He drew where he was and what was happening at his New York school situated close to Ground Zero, writing only "Run for your life." Tyler was able to release feelings, tell stories, and express worries and concerns on his memory book page.

Thirteen-year-old Melissa's dad died of cancer. She shared her funniest memory of him in the following memory book page.

> He came home from getting his hair shaved off after being diagnosed with lung cancer. During his cancer he always kept a good attitude. That's just my Dad's personality—a good sense of humor. Why do the good people have to die?
>
> (Goldman, 2000, p. 90)

Memory picture albums are a useful tool in creating dialogues and sharing feelings. Henry, age 9, created a memory picture album called "My Life" about his dad who had died of cancer. He chose pictures he loved to make an album about his life before and after dad died, writing a sentence about each picture.

Bereaved children can acknowledge a death through creating a memory table. Girls and boys can bring treasured objects reminding them of their person or favorite pictures and leave them on the table. Some may wish to share a memory, and others may choose to just display their memory object. Memory tables can be used in a support group, a classroom, or a family home. Children may decide to silently share by displaying an object or picture, or joining together in a memory circle and talk about what the picture or object means to them.

Expressing memories through artwork is an invaluable tool for grieving children. Memory murals and memory collages are memory projects that allow girls and boys to creatively express feelings and thoughts about a loved one. Ten-year-old Josh prepared a collage of magazine pictures that reminded him of his big brother, Nathan, who had accidentally drowned. He included Nathan's favorite foods, clothes, music, and sport stars. Zack, age 9, drew the cover of the memorial booklet for his friend Andrew, showing Andrew "shooting hoops in heaven." Since Andrew's death, Zack had been playing basketball, and assumed Andrew was doing the same in heaven. Zack was able to continue to actively remember his friend through his drawing.

Memory work resources are meaningful tools to promote discussion and expression of memories. They enable families to dialogue about their common loss issues. Several resources for conducting memory work with grieving children can be found at the website *Children's Grief and Loss Issues*, http://www.childrensgrief.net.

CASE EXAMPLE

Caring adults working with bereaved children may need "to focus on ways to transform connections and place the relationship in a new perspective, rather than on how to separate from the deceased" (Silverman et al., 1992, p. 503). Many young people place their loved one in a place called "heaven." Michelle was 7 years old when her mother died in a car crash. Michelle asked in a therapy session, "What do you think heaven is?" Reflecting the question back to her, "What do you think it is?" resulted in her drawing a picture of her image of heaven. By reflecting on her own question, Michelle was able to access Mom's memory, honor her, remember her life, and symbolically send her mother love.

What is heaven? This is what heaven is to me. It's a beautiful place. Everyone is waiting for a new person, so they can be friends. They are also waiting for their family. They are still having fun. They get to meet all the people they always wanted to meet (like Elvis). There are lots of castles where only the great live, like my Mom. There's all the food you want and all the stuff to do—There's also dancing places, disco. My mom loved to dance. I think she's dancing in heaven. Animals are always welcome. (My Mom loved animals.) Ask her how Trixie is. That's her dog that died. Tell her I love her.

(Goldman, 2000, pp. 79–80)

CONCLUDING THOUGHTS

Giving young people the opportunity to release their emotions in a safe haven is the underlying thread inherent in working with grieving children. Research indicates that bereaved children may show more depression, withdrawal, and anxiety, lower self-esteem, and less hope for the future than non-bereaved children (Lutzke, Ayers, Sandler, & Barr, 1997). Support for bereaved children is therefore essential in helping to reduce negative outcomes related to unresolved or unexplored grief. Haine and her colleagues (2008, p. 114) explain that the primary goal of bereavement interventions for children is

> to normalize the grief process and to provide information that can reduce anxieties about the future, including . . . It is acceptable to talk about the parent who has died; it is not unusual for children to think that they see their parent who has died or to dream about the deceased parent; and children will never forget their deceased parent.

According to Silverman et al. (1992, p. 502), "Memorializing, remembering, and knowing who died are active processes that may continue throughout the child's entire life . . . This is not a matter of living in the past, but rather recognizing how the past informs the present."

Including children in memory activities helps to keep their loved one alive in their hearts. Grieving children are a growing segment of our youth; and their grief issues arise at younger and younger ages. Adults need to prepare to respond to children's questions and create safe havens for memory expression. *Memory work* is an important grief resolution intervention to help children remember their person who died. Encouraging safe expression of these memories through discussion and examination of thoughts and feelings helps build a relationship of trust through exploration of sensitive spaces.

References

Goldman, L. E. (2000). *Life and loss: A guide to help grieving children* (2nd ed.). New York: Taylor & Francis.

Goldman, L. E. (2005). *Raising our children to be resilient*. New York: Taylor & Francis.

Haine, R., Ayers, T., Sandler, I., & Wolchik, S. (2008). Evidence-based practices for parentally bereaved children and their families. *Professional Psychology: Research and Practice, 39*(2), 113–121.

Lutzke, J. R., Ayers, T. S., Sandler, N. S., & Barr, A. (1997). Risk and interventions for the parentally bereaved child. In N. Sandler, & S. Wolchik (Eds.), *Handbook of children's coping* (pp. 215–242). New York: Plenum.

Silverman, P., Nickman, S., & Worden, J. W. (1992). Detachment revisited: The child's reconstruction of a dead parent. *American Journal of Orthopsychiatry, 62*, 494–503.

63
Memory Boxes
Jordan S. Potash and Stephanie Handel

CLIENTS FOR WHOM THE TECHNIQUE IS APPROPRIATE

Memory boxes are suitable for clients of all ages who are able and willing to engage in memory work. They may be less appropriate when the bereaved are preoccupied with post-traumatic symptoms or profound guilt following a violent or problematic loss, when other therapeutic methods may be required before memory work is feasible.

DESCRIPTION

Prepare the following materials: boxes (craft cigar boxes, recycled boxes, or origami boxes in assorted sizes); tissue paper (assorted colors); glue varnish (for example: Mod Podge or white glue thinned with water); white glue or hot glue gun; drawing paper (assorted colors); scissors; brushes; assorted natural objects, fabrics, craft items and stickers; magazine collage images; inspirational phrases or words.

Memory boxes can be completed in a single session or over several with either individuals or groups. We have found, however, that one hour is generally insufficient.

Step 1: Explain memory boxes. Discuss with the client how memory boxes are useful for storing mementos that remind the client of the deceased. Memory boxes are not intended as a way to replace the loved one, but to help memorialize the dead by giving the client a personal space to safely keep items. Even though it might hold difficult memories, it contains what is precious to the client, thereby promoting feelings of connectedness to the loved one. As boxes are a contained space, clients can choose when to open and explore their contents, thereby providing a perceived sense of control. They are also organic spaces, as contents can be added, removed, or replaced. Clients are free to decide on the size, color and other features that will make them personally meaningful.

Step 2: Choose box. In selecting their box, clients should consider both emotional and practical reasons in choosing the appropriate shape and size, given their understanding of their grief. Clients should keep in mind how the memory box will be used and where it will be stored. Smaller boxes may be better for certain living situations and for their ability to be hidden or kept private. As several factors are important, the size of the box is not an indication of the extent of feeling for the deceased. If the therapist or facilitator is unable to purchase white craft boxes, clients can be led in creating a simple origami one with a lid. If using a recycled box, clients may first want to paint it with white acrylic paint or gesso to cover packaging labels.

Step 3: Select colors. Clients can begin by selecting 2 to 3 colors guided by one of the following directives:

- Favorite colors: of the deceased, client's, or both.
- Memories: meaningful physical or tangible characteristics of the deceased and signifying colors, such as colors that relate to the loved one's hair, eyes, home furnishings, or favorite flower, sports team, food or clothing.
- Emotions: select colors that symbolize their feelings, both those that have been shared publicly and those that are kept private.
- For some clients, it may be useful to offer a guided visualization to help them discover personally meaningful colors on these or other themes.

Step 4: Apply tissue paper. Clients can cut or tear the tissue paper and place it in a purposeful or random manner. The glue varnish should be applied as both an adhesive and as a finish. Clients should fully cover the outside and inside of the box paying attention to what they want seen on the outside and inside surfaces.

Step 5: Embellish memory box. Clients may want to further decorate their memory boxes with images, words and items that represent the deceased, their relationship to the deceased or their emotions. To parallel the purposeful selection of items, it can be helpful to explore with the client the many aspects of a relationship and related symbolic representations. Relationships can be complex and multi-dimensional, which the memory box can help express.

(a)

Figure 63.1 (a) and (b) Inside and outside of a sample memory box. The box holds a child's letters and drawings.

Step 6: Select or create items to place in memory box. When completed, clients can select or create items to place in the box. Some suggestions include photographs, memorial objects, and funeral cards. If a client does not have tangible items or memories of the deceased, drawings and written notes may be placed in the box [see Figure 63.1(b)]. The notes might be memories that have been shared by others who knew the deceased, as well as notes to the deceased about life without them.

CASE EXAMPLE

At Camp Forget Me Not/Camp Erin, a weekend camp in Washington, DC, for children and adolescents who have experienced a death, we facilitated the creation of memory boxes in art therapy groups for children 6–12 years old (Figure 63.1(a) and (b)). We had copies of Adinkrah, the symbolic language of the Asante people of Ghana. Traditionally, the symbols are stamped on cloth to represent the characteristics of the deceased. The campers were invited to select images that correlated to how they remembered their loved one. Each child was invited

Figure 63.1 Continued

to write a memory on special paper to place in the box, as a starter to all of the other treasures they might add once they returned home. Time was allotted for some brief group process during which children shared their creations and explained the symbolism behind colors, pictures and words.

CONCLUDING THOUGHTS

Memory boxes are a widely used technique for facilitating grief work that was even showcased on *Sesame Street* when Elmo's cousin Jessie created her own memory box to memorialize her deceased father (Delfico, 2010). In her own series of art boxes following the death of her son, Kaufman (1996) observed how "in the very creation of boundaries or contained space, it is possible to permeate, to create boundless space" (p. 246). The boxes helped her contain difficult and paradoxical feelings, while allowing her to create meaningful memorial objects. She also noticed how the boxes allowed her to transform ordinary objects by making them special as they took on new meaning. At the same time, she could observe her interaction with the box as a way to self-monitor her emotional state. In another example, the Memory Box Project developed in the 1990s in Uganda has provided hundreds of thousands of children and adults living with HIV/AIDS the opportunity to explore and process their grief while holding onto memories. It has been integral to the collective healing and support of families and communities in Africa (IRIN, 2003). Given the emotional responses that clients can have, it is important to effectively manage the art making process. Hrenko (2005) demonstrated her effective use of memory boxes at a camp for children affected by HIV/AIDS by carefully navigating the boundary between art therapy and recreational crafts. Therapists and facilitators should also take special care to understand clients' associations to boxes in regard to memory work, particularly those related to coffins or urns. Although not appropriate for every client, memory boxes may be particularly useful in cultural contexts that limit discussion about difficult emotions or traumatic experiences (Chu, 2010). Lastly, therapists and facilitators are advised to create their own memory boxes to observe and assess potential emotional reactions and difficulties in the creative process.

References

Chu, V. (2010). Within the box: Cross-cultural art therapy with survivors of the Rwanda genocide. *Art Therapy, 27*(1), 4–10.
Delfico, C. (Producer) (2010). When families grieve [Television broadcast]. New York: Sesame Workshop.
Hrenko, K. D. (2005). Remembering Camp Dreamcatcher: Art therapy with children whose lives have been touched by HIV/AIDS. *Art Therapy, 22*(1), 39–43.
IRIN (2003). AFRICA: Memory boxes to help say goodbye. *IRIN: Humanitarian News and Analysis.* Available at: http://www.irinnews.org/report.aspx?reportid=46926#.TjivR1jWN6U.email.
Kaufman, A. B. (1996). Art in boxes: An exploration of meanings. *Arts in Psychotherapy, 23*(3), 237–247.

64
Natural Reminders

Carrie Thiel and Christine Barrett

CLIENTS FOR WHOM THE TECHNIQUE IS APPROPRIATE

This technique is appropriate for groups of children who are grieving the death of a family member. This technique is not likely to be beneficial for very young children or for individuals whose cognitive functioning prevents them from communicating abstractly.

DESCRIPTION

When children have lost someone close to them through death, it can be helpful to include them in a grief support group with children of similar ages who have experienced similar losses (Grollman, 1995, p. 17). Our organization, Tamarack Grief Resource Center, specializes in outdoor-based grief support. At times it is not practical for groups to meet outside. In recognition of the healing benefits of interfacing with natural objects, the Natural Reminders activity is an example of a grief group activity utilizing organic materials conducive to indoor settings.

The objectives of our school-based grief support groups include: allowing participants to honor and remember the loved one who has died; providing safe space for expressing the emotions connected to the loss, exploring ways to support oneself and others while moving through grief, offering companionship while bereaved individuals and families reconstruct their identities and families after loss, and making use of natural settings and/or materials for creative metaphors of loss and life.

One activity that meets these objectives and that we have used successfully in a children's grief group is called *Natural Reminders*:

Step 1: Gathering materials: In this activity, the leader gathers together various items from the natural world, or somehow symbolic of something from nature: leaves, pine cones, rocks, seashells, branches, flowers, feathers, sand, etc. I have also used photographs of natural settings, polished colored glass craft stones, silk flowers, candles (unlit, but as a reminder of fire). We suggest using items related to nature because of the powerful healing potential of these organic reminders of the life cycle, special times spent with loved ones, the connection to something bigger than oneself, and the feeling of tranquility that natural settings provide (Miles, 1993; Santostefano, 2004).

Step 2: Preparing for the activity: Once these items have been gathered, there are options for how to use them in the group. Some leaders place them all in a basket that is passed around the group. Some prefer to place all the items upon a pretty cloth or placemat so that everyone can easily see each item at the same time. It helps to have a small table for this option, and set it up before group members arrive.

Step 3: Beginning the activity: When the time comes during the group session for this activity, children are asked to gather around the table, and to look at all of the objects without touching them. Then we say something like this:

> The activity we are going to do today is based on the idea that all around us are reminders of the person who died, and of the times we spent with them, and of our feelings about them. The memories and emotions those reminders bring up for us can be pleasant, unpleasant, happy, sad, or a combination of many emotions. We might remember special times with the person who died, or something about the way they were, or how we feel. Sometimes, it can be helpful to share those feelings and memories with others who understand. Or you might just feel like keeping those feelings to yourself. Either way is okay.
>
> Being in nature, especially, can help us remember our feelings about the person who died, and can help us feel good about being alive, because it reminds us we are part of the big picture of life. We are part of the seasons and of everything around us. Sometimes, just being in a wild and beautiful place can feel very comforting and soothing
>
> On this table are several objects I have gathered from nature, and also pictures or symbolic items that represent something in nature. Take a few minutes and look at the things, and see if any of these objects bring to mind memories or emotions or thoughts about the person who died, or perhaps about the way you feel when you are in a natural setting. Don't say anything just yet. Simply look, and think and remember. After a couple of quiet minutes, we'll go around the circle and each person will have the chance to pick up the object and say whatever you want to about what the object reminds you of, or, if you don't want to talk you can just hold up the object to us. After you've shared, you can set the object back down so someone else can use it if they want to.

Step 4: During the activity: After a minute or two of silence, we ask for someone to start, and then we go around the circle until everyone has had a chance to share. As each person speaks, we validate what he or she has said with an empathetic response. If someone chooses not to speak, we validate that choice as well.

Step 5: Closing the activity: Finally, we wrap up the activity by saying something like:

> Thank you all for sharing your thoughts, memories and feelings with us today. It's helped us know you, and your special people who have died, better. We also feel like we understand your feelings better, too. Sometimes, when someone has died, people who love them like to keep special objects that remind them of that person so that whenever they look at that object, they think of how much they love the person and how glad they are to have known them. Or, sometimes people will go spend time in nature to help them remember the person that died, and to just have fun and enjoy being alive. Maybe next time you are able to spend some time in nature, you can look around for special reminders, and remember to enjoy the beauty and life all around you. Or maybe you can find a quiet place to sit and miss the person for a little while, and just feel those feelings.

CASE EXAMPLE

John, an 11-year-old boy who had lost his mother when he was 4, was part of a children's grief group in which the Natural Reminders activity was used. When it was his turn to select an object from among those spread out on the table, he chose a pine cone and a candle, saying that though he didn't have a direct memory of his mom, he had pictures of them camping that meant a lot to him. He liked to think of his mom whenever he went camping. Through this activity, he was able to articulate a connection between his mom and their shared past, and his current life experiences.

Marie, another 11-year-old student in the same group, whose mother had died the previous year, was often tearful, and had not previously chosen to speak during sharing activities. On the day we did the Natural Reminders activity, she chose a flower, held it up and told us her mom had liked to garden. Though we were surprised when she spoke, no one made too big a deal of it, and from then on, she spoke during most of the activities. This gentle, non-threatening, symbolic activity had unlocked something inside her, helping her move forward sharing the experience of her grief.

CONCLUDING THOUGHTS

By demonstrating ways to remember and honor loved ones who have died, and by encouraging children to seek spaces of solace in natural settings, caring adults show children how to stay connected to their loved ones in life-affirming ways. They also offer healthy coping strategies for grieving children to manage the strong emotions they feel. This group activity could easily be adapted for use with participants of any age, and is a simple, non-threatening way to help meaningful conversations begin to flow.

References

Grollman, E. A. (1995). *Bereaved children and teens: A support guide for parents and professionals.* Boston: Beacon Press.

Miles, J. (1993). Wilderness as healing place. In M.A. Gass (Ed.), *Adventure therapy* (pp. 43–56). Dubuque, IA: Kendall/Hunt.

Santostefano, S. (2004). *Child therapy in the great outdoors: A relational view.* Hillsdale, NJ: Analytic Press.

Part XII
Renewing the Bond

65
Introducing the Deceased

Lorraine Hedtke

CLIENTS FOR WHOM THE TECHNIQUE IS APPROPRIATE

People who are living with grief both soon after a person has died as well as when the death occurred many years earlier. The technique is appropriate for adults and children alike, but needs to be used with discretion in relationships between the living and the deceased where an infraction, such as abuse, has occurred.

DESCRIPTION

Many bereavement practices in recent times focus on the internal emotional state of the bereaved person (Klass, Silverman, & Nickman, 1996). The dominant model of grief psychology treats the bereaved person's experience as if it were a journey through a landscape of signposts, arriving at an accepting destination. Well-intended counseling practices that privilege feelings, utilize empty chair conversations, or assign rank to quantify experiences of loss, have often left the deceased person out of the conversation. The physical death has created license for grief psychology to silence the stories and relational legacies of the dead. The focus has been directed towards the bereaved's return to an individual status (Hedtke & Winslade, 2004) ignoring the longstanding relationship that has gone missing.

Challenges to the modern practices of grief psychology can be found in various corners of professional writing over the past two decades (Klass et al., 1996; Neimeyer, 2001). The theoretical challenge has suggested that the relationship between the deceased and the living needs to be accounted for in the ongoing experience of the bereaved. Small spaces have been prized open for new ideas for conversation to emerge. Such spaces, however, have still to be plumbed for therapeutic value. The need persists to answer the important question: if the goal of grief counseling is not "completion" or "acceptance," what is the therapeutic goal in this new practice? I would suggest introduction as one example of the emerging focus. It stands practically and theoretically in contrast with the encouragement of individuals to "let go," "move on" and find "closure."

If we assume that our stories outlive our biology, and we are not the exclusive owner or teller of our stories, then others can tell our stories if we are no longer alive to tell them. For example, when we tell a story about a deceased parent or grandparent, we can be said to introduce this person to our listeners. As a counselor, I encourage people to introduce me to the deceased by telling me stories of their relationship. I inquire about the particular meaning that the connection held while the person was alive and I assume that this meaning (and therefore the relationship) continue to evolve after death. Introduction allows both the bereaved person and me to notice where the deceased continues to feature in the life of the living. I can become an immediate audience for the bereaved to specify what was important, and what will become important, as the deceased is introduced. I can become the audience to hear the stories that matter and to serve as a springboard for the bereaved to venture into larger communities and make more introductions.

The value of conjuring up such stories lies not just in the sweet nostalgia of reminiscence until acceptance fades the recollected moments. The introduction also calls forward relational connections to serve as resources for the bereaved that can mitigate some of the pain of loss. Asking the bereaved to introduce their loved one, and to take up the role of being a ventriloquist for the deceased, ameliorates the pain of grief by reincorporating the dead person's narrative legacies into ongoing life. Introduction affirms and inspires a relational counseling approach in a very practical fashion and answers the question, "If not letting go, then what?" To initiate such an introduction, these are the kind of questions I might ask a bereaved person:

- *Could you introduce me to your loved one?*
- *Who was he to you? What did knowing him mean to you?*
- *Are there times, places or ways in which you recall her importance to you?*
- *Do particular stories come to mind that he would want known about his life?*
- *What kind of things did she teach you about life, and perhaps about how you should manage the challenges facing you presently?*
- *What might he say he appreciated about who you are and how you might find your way with the challenges facing you now?*
- *If you wanted to grow a closer relationship with her over the upcoming years, how might you go about doing this?*
- *What difference might it make to keep his stories and memories close to you?*

CASE EXAMPLE

We can bear witness to the importance of an introduction by way of a brief example. When I first spoke with Dominic, he introduced me to his beloved wife of over 50 years, who had died two years before we spoke. During our conversation he spoke of how Rebecca's love of music and social justice had inspired her students, their nine grandchildren, and how much he had valued their connection over the years. Her passion for nature and for music had helped as she had fought against the pain of a debilitating illness that ultimately had led to her death.

Our conversation began with the simple question, "Could you tell me your wife's name and a bit about her?" Dominic had no trouble sharing touching memories, nor did he find it hard to recount stories that made him laugh. The years of his marriage were the basis for a rich relationship and he was eager to introduce his wife to me posthumously. As he spoke, it was as if she entered the room and sat with us listening to her stories being told. He told how, just following Rebecca's death, he had been given very helpful advice that guided him.

> *I received a phone call from a friend of mine who was 101 and was a long time peace activist we both knew. He told me how he had lost his wife after 62 years of marriage and it was very hard for him. He explained how he had quickly learned that he drew strength from her memory and he spoke to her every morning. He had a picture of her on the wall.*

Dominic referenced this phone call as the inspiration to keep speaking, in his head, to his wife and to consult her opinion on important matters. I inquired what matters she might deem as important enough for a consultation, hoping to continue to give her voice an outlet in our current conversation.

> *All matters I suppose, but mostly of those involving the children and grandchildren. But also about us. When I picked up her ashes, I didn't know what I was going to do with them. But when I got them home, I put them on the hearth right next to where she sat and read. I imagined her presence encouraging me to do this. And that is very peaceful for me to have them [her ashes] here. And it's a double box too, so there is room for me someday. I like this thought.*

Without asking about his wife and their many shared moments of joy, the counseling conversation, I believe, would have rung hollow. If I were only to focus on his adjustment to being alone, I would not have been introduced to her and would not have learned about how she is entwined in what continues to give him daily meaning. Or worse, had I not asked of their connection, her voice would have been driven underground to a place where many bereaved people are often left to doubt their sanity, yearning for a place to continue the connection in new ways.

CONCLUDING THOUGHTS

Whether I am speaking to bereaved people in a support group or in a private session, I must always start with a proper introduction to the deceased. Anything less has always struck me as rude. For the bereaved person, the deceased continues to feature in consciousness and to not acknowledge this leaves out a significant relational reality. Introduction flings back the door that was prized open in the theoretical focus on continuing bonds. It opens onto a wide relational space ready to be constructed in stories, songs, recipes, rituals, quiet meditation, and unlimited ways to create future connection.

References

Hedtke, L., & Winslade, J. (2004). *Remembering lives: Conversations with the dying and the bereaved.* Amityville, NY: Baywood.

Klass, D., Silverman, P., & Nickman, S. (Eds.). (1996). *Continuing bonds: New understandings of grief.* Philadelphia: Taylor & Francis.

Neimeyer, R. A. (2001). *Meaning reconstruction and the experience of loss.* Washington, DC: American Psychological Association.

66

Envisioning Connection through Guided Imagery

Courtney Armstrong

CLIENTS FOR WHOM THE TECHNIQUE IS APPROPRIATE

Adults, adolescents, or children processing the death of someone close and who want to cultivate a healthy continuing bond or settle unresolved emotional issues with the deceased. The technique may be contraindicated for clients who have trouble visualizing or for clients whose spiritual or religious beliefs preclude them from feeling comfortable imagining a conversation with a deceased loved one. Caution should also be used with persons who exhibit unhealthy emotional dependence on their relationship with the deceased loved one.

DESCRIPTION

Through a guided imagery exercise, the bereaved client senses the loving presence of the deceased now connecting with the client from a place of greater clarity, understanding, and compassion and able to provide emotional support as needed.

I have found this exercise to be incredibly healing for clients, perhaps effecting change more profoundly than any other technique I use (Armstrong, 2011). The "healing" point seems to occur when the client *experiences* a deep feeling of connection with their deceased loved one and really senses that their loved one is okay and wants the bereaved person to be okay too. Clients who are resistant to doing empty chair—or other reconnection types of exercises—are usually quite receptive to this imagery exercise. Moreover, once clients experience this healing reconnection, they are better able to resolve traumatic memories, guilt, and resentment because they sense that the deceased is now able to come from a place of enlightenment and offer compassionate support.

Envisioning connection imagery script

Sit or lie down in a place where you can get comfortable and begin by taking a few slow, deep breaths. Just follow the natural rhythm of your breath as you ease into a more relaxed state. When you are ready, imagine yourself in a beautiful place. This could be a place that you have been before or a special place that you enjoyed with your loved one. Explore this place with your mind's eye, taking in all the natural beauty there . . . whether it be water, or trees, or mountains, or a garden . . . this is your special place and you can design and adjust it any way you like. Continue looking around your special place taking in all the interesting scenery there . . . tuning into any soothing sounds you would hear there . . . inhaling the pleasant aromas . . . and basking in the wonderful feel of the air . . . the warmth of the sun on your skin, or a cool breeze blowing gently across your face . . . let all of it lift and support you.

As you settle into this scene more and more, you may notice a luminous light and a sparkling energy radiating all around and through things. On an inhalation, imagine you can breathe in this healing, brilliant light. The light can be soft and gentle, or bright and energizing; your inner mind will adjust it to be the right color and intensity for you . . . whether it is pure and white, or warm and golden, or iridescent with many hues.

Imagine the light moving through each area of your body . . . taking special care around your chest and heart area . . . here the light gently loosens any tight places . . . lifts the heavy places . . . and tenderly fills the hollow spots . . . it continues . . . dissolving grief's hard protective shell . . . and mending the torn, broken places . . . as more and more, you are aware of a safe, sweet, compassionate love shining all around and through you.

And you sense that within this light is the light of your loved one . . . coming from a renewed place of healing . . . even if you can't see them clearly, you can sense their intention to comfort you and let you know they are alright now. Perhaps you can imagine them gently holding your hand . . . or caressing your face . . . or giving you a warm hug. Your loved one lets you know that all of the pain and sorrow are understood . . . all the confusion and anger . . . all the yearning . . . all the tears . . . everything is understood and accepted.

And they let you know that they're here to walk beside you, support you, comfort you, and get you through . . . So you can just open up as they send this healing, loving energy throughout your heart . . . your spirit . . . your body. And as you connect with them, they let you know that they are okay and they want you to be okay too.

If there is anything you want to say or ask your loved one, you can do that now too. They may answer you quickly or slowly . . . and it could be in the form of words, pictures, songs, or feelings they send to you . . . just stay open and listen . . . their message will come through.

You can continue sitting with this as long as you like. . . enjoying the awareness of being in their presence . . . realizing they are available to you whenever you want to call them up. They are not gone . . . they are not lost . . . they are forever with you and your heart.

CASE EXAMPLE

Cassie was a 22-year-old woman who came to therapy because she was tormented by intrusive images, nightmares, and intense guilt related to her boyfriend Jonathan's fatal drug overdose that occurred more than a year ago. Although Cassie deeply loved Jonathan, she broke up with him a few weeks before his death because of his increasing substance abuse and erratic behavior. She was particularly haunted by images of the pained look on Jonathan's face as he tearfully shuffled down her driveway the day they broke up. This was the last time she saw him alive.

Cassie and I spent our first two sessions reflecting on her relationship with Jonathan, exploring her spiritual beliefs about death, and looking at her future goals. During our third session I explained to Cassie that guided imagery could help her resolve unfinished business with Jonathan and work out a healthier type of enduring bond with him. She said she was open to trying it, but also a little skeptical.

Drawing from the above imagery script, I guided Cassie through the process. About 10 minutes into the imagery exercise, she began to softly cry and smile at the same time, stating that she indeed was getting the sense that Jonathan loved her and wanted her to stop feeling guilty for "his mistakes." I encouraged her to continue silently talking with Jonathan as long as she liked and to signal to me when she felt she was done. Within 10 more minutes she opened her eyes and said, "Wow! That was incredible! For the first time, I can say that I really do feel like he is okay now and he wants me to go on with my life." We only had a couple of sessions after this because Cassie's mood stabilized and the grief lifted. She planned to return to college at the beginning of the next semester, and started to date again.

CONCLUDING THOUGHTS

Guided imagery has been used for decades to alter emotional states and promote healing. Imagery seems to facilitate emotional shifts because it speaks the sensory language of our emotional brain where our affective memories and attachment symbols are stored. Therefore, guided imagery seems to be a very suitable intervention in grief therapy as grief is often complicated when there are unresolved affective memories or excessive yearning for a connection to a deceased loved one/attachment figure. Similarly, research has empirically demonstrated the value of using such techniques in the resolution of complicated grief and the freeing of the bereaved to pursue goals of autonomy and relatedness. As Shear and her colleagues (2006) state, "The imaginal conversation with the deceased is a powerful component of our treatment . . . The net result of this exercise is that the patient feels deeply reassured and connected to the deceased." At its best, this type of activity can relieve grievers of unhealthy emotional ties to the deceased and encourage them to move back out into the world sensing the deceased in a new type of supportive role. If grievers have been overly reliant on the deceased, caution should be used so as not to foster increased emotional dependency on the deceased. In these circumstances therapists would want to encourage clients to imagine the deceased supporting the grievers in their efforts to become independent and take care of themselves.

References

Armstrong, C. (2011). *Transforming traumatic grief: Six steps to move from grief to peace after the sudden or violent death of a loved one.* Chattanooga, TN: Artemecia Press.

Shear, K., Corscak, B., & Simon, N. (2006). Treatment of complicated grief following violent death. In E. K. Rynearson (Ed.). *Violent death* (pp. 157–174). New York: Taylor & Francis.

67
Correspondence with the Deceased

Robert A. Neimeyer

CLIENTS FOR WHOM THE TECHNIQUE IS APPROPRIATE

Adults and older children who experience separation related distress and other troubling feelings bearing on their relationship to their deceased loved one. Letter writing to the deceased can be premature for clients who are preoccupied with troubling imagery, anger or posttraumatic reactions to the circumstances of the death itself, which might call for trauma-focused interventions before the attachment-related issues that are the focus of corresponding with the deceased can be addressed.

DESCRIPTION

Letters to the lost or "unsent letters" (Neimeyer, 2002) are a straightforward attempt on the part of the survivor to reconnect with the deceased in narrative form, in an effort to say "hello again" (White, 1989), rather than a final goodbye. In some religious contexts these same missives might be labeled "letters to heaven." The most therapeutic letters appear to be those in which the griever speaks deeply from the heart about what is important as he or she attempts to *reopen* contact with the deceased, rather than seek "closure" of the relationship. Some people find it beneficial to consider what the other has given them, intentionally or unintentionally, of enduring value. Additionally, letter writing offers an opportunity to use words that heretofore have remained unspoken, and to ask the questions that remain unasked. Often little more is required than the suggestion, in an appropriate moment in which the client is yearning for contact with the deceased, that he or she might write to the deceased about what he or she feels, needs and wishes at this point in bereavement. However, the following therapeutic prompts can be helpful in initiating this type of written dialogue, especially for those who may be stuck in their grief:

- *What I have always wanted to tell you is . . .*
- *My most treasured memory of you is . . .*
- *What you never understood was . . .*
- *What I want you to know about me is . . .*
- *What I now realize is . . .*
- *The one question I have wanted to ask is . . .*
- *I want to keep you in my life by . . .*

Continuing bonds, by their nature, are personal and individualized, and like imaginal dialogues of a spoken variety, can invite a response from the other. Thus, many grievers use letter writing to initiate an ongoing correspondence "with" the deceased, letting the conversation evolve as their life does. Others use such writing to begin a therapeutic journal, designed to branch out in a variety of literary directions. Still others take advantage of contemporary online media by opening an email account in the loved one's name to which personal messages can be sent, or by continuing to share postings to or about the deceased loved one via Facebook or other social networking sites. Although the bereaved can continue such dialogues indefinitely, I find they commonly taper off after a few months, and sometimes after a significant exchange in which the client completes "unfinished business" reflected in anger or guilt in relation to the deceased. The common tendency for such written exchanges to fade over time into a more internalized dialogue with the loved one accords with evidence that such attachments take a more psychological or spiritual form as they become more secure (Field, Gal-Oz, & Bonanno, 2003), although writing may continue to prove useful on significant anniversaries or other occasions as therapy (or life) proceeds.

CASE EXAMPLE

When Fred lost his "sweetheart" Shirley after a 55-year marriage, he understandably grieved deeply. But several months after her death, he also felt strangely relieved from the care-giving burden he had lovingly assumed during her long years of illness. Pursuing therapy to sort out these mixed feelings, he accepted the therapist's invitation to write about his conundrum to Shirley and seek her counsel, though the idea at first surprised him. In part, the first letters in the "exchange" read as follows:

Shirley, My Love,

Well, today was the day to seek the shrink . . . Dr. Neimeyer's waiting room invites calm as does his therapy suite. He is thoroughly relaxing and non-threatening. Yet, as with any good therapist, you sense he's no push-over. He completely avoided the typical clinical protocol of intake forms, etc., and said simply, "How can we use this hour to help you?"

I jumped right in and told him about your death five months ago and my sojourn since. And that I was having some difficulty with doing as well as I was, with feelings of guilt [for feeling] release after the protracted and intense care-giving . . . After asking a number of questions, he led me to the understanding that my recovery was not unusual [for someone in my position] following the release of the beloved from the great pain and suffering, [which] offers a new sense of freedom. He commented that my journaling was right on target with the most current grief therapies, and is what has put me in the relatively healthy place where I am. He read some of my writing and was obviously moved by it and said so. He said I dealt with you and your death in a moving and tender way. He did suggest that I stretch myself and conjure up what your thoughts and expressions would be to the things I am saying and writing now. So, that I will try. But it was so comforting to be really understood and affirmed. He said the next task I might consider would be to re-configure our relationship in light of your death. Not to say a final goodbye. But to find a way to continue the relationship on a different level and find your voice speaking to me and your presence still bearing upon me. Nothing spooky about that. Just simply to find your voice and your presence still with me. So, I shall try. Bear with me, my love.

Fred

He then continued with a new letter, only written with "Shirley's" words this time:

Freddie. It's about time you listened to me! How long have we known and loved each other. And me not to talk to you? That's unthinkable! Now, what Dr. Neimeyer says is exactly right. You just sit still and listen. That meditation you do each morning will probably help if you focus on it.

First of all, let's deal with the more mundane stuff—what you are doing with your time and energy. Now, that is fine with me as long as you don't do anything foolish. You don't have me to worry about. But that doesn't mean you can be reckless. There are still our children who would be heartbroken if anything happened to you. But go ahead and try some new ministry in the inner city if that's what God is calling you to do. Just don't be disappointed if no one stands and cheers! You have much to give and contribute. You have a loving heart and a good mind. Don't waste them on trivial things . . . Rekindle the dream you had for the "beloved community" back in seminary days and earlier. I am with you on this one. Just be sure to include the little children as you go along in some way.

Well, tomorrow we will get into other stuff. But, sit on that tonight. And we will chat some more tomorrow.

Love always, Shirley

CONCLUDING THOUGHTS

Narrative therapy techniques, such as corresponding with the deceased, are used in various therapeutic approaches to grief therapy, even those that otherwise differ in terms of their conceptualization of grief distress and how it should be treated (e.g., Boelen, de Keijser, van den Hout, & van den Bout, 2007; Neimeyer, Burke, Mackay, & Stringer, 2010).

Indeed, it plays a major role in empirically supported therapies for complicated grief (Wagner, Knaevelsrud, & Maercker, 2006), and when tailored to clients' deep needs in a given relational moment with the loved one, can serve to articulate, honor or renegotiate their continuing bond with the dead.

References

Boelen, P. A., de Keijser, J., van den Hout, M., & van den Bout, J. (2007). Treatment of complicated grief: A comparison between cognitive-behavioral therapy and supportive counseling. *Journal of Clinical and Consulting Psychology, 75*, 277–284.

Field, N. P., Gal-Oz, E., & Bonanno, G. A. (2003). Continuing bonds and adjustment at 5 years after the death of a spouse. *Journal of Consulting and Clinical Psychology, 71*, 110–117.

Neimeyer, R. A. (2002). *Lessons of loss: A guide to coping.* Memphis, TN: Center for the Study of Loss and Transition.

Neimeyer, R. A., Burke, L., Mackay, M., & Stringer, J. (2010). Grief therapy and the reconstruction of meaning: From principles to practice. *Journal of Contemporary Psychotherapy, 40*, 73–84.

Wagner, B., Knaevelsrud, C., & Maercker, A. (2006). Internet-based cognitive-behavioral therapy for complicated grief: A randomized controlled trial. *Death Studies, 30*, 429–453.

White, M. (1989). Saying hullo again. In M. White, *Selected papers.* Adelaide: Dulwich Center.

68

Guided Imaginal Conversations with the Deceased

John R. Jordan

CLIENTS FOR WHOM THE TECHNIQUE IS APPROPRIATE

Those seeking to reconnect with the deceased, to "finish business" with the loved one and to do reparative work on the psychic connection with the deceased. The technique should be used with great caution, if at all, with clients who are suicidal, are traumatized, or have dissociative or psychotic experiences. Likewise, clients who are very recently bereaved or who are likely to be overwhelmed by the emotional intensity evoked by the technique may need to wait until they feel more in control, and the therapeutic relationship has developed to function as a "holding environment" for strong affect.

DESCRIPTION

Prompting a guided imaginal conversation with the deceased is a powerful technique, one that should not be used casually or outside the context of an ongoing and secure therapeutic alliance with a client. It also should be used only after the client has been given informed consent about the technique, its possible risks and benefits have been explained, and the therapist and client have reached a consensus about the goals for the procedure. These could include taking leave of the deceased (when this has been denied by the location or manner of death); settling of "unfinished business" about aspects of the relationship that were troubling, hurtful, or confusing; renewal of the emotional bond with the deceased, and development of images of the deceased as being physically and psychologically healed and at peace (to help deactivate the trauma and "rescue of the deceased" responses); invocation of assistance from the deceased in coping with life since the death; resolution of ambivalent feelings about the process of healing and building a changed life; and other purposes that may be agreed upon by the therapist and client. For most clients, this is a middle- to late-stage therapy technique. It is ideal for clients who have been able to integrate the loss on a cognitive and emotional level and to gain some capacity to "dose" or regulate their grief. This ability to voluntarily choose when to go towards or away from their grief usually indicates that the mourner can tolerate an intense "encounter" with the deceased through the technique, and make good use of it in their bereavement recovery.

Steps in leading the guided imaginal conversation

1. *Relaxation*: Extra time should be scheduled to conduct the technique without the client or therapist feeling rushed—generally at least 90 minutes. The procedure begins with a method that helps clients reduce their physiological and psychological arousal in preparation for the conversation. I often begin with a brief exercise that asks clients to become aware of and follow their diaphragmatic breathing (i.e., breathing from the belly, rather than from the upper chest). With eyes closed and sitting in a relaxed posture, clients are simply asked to begin with a deep, relaxing breath, and then to keep their attention focused on their breathing for a few moments, allowing thoughts that may enter the mind to come and then leave without a struggle. This simple process seems to help almost anyone relax, while also setting a norm of openness to whatever experience is about to follow.

2. *Entry*: Following this, eyes closed, the client is invited to imagine walking into a room with two comfortable easy chairs facing each other, ready for the occupants to have a conversation. As the client enters the room, he or she sees that the deceased is there, already seated in one of the chairs, smiling and waiting to greet him or her. As a very important part of this technique, the client is asked to imagine that the deceased is completely healed of all physical illness or injury, and is psychologically at peace. Moreover, the motivation of the deceased is to come and hear whatever the mourner needs to say. This is true regardless of whatever has happened during the relationship in the past, and whatever state the relationship was in at the time of the death. *It is crucial that the mourner be asked to imagine the deceased as healed at every level, and now ready and wanting to be an empathic listener to the mourner's concerns and feelings about any issue.*

3. *Conversation*: Having set this psychological stage, the mourner is now invited to "tell _____ whatever you need them to say to him (or her)." Clients can do this in silence, within their own minds, or out loud, as they choose—although enacting the conversation through vocalization seems to deepen the intensity of it for many people. To help them begin, the clinician may want to offer the client a prompt such as "*What do you want _____ to understand about what their death (or the relationship) has meant to you?*" The prompt can also target an issue the client and therapist have previously identified, such as "*What do you want to say to _____ about the regrets that you have about the relationship?*" or "*What do you wish that you could have said to her before she died?*" After the client has begun, the therapist's job is usually to be silent, allowing the client to have the conversation in whatever fashion they need to do so. After completing what they wish to say to the deceased, the client can then be asked to imagine what the deceased would say in response. This is often a key part of the experience, as the client "hears" what the perspective of the deceased might be. This can allow the mourner to begin to see him or herself, the relationship with the deceased, and the death in a new light, one that can help to shift the narrative that may feel troubling or stuck for the client. Again, this can be done in silence, or out loud.

4. *Closing down*: The guided imaginal conversation should be closed down by asking the client to visualize a leave-taking from this session with the deceased. It should be noted that this does not have to be a "final farewell," as the client can use the technique to return for further conversation with the deceased as needed in the future (part of re-establishing a continuing bond). After the leave-taking, clients can then be brought back to following their breath for a minute or two, and then asked to open their eyes.

5. *Debriefing*: If the client has done the technique in silence, he or she can be invited (though not required) to debrief by sharing some of what transpired during the conversation. It is valuable to ask about what the conversation with the deceased means to the client, particularly what their reactions are to what they have "heard back" from the deceased.

Lastly, having done the technique, it is important to find out about the client's current physical and emotional state. If there are concerns about how clients will handle their reactions after leaving the session, plans should be made for self-soothing, support from friends or family, or contact with the therapist as needed. Clients can also be encouraged to continue to reflect on and journal about the experience, perhaps bringing this to the next session for discussion.

CASE EXAMPLE

Nancy, age 29, was referred for grief counseling by her therapist 18 months after the death of her husband, Brad, from a degenerative neurological disorder. During the last year and a half of his life, as his physical pain increased and his mobility deteriorated, Brad had become depressed, hostile, and overtly suicidal, though it was unclear from the circumstances whether his death was self-inflicted or not. Although she had been a devoted caretaker for Brad and a fierce advocate for him with the medical care system, Nancy reported significant guilt about a decision to separate from him a month before his death, feeling that she abandoned him to die alone. She also had intense yearning for him, wondered whether he was still suffering, and whether she would ever be with him again. A complicating factor was that over the course of therapy, Nancy began dating another man, and felt highly conflicted about whether this represented a betrayal of her husband.

As part of a series of 12 sessions with Nancy, two sessions of guided imaginal conversation were used to address the several problematic aspects of her grief noted above. In the sessions, she was able to visualize an encounter with Brad in which his body was free of pain and disease, his mind was clear, and his mood was peaceful and loving towards her. In one of the sessions, he was surrounded by the small animals that the couple had often befriended and for which they shared a great love. Crucially, she was able to hear him state clearly to her: "I'm okay now. I need you to remember me, but I don't need you to protect me anymore." She also heard from Brad that they would be reunited again, and that the animals would serve as messengers between the two of them while she was on Earth.

Nancy experienced these conversations as liberating, and reported considerable relief from her guilt in the coming weeks. She felt surer that her husband's spirit continued in some way, and described several encounters with animals in which she felt a strong sense of connection with him. She reported a diminution of the intrusive, troubling memories of Brad's tortured physical and emotional state near the end of his life. Lastly, she reported that she felt that she had his permission to go on with her life here, including the new relationship. The therapy went on for a number of sessions after the two guided imaginal conversations, both to consolidate the meanings that they had for Nancy, and to work on additional grief, family, and life issues. Nonetheless, for both the clinician and the client these two sessions appeared to be a turning point in her healing process after a very difficult and troubling loss.

CONCLUDING THOUGHTS

The use of techniques that allow the mourner to psychologically encounter, repair, and rework the relationship with the deceased appears to offer great promise for bereaved persons who are dealing with sudden, unexpected deaths and troubled relationships with the deceased (Brown, 1990; Jordan & McIntosh, 2011; Smith, 1996), and play a major part in evidence-based treatment for complicated grief (Shear et al., 2005). They offer hope that the relationship with the deceased, as a living entity that continues to evolve and grow after the death of a loved one, can become a source of healing from the wounds of loss. When used skillfully at the right time with the right client, guided imaginal conversations can be a powerful means for fostering integration of the loss and psychological growth in bereaved clients.

References

Brown, J. C. (1990). Loss and grief: An overview and guided imagery intervention model. *Journal of Mental Health Counseling, 12*(4), 434–445.

Jordan, J., & McIntosh, J. L. (Eds.). (2011). *Grief after suicide: Understanding the consequences and caring for the survivors.* New York: Routledge.

Shear, K., Frank, E., Houch, P. R., & Reynolds, C. F. (2005). Treatment of complicated grief: A randomized controlled trial. *Journal of the American Medical Association, 293,* 2601–2608.

Smith, B. J. (1996). Uncovering and healing hidden wounds: Using guided imagery and music to resolve complicated and disenfranchised grief. *Journal of the Association for Music & Imagery, 5,* 1–23.

69
Chair Work

Robert A. Neimeyer

CLIENTS FOR WHOM THE TECHNIQUE IS APPROPRIATE

Adults and adolescents burdened with "unfinished business" with the deceased, whether in terms of intense separation distress, anger, guilt or other issues, or who simply want to reorganize an ongoing bond with them of a more fluid and accessible kind. Facilitated dialogues using chair work may be contraindicated for clients who struggle with intense traumatic distress, who are unable to suspend disbelief to engage in an imaginal conversation, or who hold religious beliefs that preclude symbolic conversations with the dead.

DESCRIPTION

Like correspondence with the deceased, chair work and other forms of imaginal dialogue have as their goal reanimating the relationship between the client and the lost figure, either to affirm lasting love and enhance secure attachment, or to address specific difficulties in the relationship (e.g., express disappointment, establish boundaries, extend forgiveness). Importantly, I rarely assume that the goal of imaginal dialogue with the deceased is to "say goodbye," in the sense of "seeking closure" or "withdrawing emotional energy" from the deceased in order to invest it elsewhere, a practice that nonetheless may be appropriate when the living relationship with the deceased was marked by oppression or abuse, making a kind of "divorce" or separation in death the better outcome. Far more commonly, the goal is to renegotiate the relationship as a living resource for the client and therapist to access in their mutual work, and typically for the client to draw upon in the form of affirmative and clarifying inner conversations beyond the bounds of therapy.

My practice of chair work is influenced both by the rich tradition of emotion-focused therapy (Greenberg, 2010) and dialogical self theory (Rowan, 2010), which add usefully to more basic imaginal procedures for facilitating symbolic encounters or conversations with the deceased through the use of positioning and choreography to augment a verbalized or imagined exchange. As I use the terms, *positioning* refers to the projection of the deceased (or relevant others, or aspects of the self) into the various chairs, whereas *choreography* refers to the artful sequencing of steps in the encounter, which commonly involves movement of the client (and sometimes the therapist) among the chairs, both in the active stages of the encounter and during subsequent processing. Here I will offer a personal distillation of procedures I find useful in the context of grief therapy, referring the reader to the more ample presentation of related techniques in the references below.

1. *Setting the stage*: Chairing is a very flexible technique that can be performed with minimal prompts—in the limiting case, two simple chairs that can be placed face to face, the client seated in one, the deceased symbolically placed in the other. In a small office with only two chairs, the therapist can offer his or hers to the client, crouching or kneeling at right angles to two seats so as to be less imposing and intrusive during the facilitated dialogue. Alternatively, a third chair can be brought in and "offered" to the deceased directly across from the client, with the therapist retaining his or her original seat. However, my preferred staging using four chairs as the corners of a "square" is pictured in Figure 69.1 and diagrammed in Figure 69.2, which also adds notation suggesting the choreography of the session, as described below. This permits maximum flexibility in assignment of positions, and representing a default arrangement for therapy, permits fluid shifting into and out of chair work without rearrangement of furniture.

2. *Initiating chair work*: Chairing can be planned, as when a client fearful of confrontation with the deceased is prepared through previous discussion with the therapist or through homework to consider what needs to be voiced in an encounter to follow. More commonly, however, I find that a client's readiness for the technique is suggested by spontaneous comments such as, "*I just want to say to him that . . .,*" "*She'd understand if she were here,*" or other indications of need to address the deceased, or hear from him or her directly. In such cases, without an elaborate preamble, I typically gesture toward the empty chair opposite the client, if our initial juxtaposition to one another reflects the positioning in Figure 69.2,* and simply say something like, "*What would you say to _____ now about that, if she were seated right here with us, and could hear you?*"* If the client initially is positioned opposite me, I will commonly gesture to the empty chair to my right, with the simple invitation, "*Why don't you come over here for a moment . . .?,*" and then extend encouragement to address the deceased in the empty chair opposite, as above. I keep instructions minimal, and do the briefest of acceptance checks on the client's readiness to engage in the imaginal dialogue (e.g., "*I wonder if you would be willing to say that, right now, to him?*"), indicating the empty chair with a slow wave of the hand. In my experience, elaborate prologues and stilted descriptions of the procedure heighten the client's apprehension and deaden the subsequent interaction, bleaching it of spontaneity.

3. *Prompting for honesty and directness*: As the client begins to speak, I redirect my eyes to the empty chair, slightly pivoting in its direction, to reinforce the reality of the encounter and to discourage continued eye contact with me, as I direct the client to

---

* In my basic four-chair configuration, I find that 60% of the time, when I take a chair or "mark" my positioning by leaving a clipboard on the seat, my client will from the first session on take a chair at right angles to my own, typically to my right. Such a position approximates common "living room" conversational positioning, offering the prospect of easy eye contact at a 45-degree angle without it being obligatory, or without visual disengagement by the client seeming defensive, as a gaze that wanders forward would feel natural. Some 30% of the time, however, the client will take the seat directly opposite mine, perhaps signaling greater readiness for direct encounter with high levels of eye contact being the norm. My usual practice is to allow clients discretion regarding initial positioning to enhance their comfort or to construct the relationship with me for which they are ready, and then reposition them as our work requires. This is not the space for a detailed discussion of proxemic factors in therapy, however, beyond those necessary for the present discussion of chairing.

Figure 69.1 Representative staging for chair work offering four positions

the "deceased" with my gaze. Once the dialogue is established, however, I will reorient to the client periodically to follow his or her nonverbal gestures and expressions, as well as to affirm and underscore his or her statements with a head nod or facial signal. I encourage the client's use of first-person "I" language through the use of an incomplete statement relevant to the therapeutic task: "*What I need you to know is . . .*" or "*Tell him about how you are doing now, and what you need from him now. Maybe start by saying, 'Dad, the truth is that I . . .'*" If the client slips into third-person language (e.g., "*I guess I'd tell him that . . .*"), I simply quietly model, "*What I want to tell you is . . .*", and then redirect my gaze to the empty chair. I tag and underscore statements of feeling, and other language that intensifies the connection: "*Tell her more about that 'black hole' you feel,*" or "*What more can you say about what you still need from him, now?*"

4. *Choreographing the exchange*: At a resonant moment of the exchange, when the client has voiced something poignant that calls for the response of the other—much as it might if voiced in a family therapy session—I meet his or her eyes, gesture toward the opposite chair and say something like, "*I wonder if you could come over here now . . .*", and as the client does so, continue, "*. . . and now, just loaning _____ your own voice, what would you say back to [your daughter/your mother, etc.] as she says to you, 'I'll never forgive myself for not being there to protect you . . . you were always there for me . . . and I let you down when you needed me most' [paraphrasing the client briefly]? What do you want to say to her about that?*" I then redirect my gaze to the client's original seat and await the reply, again shaping toward honesty, immediacy, and depth. Once more, typically after a few minutes, I listen for a poignant expression, watch for the

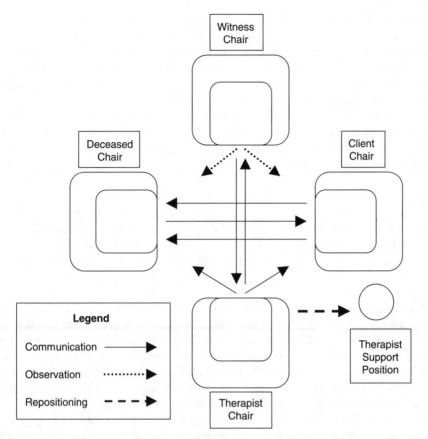

Figure 69.2 Basic configuration for chair work, with positioning and choreography of imaginal conversation between client and the deceased

emergence of strong emotion, wait for a pregnant pause, and then, just as I would in any other couples or family session, redirect the client to his or her original seat and invite a response. I continue to orchestrate the interaction in this way to a point of natural completion of the exchange or until the client meets with an insuperable impasse or meets my eyes with an obvious need to process that which has emerged, which might typically range from 5 to 15 minutes of interaction between the two positions.

5. *Shifting into processing*: During the imaginal conversation I work consistently to minimize slippage into commentary (e.g., "*I don't know if he'd want to hear that, because . . .*" by interrupting tactfully and reframing the statement into dialogue (e.g., "*I don't know if you really want to hear this, but . . .*") to retain the strongly experiential quality of the work, within which nearly all change occurs. However, once novel material has emerged and a given episode of dialogue concluded, commentary is frequently essential to harvest its implications. To foster this, I commonly invite the client to shift to a third "witness" chair (see Figure 69.2), and say something like, "*I imagine that a part of you was listening in to the dialogue that just unfolded here . . . What caught your attention about the relationship between the two of them, or what did you observe that seemed important?*" Although in canonical emotion-focused therapy clients are simply directed back to their original chair for the purposes of such processing, the fact that they are back in their familiar position, oriented inadvertently toward the seat occupied by the

"deceased," discourages self-observation, and tends to concentrate unduly on observations about the other (e.g., "*He didn't seem to be really listening to me*"). In contrast, when offered the "meta-position" of the witness chair, the client is more likely to grasp features of the relationship (e.g., "*I can't believe how much it still sounds like it did when I was a little girl*") or to share observations about the self (e.g., "*I really seemed to have a hard time standing up to her!*"). I follow the client's lead in making interpretations, sometimes volunteering an observation and inviting the client's sense of it (e.g., "*Did you notice his tone of voice when he said _____? What did you make of that?*"). Ultimately, we shift back into our original positions to bring the session to a close, or to pursue another line of work.

Variations

The schematic outline above invites many elaborations. Here I will note only a few of these briefly, deferring to written or videotaped extensions of this work to provide more ample illustrations than a brief chapter permits (Neimeyer, 2004; Neimeyer, Burke, Mackay, & Stringer, 2010).

1. *Voicing nonverbal meanings*: In the course of the imaginal conversation, the therapist can note significant gestures, expressions or bodily positions, and ask the client to voice these into the dialogue without further commentary or interpretation (e.g., "*What are you doing with your hands right now? Can you do that again, more forcefully? What are you trying to do there?*" "*Just reach him, I guess.*" "*Could you say that to him directly, 'I'm really trying to reach you, to get through to you'?*"). The dialogue then continues with this new communication taken into account.

2. *Moving into alignment*: As depicted in Figure 69.2, the therapist can signal greater support for a client during a difficult exchange by shifting position to kneel or crouch beside him or her, looking at the deceased, and continuing as before (e.g., "*Could you tell him that again, even more strongly . . . 'Dad, you just weren't there for me'?*"). Still stronger support, as in the context of "unfinished business" deriving from emotional, physical or sexual abuse of the client by the deceased, can be signaled by the therapist's literally standing alongside the seated client while prompting the client toward a position of strength (e.g., "*Try telling him, 'You can never hurt me again.'*"). I find that the more acute the angle between the client and therapist, the more intense is his or her sense of being supported by my positioning. However, I rarely align with the deceased in this way, as it can easily be experienced as a "two-on-one" joining against the client, who is thereby triangulated out.

3. *Interviewing the deceased*: Inviting the client to role play the deceased, the therapist can interview him or her about the client's strengths, needs, and special qualities, or about particular concerns in the relationship, after first learning from the client how it would be appropriate to address him or her (e.g., "*Sarah, I've been talking to your daughter Rebecca here for the past few weeks, and she's a little concerned that if she moves to another city other than this one that she has always shared with you, she'll be abandoning you in some way. What do you think of that?*" or "*Mr. Davis, what do you consider your son's special qualities as man, the things you were most proud of in him? What fatherly advice would you give him now?*"). This often allows the client to access voice of the internalized other, with the therapist asking questions that client might not, to healing effect.

4. *Dialoguing with other parts of the self*: Rather than have an imaginal dialogue with the deceased, the client could usefully engage another aspect of the self (e.g., this

frightened little girl in her), a source of wise counsel (e.g., God or the self as spiritual seeker), or even his or her symptomatology (e.g., having a dialogue with his personified "grief" or "suffering," staying close to the client's own language, to learn more about its role and purposes in his or her life).

5. *Doubling for the client*: From the "support" position standing close alongside the client, the therapist can gently ask permission to touch the client's shoulder in the course of an imaginal dialogue, noting briefly than in doing so, he or she will "stand in" for the client for a single conversational turn. This allows the therapist to articulate an implicit feeling or need hinted at, but not fully voiced by the client (e.g., "*When I place my hand on your shoulder, let me offer something, just to see if it feels emotionally true to you. If it does, then when I take my hand away, you can continue, just as if you had said that.*"). If the therapist is attuned to the client's affective meanings, this can be a powerful way of prompting the interaction toward greater depth and clarity (e.g., "*The truth is, Mom, I'm still trying to win your love.*"). As in nearly all therapy, the power of the statement is inversely correlated with its length.

6. *Using the empty chair*: Instead of rotating the client to the empty chair to speak on behalf of the other, the therapist can simply prompt a monological voicing of the client's position vis-à-vis the other (e.g., "*What do you need to tell her about that? Can you say that to her, now?*"). Not repositioning the client into the chair of the other can effectively silence that position, which may be appropriate in cases of oppression or abuse, allowing the client to speak his or her truth without broaching contradiction or retribution.

The following case briefly illustrates some of these procedures.

CASE EXAMPLE

Maria, at 45, sought therapy for a longstanding low-grade depression that had characterized much of her adult life. Though she had been reasonably successful in her career as a nutritionist, she felt unfulfilled, lonely, and vulnerable to feeling "left out" of social arrangements, leading her to retreat into a private world filled with books and solitary walks. Though married from the age of 20 to Tony and reportedly having experienced little conflict with him, their somewhat "roommate-like" relationship did little to mitigate her sense of aloneness in the world, even if it was hard for her to say what needed to change.

As we explored the origins of her chronic susceptibility to sadness (which had proven unresponsive to several attempts at pharmacotherapy and marriage counseling), we found that it dated from a difficult time in her early twenties, when she miscarried an unplanned pregnancy, and shortly thereafter chose to terminate a second pregnancy because, Maria said, she and Tony "were not ready to be parents." Asking if she knew the sex of the child, I watched her eyes fill with tears as she said she was "a baby girl." Seeing her obvious emotional investment in the baby, I gently asked if she had given her a name. "Olivia," she whispered, voicing her daughter's name for the first time in over 20 years. It soon became clear that much of what she had experienced as depression was better understood as grief tinged with regret and guilt about the fateful decision that left her childless, with much to be said about and to the child who she and Tony chose not to bring into the world and into their home. Wondering aloud if this were the case, I saw her nod slowly and sadly, opening the prospect of an imaginal conversation in the place of the one that had never taken place.

Standing, I collected a lap blanket thrown over the arm of one chair, and rolled it into a small bundle, laying it gingerly on a cushion in the empty chair opposite Maria to represent Olivia. "What might you say to her now," I asked, "if she could hear and understand what she could not at that difficult time?" Quietly, looking down, Maria replied that she felt like the child, helpless and unprepared, and then fell silent for several seconds. Lifting her right hand to her throat, she noted, "I feel very . . . constricted about it . . . I was so idealistic about being a parent, so afraid of the responsibility . . . It was easier to let Tony make the decision, and I just went along with it. But I've had to live with it ever since." Prompting her toward still greater depth, I offered, "I have had to live with this decision, rather than with you." Maria, weeping openly now, modified this and stated to Olivia, "I have had to live with this decision . . . I would rather have lived with you."

Continuing, I asked her to tell her daughter what she would have wanted for her. "Two loving parents," was her reply, "who were not afraid of you. I was afraid I would not be what you needed . . . But I still loved you." "I do love you," I offered in the present tense. Maria repeated this movingly, then hesitated, and added, "What comes to me is that it should have been enough . . . but I had my own needs." Encouraging her to voice these, I listened as she spoke to her daughter about her own need for "support, and for enough commitment in the marriage relationship." But Tony, she said, "had one foot out the door always . . . and I do the same thing." Looking directly into my eyes, she broke the frame of imaginal dialogue, and remarked, nodding sadly, "It wouldn't have worked for either of us to have someone too needy or clingy." "Like Olivia," I suggested. Nodding, Maria added, "or each other."

Moving to the witness chair to process the experience, Maria connected her decision at age 22 to her own experience as a child of a "dad who was irresponsible in all roles," leaving her to be raised by a single mother who was woefully inadequate to the task. She immediately flashed to Tony's critical absence on work-related travel when she miscarried the first child, and the way in which "he had never connected to [her] losses, but was just absent to it all." Maria at 22, she noted, "carried around a lot of anger about that, and it came out as distance, which he enjoyed." "So even in your distance," I noted, "you gave him what he wanted." Furrowing her brow, Maria added, "and what I want." We went on to discuss her stance of self-protection from further abandonment, cultivated across a lifetime, purchased at the price of great emptiness. Further chair work between Maria at 45 and Maria at 22 followed, leading to deepened self-compassion, and a joint resolve to face their shared grief over their losses, and to "look for an opening" to greater intimacy in relationships in general, and her marriage in particular.

CONCLUDING THOUGHTS

As a vividly experiential intervention that invites immediacy and vulnerability with the deceased, with the therapist, and with the client's self, chair work requires a sense of discernment on the part of an experienced therapist, as well as some delicacy in guiding the imaginal dialogue toward a more satisfying resolution. Because it is typically emotionally intense, it should be used only once a strong therapeutic alliance is in place and the client has demonstrated an ability to engage in adaptive emotional modulation and meaning making in relation to other material. Imaginal dialogues play a central role in demonstrably effective therapy for complicated grief, as assessed in a randomized controlled trial (Shear, Frank, Houch, & Reynolds, 2005), and fit broadly with a dialogical theory of self that carries rich practical implications for grief therapy (Neimeyer, 2011). With sufficient training and attunement on the part of the therapist, and courage and openness on the part of the client, chair work can promote healing conversations with the self and deceased that transcend even the silence of the grave.

References

Greenberg, L. S. (2010). *Emotion focused psychotherapy*. Washington, DC: American Psychological Association.

Neimeyer, R. A. (2004). Constructivist psychotherapy. On *Series 1: Systems of psychotherapy* [VHS video/DVD]. Washington, DC: American Psychological Association.

Neimeyer, R. A. (2011). Reconstructing the self in the wake of loss: A dialogical contribution. In H. Hermans, & T. Gieser (Eds.), *Handbook on the dialogical self.* Cambridge: Cambridge University Press.

Neimeyer, R. A., Burke, L., Mackay, M., & Stringer, J. (2010). Grief therapy and the reconstruction of meaning: From principles to practice. *Journal of Contemporary Psychotherapy, 40*, 73–84.

Rowan, J. (2010). *Personification.* New York: Routledge.

Shear, K., Frank, E., Houch, P. R., & Reynolds, C. F. (2005). Treatment of complicated grief: A randomized controlled trial. *Journal of the American Medical Association, 293*, 2601–2608.

70

The Life Imprint

Robert A. Neimeyer

CLIENTS FOR WHOM THE TECHNIQUE IS APPROPRIATE

Adolescents and adults reorganizing a continuing bond with the deceased typically benefit from the life imprint. However, those who are struggling in the immediate aftermath of a loss may find it premature.

DESCRIPTION

In a sense, we are all "pastiche personalities," reflecting bits and pieces of the many people whose characteristics and values we have unconsciously assimilated into our own sense of identity. This "inheritance" transcends genetics, as we can be powerfully or subtly shaped not only by parents, but also by mentors, friends, siblings, or even children we have loved and lost. Nor are these life imprints always positive: at times, we can trace our self-criticism, distrust, fears, and emotional distance to once influential relationships that are now with us only internally. In therapy with the bereaved, whether individual or in a group context, I often innovate upon Vickio's (1999) *life imprint* concept and extend it into a therapeutic assignment, which can be undertaken as homework or used as an exercise in group therapy or workshop settings. This involves encouraging clients to reflect upon someone they have loved and lost, and privately to trace his or her imprint on their lives at any of the following levels that apply, writing a phrase, sentence or (in homework applications where more time is available) paragraph about each. Then, at the client's discretion, I invite them to discuss their observations with one or two partners in the context of group work, or with me in the context of individual therapy. The basic framework for reflecting on this follows:

> The person whose imprint I want to trace is: _____
> This person has had the following impact on:
>   *My mannerisms or gestures:*
>   *My ways of speaking and communicating:*
>   *My work and pastime activities:*
>   *My feelings about myself and others:*
>   *My basic personality:*
>   *My values and beliefs:*

The imprints I would most like to affirm and develop are:_____
The imprints I would most like to relinquish or change are: _____

I include the latter two prompts in recognition that life imprints are sometimes ambivalent, so that even a loved figure (e.g., a devoted mother) may exemplify some traits (e.g., a tendency toward martyrdom) that the client would prefer to let go of in her own life. In cases of extremely conflicted relationships, for example, with a critical and rejecting father, the client might discover a "negative imprint" that has powerfully shaped his or her life by modeling "what *not* to be." But like a photographic negative, such imprints are no less influential and important for being reverse models for the client's later construction of self.

Usually clients find this a very affirming exercise, one that strengthens their sense of a continuing bond to their deceased loved one, while also conveying that this person continues to live on, in a significant sense, through the client's own life. Moreover, the subsequent sharing phase, especially in a group work setting, commonly leads to a sense of affirmation and joy as clients tell stories of the loved one's life and impact to responsive others. However, even when the imprint revealed is negative, this can usefully focus discussion on what might be done to relinquish it, often in the form of a healing ritual. Special care should be taken when clients have lost a largely negative or ambivalently regarded figure, such as an abusive or neglectful parent; in such cases more time should be spent processing the conflicted feeling the life imprint can engender.

CASE EXAMPLE

Pursuing the use of the life imprint in a joint therapeutic session, Cristina and her adult daughter Nuria each took a few minutes to write about the impact of Jose, the recently deceased husband and father of the family, on their sense of who they were as individuals. In subsequent sharing prompted by the therapist in the same session, Nuria looked on intently as Cristina described movingly how she now carried the confidence her partner had always had in her, as when he supported her to study for an advanced degree despite her own insecurity about her ability to do so, and how his undying love for her, even after they had lost an earlier child to stillbirth, instilled hope in her and let her embrace the decision to "try again." Cristina was then affirmed as Nuria, the product of this second attempt at building a family, related how the memory of her father's playful engagement with her through her youth, and his dying expression of pride in her as she entered womanhood, now gave her conviction to live passionately and to pursue her own ambitions. Through a veil of tears, each woman then gazed into the eyes of the other and embraced, feeling Jose's presence as another set of arms wrapped around them both.

CONCLUDING THOUGHTS

Writing and disclosing about the bond with the deceased is coherent with evidence on evolving narrative practices in grief therapy (Neimeyer, 1998; Neimeyer et al., 2009). Variations on the basic life imprint include having the client note his or her mood in a word or two or phrase following the reflective writing portion of the assignment, and then again following the social sharing. This commonly reveals a shift from a sense of grief to celebration, although many individual variations are possible, which might suggest whether further journaling or guided disclosure might be more therapeutic for a given person. Likewise, I have found the life imprint to be strong medicine to administer when the client is actively losing a loved one to debilitating illness, when it can shift attention usefully from a preoccupation with managing the disease to appreciating the life legacy of the ill or dying person. Finally, some clients have innovated further on the method by using it as an "interview" structure to document the imprint of their loved one on mutually known others, which greatly extends and validates the deceased person's impact on the world. Honoring the life and legacy of the lost loved one seems to mitigate grief in the great majority of cases, and helps focus the client on life purposes and activities that continue to connect their lives with those who have gone before.

References

Neimeyer, R. A. (1998). *Lessons of loss: A guide to coping.* Memphis: Mercury. Translations: *Aprender de la perdida.* Barcelona: Paidos [2002, 2007, Spanish]; *To those who have lost something important.* Tokyo: Shunjusha [2006, Japanese]; *To love and to lose: Coping with loss.* Athens: Kritiki [2006, Greek].

Neimeyer, R. A., van Dyke, J. G., & Pennebaker, J. W. (2009). Narrative medicine: Writing through bereavement. In H. Chochinov, & W. Breitbart (Eds.), *Handbook of psychiatry in palliative medicine.* New York: Oxford University Press.

Vickio, C. (1999). Together in spirit: Keeping our relationships alive when loved ones die. *Death Studies, 23,* 161–175.

71

Reaching through Sorrow to Legacy

Thomas Attig

CLIENTS FOR WHOM THE TECHNIQUE IS APPROPRIATE

Anyone, adult or child, living with sorrow in bereavement, whether the death occurred recently or years ago. Seriously troubling aspects of the client's experience, e.g., traumatic circumstances of the death or negative aspects of the relationship (including, but not only, abuse) should be addressed prior to using the technique.

DESCRIPTION

Remembering the dead plays a vital role as the bereaved relearn the world in grief. It can seem as if the world reminds them of their loved ones no matter where they turn. At times, often while lying awake, memories flood their consciousness. At other times, they deliberately strive to recall something in particular, to remember with others, or to reflect on the significance of what they remember. Through remembering they find meanings in their losses, the lives of their loved ones, their ties with them, and their individual, family, and community lives shadowed by loss and separation from those they mourn.

The bereaved can cherish those they love and their legacies only if they remember. Failure to remember adds to their sense of separation, leaving them holding their loved ones only in the pain of missing them. Silence of the world about the dead, or in some cases insistence on silence, adds to their pain, suggesting that their loved ones were barely noticed or are easily forgotten, making the world seem cold and indifferent, isolating them in their grief, and increasing their sense of separation. They may feel guilty when they acquiesce in silence even as it deprives them of the riches of memory.

Memory brings aspects of the past into present awareness. Conscious remembering and sharing enrich present living. In memory, the bereaved can connect with some of the best in life, reclaiming and cherishing legacies, feeling the warmth of love for their loved ones and sensing the warmth of love in return, and meeting their loved ones again in praise, gratitude, and joy.

When a loved one dies, the bereaved have a world to relearn, struggling to be "at home" in the world again (soul work) and to reshape their daily lives and stretch into the new chapters of their life stories (spirit work). They meet the souls and spirits of their loved ones in the world around them, in the things, places, food and music, and social settings they leave behind. And they meet them within their selves, in aspects of their ways of being who they are that are like, or have been influenced by, their loved ones—motivations, dispositions, desires, interests, values, behaviors, habits, souls, spirits, and aspirations to be more like their loved ones.

Ironically, the bereaved often miss their loved ones most in precisely the places in their surroundings or within themselves where they can, potentially, feel most connected with them. Those places in the worlds of their experience remind them not only of separation but also of stories of their loved ones' lives, their characters, and how they touched and shaped them, their families, and their communities. If the bereaved flee from the pain of separation in those places, they will miss that deeper connection with them and what they still love about them. If they can reach through, or look past, that pain, they can reconnect with the dead and find love in separation. As they reach through the sorrow in separation that shadows positive memories, they can recognize and harvest the legacies of those they mourn: memories themselves; material inheritances; and practical, soulful, and spiritual lessons for, and influences in, living.

The technique I recommend here invites the bereaved to reflect on their experiences of reaching through sorrow to legacy. It is an exercise I have used with groups in workshop settings. Guided imagery and reflection, followed by discussion with a partner and then the whole group, heighten awareness of the varieties of experiences of remembering the dead, show how reaching through painful reminders of separation is possible, and support harvesting of precious legacies. This exercise can very easily be adapted for a counseling setting where the imagery and reflection are followed by discussion with the counselor.

1. *The set-up*: After cautioning participants to care for themselves by turning their attention away from my voice if they feel the need, I tell them I will ask them to reflect on features in the world that remind them painfully of someone they love who has died. I ask them to choose a partner for processing later. I ask them to find a comfortable position, close their eyes, and attend to their breathing to promote centering and relaxation.

2. *Focusing on a particular person*: Reflection begins with remembering someone very close to them who has died. I ask them to bring an image of the person to mind and to remember him or her as vividly as possible. I urge them to set aside memories of troubles between them and the person they are remembering (reminding them that we are all, after all, imperfect people in imperfect relationships). Instead, I encourage them to recall a few things about their loved one at his or her best, what is most precious or irreplaceable about him or her, what they are most grateful for, or what they miss most.

3. *Recalling sorrow*: Once they have their loved one fully in mind, I ask them to recall returning home from his or her funeral or memorial service to the world where he or she was newly dead, remembering themselves in familiar surroundings and daily life and facing the future in physical separation from their loved one. I ask them to think of the things, places, people, and the life they have to live that their loved one left behind: the personal effects (e.g., items used every day or clothing); things he or she played with, worked with, created, or gave to them; places in or away from their home; members of their family or friends; activities or experiences he or she used to be a part of; their own responsibilities, hopes, and dreams. I ask them to think of how first meetings with any of these things could remind them of their loved one's absence. And I ask them to remember their sorrow and its hold on them in such encounters.

4. *Attending to one particularly painful reminder of separation*: I then ask them to focus on one particular thing, place, person, or aspect of their own life or character that was especially challenging to face because of how powerfully it reminded them of

separation from their loved one. I ask them to recall the intensity and poignancy of their feelings of sorrow over separation in their first meeting with it.

5. *Reaching through sorrow to legacy*: Having done so, I ask them to do their best to reach through the pain of that sorrow and to attend to other memories held in the thing, place, person, or aspect of their own life or character they are thinking of. *"How or why did your loved one come to care about it so deeply?" "How did your loved one pour his or her soul or spirit into, influence, or even change, it?" "How does it remind you of aspects of your loved one's life story that you hold dear?" "How does it remind you of some of the most precious or joyous times in your life together?" "How is it in itself, or does it remind you of, practical, soulful, or spiritual legacies, or gifts, from your loved one?" "Does it remind you of life lessons or changes in yourself and your life that derive from sharing life with your loved one?"*

If they are moved to do so, I ask them to pause to silently thank their loved one for the gifts they are then remembering. I tell them that in a few minutes I will ask them to open their eyes and to share thoughts and feelings about this experience with their partners. When I ask them to open their eyes, I thank them for their good efforts. Then I ask them to turn to their partners to discuss this experience by taking turns responding to these questions: *"What thing, place, person, or aspect of your life or character did you have in mind?" "What other memories, besides the reminder of separation, does it hold?" "What was it like for you to retrieve those memories; recognize delights, lessons and legacies in them; and reconnect with your loved one?"*

CASE EXAMPLE

Upon completing this exercise in a workshop, a middle-aged woman, Mary, asked if she could tell the story of the locket she was wearing around her neck. When I said she could, Mary said she had had a turbulent relationship with her mother, always sensing that her mother had not loved her as much as her siblings.

A year prior to the workshop, Mary's mother was dying after a long struggle with cancer. While Mary attended at her bedside, her mother acknowledged how challenging their relationship had been at times but insisted that she held each of her children in a special place in her heart. Mary found it hard to believe, but did not want to argue as she had so often before. When her mother asked her to think of their lives together, Mary acquiesced. They spent quite some time reminiscing about important times when Mary was growing up, entering adulthood, and beginning a family of her own, laughing and crying as they did. After a "wonderful conversation," her mother took the locket she had worn for many years from around her neck and pressed it into Mary's hand. Mary was deeply touched by the gesture.

After her mother's death, the locket was very challenging for Mary, reminding her of her mother's absence more than anything else. She wore it occasionally, but only reluctantly and usually after crying before putting it on. It was several months before it occurred to Mary to wonder whether her mother kept anything in the locket, and she decided to open it. As she did so, she found it contained a picture of herself as a little girl and a locket of her then curly, blonde hair. Through all the years Mary had doubted her mother's love for her, her mother had held these memories of her childhood in the locket that she wore so close to her heart. Mary said that she now wears the locket most every day, not in sadness at her separation from her mother, but in recognition of how her mother held her close even when she made it difficult for her to do so.

CONCLUDING THOUGHTS

As workshop participants move through discussion, they regularly move from sadness, even tears, as they recall the pain of separation, to smiles, even laughter, as they recall precious memories and other legacies they still hold. Few report surprises like Mary's, but nearly all report success in reconnecting with cherished legacies.

I have long held that nothing is more difficult for the bereaved but also more rewarding than moving from loving in presence to loving in separation (Attig, 2000). Helping grievers to reach through the sorrow of separation, as this technique does, is surely a key to helping them make this life-affirming transition.

Reference

Attig, T. (2000). *The heart of grief: death and the search for lasting love*. New York: Oxford University Press.

72

"Moments Held" Documentary

Todd Hochberg

CLIENTS FOR WHOM THE TECHNIQUE IS APPROPRIATE

Individuals in a period of transition, particularly those struggling with serious illness, impending death, or bereavement. However, building legacy using these tools does not supplant the need for professional counseling when the person is troubled by intense regret, personal or family conflict or complicated grief.

DESCRIPTION

The term *legacy* typically refers to that which one leaves to family, community, profession or society, often referring to accomplishments, values or progeny. Legacy practitioners generally guide clients through life review. I view legacy work as a personal, emotional and spiritual exploration of one's place during the time of a life transition in addition to oral histories—the stories that often inform through metaphor who we are and what we value. The majority of my work is done with individuals nearing the end of life. Considering the importance of meaning-making when one's world is disrupted by serious illness, impending death or loss, the telling of one's story may possess great therapeutic benefit. Legacy is thus more akin to the Jewish tradition of an ethical will, sharing values and gifts of emotional relevance with loved ones and others (Baines, 2002).

This activity may also be considered ritual. It can reframe or transform an experience or perspective and open space to begin to integrate challenging circumstances or feelings (Harvey, 1996; Sontag, 2003).

I use the documentary form in my work. As storytellers, photographs are powerful aids to narrative and expression of emotion. Images may ultimately serve as touchstones for feelings and memories pertaining to a specific experience or transition circumstance; their use over time may contribute to one's emotional healing. (See Figure 72.1.)

The additional use of video affords individuals an opportunity to speak, be heard and potentially share what they may want to say to family and friends at a time of their choosing in a supportive, creative space. This video work begins with a few open-ended questions that then lead into deeper discussion. My approach is to record thoughts and feelings spontaneously, in the moment, yet some clients feel they need preparation time, in which case I provide the questions in advance of our meeting. The questions are tailored to the individual yet are broad enough that the client can interpret and go where he or she needs to in formulating a response.

Figure 72.1 Bob

Source: Photograph copyright Todd Hochberg.

As example:

- *Can you tell me something about yourself?*
- *What have been your passions in your life?*
- *What is most important to you right now, today?*
- *Describe your family, those relationships and significant others.*
- *How has your life changed since your illness began? And today?*
- *What has buoyed you most through this time of illness?*

Answers lead to further conversation and may diverge entirely from the planned questions. Often stories emerge that illustrate and inform the individual's current sense of self and challenges.

The sessions are 2–3 hours in length distributed over one or two visits. The resultant album of images and edited video DVD are delivered at a meeting with clients where we view and discuss the work, and these sessions are often therapeutic as well. Watching and listening to themselves reveal deep personal truths and feelings offers validation, inspires new self-inquiry and engenders pride and joy in the creation that will endure. Family and others who view the work are offered a new perspective on the client's place in their shared lives, often opening a dialogue that enhances relationships and new meaning at this crucial time for all. It is a privilege to sit beside those who engage in this process.

CASE EXAMPLE

Bob was a 46-year-old cancer patient with a second metastasis to his lungs, undergoing chemo-therapy. Two and a half years into his illness, he had a sense now through consultation with his oncologist that he would likely not live another year. He chose to do this work, embracing the process as he did everything and everyone he encountered now in his life. Bob spoke warmly of his love for his wife of 17 years, Adriana, and his two adopted children ages 12 and 11. We began at their dinner table with storytelling and laughter. The children, excited by the presence of the camera, quickly usurped my role as interviewer. Shyly yet certainly, they asked mom and Bob questions they had never asked before about their past and relationships to them and each other. There was discussion about Bob's long illness and its impact on the family. Bobby admitted, when prompted by his sister Melissa, that he was fearful about being in Bob's presence for nearly two weeks after his surgery. The deep wound in his neck altered Bob's appearance. Bobby repeated, turning toward Bob in a tender, heartfelt apologetic tone, "It's not that I hated you, I was just scared." In another private session, Bob shared, "When I grew up, my grandfather passed on a bunch of skills to me of being able to repair things, do things. Then my father added to that . . . I still have the first car I ever owned [a 1969 Roadrunner], and always had a dream of Bobby and me working on it together . . . It really hurts me knowing that maybe that dream may not come true. I had so many things planned for us to do as a father and son team . . . now I just don't know." Tearfully, he also talked about his fear of not being present at his daughter's wedding years from now to walk her down the aisle.

Upon later sharing the photos and video with the family, they responded with smiles, laughter and tears throughout the 45 minutes. When the DVD ended, the living room was quiet. With a start, Bobby burst out with a grin, "I didn't know I was getting the Road Runner!" I then watched as Melissa silently, solemnly, stood up from her rocking chair and walked toward

Figure 72.2 "I just don't know what is going to be when I wake up. I try to cherish every day now."

Source: Photograph copyright Todd Hochberg.

Figure 72.3 "I like to spend time with my dogs when I'm out walking. Brownie, a Golden Retriever and Murray, a Smooth Collie, are both buried here."

Source: Photograph copyright Todd Hochberg.

the couch and snuggled beside Bob, leaning her head into his shoulder and pulling his arm around her.

Bob had shared much with me about his children and his dying that he had not as yet shared with them directly and yet he assured me that he wanted to, made easier through the conduit of this work (later explaining to me that at the time, as a father, he could not speak directly to them about his own death). The kids became ever closer to dad, opening communication and exploring uncharted relational territory together. They all agreed that they hadn't had fun like the time spent in this work since before Bob's initial diagnosis two years earlier. After Bob's death, the family used the images and video to lovingly remember their precious time together and that which Bob held dear, including displaying of the images and playing the DVD at the visitation and funeral. Adriana shared that now, four years later, watching and hearing his voice brings them great comfort.

Video clips of Bob may be viewed at www.momentsheld.org.

CONCLUDING THOUGHTS

Complementary to traditional therapeutic modalities, legacy work can be very effective for both the dying and the bereaved. As a family process/activity much gold can be gleaned. "A project" is oftentimes what a family seeks as a diversion that simultaneously serves to validate and strengthen bonds of love. For individuals who find daunting solitary inwardly probing legacy activities like journaling, this guided process may be very appropriate. As Bob put it, "We've all been given journals to write in . . . the pages are blank . . . we wouldn't have done this on our own," and "I like this a lot . . . it comes from my heart . . . we just wouldn't have had this time, the kids and everything. We had a lot of fun . . . it was very rewarding . . . [When] I pass away; they do have something instead of nothing . . . I thought I was leaving them nothing."

References

Baines, B. K. (2002). *Ethical wills*. Cambridge, MA: Da Capo Press.
Harvey, J. H. (1996). *Embracing their memory*. Needham Heights, MA: Allyn & Bacon.
Sontag, S. (2003). *Regarding the pain of others*. New York: Picador.

Part XIII
Revising Goals

73

Goal Setting for Self-Care
During the Grieving Process

Laura E. Holcomb

CLIENTS FOR WHOM THE TECHNIQUE IS APPROPRIATE

Most bereaved adults can benefit from some form of goal setting and activity scheduling, especially those who have been widowed or who are experiencing complicated grief. These techniques are less feasible to implement with children, and less relevant for those engaging in adequate self-care.

DESCRIPTION

After the loss of a loved one, intense grief can cause even basic self-care activities such as daily hygiene, eating, intake of adequate fluids, and getting enough sleep to become challenging. Self-care behaviors important to managing health problems, such as blood glucose monitoring for Type II diabetes or remembering to take medications for hypertension, may be neglected. Social contact may also be avoided.

Two groups of grievers who may have special difficulties with self-care are bereaved spouses and those with complicated grief. The bereaved spouse may struggle with taking on responsibilities once performed by the deceased spouse (Caserta & Lund, 2007), such as housework, household maintenance, preparing meals, or paying bills. They may also avoid social activities that they previously enjoyed with the spouse. Those with complicated grief engage less frequently than healthy non-grievers in personal contact with others, eating meals, going outside, starting work (including housework or volunteer activities), and exercising (Monk et al., 2006).

Therapists can assist the griever in reducing the overwhelming snowball of self-care challenges into manageable parts by providing guidance in setting appropriate self-care goals, monitoring progress, and providing support for maintenance of these goals. The following series of steps may be helpful to use with those experiencing grief-related problems with self-care:

1. *Identify self-care problems*: During the initial interview, ask about important self-care behaviors such as intake of food and fluids, personal hygiene, sleep hygiene, social contact, management of chronic health problems, and keeping up with household management. If further information is desired, it may be helpful to ask the griever to keep a log of frequencies of behaviors in question. While keeping a log may seem

daunting for some experiencing intense grief in early bereavement, for many, the act of keeping a log may be a helpful intervention in itself, resulting in an improvement because of increased focus on the behavior and anticipation of reporting back to the therapist.

2. *Prioritize self-care problems*: Assist the griever in determining which problems are in most urgent need of addressing, starting with any problems with potential to result in significant harm in the short term.

3. *Then focus on one problem at a time*: Some grievers may have difficulty staying focused if there are multiple problems concerning them. Gently bring them back to the problem in question.

4. *Choose an appropriate goal to address the problem*: The goal should be one that takes the griever just a small step forward. They should be able to imagine successfully engaging in the behavior necessary to reach this goal. If there are multiple options, ask which goal seems easiest to implement at this time.

5. *Phrase the goal carefully*: Start the goal with "I will . . .," as the griever can only control his or her own behaviors. The goal statement should make clear what specific behavior they will be engaging in, for what duration, and when/how often the behavior will occur. It should be clear how to know when the goal has been accomplished. Examples of good goals are, "I will call at least one person each day" and, "I will walk around the block every other day at 3 p.m." Examples of poor goals are, "I will try to get more sleep" and "I will get out of the house more." (These guidelines roughly follow SMART goals: Specific, Measurable, Achievable, Relevant, Timely (Sage et al., 2008).) Also consider using the "Implementation Intention" goal format of "If situation X is encountered, then I will do Y," where a goal is associated with a situational cue (Gollwitzer & Oettingen, 2007). One example of this format is, "If someone calls and invites me to go out to lunch, I will accept, even if I don't think I will be good company."

6. *Consider possible obstacles*: Discussing how to prevent or handle possible obstacles to reaching the goal may increase chances of success.

7. *Monitor progress*: Provide praise for progress! Modify goals and troubleshoot if necessary.

CASE EXAMPLE

Jim, a 69-year-old man, was referred to grief therapy by his primary care provider. His wife of 44 years, Pat, had died of Alzheimer's Disease two months ago. Jim had gained 50 lbs. in the last two years prior to his wife's death, eating foods ordered for delivery to his home, as Pat was no longer able to do the cooking. He no longer played golf with friends, as his caretaking responsibilities for Pat increased. Jim was recently diagnosed with Type II diabetes.

Since Pat's death, Jim had been surprised at the intensity of his grief. He had felt Pat slipping away for a while but the lack of her physical presence and losing his role as caretaker left him feeling lost. He had been spending a lot of time watching TV, eating only home-delivered food and pre-packaged foods high in fat and calories, and taking frequent naps to escape his pain and loneliness. He rarely left the house. He had not been checking his blood sugars and had been forgetting to take metformin. His last hemoglobin A1c (HbA1c) level was 8.3, which he understands is too high.

Jim was able to help identify his self-care problems that needed addressing—obesity, poor eating behaviors, lack of exercise, lack of social contact, excessive sleep, and non-adherence to his medication regimen. But he felt overwhelmed and unable to figure out where to start in addressing these problems. The therapist suggested to Jim that not taking diabetes medication seemed the most harmful problem in the short term, and he agreed that this would be a good place to start.

He agreed upon the initial goal of, "I will move my medications from the medicine cabinet in the bathroom to a basket on my kitchen table when I get home from this appointment," so that he would be more likely to see them and remember to take them. He thought a possible obstacle to following through with this goal was that he could forget to move the medications, so the therapist wrote a reminder on a sticky note that he attached to his wallet.

The following session, Jim indicated that he had moved the medication to the kitchen table and remembered to take it first thing in the morning when drinking coffee at the table. However, on several days he forgot the late afternoon dosage, as he was typically sitting on the couch watching TV and did not see the medication basket in the kitchen. He and the therapist agreed upon additional goals of, "I will put an alarm clock in the basket with my medication when I get home today" (again written on a sticky note), and "Each morning when I take my medication, I will set the alarm clock for 4 p.m. to remind me to take my late afternoon dosage."

During continued therapy, Jim and the therapist spent part of each session focusing on goal-setting work, and part of the session focusing on Jim's feelings about loss and change, helping him to find meaning in his prior caretaking experience and his wife's death. He was able to follow through with goals to call friends to play golf regularly, to keep logs of his blood sugars, to ask his primary care provider for referral to a nutritionist, to take a cooking class and start to prepare healthier meals, and to decrease the length of time he spent sleeping or napping. He began to lose weight and his blood sugars improved. With each goal he successfully completed, he felt less overwhelmed and better able to cope with the continued grieving process.

CONCLUDING THOUGHTS

Focusing on goal setting and behavior change during grief is consistent with Stroebe and Schut's Dual Process Model of coping with bereavement (as cited in Caserta & Lund, 2007), which states that grief work involves not only loss-oriented work but also restoration-oriented work, and that the bereaved alternate between the two. Restoration-oriented work such as goal setting allows for a break from the intense emotional experience of loss, and has been associated with increased self-care and daily living skills, as well as increased self-efficacy and personal growth (Caserta & Lund, 2007). Problem solving and goal setting can also help with depressed mood.

References

Caserta, M. S., & Lund, D. A. (2007). Toward the development of an inventory of daily widowed life (IDWL): Guided by the dual process model of coping with bereavement. *Death Studies, 31*(6), 505–535.

Gollwitzer, P. M., & Oettingen, G. (2007). The role of goal setting and goal striving in medical adherence. In D. C. Park, & L. L. Liu (Eds.), *Medical adherence and aging* (pp. 23–47). Washington, DC: American Psychological Association.

Monk, T. H., Houck, P. R., & Shear, M. K. (2006). The daily life of complicated grief patients: What gets missed, what gets added? *Death Studies, 30*(1), 77–85.

Sage, N., Sowden, M., Chorlton, E., & Edeleanu, A. (2008). *CBT for chronic illness and palliative care.* Chichester: Wiley.

74
Defining and Envisioning Self

Vicki Panagotacos

CLIENTS FOR WHOM THE TECHNIQUE IS APPROPRIATE

Adults having difficulty reconstructing their lives after partner loss beyond 18 months of bereavement. Because this technique involves hypnotic imaging and fantasy, it is inadvisable for those with a history of psychotic disorders unless practitioner has level of competency with the clinical population.

DESCRIPTION

With time, surviving partners' focus shifts from the primary loss to an overwhelming number of secondary losses—the many practical roles their partners filled that they often took for granted. The struggle to fill these roles, coupled with life having lost its sense of meaning, often causes the bereaved to slip into depression. Hollis (1996) says that once we realize we can live without happiness but not without meaning, we have to start re-imagining ourselves. It is with the process of re-imagining that many individuals need help. The client intellectually knows what they need to do but *they can't imagine themselves doing it*—and not due to a lack of imagination. Every bereaved client is a visionary; the problem is they have no emerging vision and have misplaced their ability to evolve. The goal of this technique is to provide a tool the client can use to excavate their separate identity supported by guided imagery for self-mastery.

Sessions are 1–2 hours except for a 2-hour first session when the client completes a timeline, noting age and a short description of the best/worst life experiences. These shape the therapist's choice of guided imagery in each of the sessions that follow.

> *Sessions 1–3*: Sessions are tailored to help the client reveal and develop a separate identity by answering four questions: *(1) What do you want to include in your life?; (2) What don't you want to include in your life?; (3) What do you have in your life that you want to eliminate?; and (4) What do you have in your life that you want to keep?* I use a large pad of presentation paper and write each question at the top of a page. Clients often start with global answers to Questions 1 and 2 (e.g., "I want to feel better" or "I don't want to feel this way"). Therefore, I begin with Question 3—what they have that they want to eliminate. By the end of the third session the client is deeply involved and has actively edited their answers to all questions. Each of these initial sessions ends with a

few minutes of relaxation and present tense guided imagery, focused on connecting the client to the early childhood experiences of a drive to discover.

Sessions 4–8: In Session 4, clients are given a final list of what they have said they want to include in their life, which includes converted answers from Questions 2, 3, and 4 (e.g., "I don't want to move" converts to "I want to stay where I am living"). Weekly homework assignments are commenced in order to break the goals down into smaller steps. Items on the final list, as well as homework, are supported by 30-minutes of guided imagery using story, metaphor and direct/indirect suggestions to address client's wants as well as concerns. In this way the client can step into and rehearse their desired outcome prior to actually doing it.

CASE EXAMPLE

Session 1: Ida (age 44) had been widowed 19 months prior, leaving her alone to raise two children, ages 9 and 11. She had an active career prior to marriage but hadn't worked for 12 years. Since the death she had become isolated and limited her activities to childcare. She was experiencing panic attacks and had lost her desire to dress/groom herself. A friend from her previous grief group recommended she see me. During the intake interview she said her husband had made most of the decisions and had taken good care of the family. Ida's timeline showed no history of unresolved loss or prior childhood trauma. As I started to explain the process, the client exclaimed "I don't know what I want! That's why I am here!" I assured her that it was common and continued to move through the questions stopping at what she currently had that she would like to eliminate. She said she wanted to eliminate her fear of the future, specifically her panic over not knowing if she had enough money, and her anxiety about not being able to get a job if she needed to work. For the rest of the session we continued to work on what she wanted to eliminate. With a few minutes remaining, I asked if she would like to close her eyes for some relaxation and guided imagery. Ida agreed. The following are a few images used:

> *I wonder if you would be willing to go back to the time . . . when you are 2 and 3 years old . . . when you can't be held back from finding out what you don't know. . . as you learn to crawl and then wobble . . . tip and then hit the floor . . . often . . . before you start to walk. One day you catch a glimpse of a staircase . . . and you look up and wonder what is at the top. You are so intent upon exploring the unfamiliar that you turn around and go up the stairs . . . backwards . . . on your bottom . . . and once you have taken a good look . . . your fascination turns to how you are going to come back down . . . and then you realize you can fold forward onto all fours . . . and come down one step at a time . . . peeking between your legs . . . so you know when you have cleared the last step . . . and you know to stand up and move toward the rest of your life.*

Sessions 2 and 3: Ida was more relaxed and actively engaged in answering questions. By Session 3 she was wearing makeup and proceeded to ask me to change wording, eliminate and add items to her lists. The following is one of several images used to end these sessions:

> *It is clear from listening that you are adapting to what has taken place in your life . . . as you connect to the strengths you have always possessed . . . resources you might have forgotten to remember . . . like the time when you graduated from a tricycle and are now balancing on a two-wheeler. Sometimes you choose to ride standing up . . . sometimes sitting down . . . sometimes with no hands at all . . . until you decide . . . to put your hands onto the handlebars and steer yourself in the direction you want to go.*

Session 4: Ida shared that she seemed to never be without her questions and had even dreamed about them. I handed her the final typed list of what she had said she wanted to include in her life and watched her somberly read it. She said she had a hard time thinking she had created the list. I asked her if she would consider choosing something she could do the following week that would move her closer to one item on her list. She had wanted to reconnect to women friends and agreed to invite a few friends to meet for dinner at a restaurant.

Session 5: Ida reported she had enjoyed dining with friends and had decided this week's homework would be to invite a friend and her children to go to a performance of The Nutcracker.

Session 6: One of Ida's wants was to talk to a financial planner, but she said she didn't feel smart enough and was too intimidated to make an appointment. I wrote two words at the top of a blank page of paper—possible and impossible—and asked her to tell me what would be possible and what would be impossible if she didn't get help. It soon became clear that she could not get what she wanted without speaking to an expert. I wondered aloud if she might make the financial appointment—while giving herself permission to cancel. She agreed. The following is part of the guided imagery used for this session.

> *You have been on a crooked road but a road forward nonetheless. Sometimes a part of you can feel held back. Feeling held back reminds me of how elephants are trained in India. The people bring an elephant from the wild and chain it to a steel pole for weeks . . . before they remove the chain and replace it with a rope. In another couple of weeks they remove the rope and tie the leg of the elephant to the pole . . . with a long strand of dry grass . . . and the elephant never leaves. Isn't that interesting? The elephant is initially physically held back, but eventually it is held back only by the illusion that it can't move. We humans also fall for illusions, don't we? Recently you found you are stronger than you ever thought possible . . . and it probably won't be long before you find out you are smarter tomorrow than you think you are today.*

Session 7: Ida reported that she'd made the appointment with the planner and agreed with what we had talked about the week before. "He is working for me, so he's the one who has to be smart." For homework she decided to have a Chinese take-out dinner party.

Session 8: Ida said she no longer felt frozen and thought she would be able to keep her new focus. We ended with guided imagery using age progression—moving two years out to look back on all that Ida had accomplished. This consolidated her change, and gave her hope.

CONCLUDING THOUGHTS

Bereaved clients need an uncomplicated way to organize their thoughts in order to effectively reconstruct their lives after the loss of a partner. By providing a simple four-question format, clients have the manageable opportunity to reclaim their locus of control—and ultimately define what they want to include in their life. By adding guided imagery the cognitive process is supported by the unconscious—the seat of creativity and motivation. Handelsman (1984) proposes that the primary benefit of using hypnosis with the grieving is not just what takes place during trance, but what the process provides: a sense of mastery. By weaving open-ended stories and metaphor with direct/indirect suggestion, clients are able to access their existing strengths/resources, experience the outcome of behavior and modify their perceptions.

References

Handelsman, M. (1984). Self-hypnosis as a facilitator of self-efficacy. *Psychotherapy, 21*, 550–553.

Hollis, J. (1996). *Swampland of the soul.* Toronto: Inner City Books.

75

Mind Map for Coping through the Holidays

Melissa Axler

CLIENTS FOR WHOM THE TECHNIQUE IS APPROPRIATE

Families planning how to move forward and incorporate new ideas for celebrating the holidays while holding onto traditions shared with their loved ones. Mind maps may be premature for clients struggling with traumatic grief or the establishment of basic self-care, when more intensive emotion focused work may be indicated.

DESCRIPTION

Many of my clients greet the holidays with great trepidation. It is a time of year that brings memories flooding back and provides an opportunity for reminiscing. However, it is also a time that clients approach anxiously with a "here we go again" attitude. Their anxiety for the holidays begins early in November and seems to conclude just after children return to school in January. It has been my experience over the years that clients will typically try to avoid dealing with the holidays. With this thought I developed a Venn diagram *mind map* that can be used during this difficult season to help families celebrate in a way that provides meaning and continuity with their traditions as well as the creation of new memories.

- *Beginning the diagram*: Starting with a large circle in the middle of a big piece of paper on an easel or whiteboard, write the word Christmas Holidays in big letters through the middle of the circle. Brainstorm with the family and come up with ideas for enjoyable things that they might like to do. What days are important to them over the holidays? It might become evident that Christmas Eve, Christmas morning, Christmas dinner, Boxing Day, New Year's Eve and New Year's Day may all be important. (Of course the specific days of relevance will depend on the client's cultural and family traditions, and the circles will be labeled accordingly.) Each of these days now forms a circle attached to the main big circle and the ideas of what might make that day or evening special can be written into the circle itself.
- *Completing the circles*: Inside each circle, clients can write special foods the family likes to eat—either traditional or new; activities that they might like to continue such as attending a religious service as well as novel activities that could add to the celebration; people who the family would like to include in their celebrations as well people they might like to avoid. Similarly, each of the many circles linked in to the central

circle can be detailed in its own contents, helping families visualize and plan a holiday that can be rich with affirmation of their traditions and loved ones, including the deceased.

The mind map should be left in a prominent place so that the whole family is able to see it. It should be stressed that this mind map is *a work in progress* and that being said, all members of the family can add to the mind map if they think of something else they might like to do. I think it's also helpful to have several different colors of markers available so that each day has its own color.

The families that I have worked with using this mind map have found it to be a success. They report back that it keeps them happy and focused on the present holidays and what they mean, rather than only on what they had lost. It allows an opportunity to see what old traditions they want to keep and what new experiences they want to add. It gives the family something positive to look forward to. On the flip side it helps prevent them family from moping around and thinking about how unhappy they are without their loved one. My clients also tell me they find this activity easy, as it provides time for them to be together to laugh, to share and to shine some light on the shadow of sadness that had previously surrounded them.

CASE EXAMPLE

Christmas had been an exciting time for Rebecca, Alex and their young children, Jamie, Max and Emily. For 15 years the house had been filled with joy, excitement and a love of the holidays. When Alex died in the fall after being diagnosed with stage-four lung cancer, all of that changed. For the next two years Rebecca described how she and the kids successfully avoided the holidays by traveling to Disney World and Cuba. However, as they approached the third holiday season without Alex, Rebecca said it was time to stop running and deal with the reality. On the white-board in the therapist's office, she and Rebecca began to create the mind map explained above. The map created in the office was then recreated at home on an easel with the additional input of the children. In addition to the circles that Rebecca had drawn and filled in her therapy session, her children added others, until they eventually had 14 meaningful circles. Some of the ideas that excited the children left Rebecca a little anxious, as they were now inventing what were to become new traditions for the family. The mind map was posted in a prominent place in their home so that as ideas came up they could be added. This was the first holiday season in three years that Rebecca and her children were truly looking forward to in spite of missing Alex.

CONCLUDING THOUGHTS

The straightforward adaptation of a Venn diagram I have described here stands, in a sense, at the intersection of more elaborate visual expressive arts therapies (Thompson & Berger, 2011) and cognitive techniques for restructuring goals, such as those used in therapies for complicated grief (Shear, Boelen, & Neimeyer, 2011). It provides a helpful visualization of a changing life in the wake of loss, while also assisting with concrete planning. Although I have used this activity primarily with families sharing a generally Christian or Jewish tradition, I believe that this activity can be used with other cultures and ethnic groups at other times of the year, perhaps at the time of an anniversary, when many individuals celebrate the life that was lost and honor that person in a unique way. I have also used this concept with couples who are rebuilding their relationships, and anticipating life without their partner, or with another. By presenting the mind map as one option towards healing, clients can shape the technique in a way that provides the most meaning for them.

References

Shear, K., Boelen, P., & Neimeyer, R. A. (2011). Treating complicated grief: Converging approaches. In R. A. Neimeyer, D. L. Harris, H. Winokuer, & G. Thornton (Eds.), *Grief and bereavement in contemporary society: Bridging research and practice* (pp. 139–162). New York: Routledge.

Thompson, B. E., & Berger, J. S. (2011). Grief and expressive arts therapy. In R. A. Neimeyer, D. L. Harris, H. Winokuer, & G. Thornton (Eds.), *Grief and bereavement in contemporary society: Bridging research and practice* (pp. 303–313). New York: Routledge.

76
Worden's Paradigm in Wartime Bereavement

Joan Beder

CLIENTS FOR WHOM THE TECHNIQUE IS APPROPRIATE

Adult clients who have experienced a death due to war. However, not all families experiencing such losses will require the help of a professional counselor in addressing the tasks of grief, as many will do so on their own and with the support of military ritual.

DESCRIPTION

In wartime, "the inevitability of violent dying makes it expected and acceptable" (Rynearson, 2001, p. 111). While "expected" in the abstract, it is often unexpected and unwelcome by those who await a soldier's return. The notification of the death of a soldier to the next of kin begins a series of stressor events that require numerous adaptations by the grievers, including expected bereavement responses.

Numerous factors influence the ability of those bereft by wartime dying to move on and accept their loss. The factors include the political climate of the country; the service person's philosophical agreement with war in general and the specific reasons that the person chose to enlist; the support of the war by the family members; the state of the family when the service member departed; the type of death (in battle, in noncombatant situations); the level of unfinished business between the mourner and the deceased; the myriad of post-death bureaucratic military processes involved for the family, and the demographics of the family (the majority of current deaths in Iraq and Afghanistan are of service members who are young adults, often in newer marriages with young families); the level of information supplied surrounding the death and supports available to the family (Rando, 1993; Beder, 2003). Balancing the above-described stressors and other factors that facilitate the grief process, are the military funeral rituals, which include an honor guard, flag-draped casket, a 21-gun salute, the sounding of Taps and the presentation of the casket-folded flag. The sense of honor and ritual is often comforting to the bereaved as it facilitates a formal and public acknowledgment of their loss. Through the ritual, a family is supported in their grief and the meaning of the soldier's death is honored, enabling the family to begin their grief work (Schading, 2007). It may be very difficult for family members to "move on" in their grief until some of the compounding factors have been addressed.

I have found Worden's Task Model (2009) to be helpful and applicable in many military death situations; I especially endorse that, within the model, the mourner is directed to take action on their own behalf. For the counselor, it creates a path and a plan for us to follow while helping locate the mourner in their bereavement trajectory. The tasks are: (1) to accept the reality of the death; (2) to work through the pain of the grief; (3) to adjust to an environment in which the deceased is missing; and (4) to emotionally relocate the deceased and move on with life.

Accepting the reality of the loss means that the mourner must face the fact that the person has died. While this sounds self-evident, for the family who has had a service member who has been deployed for months, acceptance may be elusive as the mourner is more prone to denial, falsely believing that the deceased is still engaged in battle. Additionally, in wartime death, there frequently are no remains to bury or the remains may take a long time to arrive, thus delaying funeral rituals and delaying acceptance. On the other hand, military funeral ritual, for many, facilitates the beginning of emotional acceptance. The counseling effort helps the mourner break down denial to be able to begin accepting the loss. The underlying strategy is to gently pierce the denial by bringing the deceased into the counseling room and counseling effort.

The second task, working through the pain of the grief, involves experiencing the sadness and emptiness of life without the deceased. In the counseling it is important for mourners to give voice to their emotional pain; most grief counseling is based on the assumption that emotions need a voice or the individual may carry this pain throughout life, creating periods of depression and anguish (Rando, 1993). For the wartime bereft, this can be especially complex as feelings, usually anger-related to the war effort, the hardships of repeated deployments and lengthy separations, become entangled with other emotions. If the mourner is struggling with unfinished business, it is helpful to encourage the griever to say aloud the things that were unsaid to the deceased, to finish the unfinished business by voicing it. This second task may be heavily impacted by society's political reaction to the wartime effort, with a predominant view that the war was unjust or unnecessary, compounding the mourner's sense of violation. Also, in wartime, the number of soldiers who die can, in time, inure society to personal loss, making much-needed social support less and less available (Beder, 2003).

Task 3 involves adjusting to an environment in which the deceased is missing, and touches several areas. External adjustments include the day-to-day roles and tasks that the mourner has to assume with the absence of the deceased. Internal adjustments are more complex and are concerned with a new definition of self as a widow (or widower) or bereaved parent. These new self-definitions require internal reorganization and may impact self-esteem and a sense of identity. Counselors need to be alert to this dynamic as we might make the assumption that the depression we observe in our client(s) is due exclusively to the death while it may be equally related to the loss of self-esteem and position created by death. Oddly, Task 3 may be facilitated for the wartime griever: some of the lifestyle adjustments may have been made because of deployment separation, although the adjustment was believed to be temporary.

Task 4, the final task, of emotionally relocating the deceased and moving on with life, is especially difficult for anyone who has sustained a loss, wartime or otherwise. The counseling effort is geared to help mourners find a special and secure spot for the deceased in their emotional life while at the same time being able to go forward with their life and plans (Beder, 2003). In wartime, the designation of "hero" may enable the griever to be able to memorialize the deceased in a positive and meaningful manner.

Worden's (2009) Task Model provides a template from which we can help those grieving a wartime death. It must be understood that this is not a smooth, linear process occurring in a fixed progression with tidy completion of one task before moving onto the next. Tasks can be partially completed and can be reworked and revisited; grieving is a fluid process with many stopping and starting points.

CASE EXAMPLE

Peter was from a military family; Mary was not. They met in high school, married and had two children. As part of Peter's family legacy, he enlisted soon after the 9/11 bombing of the World Trade Center. He returned home after 15 months in Iraq and redeployed twice (also for 15-month tours) more. When Mary opened the door to the Army representative, she knew immediately that her life as she had known it was over. Her boys were 6 and 8. For the last 5 years, since Peter had enlisted, Mary had been managing all the home details. Mary lived a distance from her family and Peter's family were scattered across the US, living in military facilities and inaccessible to Mary. Intellectually, Mary was ready for the knock at the door, was almost expecting it, but she emotionally crumbled when she received the news. The funeral rituals were completed in a fairly expedient manner. Soon after, at the urging of friends, Mary sought counseling. Acceptance of her loss, Task 1, was slowly being accomplished.

Task 2, working through the pain of the loss, required that Mary give voice to her anger about Peter's choices to redeploy for a second and third time, knowing of the strain it imposed on her and the children and Peter's adherence to his family's urging and military orientation. Once the anger was spent, Mary was more able to look at the deeper feelings of pain and loss around Peter's death. This was not easily accomplished and took many weeks in the counseling effort.

Task 3, adjusting to the environment in which the deceased was missing, was somewhat easier for Mary as she had been "holding things together" for such a long time and had become proficient at managing the home and family details. The future concerns were deeper: would she have enough money, would/should she marry again, what about a father for the boys?

Task 4 required Mary to be able to place Peter in a memory location that had begun to fade with his extended time away from her and the children. While she remained faithful to him and would have welcomed him home, the distance from him had changed the nature of their relationship, filling her with some uncertainty about their future as a family.

CONCLUDING THOUGHTS

Death in wartime is complex due to the political climate, culture of the military and extended absences of service members. Counselors are challenged to work with levels of anger and denial that may be absent in other bereavement situations. A familiarity with military culture and the nuances of military separations is helpful in working with this cohort. Tapping into the resilience of the bereft and using the Task model outlined above will help facilitate the work.

References

Beder, J. (2003). War, death and bereavement: How we can help. *Families in Society, 84*(2), 163–166.

Rando, T. (1993). *Treatment of complicated mourning*. Champaign, IL: Research Press.

Rynearson, E. K. (2001). *Retelling violent death*. Philadelphia, PA: Brunner-Routledge.

Schading, B. (2007). *A civilian's guide to the U.S. military*. Cincinnati, OH: Writer's Digest.

Worden, J. W. (2009). *Grief counseling and grief therapy: A handbook for the mental health practitioner* (4th ed.). New York: Springer.

Part XIV
Accessing Resources

77

Poetry and Bibliotherapy

Ted Bowman

CLIENTS FOR WHOM THE TECHNIQUE IS APPROPRIATE

Mourners of nearly any age, any circumstance, as long as care is taken with language, literacy, developmental, cultural, and ability considerations and after gaining perspective about the losses and resulting grief of the individual, family or group. However, for mourners struggling with basic self-care, stabilizing interventions should be given priority.

DESCRIPTION

Poetry therapy and bibliotherapy involve the creative use of literary sources, writing, and storytelling for therapeutic purposes. Like its siblings—drama, art, music and dance therapy—it is a legitimate tool that complements other therapeutic and caring processes (Bowman, 2011). But ironically, because people of all cultures across time have told stories through song, words, and later via the printed word, this method can be overlooked or misunderstood. Further, common usage can cause therapists to under-use poetry and literary tools as specialized techniques. Similar to other creative arts, poetry therapy is a disciplined (formal) use of traditional (informal) ways of understanding and responding to life events.

Psychiatrist Peter Lomas argued that "the limitation of technique is at no time more apparent than when the therapist is faced with naked grief . . . in the grip of an experience that is too painful for words" (Lomas, 1999). Grievers may, therefore, benefit from processes that augment the words and stories they tell.

Given this context, here are three ways to integrate bibliotherapy into grief work:

1. *Ask your clients if they have written about their experiences.* Ask if they are now keeping a journal. Ask if they have found or been given any readings, poems, memoirs useful for their loss and resulting grief. Such inquiries show an interest in their resourcefulness. It also points toward topics and issues for exploration in the re-storying of lives. Clients are empowered when they find "word mirrors" for disruptive changes and the resulting grief.
2. *Bring a story or poem and use it as a prompt.* Prompts are the use of literary sources in therapeutic work. Stories evoke stories. Often hearing or reading another story will invite clients to share their story, and there are many anthologies that can serve this

prompting function (e.g., Bowman & Johnson, 2010). A note of caution, however: choices of prompts should always be selected with the client and his or her experience in mind. Do not casually thrust your favorite poem on others. The effectiveness of bibliotherapy depends on the facilitator's ability to choose material that speaks to the client's needs (Hynes & Hynes-Berry, 1994, p. 18).

3. *Ask clients what they might say to the author of a prompt you bring.* For example, in this variation on the previous principle, you could bring these lines about death from a Mary Oliver poem: "It's not the weight you carry/but how you carry it–/books, bricks, grief–/it's all in the way/you embrace it/balance it, carry it" (Oliver, 2006). "*What do you think about Oliver's statement? If she were here, what might you ask or say to her?*" The client can stay with the third person. Often it is easier to talk about someone else's experience before revealing one's own suffering or questions.

CASE EXAMPLE

Ralph, a recent widower, struggled with the finality of death. He self-critically noted that he knew this was unreal. He was a rational man and had always used his intellect and clarity of plans to get him through challenges. He had actively participated in the funeral, the burial, even some cosmetic changes in the home he and Annette had shared for over 30 years of their 42-year marriage. Ralph thought that with those acts done, he could move on. Now, he was confused by the ambiguity of what grief scholars have come to call continuing bonds. It was as if Annette was still present in his life. He thought he was hallucinating or that he was not well.

Ralph agreed to participate in a complement to our "talk therapy." I introduced metaphor to Ralph and asked that he join me in an exercise of finding other words for death and for his experiences of Annette's presence: "Ralph, here are a few phrases from poetry and memoir that may or may not be words you could find useful in your grieving. Take a few moments with each of these phrases. Write your own version beside my selections."

> *Grief is a circular staircase/I have lost you.*
> *Grief is the ceasing of Annette's own brand of magic in daily life.*
> *What got me thinking about voice was its loss . . . I ached to hear what I could not.*
> *Who do the dead think they are . . . leaving themselves all over my books, my face . . .*
> *I find you where I found you years ago.*

"Ralph, do any of these come even close to what you have been experiencing?"

The introduction of this sort of material helped divert Ralph from continuing to rationally question what seemed like strange, perhaps even "crazy" thoughts and experiences following Annette's funeral. While a skilled therapist certainly could discuss those thoughts with Ralph, the introduction of metaphorical words and phrases prompted him to move from a predominately rational way of addressing his grief toward different words and ways of conveying his experiences. In addition, giving Ralph the sources for the prompts provoked him to reconsider his belief that his bereavement was strange.

CONCLUDING THOUGHTS

When we express our truths, either in response to literary works or to other prompts, we empower and develop our voice (Chavis, 2011). Reading poems and stories and writing personal reactions to literary stimuli affect emotions, cognitions and behavior in ways many other methods do not. Complementary with most frameworks of grieving and with most psychological methods, poetry, literary sources and writing can easily be part of the therapist's repertoire.

References

Bowman, T. (2003). Using literary resources in bereavement work: Evoking words for grief. *The Forum, 29*(2), 8–9.

Bowman, T. (2011). Helpers and bereavement care: A bibliotherapeutic review. *The Forum, 37*(1), 9, 10, 24.

Bowman, T., & Johnson, E. B. (2010). *The wind blows, the ice breaks: Poems of loss and renewal by Minnesota poets.* Minneapolis, MN: Nodin Press.

Chavis, G. G. (2011) *Poetry and story therapy: The healing power of creative expression.* Philadelphia, PA: Jessica Kingsley.

Hynes, A. M., & Hynes-Berry, M. (1986–1994) *Bibliotherapy: the interactive process: A handbook.* St. Cloud, MN: Northstar Press.

Lomas, P. (1999) *Doing good? Psychotherapy out of its depth.* Oxford: Oxford University Press, pp. 73–74.

Oliver, M. (2006) *Thirst: Poems.* Boston: Beacon Press, pp. 53–54.

78
Bibliotherapy with Children
Joanne C. Robinson

CLIENTS FOR WHOM THE TECHNIQUE IS APPROPRIATE

Bibliotherapy can be used with clients of any age, especially children who are struggling with loss and grief. This technique may not be appropriate or may need to be adapted for those clients with complex bereavement, or difficulties with concentration, reading or verbal reasoning.

DESCRIPTION

Bibliotherapy is a technique that purposefully uses books in a creative and therapeutic way, often combining cognitive behavioral therapy and narrative therapy approaches. Personal construct theory offers an alternative approach to explore how children make sense of their experiences. Within personal construct therapy, Mair (1988) outlined a story-telling psychology and Ravenette (1979) routinely told and elicited stories with children as a therapeutic technique. Stories serve to normalize experiences, and establish similarities and differences to the child's own situation. In therapy, I often find that children engage well with stories and identify with characters to the extent they report no longer feeling alone in their loss.

When children experience loss, the event itself can become enmeshed in the child's sense of self and affect the child's important relationships. Children may struggle to talk about their loss directly and for some parents talking to their child about death is either tricky or avoided altogether. Through the discussion of storybook characters, children are able to integrate concepts of dying and find personal meaning in their grief, increasing their understanding of self in relation to others and the world.

In therapy, books also help children to distance usefully from their experiences of loss, which facilitates construal from alternative perspectives and fosters therapeutic change in a developmentally appropriate way. Children are invited to discuss particular themes that emerge from reading a story, using questions such as: *"In your own words, tell me about the story. Would you change anything in it? If so, what would you change? How would you like the story to have ended?"* Such questions help children to "re-story" their life so that they are able to anticipate a more hopeful future (Malchiodi & Ginns-Gruenberg, 2008). The exploratory approach to conversations between the child and the therapist makes bibliotherapy a collaborative, interactive technique.

Choosing one or two suitable books to use is important. The books need to be meaningful to the child, developmentally appropriate and relevant to the child's situation. For example, is the child grieving for the loss of a parent, friend, and or pet?; does the child feel responsible for the death?; was the death anticipated or sudden? A particular book may be explored in one therapy session. However, parallels to the stories and characters may be referred to throughout the course of therapy. Two books that I have found popular with children are discussed below.

A Terrible Thing Happened (Holmes, 2000) is just one of many books that can be used with children when facilitating conversations around loss. It addresses common feelings and behaviours that children experience following a traumatic event through a character called Sherman. The therapist first introduces the book to the child, emphasizing that talking about the child's own situation is not initially necessary. The therapist then reads the story aloud and invites the child to consider which part of the story he or she connected with the most. The child is then asked if he or she is like any of the characters and if so, how they are alike.

Second, the *Harry Potter* books by J. K. Rowling are very much part of children's lives today. Harry Potter is a well-known character whom children often identify with in therapy due to Harry's struggles with having lost both his parents (Noctor, 2006). Despite being surrounded by others at Hogwarts, the school of witchcraft and wizardry, Harry at times feels alone. He learns to use the "Patronus charm," which involves recalling his happiest memory of his parents, to defeat the Dementors, creatures that destroy happiness and hope. In therapy, I discuss with children how Harry was able to think about his experience of loss in a different, positive way in order to seek strength to overcome the sadness and despair brought about by the Dementors. Helping children to remember significant aspects of their relationship with the person who died can be empowering in creating a more hopeful future, just like Harry Potter did. Children can be encouraged to use their imagination through questions such as: *"What do you think it was like for Harry? Are you like Harry in any way? What do you think Harry Potter would do? If Harry Potter were here now, what do you think he would say/do to help you with your loss?"*

CASE EXAMPLE

Jenny was 9 years old when I first met her. At 5 years old she saw her mother die from a heart attack. Jenny was under her mother's bed at the time, playing a game. Her mother got up from the bed and collapsed. In therapy, Jenny told me how she thought her mother was playing with her and it had not occurred to her that she had died. It was only when her mother would not get up that she became upset and shouted for help. When I first met Jenny, she was tearful, yet brave in being able to recall the events of her mother's death. She told me she had not talked about what had happened much and had tried to push any memories away. She said she wanted to talk about it but worried it might be too difficult. I introduced Jenny to the idea of reading a story together about when people we love die, and then talking about it together. I wondered what this might be like for her. Jenny agreed to give this a go.

I invited Jenny to read aloud the book entitled A Terrible Thing Happened. *She quickly identified with the main character, Sherman. Relating the story to her own experience, I heard how she was like Sherman because he got "stressy" when he tried to ignore his thoughts. Jenny told me she sometimes felt angry, sad and worried. When worried, Jenny would check to see if her father was well. As Jenny read the story, she began to wonder whether pushing away her thoughts was helpful. By questioning her behavior, Jenny began to explore different ways of coping with her thoughts. Jenny said Sherman had given her ideas of things to do, such as coloring and going to the park with her sister.*

A week later, Jenny returned to therapy smiling, having watched the film Harry Potter. "He was very sad. When he went to school he made lots of friends, which helped him when he found out his parents had been killed." Jenny said she had friends too who were nice to her. I wondered in what other ways Jenny was like Harry Potter. Jenny said that Harry thought about his parents and saw them in the magical Mirror of Erised, which showed whatever the heart desired. Jenny drew a picture of the mirror. Inside she drew herself with her mother and father. She told me that they were "happy and swimming on holiday." She said because she was happy her "mum was happy too." I reflected that Harry Potter had used his happiest memory of his parents in order to defeat the Dementors. Jenny shared her happiest memory of her mother tucking her up in bed, saying, "I love you. Sweet dreams." Jenny experienced a "warm, fuzzy feeling in her tummy" when remembering this. Like Harry Potter, Jenny recalled this memory when she felt sad, or when she found it difficult to sleep and it helped her to respond positively to any thoughts she had of her mother.

CONCLUDING THOUGHTS

From Jenny's perspective, using stories to help children who are hurting *"makes you feel you are not alone and it gives you ideas about what to do when you are feeling sad."* Stories also help children to remember what was important about their relationship with the person who died. Jenny reported that Harry Potter helped her *"to think of happy memories of my mum and I found ways to have fun with my dad and sister and be happy."*

Bibliotherapy allows children to explore the impact of loss in a safe, developmentally appropriate way. Discussing characters from stories gives hope and confidence to children so that they may anticipate a positive future. It allows children to reconstrue their loss, so that they are able to remember the loved person without the pain and hurt.

References

Holmes, M. M. (2000). *A terrible thing happened*. Washington, DC: Magination Press.

Mair, J. M. M. (1988). Psychology as storytelling. *International Journal of Personal Construct Psychology*, *1*, 125–137.

Malchiodi, C. A., & Ginns-Gruenberg, D. G. (2008). Trauma, loss, and bibliotherapy: The healing power of stories. In C. A. Malchiodi (Ed.), *Creative interventions with traumatized children*. (pp. 167–185). New York: Guilford.

Noctor, C. (2006). Putting Harry Potter on the couch. *Clinical Child Psychology and Psychiatry*, *11*(4), 579–589.

Ravenette, A. T. (1979). To tell a story, to invent a character, to make a difference. In Ravenette, T. (1999), *Personal construct theory in educational psychology*. London: Whurr.

Rowling, J. K. (2004). *Harry Potter* (boxed set). London: Bloomsbury.

79

Grief and Loss Support on the Web

Gloria C. Horsley and Heidi Horsley

CLIENTS FOR WHOM THE TECHNIQUE IS APPROPRIATE

Web-based resources can support many of the bereaved who seek information, encouragement and companionship in their grieving. In cases of more complicated bereavement, however, it should supplement rather than supplant professional counseling.

DESCRIPTION

Losing a child, a spouse, a sibling, a parent or other loved one can be a deeply isolating experience. At times, people feel that they are the only ones who have ever known such anguish. It may seem as if darkness surrounds them. Some people lose hope, and search for it in the virtual universe of the World Wide Web, where a broad range of resources and virtual communities offer advice and companionship on the quest for healing after loss. Our goal in this brief chapter is to illustrate these resources through a discussion of the work of the Open to Hope Foundation, a content-rich, heart-based on-line community forum designed to help people cope with their pain, heal their grief, and begin investing in their futures. Content on Open to Hope's website (www.opentohope.com) includes radio shows hosted by grief professionals, video interviews of grief experts, and articles written by clinicians specializing in bereavement as well as ordinary people going through loss. In addition to these content-based resources, the site offers myriad possibilities for on-line conversation as a means of fostering virtual community among the bereaved suffering specific losses.

The Open to Hope site is also heavily trafficked by therapists, health-care workers, professors, students and others interested in supporting the bereaved or understanding the subtleties of the grief process. The site currently has about 300 contributing authors, with new authors joining regularly. The site's library contains approximately 3,000 original articles, 500 radio shows, and 60 videos. All are free to the public for reading, listening, viewing, and downloading. The site also has a number of forums where people can tell their stories and receive support from others who have had similar experiences. Site visitors also have the opportunity to add comments to articles and to receive a response from individual authors. Those who write articles for the site are vetted by the editor before their material is posted. All materials are catalogued so they are searchable on the site 24 hours a day. The site also maintains an on-line interactive calendar, which allows organizations and individuals to post information about conferences, workshops, and other events related to grief, loss, hope and healing.

CASE EXAMPLES

The best case examples available to us are the on-line comments of those who visit the website after the loss of a child, a spouse, a parent or other loved one. We have also included posted comments from a clinician and an educator.

Death of a parent

Ash: *I lost my dad in mid July of 08. It was unexpected and he was only a few months away from his 70th birthday. I'm 25 and none of my friends know what it's like because their parents are still alive. It hurts to know I'm so alone but it is a relief to know there are others out there in similar situations and others who understand why the little things can be the biggest triggers.*

Alex: *My mother died exactly 1 month ago today of a sudden stroke. She was 65 and perfectly healthy. I feel like I am really losing my mind . . . you have given me hope. Just to know that there is someone else out there who is working through the same things and that I will survive this.*

Death of a child

Louise: *I buried my 34 yr. old daughter 6 months ago today. I have read many books, gone to a grief counselor, have a wonderful husband, son and many friends trying to help me get through this. I come to this website every day looking for understanding from the only people who truly know the feelings of losing a child, those who have gone through this pain.*

Frank: *My wife and I lost our 1-month-old son to crib death this year. We listen to your show Open to Hope on our computer every night. We put the computer by our bed and listen when we are ready to go to sleep. It makes us feel that we are not alone in our grief. I hope you won't mind if I tell you we usually don't get through an entire show because we fall asleep.*

Death of a spouse

Kathy: *I lost my husband 4 months ago to cancer. We were married 26 years and have 2 beautiful daughters. I still have not removed his toothbrush, I sleep on his side of the bed and I still wear my wedding band and the list goes on. Thank you for your articles. Sometimes I feel I'm really losing my mind and it helps me to know I can share with others.*

Lisa: *I am glad that I stumbled onto this website. Since my husband of thirteen years died of lung cancer I have been on a number of grief sites. When I read the posts on this site I almost fell outta my chair because of the things that I read . . . as they are the same feelings that I've said out loud to myself. I am pleased that I have finally found a place where I can share my loss with others.*

Comments from professionals

Pamela Gabbay, M.A., FT, The Mourning Star Center for Grieving: *Reading Open to Hope every morning has become a part of my daily routine. My "daily dose of Open to Hope" has given me numerous resources and wonderful articles to pass along to my colleagues and families.*

Darcy Harris, Ph.D. FT, Thanatology Coordinator at Kings College, Canada: *I often refer my students to the YouTubes (with interviews of grief professionals). It is fun for them to hear and see leaders in the field of Thanatology.*

Richard, Social Work Student: I am currently taking a class in grief and loss. My professor directed the class to the Open to Hope web site and asked us to pick a YouTube, radio show, or article to comment on. I have really learned a lot about how bad experiences can be turned around to do good in the world.

CONCLUDING THOUGHTS

The Internet is an important resource for both professionals and the lay public who are dealing with issues of grief, loss and recovery. In 1983, when our son and brother, Scott, was killed in an automobile accident at age 17, there was little support for those who had suffered loss. Giving a voice to grief and supporting those who have suffered loss was the impetus for starting The Open to Hope Foundation. Currently www.Opentohope.com is the most visited grief and loss site on the World Wide Web.

Further resources

Christ, G., Kane, D., Horsley, H. (2011). Grief after terrorism: Toward a family focused intervention. In R. A. Neimeyer, D. L. Harris, H. Winokuer, & G. Thornton (Eds.), *Grief and bereavement in contemporary society: Bridging research and practice*. New York: Routledge.

Gilbert, K. R., & Horsley, G. C. Technology and grief support in the twenty-first century: A multimedia platform. In R. A. Neimeyer, D. L. Harris, H. Winokuer, & G. Thornton (Eds.), *Grief and bereavement in contemporary society: Bridging research and practice*. New York: Routledge.

Horsley, G., & Horsley, H. (2011). *Open to Hope: Inspirational stories of healing after loss*. New York: Open to Hope Foundation.

Horsley, G. C., & Horsley, H. (in press). Open to Hope: An international online bereavement community. In K. Gilbert, & C. Sofka (Eds.), *Technology communication in grief counseling and research*. New York: Springer.

Part XV
Grieving with Others

80

Orchestrating Social Support

Kenneth J. Doka and Robert A. Neimeyer

CLIENTS FOR WHOM THE TECHNIQUE IS APPROPRIATE

Many adolescents and adults early in loss seeking affirmation and reengagement with others benefit from exploring sources of social support. However, those who are at some distance from their loss, whose social worlds are already responsive, or whose struggles seem more internal may find doing so less relevant. Moreover, this technique should follow an assessment that an individual has a viable and available support system. If the client does not, then this technique may increase a sense of isolation.

DESCRIPTION

Although grief is commonly viewed as an internal experience, in fact we grieve in a social world. Most bereaved people spontaneously seek out others who can assist them with practical tasks (e.g., running an errand, consulting about a technical problem), whom they trust to understand their feelings surrounding the loss, and who can help them reengage once-pleasurable activities after a loved one's death. And research suggests that such social support, when available, is indeed associated with better bereavement adjustment (Vanderwerker & Prigerson, 2004). Conversely, many of the bereaved report being hurt by the unintentional insensitivity or even malicious comments of others, and evidence indicates that the frequency of such negative interactions predicts more intense and protracted grief symptomatology, especially when the deaths result from violent causes (Burke, Neimeyer, & McDevitt-Murphy, 2010). Thus there is good reason for counselors to join with clients to review how well their close relationships accommodate their needs following bereavement.

One practical tool for therapists undertaking this task is the *DLR approach* utilized by Doka (2010). DLR is a useful mnemonic for considering who in the client's social field is a *Doer*, a *Listener* or a *Respite figure*. To this basic DLR inventory we might add an X, for *Negative or destructive relationship*—the kind of people the bereaved person would do well to avoid or engage in limited, necessary ways. More subtly, of course, therapists can assist clients in considering how to minimize the burden on a limited number of support figures, and how to "titrate" the sharing of feelings and needs so that a potential supporter is not overwhelmed. More specifically, clients can be prompted to consider who in their present lives would fit each of the following categories:

- *Doers (D)*: people who can be counted on to get things done (e.g., assisting with house-work; consulting on a computer problem).
- *Listeners (L)*: friends who can lend a sympathetic ear, without becoming reactive, prematurely advice-giving, preachy or critical.
- *Respite figures (R)*: support figures with whom to engage in specific activities for the purpose of simple enjoyment (e.g., visiting a gallery; exercising).
- *Negative or Destructive figures (X)*: people who are better off avoided, or if essential to interact with (e.g., a critical parent or relative), to engage in limited interaction.

Thinking about *who* to seek out for *what* is critical in rebuilding the world after loss, as turning to those who are likely to disappoint in a given domain is a recipe for pain, resentment, and self-protective isolation. In addition, bear in mind the need to distribute the client's needs across several figures to avoid burning out any one person. Consider the following suggestions:

- Begin by asking the client to list their support system (after assessing that the client has a viable and available support system). Once they write the list, work with the client to make sure the list is complete. *Did the client include friends and neighbors, supportive individuals in their work, school, faith communities, and organizational affiliations?* This is a particularly valuable step as it reaffirms that the client is not without support and resources in the current crisis.
- Identify people in each D, L or R category, noting that some may fall into a few categories. It may help to have clients identify their "top 5 or 6" individuals in each category and have clients program their numbers into their mobile phone.
- Schedule at least one D, L and R interaction each week.
- Play to the strengths of each potential support figure; someone good at home repair might be bad company at the symphony; and enjoyable respite figures might be uncomfortable with strong emotions.
- Coach the client to actively reach out to help would-be supporters understand their needs, as others often hold back out of a fear of intruding.
- Practice assertive responses to critical or nosy people; mitigate contact with "Xs."
- Consider the value of *not talking* at times about the loss in regulating one's own emotions and those of the other.

CASE EXAMPLE

Maria was a 58-year-old Hispanic woman who had been a teacher's aide for nearly 30 years. She entered counseling about 8 months after the death of her husband, Hector, who had died within a year of being diagnosed with pancreatic cancer. In the 6 months prior to Hector's death, Maria had taken a leave of absence from her school to care for him. In counseling, Maria complained of loneliness and lack of support.

As we analyzed Maria's support system, it seemed both substantial and viable. She had a large extended family in the area, a number of friends from her work, and a number of other friends and neighbors who had been helpful to her during Hector's illness. Moreover, she was an active member of an Evangelical Church and seemed to have a number of active associations there. Part of the difficulty, Maria realized, was that Hector's illness and her caregiving had isolated her from her network—disrupting opportunities to connect. During that time, she was so devoted to Hector's care that she refused numerous offers for assistance. Hence we began to address strategies to re-engage with family and friends.

Here we used the DLR list, labeling her support system as doers, listeners, or respite persons. In counseling, Maria reframed her isolation from "I always ask the wrong person" to "I ask the right person to do the wrong things." This exercise allowed Maria to use her support system more effectively.

In addition, it led her to a new appreciation of her longstanding friendship with Lydia, a co-worker for many years. Maria had been disappointed that Lydia was not more present during Hector's illness. Moreover, Lydia was always willing to go to a movie or out for coffee but even then conversations remained light and superficial. She rarely asked Maria how she was doing and seemed uncomfortable when Maria talked about her loss. Maria now recognized that Lydia's gift was respite. She also acknowledged that Lydia's own experience of having so many recent losses of husband, mother, and siblings was a factor in her strategy of avoidance of any discussions of grief. Maria was able to reframe time with Lydia as "time away" from her grief and looked forward to those opportunities for respite.

CONCLUDING THOUGHTS

Most bereaved people as well as those who care about them intuitively recognize the importance of reengaging the social world in the wake of loss. But common injunctions to become more socially active are often too general to be helpful, so that the bereaved feel disappointed or rebuffed when they turn to someone for understanding, only to be met by awkwardness, avoidance, facile advice or hackneyed consolation. In such cases a systematic review of who in their families, workplaces and broader networks can address their needs for practical help, emotional support and simple enjoyable companionship can be remarkably helpful, particularly when this is coupled with judicious consideration of which relationships should be avoided when the client is feeling vulnerable. Collaborating in activating a broad support network that meets different needs on the part of the griever also mitigates the potential problem of a client's growing dependence on a professional therapist, with a corresponding constriction of natural sources of counsel, care and companionship.

References

Burke, L. A., Neimeyer, R. A., & McDevitt-Murphy, M. E. (2010). African American homicide bereavement: Aspects of social support that predict complicated grief, PTSD, and depression. *Omega, 61*, 1–24.

Doka, K. (2010). Grief, illness and loss. In M. Kerman (Ed.), *Clinical pearls of wisdom* (pp. 93–103). New York: W. W. Norton.

Vanderwerker, L. C., & Prigerson, H. G. (2004). Social support and technological connectedness as protective factors in bereavement. *Journal of Loss and Trauma, 9*, 45–57.

81

Addressing Therapeutic Ruptures in Bereavement Support Groups

Christopher J. MacKinnon, Nathan G. Smith, Melissa Henry,
Mel Berish, Evgenia Milman, and Laura Copeland

CLIENTS FOR WHOM THE TECHNIQUE IS APPROPRIATE

Adolescents or adults who are experiencing an uncomplicated grief trajectory in the context of a bereavement support group. The strategies below may not be suitable for groups with members displaying a more prolonged/complicated grief response, or for those clients whose persistent anger or inability to work with a group make them better suited for individual therapy.

DESCRIPTION

Ruptures are a well-documented therapeutic phenomenon in both individual and group psychotherapy. They are characterized by an event that can potentially negatively impact the therapeutic relationship (Safran, Muran, Samstag, & Stevens, 2001; Yalom & Leszcz, 2005). Rupture events involve intentional or unintentional communications that entail misunderstanding, devaluing, or inappropriately judging another's comments. Anger, frustration, and disappointment can result.

Although bereavement support groups can facilitate psychological adjustment for mourners, therapeutic ruptures are common in this context and can have deleterious effects on members. We observed a tendency towards therapeutic ruptures between group members during the course of our clinical research study that involved the development and evaluation of a professionally-facilitated 12-week meaning-based group counseling intervention for uncomplicated bereavement (MacKinnon et al., 2011).

Therapeutic ruptures can assume a particular guise in the context of bereavement groups. Grievers often have heightened awareness of the expectations and corresponding judgments of others, rendering them vulnerable to painful emotions. For example, bereft individuals may report feeling misunderstood and isolated in their grief, contributing to social withdrawal, symptoms of anxiety and depression and feelings of meaninglessness. This heightened awareness of social feedback can increase the likelihood of therapeutic ruptures occurring in response to comments made by other group members.

In addition, the group setting itself may result in common and potentially overlooked ruptures. Specifically, members typically do not recognize ruptures when they occur, nor do they know how to deal with them. Facilitators likewise may fail to observe them, as their attention is divided between the complexities of group functioning and the expressions of grief. Thus, facilitators need strategies to negotiate such ruptures lest they impair group functioning. Leaving them unaddressed risks the occurrence of therapeutic failures, such as members skipping sessions or dropping out of the group entirely in order to protect themselves from feeling increasingly misunderstood.

The following techniques can be modified to fit the context of each group. Initial prompts involve the identification of the rupture, with later focus on repairing it.

1. *Establishing group norms early-on*: Explaining rules regarding group functioning can prevent ruptures, especially when these are co-constructed by group members. Common norms include punctuality, not interrupting others, and not compelling members to disclose material they do not wish to share. Ensuring feelings of safety for participants can be particularly important when adjusting to grief, as death is often an unpredictable event that shatters feelings of security. With regards to ruptures, facilitators can prepare group members by emphasizing that they are a normal and expected phenomenon in groups, and that they need to be addressed. For example, facilitators can explain that people may grieve differently and be more sensitive to the words of others during grief. As a consequence, they may object to particular comments from other group members. Voicing these disagreements in the controlled context of a group may lead members to better understand themselves, empathize with others, and more freely communicate their needs with others outside of the group. Prompts for establishing norms include:

   What rules do we need to foster feelings of safety?
   What rules do we need to establish if members start to feel less safe during the course of our discussions?
   How might we be vigilant about not pushing each other to share more than we're comfortable with?
   What are the risks of raising (or not raising) our objections to comments made by other members?

2. *Addressing ruptures as they occur*: It is important that group members learn to speak up when a particular comment "doesn't sit well with them." Facilitators can model this immediacy by commenting closely after a rupture until group members are able to identify ruptures themselves. Facilitators can also turn to group members not involved in the exchange, inviting them to comment on what just occurred. It is useful for facilitators to progressively refrain from identifying ruptures, as this reinforces that the group is responsible for monitoring its own function and behavior. A useful prompt might be:

   Let's pause for a moment: Did something just happen during the last verbal exchange that the group may wish to attend to?

   Once the rupture has been made explicit in the group, the facilitators should reinforce that it takes a lot of courage for participants to speak up as there are often implicit social conventions that forbid expressing disagreement. The facilitators can then gently guide the group to explore the nature of the rupture using prompts like:

   It looks like there might be some disagreement in the group. What is causing it?
   Do people feel there is some miscommunication in the group's conversation?
   How might these disparities in communication be linked to our grief?

3. *Identifying the original intention and re-framing*: Ruptures are frequently unintentional statements regarding grief that are difficult for other members to hear. Sometimes the

rupture is a failed attempt to reassure, protect, help, or give advice to another participant. At other times, the intention is that of curiosity or an attempt to make sense of another's experience. One technique to repair ruptures is to explicitly identify the implicit motivations under the surface of the original message. Stressing underlying intentions often helps reframe the rupturing participant's words in a less threatening and harmful way. Simultaneously, the facilitators protect the rupturing member from feeling he or she is being punished or shamed. Prompts to achieve this include:

> *While it seems that your words were difficult for people in the group to hear, perhaps you could share what you were thinking, or feeling, or intending to communicate in that verbal exchange?*
> *How might these underlying messages be linked to your/members' present experience of grief?*

4. *Drawing parallels with the outside world*: Ruptures often are derivatives of members' past and present conflictual interactions outside the group. While some people may go to great lengths to avoid conflict in their lives, others may believe that conflict is a necessary evil to establish trust and honesty in relationships. Some prompts are provided below to draw out these narratives of conflict, showing how these stories may be related to members' behaviors in the group, and ways these tales are linked to grief.

> *How have we learnt to deal with conflict in our lives? How do these learning experiences impact our behavior in the group?*
> *Because we want to preserve and protect the memory of our deceased loved one, sometimes we keep to ourselves stories that can't easily be shared with others. Might we risk sharing some of these untold stories with the goal of both shedding light on these narratives and feeling less alone with them?*
> *To what degree is our grief made harder when the person who saw us through the dark periods is no longer there? How might the group comfort us at this time?*

5. *Dealing with anger*: Grief is often characterized by upset expectations. Plans for the future are interrupted by death, friends neglect to provide support at critical moments, and health care providers failed to prevent an inevitable death. Correspondingly, the early stages of group formation tend to include expressions of frustration, irritability, anger, and rage. Anger that spirals out of control can be destructive to a bereavement group as the feeling of safety becomes jeopardized. Facilitators need to be active and firm when verbal exchanges become malicious, reminding members about group norms.

Techniques to de-escalate conflict are more effective if they target the group rather than individual members. Making anger the group's responsibility diminishes the tendency toward scapegoating, and highlights how grief and anger intertwine. Guiding members to explore their anger opens the door to discussing some of the untold stories of loss. For example, some members may report feelings of abandonment and rage that the deceased has died and left them alone. At other times, exploration will reveal underlying guilt and self-criticism; e.g., "I should have brought him to the hospital sooner." In these cases, facilitators can explore the adaptive and hindering properties of anger:

> *It is getting hot in the room. Let's find a way to cool things off. How can we make our group conversation more constructive, productive, and safe?*
> *How is our anger related to our grief? How do we make sense (or meaning) of our grief-related anger?*
> *How does our anger move us forward, and how does our anger keep us stuck?*

CASE EXAMPLE

It is the beginning of the eighth session of a closed 12-week support group with eight participants. Paul starts the group by stating, "I was very bothered by what was said at the end of last week's session, so much so that I almost didn't come tonight." Members react with concurrent shock and curiosity, encouraging him to elaborate. "Last week, someone said that men have an easier time grieving than women. I felt like my experience of grief was minimized and that my feelings of loss weren't as valuable as others." As ruptures were previously introduced and normalized by the facilitator, the group is able to recognize the event. One member adds, "You are so brave for saying that; thank you." Bringing the group's attention to the fact that a rupture appears to have occurred and validating the risk Paul took in articulating it, the facilitator gently explores the character of the rupture by inviting other group members to comment on what they observed. There are a few awkward moments of silence as some members report they did not see the event, while others note they witnessed it but weren't sure what to do.

Finally, Rachael comments in a defensive tone, "I think you are responding to my comment and I feel like I am being put on the spot." The facilitator reassures the group that the goal of the discussion is not to assign blame but rather to increase understanding of the event and how it relates to grief. The facilitator invites Rachael to explore the underlying intention of her message. Over the course of a few minutes, she is able to articulate that her friends are telling her she should have gotten over the death by now even though it only occurred 3 months ago. "The strange thing is, I also berate myself that I am not getting over this sooner. I see men in this group who don't cry and seem to be doing so much better than me. I wish I could grieve like a man." From her perspective, men are able to contain their feelings, which makes her inability to contain affect a source of embarrassment and shame. With encouragement and guidance from the facilitator, Paul is able to articulate that he was unaware that he was giving the message that he was coping well. In fact, he has a lot of feelings surrounding his grief that he finds embarrassing and is worried that the group will judge his expression of them.

To maximize the therapeutic gain for the group, the facilitator invites all members to share their responses to the rupture. The facilitator draws out the common narrative threads and notes the divergent ones. Members are able to identify with the feelings of shame, reporting that they too perceive they are not coping as well as others expect them to. The group is also able to recognize that each person has a different reality that can naturally contribute to miscommunications. Some members are able to make links with their broader social world and identify how messages they have received and perceived as hurtful may in fact be misunderstandings between themselves and others.

Some members are able to explore their fear of speaking up during conflict. The facilitator encourages the group to explore how members have negotiated conflict in their lives and how these behaviors can manifest in the group. This leads to a productive discussion of the untold stories of conflict with the deceased. Speaking directly to the conflict experienced with his now deceased partner, Paul adds, "It is not that I don't love him and wish to honor his memory, but I don't miss all the fights we had."

CONCLUDING THOUGHTS

All the techniques above have the goal of bringing the focus of the group's discussion back to the ways in which the rupture is linked to their experience of grief. In this way, the group becomes a socio-microcosm where participants can (1) learn to explore feelings and experiences implicit to their grief process that resurface due to therapeutic ruptures; and (2) develop ways to cope with troubling messages in their broader social world that don't fit their experiences of grief.

Our initial research suggests two competing truths for those in bereavement groups: members perceive that they are not alone in their grief through the support of others in the group, and also realize that grief is a solitary event as evidenced by miscommunications and ruptures. The challenge for members lies in articulating their inner reality and emotional needs when a rupture occurs, both in the group and in their broader social network. When this happens, ruptures can lead to opportunities for growth.

References

MacKinnon, C. J., Smith, N. G., Henry, M., Berish, M., Milman, E., Körner, A., Chochinov, H. M., Copeland, L., & Cohen, S. R. (2011). Development of a meaning-centered group counselling intervention for bereavement. Paper presented at the 13th World Congress of Psycho-Oncology, Antalya, Turkey, October.

Safran, J. D, Muran, J. C., Samstag, L.W., & Stevens, C. (2001). Repairing alliance ruptures. *Psychotherapy*, *38*(4), 406–412.

Yalom, I. D., & Leszcz, M. (2005). *The theory and practice of group psychotherapy* (5th ed.). New York: Basic Books.

82
Talking about Talking with Couples and Families

An Hooghe

CLIENTS FOR WHOM THE TECHNIQUE IS APPROPRIATE

Most bereaved who seek grief therapy, individually, as a couple or as a family will appreciate the space and opportunity to explore the process of talking and listening to the pain of grief from early in the therapy process. Exploring the ambivalences and hesitations of every family member is especially important for couples or families who have not talked about the loss for a long time. However, a "meta-conversation" about constraints on communication within families may be less relevant when such communication is fluid and well established.

DESCRIPTION

In grief literature, and more generally in psychotherapy literature, there is a strong emphasis on the importance of the expression of grief, and openness in communication between partners and family members. Indeed, the expression of grief can be healing for the bereaved and sharing grief can be a way to create a stronger bond, a sense of togetherness and relational intimacy. However, in our view, rather than approaching grief communication as a necessary condition for all bereaved at all times, we propose to consider the contextual factors, ambivalences and relational tensions at a specific moment in the grieving process of the individuals and relationships involved (Hooghe, Neimeyer, & Rober, 2011). Therefore, we want to create a space and opportunity in clinical practice for family members to "talk about talking" (Fredman, 1997), to explore how it would be for them to talk about, and listen to, the pain related to the loss. Often family members are not used to, or choose not to talk about their grief with each other. They don't want to be a burden for the partner, their children or parents, they find it hard to express their pain, they see no value in making this enormous pain explicit, they fear not being listened to, they want to keep their own grief for themselves, they feel they lack the strength to deal with the suffering of others on top of their own, and so on. Exploring and acknowledging the hesitations of all family members in therapy gives them a chance to better understand the process of talking and not talking in their family. The therapist therefore needs to attend to the possible tensions and hesitations involved in sharing: *"How would it be for you to talk about this pain you feel? What would you be afraid of if you were to express some of it to your partner? How would it be for you if we were to talk about your deceased brother? How would it be for you to listen to the struggles and grief of your daughter? Which stories would be valuable to share? Would it be a good time for you now* to talk about how you all try to deal with this loss you had? With whom would you think it would be good to share some of your grief? What might be good reasons for you to keep your grief to yourself and not share it with others?" And so on. Not only is it valuable to explore this possibility of sharing with each other in advance, it is also important to reflect on this sharing afterwards: "How was it for you to express this to your father? How did it feel for you to see your mother crying when she was talking about your deceased sister? Did you feel listened to by your partner in your grief?"

It might be that, at least for a given moment in time, *not* sharing some (or all) feelings or thoughts, with some (or all) listeners is valuable for the bereaved and/or the bereaved family. An increased understanding of the possible risks associated with talking, as well as *not* talking, and the wish to remain silent about some aspects of their grief, may give them increased tolerance for their different ways of dealing with their grief.

CASE EXAMPLES

Case 1. Five years after the loss of their baby girl, Hellen called me with a request for grief therapy. I suggested that she bring her husband for the first session. I told her that her husband Wouter perhaps could help us all better understand what she was looking for in psychotherapy. I proposed that we could talk about how it would be for them to talk about the loss of their child. Although Wouter was somewhat hesitant to come along, he was willing to cooperate in exploring how talking about the loss could be helpful for his wife. They told me that shortly after their daughter Katrijn had died during delivery, they had talked a lot about Katrijn and the pain of losing their dreams for this child. However, after a few weeks they stopped talking to each other about the loss, not wanting to burden the partner with their own grief. Moreover, they increasingly felt the tremendous difference in their ways of grieving, and did not see the value in sharing their grief with one another. Wouter talked about how he had always tried to hide his tears and to be strong for Hellen. He was raised this way, he said, "to be there for your wife, to be the rock to lean on." Besides, he added, he did not think of himself as emotionally strong enough to confront her tears and comfort her. "I walk away when I see the pain in her eyes, because I'll crash if I stay with her." Although Hellen often felt alone in her grief, she also recognized that her husband had been the one who took care of her in many ways. After the delivery, she stayed home for more than two years while he worked hard, took care of all the financial and administrative hassles and finished the house they were building. She explained that her request for individual therapy was her way of creating the opportunity to express her grief without being a burden on Wouter. Exploring these last years in terms of their not talking, they both expressed how they were touched by realizing how they had been taking care of each other in their own ways. We further explored how it would be for them to talk more about, and listen to, each other's grief. On the one hand, Wouter said it would be nice to have a limited time in these sessions in which they could talk about Katrijn and speak her name again. On the other hand, he feared that it would be so hurtful that it would disturb him in the days following the sessions. Also Hellen expressed her ambivalence about talking in the presence of her husband. She was afraid of not being able to express her pain fully, knowing that it affected him, and at the same time she also longed for a connection in what they had lost together. Exploring their desires and hesitation about talking with each other about their grief, the two partners were able to find a clearer way forward in their conversation.

Case 2. For several sessions I met with a father and his three adolescent sons after the loss of their mother to suicide more than ten years ago. It was the oldest son, Gert, who took the initiative for the family to seek psychotherapy. For the past few years his brother Stijn had been drinking heavily and the situation at home was no longer sustainable. There were a lot of fights between the sons and the father seemed to have no authority over his adolescent children. Although Gert immediately started talking about their mother in the first session, we first wanted to explore with them how it would be for them to talk about the loss of their mother. François, the youngest, said they had never talked about their mother before. He regretted this, he said, because he was only 4 years old when his mother died and he did not have many memories of her. Still, he added, he thought it would be risky to talk about this subject because of the many difficult and strained years following the loss. In his opinion, there were so many things left unspoken, such as any discussion of his father's new girlfriend, his mother's depression, the motives and circumstances of her suicide, and more. Maybe, he feared, it would all get worse if they were to talk about these sensitive themes. Stijn similarly expressed his hesitation to talk about the suicide of their mother. Doing so, he said, would silence all the other relevant issues in their family life. Moreover, he feared that by talking about the loss, his excessive drinking would be entirely linked to a so-called complicated grief process. He preferred to talk about what he called their father's ignorance and lack of interest in their lives. The father agreed that there was no use in digging up history, but instead preferred to talk about how they could stop the fighting and Stijn's drinking. Clearly, there were many different meanings associated with the sharing of grief experiences in this family. We noted that for some of them there was a wish to share more of the story about their mother/wife, and to talk about the way this loss affected them all in different ways. Moreover, they all longed for an improved connection with each other. At the same time they all had their own reservations related to this talking and listening to each other. It could cause increased tension or blame related to the cause of the suicide. In addition, it could conceal other issues, or, they feared, it could lead to the simplification of diagnosing one of them with a complicated grief disorder. In the following sessions we discussed the complexity and ambivalence related to talking and not talking about their mother. As they all expressed how they missed the connection to the good stories about mother, we explored how it could feel safe for them to share some of the memories of earlier years when they were a young family. They all agreed it would be best, at least for now, not to talk about the time following the suicide, but keep the conversation limited to the time prior to the loss. To this end, they all brought pictures and objects that reminded them of their mother and shared stories of the good times they had had together. Gradually, connection was made between family members, and space was created to talk cautiously about their different ways of grieving. After some time they ended the therapy, which, they said, had resulted in decreased tension at home, while also acknowledging that it was too early for them to talk about some issues related to the circumstances of the suicide and their father's new girlfriend. Perhaps, they said, they would contact us again when the time was right to talk some more.

CONCLUDING THOUGHTS

Talking about, and listening to, the devastating pain that the loss of a loved one can elicit is a process characterized by dialectic, dialogic and dynamic features (Hooghe et al., 2011). Working with bereaved families, it is valuable to explore the meanings associated with sharing their stories of grief with each other, and the process of this sharing since the loss. We propose that exploring this process of talking and listening is appropriate in nearly every first session with the bereaved, and throughout the ongoing therapy process.

References

Fredman, G. (1997). *Death talk: Conversations with children and families.* London: Karnac.

Hooghe, A., Neimeyer, R. A., & Rober, P. (2011). The complexity of couple communication in bereavement: An illustrative case study. *Death Studies, 35,* 905–924.

83

The Workplace Study Circle

Barbara Barski-Carrow

CLIENTS FOR WHOM THE TECHNIQUE IS APPROPRIATE

Managers and employees of companies or organizations in which a worker has experienced recent bereavement. Although it assists both the grieving employee and others in the workplace in adapting to this transition, it is not intended as a substitute for professional therapy when accommodation to loss is complicated.

DESCRIPTION

The Study Circle is a structured, yet informal, adult educational format that has been used by local groups for over 100 years. Originally, participants met in small groups for a series of sessions to study such subjects as history, art, languages, literature and current political issues. I discovered the Study Circle's power in helping people deal with others who have experienced grief and trauma. When used in the workplace, a grief-focused Study Circle enables managers and co-workers to prepare each other to interact helpfully with fellow employees who are returning to work after having experienced a significant loss in their lives.

As an educational format, a Study Circle is not a seminar, group therapy, psychotherapeutic technique or a training workshop. Sessions focused on issues of employees returning to the workplace after suffering a loss can be held in the workplace, for example, in a lunchtime setting. These sessions give managers and employees an opportunity to create a learning dialogue in a safe environment. Each session provides a structured format to exchange thoughts and feelings about a very sensitive topic and allows participants to gain an understanding of how to acknowledge a co-worker when that person is vulnerable.

In selecting participants, usually from 10 to 12 per group, include managers and employees, men and women, extroverts and introverts, creating a mix of people where the energy will evoke a lively exchange of ideas. Participants should make a commitment to participate in the Study Circle actively.

Study Circle sessions usually last an hour. Participants are given a handout ahead of time describing the topic, theme and questions to be discussed, providing participants a chance to think about the issues, feel more at ease during the session and create more interaction within the group.

The group leader does not have to be a trained or skilled facilitator, therapist or grief counselor. The person only needs to be interested to lead the group into discussion and be an attentive listener. The leader's job includes keeping the group focused, encouraging everyone to participate, raising questions for group discussion and creating a collaborative learning atmosphere where all members feel free to express themselves and share their ideas.

Value of a Study Circle on grief

In many cases, people who have experienced grief, especially after a sudden unexpected loss or a traumatic experience, need private counseling or psychotherapeutic help. If such grieving employees come back to work with their grief or trauma still somewhat unresolved, it is important that the person's managers and co-workers be sensitive to the person's issues and needs. The workplace treatment of the grieving person can either foster the person's healing or hinder it. And while the counselor or therapist may see the grieving person one hour each week, the person's managers and co-workers interact with the person eight hours each day, five days a week. Thus, it is important to educate managers and co-workers in the grieving and healing process but this does not necessarily imply education by a specialist. Because many managers and co-workers have personally experienced some form of grief or traumatic life experience, they already have a very good idea of how the person returning to work would like to be treated. During the Study Circle the group members become each other's teachers.

Topics for sessions

A Study Circle must always have a topic that each participant considers important and of practical value for his/her life. As a framework for discussion, the topic gives the facilitator and group a clear focus and direction for the session.

Topic 1: *Putting out a welcome mat*: In this first session, managers and employees discuss how to create a welcoming home environment where a returning grieving employee can feel safe when he or she returns to work. Safety and security issues are at the heart of an employee who is returning to work after a trauma. "*Will I still have my job? How are co-workers going to treat me? Will I be able to take a work break during the day, if I need one?*"

Topic 2: *Lending a listening ear*: This session helps create bonds among participants because most managers and employees have experienced a trauma in their life or work and many have had a difficult time when they returned to work. Here, participants have a choice whether they want to tell their "trauma story." Some may choose not to share their feelings with their co-workers or their supervisors, while others want the rest to know how they felt in their grieving process. This sharing of personal stories can be very therapeutic for both managers and co-workers. For example, in one Study Circle a woman stated her boss listened to her at lunch for a whole year while she talked of how her son was shot. After the year, she stated she was okay, but she had needed that "listening ear." Hearing other group members discuss what kind of listening is helpful in such circumstances assists co-workers in offering something similar to the returning employee.

Topic 3: *Offering a helping hand*: This session offers managers and co-workers the opportunity to take the initiative in restoring their personal and professional connection with the returning worker. The need to belong and be part of a workplace group is essential for a returning employee. We humans need this sense of connectedness and belongingness in many different ways in our lives. The workplace provides us with an opportunity to meet and develop lifelong friendships. These bonds grow stronger when grief is allowed to be shared.

CASE EXAMPLE

When Jim's wife died, a group of managers and employees at his plant, who had participated in the Study Circle on grief and loss a month before, got together to respond. Instead of acting individually, a dozen or more of his co-workers came as a group to his wife's wake. This showed their solidarity with Jim. When Jim returned to work, he told his managers and others how impressed he was with the strong support he had experienced from his co-workers. Instead of expecting him to get back to work as if nothing had happened, the manager suggested (from what he had learned in the Study Circle) that Jim might need some extra time to take care of the many legal matters required after a family member dies. The manager suggested that Jim might take time off work, as needed over the next few weeks, to deal with such matters. Jim's co-workers, sensitized to his situation from their Study Circle experience, made him feel welcome again, volunteered to cover for him when he had outside things to attend to, listened with an open ear to his stories, and made him feel connected to the workplace community.

CONCLUDING THOUGHTS

A Study Circle focused on grief and loss has wide application in any work setting. All employees have had first- or second-hand experience with death and other major losses, and in a Study Circle each of their suggestions on what to say and how to behave—especially what *not* to say and how *not* to behave—to a grieving co-worker are immensely valuable to others. Bereavement professionals could easily coach managers or other employees on how to lead a Study Circle, and help ensure that grieving employees returning to the workplace would be welcomed, listened to and made to feel a part of the working team.

Further reading

Barski-Carrow, B. (2000). Using study circles in the workplace as an educational method of facilitating readjustment after a traumatic life experience. *Death Studies, 24,* 421–439.

Barski-Carrow, B. (2010). *When trauma survivors return to work: Understanding emotional recovery: A handbook for managers and co-workers.* Lanham, MD: University Press of America.

84
The Kindness Project

Joanne Cacciatore

CLIENTS FOR WHOM THE TECHNIQUE IS APPROPRIATE

Children, adolescents, and adults who have experienced the death of any family member or friend and who wish to intentionally remember them through mindful service to another. Focusing on kindness to another may feel premature to mourners in the early aftermath of loss, and especially traumatic loss, who may understandably be focused more on their own suffering or anger than on the well-being of others.

DESCRIPTION

I started the Kindness Project in 1996 as a way for grieving parents anonymously to remember and honor a child who died. Since then, more than 1,000,000 Kindness Projects have occurred globally in the U.S. and abroad in Romania, Australia, Paraguay, Bermuda, the Netherlands, Spain, Mexico, New Zealand, Chile, Italy, Malta, and other countries. The idea came to me in 1996 when, just months after the death of a baby daughter, I wanted to spend her holiday gift money on underprivileged children anonymously. This sparked a pattern of random acts of generosity, which I discovered were often more healing to me than beneficial for the recipient. I created a "kindness card" that could accompany the good deed, and began telling others about it. The idea quickly spread through the bereaved parent community, and on July 27, 2011, the day we would declare International Kindness Project Day (www.kindnessproject.org), more than 10,000 people around the world united to use free Kindness Project cards to commit random acts of anonymous kindness in memory of a loved one who died (Figure 84.1(a) and (b)). While these good deeds do not eradicate grief, nor should they do so, they do provide a means through which the mourner can redirect painful emotions into feelings of love and compassion and hope.

CASE EXAMPLE

Ann is a middle-aged woman who experienced the death of her baby, Joshua, to sudden infant death syndrome several years ago. Through the Selah Grief Model (see Chapter 3 in this book), she was able to pause and be with her suffering, to actively approach her grief, and then discover meaning through service to others. Ann was now a leader of a local support group, helping other parents whose children died, and I was her counselor and mentor. One of her favorite

Figure 84.1(a) and (b) Kindness cards in English and Spanish

mindfulness strategies was the Kindness Project, and she participated frequently. This particular October day happened to be the third anniversary of her baby's death. I received a call from Ann, sobbing, as she recounted the story: She was engaging in active self-care, taking the day off work and treating herself to a favorite meal at a favorite restaurant. Minutes after her meal arrived, a large crowd was seated across from Ann, and at center stage a visibly pregnant woman about to enjoy a baby shower. Ann described feeling nauseous, confused, and overwhelmed. She felt rage erupting in her, shocked that it was directed toward a pregnant stranger. She described how she wanted to turn to the innocent woman, seething, "Save your receipts, because some babies die!" I replied with gentle hesitation, "Did you say that?" She had not, but her mind was whirling with silent gasps of self-loathing and disbelief, and she left her unfinished meal and headed toward the door. She paused, took a deep breath, took out a Kindness Project card, wrote Joshua's name on it, pre-paid the restaurant bill of the shower party in full, and called me weeping. We spent almost an hour on the phone discussing how it felt: bittersweet, stinging, honoring, painful, shameful. Several hours later, I received an email from our website inquiry form. The email read:

> *Today we received one of the nicest gifts ever. I was at Mona's Café having my baby shower when our server gave us a card. Our meals had been paid in memory of Joshua Michael. If*

you know who this lovely person is, would you please relay my message? Tell them that they truly touched our lives today. Tell them that their little boy is lucky to have such a loving family. And tell them that Joshua is an angel who touched our lives today. We will never forget him. Sincerely, Jill Anderson

I picked up the phone and called Ann, and reading her the note, we wept affirming tears together.

CONCLUDING THOUGHTS

Ultimately, every grieving parent's wish is to be reunited with his or her child. The Kindness Project doesn't bring Joshua back to Ann. However, it does provide a means through which a parent—or sibling, grandparent, spouse, friend—can remember, honor, and remain connected to the dead.

On July 27, 2011, mourners around the world publicly expressed their experiences with International Kindness Project Day. Christine in Iowa and her teenaged son brought much-needed supplies to homeless shelters in memory of their son and brother. Sarah and Rae-Ann anonymously paid for meals at restaurants in memory of their son. Melissa randomly wrapped $20 around a Kindness Card and left it for a young boy, about 10 years old, to find. As she quietly watched from a distance, she noted his mother's elation because now they could afford to buy him his much-needed medication. Her own son would have been 10 years old this year. Deborah hand-made dresses to ship anonymously to Haitian children in memory of her daughter who died 24 years earlier. Sandie and Mark paid for the adoption of 16 dogs in memory of their 16-year-old son and left 17 potted flowers next to random cars in memory of their 17-year-old daughter. Both were killed in a car crash two years earlier. Heidi went to a bookstore and bought a stack of her favorite childhood books, then gave them to the cashier to give away to random children in memory of the daughter to whom she would never again read. Brandy and her 4-year-old daughter delivered bouquets of flowers to people in nursing homes in memory of their son and brother, and her grandparents. Angelica anonymously tended to her ill neighbor's yard in memory of her nephew. Jeanne bought coffee for the person behind her in line. That set off a chain of kindnesses that lasted through several other people as each paid for another in memory of her son. One mother said, "I am thankful that I can finally see beyond my grief and still be a light in the lives of others, thanks to my son Lucas who showed me how to love."

And on that October day in the restaurant, Joshua reached through time and space, symbolically resurrected through his mother's love, and touched the life of a stranger. That pregnant woman ended up naming her new baby after Joshua. Few therapeutic strategies are as painfully beautiful and transformative as the Kindness Project.

85

All the Stars Above

Daisy Luiten

CLIENTS FOR WHOM THE TECHNIQUE IS APPROPRIATE

Adults, adolescents and children from 6 years old. *All the Stars Above* is suitable for use in individual therapy as well as within group or family sessions. However, it may be inappropriate when clients are struggling with complicated or traumatic symptomatology and require more intensive individual treatment. It should be used under the supervision of a therapist.

DESCRIPTION

All the Stars Above is a therapeutic tool in the form of a board game. It can be used for one to eight participants. There is a special die added for larger groups, for instance, a classroom situation, as an alternative to moving around the game board, which serves to direct players to particular topics of discussion and disclosure.

To distinguish between the language of children and that of teenagers and adults, the playing cards are printed on both sides. One side is for children aged 6–12 years, the other is for teenagers and adults (12 years and older).

All the Stars Above consists of an octagonal game board (Figure 85.1). A wooden sun is placed in the middle with a tea light in it. This light can be lit for the deceased. All participants play with their own "tear," which symbolically represents pearls when they share their stories. By following the route on the board the clients pass through eight different categories of disclosure: Feelings; Memories; Environment; Dying; Funeral; Moving on together with our inner strength; What place does the deceased occupy in your life?; Assignments. Each category—recognizable by color and symbol—has its own specific set of question cards. When clients land on a particular square, they receive a corresponding question card. They read the question out loud and may answer it.

Included with *All the Stars Above* is an Indian Talking Stick. As the name suggests, it originated with Native Americans, and is used to indicate who holds the floor for a given speaking turn. Others must show respect and listen. By using this Talking Stick, all players get their turn and may express themselves in their own way. If participants choose not to talk, they don't have to. If participants would like to respond but need more time to think, they may also save the question card in an individual plastic folder until they find the answer.

Figure 85.1 *All the Stars Above* therapeutic tool for facilitating sharing regarding a loss

Source: Photo by Jessica Scholtes.

To cover a vast array of subjects with respect to grief, bereavement and dying, *All the Stars Above* provides more than 700 question and assignment cards. Participants are addressed in an open and direct style. The questions get to the heart of the matter. In this way the players have to face direct questions, stimulating them to share their experiences. Sample questions include:

- *What helps you when you are feeling sad?*
- *Did you get new jobs in the house after * died? (instead of * you name the deceased)*
- *What did you do with * when you were together for the last time?*
- *What was great fun to do all together?*

Some causes of death raise their own specific questions. Therefore *All the Stars Above* provides an extra deck of question cards in the category "Dying." Asterisks and dots at the bottom of the cards refer to the cause of death (e.g. terrorism, natural disaster, suicide). The cards can be found in the back of the card tray and can be added to the general deck if applicable.

There are eight different assignment options in the category assignments. You can choose to use all of them or a selection. Four of these eight options aim to release tension and encourage relaxing. And four options aim to express feelings and thoughts in a different way. Participants are asked to finish the sentence, to choose one out of three words and share what comes to mind, to write a poem or to draw a picture. This way, participants who do not have the words get the chance to share their story in a way that might work better for them. A 3-minute hourglass timer is supplied to set an optional time limit on the assignments.

In addition to the assignments that are part of *All the Stars Above*, the therapist may choose to use art during the board game (for instance, drawing or painting). Each participant throws the die, lands on a particular square and receives an appropriate question card. This question card is the starting point for the artwork. If the therapist chooses drawing, everyone takes a different question card and draws the answer. The hourglass can be turned two or three times so this won't take too long. Afterwards the participants can show their pictures and everyone can choose to explain something about their drawing.

CASE EXAMPLE

Patty was a happy but quiet girl of 12 years old. She smiled often and had a good sense of humor. Patty's mother had been ill for one and a half years with colon cancer. She had been in the hospital for a long time receiving treatment. When her condition improved, she was released from the hospital. Unfortunately, she got pain in her stomach not long after. Patty and her younger sister left the house to sleep at their aunt's. During that night Patty's mother died unexpectedly of heart failure.

From that moment on Patty's carefree life changed completely. She got a lot of support from her friends and the teacher at school, and her dad and aunts did a good job making "home" as normal as possible. Nevertheless, she missed her mother dreadfully. School didn't go well, she felt insecure and anxious and thought about her mother a lot. She also saw awful images from the moment she closed her eyes to go to sleep.

A few months after her mother's death, Patty came to see me in art therapy. She found it hard to talk about her mother, but she liked to draw, paint and make things about what had happened to her, about her memories and about her feelings.

As Patty was a joyful child who had not lost her sense of humor after the death of her mother, it was sometimes hard to get through to her more painful feelings. Everything was "fine" and she was doing "great," even when the doctors found out that her mother's colon cancer was heritable and the DNA test proved that Patty was carrying the same genes as her mother. The fear she had felt before had now turned into reality, but Patty's reaction was kind of cool, she didn't show much emotion when she told me about it.

I knew from experience that discussing a variety of subjects around the death of a loved one was much easier with the use of All the Stars Above, so I decided to use this therapeutic tool with Patty. Patty liked the idea of sharing stories about her mother by playing All the Stars Above and so we did.

I added the extra cards for the dying cause "disease," with specific questions about Patty's situation. When Patty at one point received the question: "Are you afraid to become ill yourself?" She threw the card back, saying: "I am already ill!" I asked her: "Is that what you think?" Patty: "Yes." I said: "I understood that you have the same genes as your mother and that means that the disease could develop more easily; it doesn't mean you are already ill. The doctor will do a check-up every year to see if you have developed polyps and, if so, the polyps will be removed before they turn cancerous . . . But I am not a doctor . . . Let's see what questions we can write down to put to your doctor."

We sat down and made a list of questions. The heart of the matter was that everyone (her doctor, her dad), including me, had asked her if she understood what the doctor explained. "Yes," she said. She had even explained to me what the doctor had said to her. What we all didn't know was that she thought she would go the same way as her mother from the moment the doctor found polyps. She thought that she would die soon after. I talked to her doctor and gave Patty the answers to her questions the next session. She felt so relieved!

CONCLUDING THOUGHTS

All the Stars Above helped Patty to give words to her thoughts, worries and feelings. It gave her an opening to talk about the tough subjects she was struggling with all by herself. Until that moment it was easier for her to avoid talking about it. Even within a family session Patty dared to discuss subjects she had been avoiding discussing before, and she found out that this helped her. *All the Stars Above* served her in moving on together with her inner strength.

All the Stars Above offers an opening to communication about a variety of aspects concerning the loss, especially in the family context (Walsh, 2006). It stimulates and facilitates the opening up of feelings and thoughts, and can promote meaning-making and resilience in the wake of loss (Neimeyer & Sands, 2011). Research with therapists who have used the technique indicates that they rate it as visually appealing and welcoming for clients (85%), usefully stimulating of client disclosure (99%) and exploration of feeling (98%), and generative of client insights (84%), and improved coping with the loss (88%). As with Patty, therapists also report that the technique helps bring forth important, but often unknown issues for therapeutic discussion (97%) (see Luiten, 2009, for more details). While preliminary, such results are encouraging, and suggest that this technique can be a useful adjunct to grief therapy and bereavement support.

References and further reading

Luiten, D. M. F. (2009). Results of a survey of *All the Stars Above*. All the Stars Above Productions. Available at: www.daisyluiten.com/all-the-stars-above/experiences.html.

Neimeyer, R. A., & Sands, D. C. (2011). Meaning reconstruction in bereavement: From principles to practice. In R. A. Neimeyer, D. L. Harris, H. Winokuer, & G. Thornton (Eds.), *Grief and bereavement in contemporary society: Bridging research and practice*. New York: Routledge.

Walsh, F. (2006). Traumatic loss and major disasters: strengthening family and community resilience. *Family Process*, 46: 207–227.

86

Group Treatment of Anticipatory Grief in Senior Pseudo-Psychosis

Robert F. Morgan

CLIENTS FOR WHOM THE TECHNIQUE IS APPROPRIATE

Elders facing anticipatory grief from constrained possibilities, particularly the death and disability of their friends and, eventually, themselves typically benefit from this group structure. It is contraindicated for inpatients with Alzheimer's or stroke, or those who have been lobotomized or electro-shocked.

DESCRIPTION

Group treatment methods can be particularly effective for otherwise isolated individuals and are re-emerging as an inexpensive alternative or adjunct to one-on-one psychotherapy. Yet they can be particularly daunting for those with cognitive impairment or the memory loss found in elder clients, particularly chronic in-patients. By applying a mixture of standard existential here-and-now group process and creative activities to make the group environment more memorable, combined with specific emphasis on the anticipatory grief of death and disability, functional memory loss can be reduced and therapeutic goals upgraded.

CASE EXAMPLE

For a year, I worked with a group of institutionalized chronic senior patients in a state mental hospital. We met every day, Monday through Friday, for 90 minutes. Initially, all 10 patients had severe memory loss to the point where remembering each other's names was difficult. None had Alzheimer's or stroke, and none had been lobotomized or electro-shocked. So they were labeled "senile psychotics." They could speak reasonably well about their distant past, but their view of present and future was blurred and dysfunctional.

In the second week I brought in food and the group looked forward to this at least. Then we began doing spontaneous and interesting things—going for a walk to the ocean, painting graffiti on the wall, telling jokes. We had "remember the years I was in High School" parties where the dress/music/events of an era were relived.

In a month, the "here and now" group process began to work. People remembered everybody's name and launched into perceptive discussions of hospital life. We had made the present both fun and safe, so they carefully ventured into it.

But there was no apparent transfer of these newly restored abilities to their home hospital ward on the rest of the day. Once out of the group room, the confusion rolled in like a fog, yet again. I understood that their normal present life outside the group was unpleasant but that didn't seem to be enough for such functional pathology.

Howard Gudeman, an existential psychologist and my supervisor, suggested they were being immobilized by a traumatic fear of death. Given their age and environment, this was no irrational fear. Most of their friends had died and a season never ended without a funeral of somebody they knew or cared for. Further, they grieved not only for their deceased or disabled friends but for themselves. They lived in a world of increasingly constrained possibilities and, for now, an unthinkable future. This was a traumatic grieving that they had never confronted. Hiding from it in their past was dysfunctional.

By this time, the group trusted me and so when I began to talk about death, they tolerated it as my own "craziness." It was a delicate intervention since I was half a century younger than most of them. But within a month they had all confronted their mortality in their own way. Some decided to live a lot longer and began special exercise and nutrition programs. Some became more religious in a sectarian way or more spiritual. It took several months, but eventually all could discuss their mortality in a calm way and even plan for it (we each wrote our own epitaph, obituary, and will).

With the death trauma reduced, the memory of all improved, both at our meetings and even over the rest of the day. The group members now functioned more normally and moved to individual problems, including hospital discharge. Shining a light on the fear of death can help any community cope more effectively (Morgan & Wilson, 2005).

CONCLUDING THOUGHTS

After developing these techniques for an inpatient population of senior and chronic patients, I have since adapted them in my practice with a wide variety of outpatient elders. They experience the same anticipatory grief from a world of narrowing possibilities leading to death or disability. Anticipatory grief occurs when a catastrophic or death-related outcome is assumed to be beyond intervention or, at times, conscious comprehension. Confrontation and planning have often led to enhanced memory, improved functionality, reduced depression, bolstered health, more realistic and meaningful five-year plans and reduced body age (Morgan, 1981; Morgan & Wilson, 2005). The introduction of the concept of anticipatory grief fits well into the four decades of research literature on death anxiety (Neimeyer, 1994), and carries clear treatment implications for elderly or institutionalized patients.

References

Morgan, R. F. (1981). *Interventions in applied gerontology.* Dubuque, IA: Kendall/Hunt.

Morgan, R. F., & Wilson J. (2005). *Growing younger: How to measure and change body age.* Charleston, SC/Grass Valley, CA: Morgan Foundation.

Neimeyer, R. A. (Ed.). (1994). *Death anxiety handbook: Research, instrumentation, and application.* New York: Taylor & Francis.

Part XVI
Ritualizing Transition

87

Therapeutic Ritual

Kenneth J. Doka

CLIENTS FOR WHOM THE TECHNIQUE IS APPROPRIATE

Carefully constructed with clients, therapeutic ritual can be used with virtually any client who would choose to plan and participate in such symbolic action. It may be contra-indicated with clients for whom ritual of any kind conjures a negative association with a religious system with which they are disaffected, or at points in their grieving when manage-ment of the raw pain of loss has greater priority.

DESCRIPTION

Gennep (1960) indicates that rituals are powerful in that they are *liminal*. By liminal, Gennep means that they strike us at the threshold of consciousness, speaking to both our conscious and subconscious simultaneously. Rituals have long been recognized as powerful interventions used to help individuals cope with loss. Even prior to written history, evidence clearly indicates that Neolithic humans developed extensive rituals to bury the dead.

Given that history, it is unsurprising that research has affirmed the therapeutic role of funeral—especially when bereaved individuals participate in the planning and actively participate in the ritual (Doka, 1984; Bolton & Camp, 1987, 1989; Gross & Klass, 1997). Rando (1984) further delineates many useful facets of ritual, including allowing individuals to act, offering legitimization for physical and affective ventilation, delineating grief (i.e., limiting grief to a certain space and time), giving a sense of control (i.e., doing something at an otherwise uncontrollable event), providing an ongoing sense of connection to the loss, allowing space to safely confront ambivalent or confused feeling or thoughts, generating social support, and offering opportunities to find meaning in the loss by applying spiritual frameworks to that loss.

Using ritual as a therapeutic tool extends this value in many ways. Here it is not just harnessing the therapeutic value of a single activity such as a funeral but rather developing rituals at varied points within the grieving process. Such rituals should not be simply assigned to a client but rather be developed drawing on the client's needs and personal narrative of loss. Because rituals vary, they can affirm a continuing bond, mark a transition in the client's grief journey, validate a relationship or legacy of the deceased, or promote symbolic recon-ciliation with the deceased. Rituals can be done individually by the client, witnessed by the therapist or others, or be done communally. Rituals can be a bridge to the client's culture or spirituality.

Rituals can be developed for a variety of contexts and allow distinct messages. *Rituals of continuity* are rituals that emphasize, even in the midst of loss, that the deceased is still remembered. An Anniversary Mass, for example, would be a collective ritual of continuity as would any ongoing memorial service. Others may choose a less public ritual; perhaps lighting a candle on the deceased's birthday or the anniversary of the loss.

On the other hand, *rituals of transition* affirm that one has entered a new place in one's journey through grief. In one case, for example, a mother whose adolescent son had died was reluctant, even after a year, to move any of her deceased son's clothes or effects from his bedroom despite the fact that one of her daughters now sharing a room with her sister requested the room. In therapy, she created a ritual much like a *potlatch* (a gift-giving cere-mony of indigenous people that, among other areas, was practiced in the Pacific Northwest) where she reverently removed the items she wished to retain and then distributed the remaining items to family or friends in a joyous celebration of her son's life. Once the material was distributed, her daughter was free to move into the room.

Rituals of reconciliation either ask for or extend forgiveness. One client used a ritual in which she wrote a letter to her often absent father, read it at the grave site and then burnt it as an offering as a way to forgive her Dad for his prior neglect.

Rituals of affirmation offer a complement to rituals of reconciliation. Rituals of affirma-tion simply provide ways to acknowledge legacies or say thanks. An example was practiced by a young man who had experienced the loss of his father in his early life, and who devel-oped a ritual to thank his deceased Dad for choosing the boy's godfather and committing the godfather's involvement in the son's life.

CASE STUDY

Mary is a widow in her forties, whose husband died 7 years ago after a 5-year, debilitating struggle with multiple sclerosis. Mary is at a point where she would like to take off her wedding ring and begin dating, but she seems unable to do so. In discussing her relationship with her counselor, it becomes clear that the ring has great meaning. Though the illness was very difficult for both, every night after a long day's struggle, when they lay in bed, they would put their ring fingers together and repeat their vows "in sickness and in health." The counselor acknowledged that she had put on the ring in a ritual that had great value, and both he and Mary agreed that it should be removed in another meaningful ritual. It was arranged that on a Sunday afternoon, Mary and her friends and family gathered in the church where she and her husband had exchanged vows. The priest met her at the altar. There he repeated the vows, now in the past tense. "Were you faithful in sickness and in health, in good times and in bad?" he intoned. Mary could, in the presence of these witnesses, affirm that she had been. The priest then asked for the ring. As Mary later described, it came off "as if by magic." As planned, the priest arranged to have both rings interlocked and welded to her wedding picture. He returned it to her in a brief ritual of continuity.

CONCLUDING THOUGHTS

In planning therapeutic rituals with clients, it is essential to follow certain principles:

- *Rituals arise from the client's narrative*: Rituals should be planned with and by the individual client. What meaning or need shapes the ritual? What elements should be part of the ritual? Who should witness it? Some rituals may be private while others may be shared.

- *Select elements for a ritual that are visible yet retain symbolic meanings*: This draws upon the liminal aspect of the ritual. The ritual should focus on these visible elements but be drawn by them to the underlying symbolism. In the preceding case, the ring was not only a band of gold but also a symbol of an honored commitment.
- *Rituals should be planned and processed*: Before undertaking a ritual, it is critical that it be carefully thought out. The powerful ritual around the wedding ring would have been far different if the priest had asked at that special moment when the ring was removed "Who gets it now?" Follow the planning through to the conclusion. After the ritual, individuals may need opportunities to process, or continue to think about, or talk about the event.
- *Rituals should use primal elements to enhance the liminality of the act*: Water, fire (such as candles), earth (e.g. flowers), and wind (music) enhance the value of ritual. Where appropriate, these elements can be incorporated in the event.

References

Bolton, C., & Camp, D. (1987). Funeral rituals and the facilitation of grief work. *Omega: The Journal of Death and Dying, 17*, 343–351.

Bolton, C., & Camp, D. (1989). The post-funeral ritual in bereavement counseling and grief work. *Journal of Gerontological Social Work, 13*, 49–59.

Doka, K. J. (1984). Expectation of death, participation in funeral arrangements, and grief adjustment. *Omega: The Journal of Death and Dying, 15*, 119–130.

Gennep, A. van (1960). *The rites of passage*. Chicago: University of Chicago Press.

Gross, R. E., & Klass, D. (1997). Tibetan Buddhism and the resolution of grief: The Bardo-Thodell for the living and the grieving. *Death Studies, 21*, 377–398.

Rando, T. (1984). *Grief, dying, and death: Clinical interventions for caregivers*. Champaign, IL: Research Press.

88

The "Barefoot Walkabout"

Joanne Cacciatore

CLIENTS FOR WHOM THE TECHNIQUE IS APPROPRIATE

Adults who are in relatively good health and who wish to integrate mindfulness practices as part of their everyday life. Being in a barefoot state while hiking a trail may pose some risk to an individual if he or she is not paying very careful attention to each step. In addition, this practice may be impractical in certain seasons, terrains and inclement weather. Clinicians and clients must exercise prudence and foresight when using this technique.

DESCRIPTION

As a result of many years of research and increasing evidence of its efficacy (Hoffman, Sawyer, Witt, & Oh, 2010), there is a widespread movement in the U.S. toward daily meditative practice. I have been no exception to this trend, and began my own practice in early 2007. Despite my own contemplative practice, cordoned off between 6 and 7am, I wanted to become what I'd named in my mind as a walking meditator. I wanted the contemplative life to permeate my consciousness all day. Every day was a rehearsal, and I often fell short. As an avid nature-lover, I hike nearly every week, at least several miles. On one occasion in 2007, I hiked up a beautiful trail in Sedona, Arizona. It was sunrise, and the crisp air danced between the rustling leaves. The sun burned through the clouds, creating vibrant shades of marmalade orange and metallic silver. The magic of the natural world awed me. Before I realized it, however, I had hiked to the top of the trail, stepped high on the majestic red boulders of Sedona; and I hadn't recalled anything about my journey there. Instead, I realized that I'd been preoccupied with many racing thoughts: grant proposals, papers to grade, and mostly, my beloved dead: my daughter, my parents, my best friend. I sat in reflective solitude at the top of this trail for about 30 minutes and considered the many present moments I'd missed in allowing my mind to wander so far "off the path." And I decided, as part of my quest toward becoming a walking meditator, that I would emulate the humble tradition of the Discalced Carmelites of the 15th and 16th centuries, returning on my path barefoot down the trail.

I was quite surprised to discover that I could learn about my grief journey through mindfully walking barefoot, perhaps because of the vulnerably present state of mind it incited. The first step forward took courage. Sharp rocks and cacti needles were an unfamiliar sensation. But I found I could avoid things that added to my discomfort. And physical pain is an effective reminder to avoid that which causes us pain; thus, with every step, I paid close attention, noticing things I'd never before seen. Footprints on the path reminded me that others, too, had been there. The colonies of ants working busily told the story of how life goes on for others, even when we feel it should stop. Cairns built by those who came before would show me the direction. Yet, no one's trail will be precisely replicable. I found that during this sojourn things will get broken: nails, skin, and the heart. And even when the sun hides itself behind the clouds, it remains a steady presence that I can trust. Some places on the trail are easier than others, and it's not all uphill. The simple things matter: sometimes, a cool, smooth rock was an oasis for which I felt immense gratitude as I rested my sore, bare feet. And as I came around the last corner of my 2-mile hike down the trail barefooted, I noticed a typical Arizona cactus (the ones that had deposited their thorny vestiges in my heels as I learned to pay attention closely) and a single, gorgeous daisy stood in camaraderie, by its side. The ultimate of all lessons: There it is—the beauty, right next to the pain. And the barefoot walkabout became a regular mindfulness practice for me and for my clients seeking a contemplative life as appropriate (Bashaw, 2011). This technique can begin as either secular or existential; however, many clients may end the experience feeling as if they have had a sublime spiritual encounter that is consistent with each individual system of faith.

CASE EXAMPLE

Darla is a 50-year-old divorced mother of two whose 24-year-old son died in an automobile crash one year prior to her seeking counseling. She described herself as once vivacious and deeply spiritual with a wide variety of interests and social activities. She was well-liked at her job in the tourist industry and had many friends. That was until Mike's death. Darla sought help at the behest of concerned others who convinced her that she was depressed and needed medications to help her cope. During our initial intake, Darla expressed doubt about her sense of self in the world. She had "lost her footing" and all her belief in a just and loving God disappeared. Darla missed Mike terribly and was having significant difficulty adjusting to life in his absence. I asked her to tell me about Mike, and she spent considerable time describing her remarkable child who was, also, deeply spiritual. The first six months we worked together, we spent merely being with—and thus validating—Darla's profound sense of loss. She began to dream about Mike, and these dreams comforted her. She brought in photographs and mementos of him, and she would recount details of their time together. Darla and Mike both loved the outdoors, and hiking was one of the few activities that she had not abandoned after his death. As the anniversary of Mike's death approached, she began to share her fears about the day. I asked if she would like to try a silent barefoot walkabout with me on that day. Darla was excited to move her therapy outside the four walls. Before the hike, we discussed the importance of being fully present in each moment, with each step. We agreed we would remain silent on the round-trip pilgrimage, waiting until the time felt right to discuss what had happened. During the hike, Darla remained quiet. At one point she stopped and began to weep. Our eyes met, and I nodded as if to assure her to take her time. We sat in silence at the top of the mountain for about an hour before descending the trail again. When we returned, we sat quietly again, and I waited until she was ready to speak. Darla broke the silence after a few minutes, thanking me for what she called an amazing experience. I asked her if she wanted to tell me about what happened, and she replied that she did not. She felt it was "too sacred" for words, but that the experience had been "powerful and life-changing."

Later that day, she went into her son's room, a room that had remained tightly closed for more than a year, and she put on his favorite music. She said that she danced around the house, singing songs they'd once sung together, for the first time since he died. She laughed and she cried and "for the first time, experienced pure joy again." The next few sessions felt different for us both. Darla was more tolerant of her own emotional state, moment by moment, and felt better able to handle stressors at work. She reconnected with a few friends at work, and began socializing on weekends. Darla began barefoot hiking regularly for the next several months. She said she felt "closer to God again" and sometimes could feel Mike's presence with her. She continued to integrate aspects of the Selah Grief Model (see Chapter 3 in this volume) through weekly therapy sessions, including a morning meditation every day, gardening, and a compilation of letters to Mike. Darla never required medication in order to regain equilibrium. She reported feeling more optimistic about the future and that her renewed relationship with God has helped her gain a once elusive feeling of hope. She says she wants to work toward being able to help others who are suffering the death of a child "one day in the future" when she is ready.

CONCLUDING THOUGHTS

Darla's experience with the barefoot walkabout is not unique: I have done this exercise with many clients since 2007, and most of them experience a shift in their worldview that is often numinous and ineffable, even for the secular humanist. Creative therapeutic strategies invite the client to a place of openness, curiosity, humility, and connectedness. And though the effects of these techniques may leave us without words that sufficiently describe the why and the how, for many, such words are inconsequential. Rather, we need only realize the potential quenching of our thirst for meaning in the aftermath of traumatic loss, the vital lesson of an inexplicable beauty which is born of pain.

References

Bashaw, M. A. (2011). Finding purpose in grief. *Raising Arizona Kids*, January, 2011.

Hoffman, S., Sawyer, A., Witt, A., & Oh, D. (2010). The effect of mindfulness-based cognitive therapy on anxiety and depression: a meta-analytic review. *Journal of Consulting and Clinical Psychology*, 78(2), 169–183.

89
The Grief Spiral

Christine Barrett

CLIENTS FOR WHOM THE TECHNIQUE IS APPROPRIATE

Groups of bereaved children, teens, adults, or mixed ages. Individual support is likely to be more beneficial in cases when a person is facing acute grief, has difficulty self-regulating or is behaviorally disruptive. The intensity of a community ritual and exposure to others' stories and emotions may be too much and cause flooding for individuals in these circumstances.

DESCRIPTION

The death of a loved one forces us on a journey through an internal wilderness. This journey within takes us through previously unexplored terrain of being and meaning—revealing new parts of ourselves as we continue to navigate life. This journey can feel ominous, isolating, and unguided. Grief camps and retreats provide opportunities for bereaved children, adults, and families to gather with understanding peers for support, camaraderie, and healing. In outdoor settings, the Grief Spiral ritual can become an embodied life metaphor illuminating the theoretical Dual Process Model of Grief (Stroebe & Schut, 1999). This model underscores the simultaneous processes of honoring significant loss while re-engaging and investing in life.

A spiral can be created in a multitude of group settings—stomped in the snow, outlined in the grass, or brushed in the sand. As individuals walk the spiral at night toward the center with an unlit dripless tapered candle, the spiral represents the journey within that we find ourselves launched upon following a significant loss. The path winds and is walked alone as a symbol of the uniqueness of the journey. A single lit candle in the center symbolizes parts of ourselves that are illuminated having walked this path—parts that are brighter, stronger or more pronounced since the loss. Participants light their tapers from the center candle and as they move along the outward spiral have the opportunity to share their experience of who they are becoming on the journey and new parts of themselves that are more present. The path is lined with tea candles. As participants move along the spiral outward, they may light one candle or more in honor of their loved one who has died. This begins to add light to the darkness—a symbol that while we cannot walk the path for another, we can add comfort, warmth, and hope along the way.

The group holds the space with their candles around the periphery of the spiral, bearing witness to one another's journey—a symbol of universality and solidarity. After each group member has walked the spiral, they stand together with candles ablaze. At this time, a facilitator may make a comment about how the space holds the energy of the words and memories that have been shared, the candlelight holds the courage and camaraderie of the individuals who have come together for this event, and the silence holds the many stories and feelings unspoken, yet present and real. After a moment of silence the group together recites, "We will remember, we will remember, we will remember," and each individual blows out his or her tapered candle. The strumming of an acoustic guitar, a poetry reading or a song can help bring the group together as the ceremony comes to a close. Participants have the opportunity to stay in the space for a time before transitioning to campfire for music and s'mores, helping to re-focus and re-center each individual before transitioning away from the event.

Logistical considerations

Prior to the ceremony, the group can choose a location of significance or beauty for the spiral ritual. Clearly delineating the spiral facilitates walking it during the ceremony, marking the path in the pine needles, trail, snow or sand. The path can be lined with yarn, hemp, pine cones, rocks, branches, or wild flowers for clarity (see Figure 89.1). The process of creating a unique spiral together provides an opportunity for reflection while establishing ownership in the ritual. With large groups and camps, a double spiral with a path circling inward and continuing outward can be created, allowing multiple people to walk simultaneously. When created as a double spiral, the Grief Spiral is often walked in silence.

Gathering as a group just prior to walking the Grief Spiral to read a poem or story and to discuss the plan and significance of the ritual can serve to focus the collective energy and help to create a calm, safe space for the walk. A facilitator can pass out tapered candles or have a basket of candles at the entrance to the spiral. The center candle is lit prior to the ritual.

Figure 89.1 The Grief Spiral

Source: Joe Danzer, Mad Hatter Photography.

CASE EXAMPLE

Molly, age 16, experienced the death of her father who committed suicide when she was 12 years old. She participated in a snow spiral on a Teen Grief Retreat. Seven adolescents and three facilitators snow-shoed to a historic homestead in the Sapphire Mountain range in Montana over a January weekend. During the afternoon the group stamped a spiral in the snow and placed tea candles along the path. That evening we gathered around the spiral as brownies baked in a Dutch oven on the campfire warming our backs. The following is a recreation of Molly's words as she walked into the spiral.

> *I'm walking this spiral in honor of my dad. When I was 12, I was babysitting and this lady came to the house frantically stating, "You have to come home right now!" Dad had been missing for a few days—but I had convinced myself that he is my hero and heroes don't die. We ran home and I remember it pouring rain and lightning everywhere. A police officer was in the living room and all of my siblings were sitting in a row on the couch sobbing. My mom came in and said, "Your dad committed suicide." He was in our bus in the backyard. I really wanted to go out and see him. I remember screaming then my knees buckled. I just wanted to hold his hand even if I couldn't see him.*
>
> *It turned out that it wasn't raining or lightning. It was cameras in the backyard. I never saw the ambulance or fire trucks. I just walked past without seeing them.*
>
> *I am one of quadruplets and we all responded completely differently. I wanted to talk about it and feel it. My brother got angry. My sister disappeared to connect with horses and disconnected from people. My other brother stayed close to my mom who could no longer parent. I took my little sister under my wing. So basically that bullet shattered our lives.*

Molly knelt in the snow to light her taper from the candle in the center of the spiral:

> *I light this candle in honor of my dad. My dad was incredibly compassionate and passionate about what he did. I hope and strive to be a bit like him in those ways.*

As Molly walked out of the spiral, she stopped to light a tea candle along the path:

> *I light this candle in honor of me. Deep inside of me there is a flicker of deep existence and hope. Let's be honest, it's been a long road. I really see myself as having perseverance and the ability to fight for who I want to be. I don't want to be a quitter. I want to believe no matter the circumstances, a piece of you exists that just keeps going.*

Eight years later, now age 24, Molly reflects on her experience with the Grief Spiral:

> *Walking the spiral was pretty divine because it was pretty cold. We were walking this path that is just ice with a candle in the center. I realized that my dad presented me with the idea that you can just opt out, but somewhere along my journey, I saw that there is one flicker of light or one bit of hope somewhere. I want to move toward the light instead of away from it.*
>
> *The deep spiral of grief is pretty isolating. You can't walk it for anyone else. You find yourself ultimately alone on the bumpy, cold, dark path. However, the circle of all these people standing around the spiral is a blatant symbol of solidarity and shared experience. We know that we will come out the other side and that there will be people waiting for us. At different times the candles actually go out, but we help to relight them for each other. That seems significant.*

CONCLUDING THOUGHTS

Whether it be a mountain, lake, or desert landscape, the great outdoors can be an ideal setting for contemplation, reflection, and natural metaphor. The Grief Spiral allows participants to enact or embody meanings as they walk the spiral inward and out. As an embodied life metaphor, the Grief Spiral integrates a person's narrative with his or her footsteps, illuminating past experiences, self-awareness, and movement forward amidst a group of understanding others.

Metaphors can facilitate the reconstruction of experiences (Santostefano, 2004). Weaving together interaction, experiential participation, and opportunities to honor self and others, the Grief Spiral as a metaphor enactment has the potential to foster hope, insight, and strength as the grief journey continues.

References and further reading

Fletcher, T., & Hinkle, J. S. (2002). Adventure based counseling. *Journal of Counseling and Development*, *80*, 277–285.

Santostefano, S. (2004). *Child therapy in the great outdoors*. Hillsdale, NJ: Analytic Press.

Stroebe, M., & Schut, H. (1999). The dual process model of coping with bereavement. *Death Studies*, *23*, 197–224.

90
Memory Boats
D. *"Dale" M. Mayer and Christine Barrett*

CLIENTS FOR WHOM THE TECHNIQUE IS APPROPRIATE

Memory boats are a creative ritual that can be utilized with clients of all ages, including adults, children, individuals, and families. However, when grief is complicated or the death traumatic, this technique would likely be insufficient unless paired with more intensive therapy.

DESCRIPTION

Societal rituals after a death allow people to pause from everyday activities and gather together to acknowledge the life, and death, of an individual. While the term ritual has many meanings, the definition here acknowledges that rituals are "special acts that offer sacred meaning to events" (Martin & Doka, 2000, p. 151). Rituals are important events for those bereaved by a death, and it is important to recognize that people grieve on both an individual level and within a social context with others, including family members and friends.

Bereavement rituals can be constructed to either acknowledge a significant event or to facilitate movement through aspects of participants' grief experiences. Those that are designed to acknowledge the magnitude or unchanging nature of an event may involve the creation of a static object including a shrine or cairn. Other rituals can be created to symbolize movement or transition. These rituals often include elements, such as burning ceremonies, or releasing something into the wind. Memory boats contain aspects of both types of rituals as the building of the boat results in a distinct, precious object of commemoration. The release of the boat into the water can be coupled with painful parts of one's grief experience that one wishes to set free.

Doka, in Chapter 87 in this volume, offers principles for the preparation and implementation of meaningful, individualized ceremonies, emphasizing consideration of planning, participant roles and use of symbolic objects and links to the decedent in their construction. In addition, timing is crucial, as there are many beneficial times, dates, and moments for a ritual to occur, such as anniversaries, birthdays, or holidays.

Ceremonies can hold extra significance in cases of sudden death. When there is no forewarning or indication of an impending death, surviving family members often do not have a chance to convey important sentiments including: "Please forgive me, I forgive you, I love you, thank you, and goodbye" (Byock, 2004, p. 3). The suddenness of the death may leave the survivors with regrets, or unfinished business, for what they did, or did not, say or do with their family member before his or her death. While the specifics of each family's situation will be different, the overall pattern of unfinished business is acknowledged as a special feature associated with sudden deaths (Worden, 2008). Although not all family members will have regrets or sorrow for things not said before a death, in situations of sudden death, a ceremony involving the making and launching of memory boats may provide surviving family members with an opportunity to say goodbye.

CASE EXAMPLE

A family grief workshop that met after school for eight weeks culminated with a memory boat ritual. This final session allowed bereaved family members to create and launch a memory boat together. A group session focused on bringing the supportive energy of the previous sessions into the natural setting and laid out the general plan for the activity. Group facilitators had assembled nature-based material such as driftwood, rocks and stones, twigs and branches, leaves, moss, flowers, and related objects on a large picnic table. In respect for the natural landscape, it was encouraged that all boats be assembled from natural materials so that no inorganic materials would be left in the creek or along the water's bank.

Families were invited to use preassembled materials as well as special tokens they found around the space. Utilizing a bark or wood platform, parents and children collectively assembled a boat in commemoration of a family member who had died. Family members wandered into the woods to search for unique and special objects, like shiny pebbles, heart-shaped rocks, or distinctive leaves to include as part of the memory boat. When the boats were complete, it was evident that each creation had been lovingly assembled, meaningful, and unique. All group participants gathered for a short remembrance ceremony and were given the opportunity to share memories with one other as they felt comfortable. From the remembrance ceremony, the families carried their boats in silence to the water's edge.

One by one, families placed their boats into Rattlesnake Creek. The pace was unhurried, and adults held onto children as they stretched to place their unique crafts upon the water. Some people chose to say a few words to those whom they had loved and lost before launching their memory boat. The boats were swept into the fast-moving current, and young family members often ran alongside the water's edge to watch their special boat travel down the creek.

One family, a mother and her three school-aged children, who had experienced the sudden cardiac death of a husband and father a few months earlier, found this ritual to be an especially powerful way to say goodbye. The hands-on aspects of building of a memory boat provided a project that all family members, whose ages ranged from a young child to a preteen, a teenager, and an adult, could work on collectively. Everyone in the family was able to contribute to the boat's creation. This ritual allowed these family members a chance to collectively say goodbye as they set their boat into the water. The launching of the memory boat into a fast-moving creek surrounded by mountains was especially meaningful for these surviving family members as they recalled that their family member, a much-loved spouse and father, had cherished the outdoors and shared his passion for the mountains and natural landscape with them. Hugs and tears were shared together as they watched their boat travel downstream in the creek's current. The presence of other bereaved families and compassionate facilitators provided support and camaraderie, which in turn helped lessen feelings of isolation that sometimes overtook this bereft family. Having others bear witness to the launching of their boat added importance to the event and offered a gentle, nonverbal reminder that they were not alone on their grief journey.

CONCLUDING THOUGHTS

This technique has been adapted for use with a women's bereavement group and at youth grief camps and family retreats, using both river and lake settings. Variations of this technique can be incorporated to meet the needs of individuals, and their collective families, so that it can be used as a meaningful tool to honor and heal many types of losses. This technique can be modified to support different age levels of grievers, for example, attaching a string to the boat and launching into calmer water would allow younger children to pull the boat back to shore if they are not ready to relinquish their boat. Some participants may not have explicit memories of the deceased; and in this case 'Boats of Honor and Remembrance' may be more appropriate.

In this ritual it is important to provide an environment of both emotional and physical safety for participants. In outdoor-based therapies, participants and facilitators are often immersed in changing landscapes shaped by wind, water, and wildlife. Facilitators are encouraged to conduct a risk survey of a natural setting prior to gathering participants and implementing rituals. Special caution is recommended around rapidly moving water to maintain everyone's safety, especially for young children or non-swimmers. Much like grief itself, the release of memory boats into moving water may be unpredictable. Pre-ritual preparation is needed so that the organizers and participants are prepared for the unexpected. As boats are launched, they may float gracefully onto the water, or they may flip, sink, and even crash into other boats or wash up on shore. Talking participants through what they might expect upon release of the crafts, as well as the unpredictable nature of how the boat will move through the space offers a powerful analogy with the grief journey. No matter how deliberately we move through the world following loss, we will face waves and currents, as well as moments of stillness that catch us by surprise. Pre-ritual discussion can help prepare participants for the acceptability and significance of not being able to control the exact outcome. A well-planned ritual with clear communication and deliberate movement in pre-determined areas can provide a meaningful, healing gathering for the bereaved.

In conclusion, the making and launching of memory boats into water create a powerful experience for those grieving the death of someone close to them. Particular benefits are present for bereft families following an unexpected death. The experience of building memory boats provides an experiential activity that incorporates family members of all ages. The building and launching of a memory boat also are a creative activity that may engage and help both intuitive and instrumental grievers (Martin & Doka, 2000). A memory boat ritual provides a meaningful opportunity to release feelings and messages within a stabilizing, supportive network of understanding others.

References

Byock, I. (2004). *The four things that matter most*. New York: Free Press.
Martin, T., & Doka, K. (2000). *Men don't cry, women do*. New York: Taylor & Francis.
Worden, J. W. (2008). *Grief counseling and grief therapy* (4th ed.). New York: Springer.

91

Supporting the "Lost Ritual" after a Suicide Death

Doreen S. Marshall

CLIENTS FOR WHOM THE TECHNIQUE IS APPROPRIATE

This technique is a guided exploration that has been used primarily with adults who were unable to engage in a formal mourning ritual (e.g. funeral) following a suicide loss. It can be adapted for other types of loss if participating in a mourning ritual was not possible or when the ritual that occurred did not feel appropriate to the client. Special caution should be used if adapting the technique for use in groups, particularly with adolescents, to ensure that commemoration does not lead to glorification of the suicide death. The clinician should consider the client's cultural meanings related to mourning rituals, his or her beliefs about suicide, and the intersection of these concepts.

DESCRIPTION

Worden (2009) has described how rituals, in particular a funeral, can facilitate a grief process. In particular, this ritual can draw a support network close to the bereaved person. Following a suicide, a funeral service may be privately held, or due to a family conflict related to the death or other circumstances, the bereaved individual may be unable to participate in a public grief ritual. This may reinforce the bereaved person's sense of isolation, particularly if they ascribe great meaning to the ritual that was held in their absence. Due to the nature of stigma, those grieving a suicide may already have more difficulty finding meaning in the loss and social isolation than others (Jordan, 2001).

When a client is unable to attend a formal mourning ceremony following a suicide death, the following questions may guide exploration of how being involved in a ritual may help facilitate the grieving process:

- *According to your cultural beliefs, what ritual would have typically acknowledged your loved one's passing? How might this be different if your loved one had not died by suicide?*
- *If a funeral or similar ritual had occurred: What do you imagine occurred at the ritual (funeral, etc.) that you were unable to attend? What role do you wish you had had in that ritual? What do you wish had been said about the deceased's life struggles and his/her suicide during the ritual?*
- *If a funeral or similar ritual did not occur: Take a moment and imagine the type of ritual you would have liked to have had for your loved one. What would have happened*

at this occasion? How would this be different or similar to rituals you have attended in the past?
- What would you like for others to know about your loved one's life (and death)? How would this ritual appropriately acknowledge and remember your loved one? What would be said about his/her suicide?
- Who would be present to support you during this occasion?
- What might be different about your grief experience had you had the opportunity to participate in a ritual?

CASE STUDY

Julie was a Caucasian woman in her thirties who sought counseling following the suicide death of her romantic partner of one year, Tina. Following her death, Tina's parents made funeral and burial arrangements in their home state about 500 miles away from where Tina resided. Tina's parents did not know about their relationship and thus, Julie was never informed of the funeral arrangements. For Julie, the inability to attend a funeral reinforced her experience of stigma, as she was unable to engage support in the way she was accustomed to following a death. The "lost ritual," as we labeled it in therapy, left Julie feeling as if she didn't know how to begin grieving this traumatic loss of her partner.

Through a guided exploration using questions similar to those above, we discovered that Julie's need to have attended a funeral was grounded in her cultural beliefs of what she felt should occur following a death. For Julie, engaging in a funeral service would have provided the comfort of participating in a ritual that honored the death transition and that was familiar to her. She also felt like it was her role, as Tina's partner, to ensure that Tina had "a proper goodbye," one that was consistent with how she knew Tina and that did not convey shame about her death. And so, led by the exploration above, Julie indicated that she wanted to plan a memorial service for Tina. This exploration, and the subsequent ritual that was held, became a grounding aspect of our remaining therapeutic work.

Julie planned a service at a local Unitarian church and spoke with a minister there who was comfortable officiating a memorial service following a suicide death. It was important to Julie that the suicide aspect of Tina's death (and her struggles in life) be acknowledged. She gathered Tina's favorite music and enlarged a photo of Tina that would sit on an easel in the chapel during the service. She chose spiritual passages that would have had meaning for Tina. She printed programs for the service that included a brief biography of Tina and information about a suicide prevention organization to whom donations could be made in honor of Tina. Consistent with Julie's cultural practices, she planned to host a repast at her home following the service for those closest to her and asked a friend to help prepare the food. She also asked me to attend the service and bring some printed information related to suicide grief and resources.

The service, attended by roughly 15 people, was among the most meaningful I have attended. Our exploration in therapy of ritual served to validate her need, to reduce feelings of stigma and marginalization, and to help her to engage support in her grief. It also helped her to share aspects of Tina's life so others could know her beyond the tragedy of her suicide, as well as to be able to publicly acknowledge the difficulties Tina had faced. The service, then, was not an idealization, but rather, an accurate, meaningful representation of Tina's life.

Of note, the service was not the ending of our therapeutic work, but the beginning. Our remaining sessions focused on Julie's coping with the devastating loss by suicide, a process that I believe was enhanced through acknowledging and supporting Julie's need for a ritual.

CONCLUDING THOUGHTS

Jordan (2011) discussed the counselor's role in "bearing witness" for those who have been affected by a suicide death. The counselor's willingness to explore and acknowledge the client's need for ritual after a suicide death can also serve to reduce the stigma associated with suicide loss. When appropriate and desired by the client, this exploration can help to facilitate the grieving process for those clients who were unable to participate in a ritual following their loved one's suicide.

References

Jordan, J. (2001). Is suicide bereavement different? A reassessment of the literature. *Suicide and Life-Threatening Behavior, 31*, 91–102.

Jordan, J. (2011). Principles of grief counseling with adult survivors. In J. R. Jordan & J. L McIntosh (Eds.), *Grief after suicide* (pp. 179–223). New York: Routledge.

Worden, J. W. (2009). *Grief counseling and grief therapy*. New York: Springer.

Part XVII
Healing the Healer

92
Wisdom Circles for when Helping Hurts

Lara Krawchuk

CLIENTS FOR WHOM THE TECHNIQUE IS APPROPRIATE

Helping professionals struggling to process the emotional impact of their work with vulnerable clients, who collectively assent to meeting in a safe place that encourages disclosure. It may be inappropriate in institutional settings marked by conflict or distrust among group members, or where participants feel coerced to attend.

DESCRIPTION

Witnessing intense client pain over time places helping professionals at risk of compassion fatigue, vicarious trauma, and even burnout. The "cost of caring" ranges from exhaustion to a complex symptomology including intense distress, total depletion, and cognitive shifts in beliefs about the world (Figley, 2002). Though it is absolutely normal for helpers to experience pain from intense work, hectic workplaces frequently fail to adequately address this experience. In an attempt to honor the emotional toll of helping, I have created a day-long retreat called *When Helping Hurts: Self-Care for the Helping Professional.* Central to this day are Wisdom Circles where professionals converge to bear compassionate witness to the joy and suffering involved in their helping journeys.

Wisdom or Talking Circles have been historically practiced in Native American communities to foster compassionate community, teach values, share respect for diverse viewpoints, and offer wisdom. Circle seating was traditionally used to acknowledge the continuity of life and relatedness of all things (Running Wolf & Rickard, 2003). In our modern retreat, the circle contains between 6 and 20 participants, in order to foster a safe space to deeply honor hurts, share struggles, listen deeply, and mend battered hearts.

Our circle follows traditional guidelines to promote meaningful sharing and self-reflection. I hold the role of "circle-keeper," explaining group guidelines, creating poignant reflection questions, and ensuring safety in the space. I participate fully in all aspects of the circle. In the center of our circle we place a few "sacred" objects or writings to personalize our space. Communication is structured by the passing of a "talking stick" that is created from a variety of natural and decorative elements, including shells, feathers, ribbons and colorful beads.

After offering an introduction to the circle process, I, the circle-keeper, invite all participants to stand for an opening exercise. This activity is created ahead of time and reflects the tone and direction I would like the discussion to follow. Activities can include inviting symbolic members into the circle, sharing important aspects of participants' lives, stating intentions for the day, or reading a reflection or poem.

After the opening exercise, the circle-keeper poses one predetermined question to the entire group and begins the clockwise passing of the talking stick for sharing. On a day of healing for helping professionals, I find that asking participants a question related to work generates powerful reflection. Each participant holds the talking piece and answers the question or quietly passes it to the next person. Only the participant holding the talking stick (and the circle-keeper, if necessary) may speak at any one time. Everyone else is asked to listen deeply. After the stick completes an entire circle rotation, the circle-keeper may pass the stick around again, for further reflection. Participants can share more of their story or respond to something that moved them from the previous rotation. The circle-keeper may send the stick around one final time or move onto a new question (Running Wolf & Rickard, 2003). After we answer the posited questions we sit quietly with the feelings and emotions that have been stirred within us from bearing compassionate witness to the struggle of self and of others (Siegel, 2010).

At this point the circle-keeper puts aside the talking stick and asks for feedback related to the circle experience. It never fails to inspire me when helping professionals are moved by the deep empathy, compassion and kindness that they too often reserve for hurting clients. Honoring our pain in a safe, relational space acts as a balm for tired souls and allows us to return to our work nourished and renewed in ways that allow us to flourish once more.

CASE EXAMPLE

At a recent healing retreat I had 20 participants. This made for a large Wisdom Circle so I limited my circle questions to allow for full participation by every member. I introduced myself as the circle-keeper, urged compassionate non-judgment of self and others, and we began. On this day, participants had already introduced themselves to the larger group and had engaged in a lively discussion about compassion fatigue. They had exhibited a high degree of respect for one another and an eagerness to share, so I felt able to delve immediately into emotionally deep topics for our circle. For our opening exercise I asked every participant to invite someone (or something) of great personal significance to symbolically join our circle. As we invited in our special someone we took a piece of colorful ribbon and tied it to the person to our left so that we would ultimately be bound together by this visible circle of color, which would be placed at our feet to demarcate our sacred space.

Participants brought in a diverse range of meaningful beings to our space. I started the exercise by inviting my father who had died 4 years prior and had been on my mind a great deal. My voice wavered as I invited him to our circle. Next, Mary, from a local hospice, invited her child into the space because he had been struggling in school and she was quite worried about him. The talking piece was passed several spaces and Kate, who worked exclusively with sexual abuse perpetrators, invited her husband into the circle because he had been such a vital support in her challenging work. Jim, our only male participant, a parole officer, invited his sister to the group because she had recently been diagnosed with cancer. Audrey, a social worker in a local nursing home, invited God to our group as her divine savior. Sarah, a chaplain from a children's hospital, invited her cat because she felt total peace when stroking kitty's soft fur. Our final participant (situated to my right) was Elaine, a woman who worked at a local hospital. Elaine took the talking stick and paused, emotion visibly swelling in her. The group remained quiet as she grappled privately with her emotions. Eventually she shared that she was inviting her son who had just been sent to prison. As she spoke, she trembled and started to sob. I silently wrapped my arm around her shoulder and she leaned in for support. Every participant in the healing circle shifted towards Elaine as she shakily joined her ribbon to mine. She looked around the circle and quietly uttered "Thank-you . . . for listening." Our Wisdom Circle had begun.

I always bring several potential questions to a circle and select the one that best fits the mood of the day. On this day I sensed much pain in the room so I decided to offer an opportunity to share this burden with others. I asked everyone to consider responding to the statement: "Share a burden that feels difficult to carry at work." I immediately passed the talking piece without sharing. Once again the contributions came quickly. Mary shared that she was struggling deeply with the death of a young woman who had died of lung cancer, leaving behind three small girls and a husband she feared could not handle their care. She passed the piece to June who shared that in her work with seriously mentally ill patients, she felt burdened by the constraints of the system she worked for. Several heads nodded and June smiled. The stick moved around and Jim shared that he was thinking of leaving his job because no one listened to him when he felt a troubled kid deserved a second chance. Sally, a therapist in private practice, shared quietly that she was having a hard time sitting with her clients' pain because she was struggling at home in an unhappy marriage. Elaine shared that it was very hard to experience children suffering while she knew her son was also carrying enormous pain. As the talking piece made its way slowly around the circle, each person shared a burden, some for the very first time, and received the powerful collective compassion and wisdom of a group of helpers collected together to support one another in the very real struggles of helping.

I sent the piece around another time. Several participants shared that it felt good to have their hurts validated by others who were also struggling. Jim remarked that his choices were becoming clearer to him now. A few thanked others for sharing painful parts of their lives. One participant thanked me for hosting the retreat. When the talking piece reached me, I observed that it felt powerful to share our burdens in the circle and thanked everyone for their wisdom. Most participants nodded and smiled. I then invited members to share their experience of this circle and several chose to do so. Themes here included gratitude for being heard, answers being found by sharing the burden, feeling deeply supported and cared for, and the healing power of stating one's truth. We ended our circle with a brief moment of silence to sit with the compassionate energy in the space and seal in the wisdom of this powerful healing experience.

CONCLUDING THOUGHTS

Wisdom Circles can provide powerful healing opportunities and can be held in a variety of safe environments. I encourage helpers to experiment with holding peer-led Wisdom Circles in their own organizations, but stay mindful that it is imperative that circles be held only where participants can speak freely and without worry of repercussions for what they share in circle.

References

Figley, C. R. (2002). *Treating compassion fatigue.* New York: Routledge.

Running Wolf, P., & Rickard, J.A. (2003). Talking circles: A Native American approach to experiential learning. *Journal of Multicultural Counseling and Development, 31,* 39–43.

Siegel, D. J. (2010). *The mindful therapist.* New York: Norton.

93

Stand in These Shoes

Jane Moss

CLIENTS FOR WHOM THE TECHNIQUE IS APPROPRIATE

Those providing bereavement support who find themselves struggling to empathize with a client whose attitudes and behaviors are challenging. It can also assist those struggling to understand the different grieving styles of close family members or friends. It may not be as effective for those in the early days of grief but may be offered in hindsight to enable sense to be made of differing grief reactions around the time of the death itself.

DESCRIPTION

Empathy lies at the heart of bereavement support. Along with our ability to sit alongside mourners as they grieve, the offering of respect, empathy and genuineness (Rogers, 1980) is the most important support we can offer. Part instinct, part natural ability, part learned technique, the gift of empathy can make the difference between someone feeling isolated and misunderstood, or supported and heard.

There are times when the most empathic among us struggles to place ourselves alongside a client whose values we do not share, or whose inability to make progress through grief frustrates us after many sessions. It is hard to admit to, but there are some we struggle to help, not because they cannot be helped, but because of our apparent incapacity to offer empathy to those whose attitudes and values are very different to our own.

Admitting this can feel like failure. I offer this technique as a way to nurture the empathy that is essential to effective bereavement support. I invite the counsellor to follow this guidance when reflecting in a journal or in the context of supervision. Begin by picturing a pair of shoes. These are the shoes in which your client stands. Notice how they look, their texture, color and condition. Are they sturdy or flimsy? Are they polished or rough? Are they new and smart or old and worn? Have a good look at these shoes. Now notice what they are standing on. Is the ground solid? Is it level? Is it at the top or the bottom of a slope? Soft grass or rough stone? When you have observed the shoes and where they stand, look up and see the person standing in them. What is the look on her face? Is he making any sound? Is she upright or slouched? What is she carrying? Who is with him? What are they doing? What can you observe? When ready, write from the prompt:

How does it feel to stand in these shoes?

Write as much or as little as you need to. When you have finished writing, read back what you have written. Underline anything that seems significant or that you find yourself surprised to have written. If you wish to, write further about these insights and matters of significance before reflecting on them further or talking about them in supervision. Ask yourself what difference this exercise has made to your feelings about your challenging client. Are you better able to empathize with their situation now?

CASE EXAMPLE

Beverly, a Cruse bereavement support volunteer in the UK, used this technique to reflect in her journal on the situation of a client with whom she was struggling to remain congruent: a young man who had lost his father. This client had, in Beverly's words:

> *never held a job for any length of time, nor did either of his parents. His father was an alcoholic and his childhood years were spent living in his grandmother's home with his mother. This client was either very late to sessions or did not turn up without canceling. I found it difficult not to tell him to go out and get any job available. I also found myself very frustrated with his issues around coming to the sessions.*

When she wrote about this client, Beverly began by describing his athletic shoes:

> *They always looked shiny and new. As I continued to write I began to focus on his shoelaces and imagined them to be pulled very tight, so tight that his feet were constricted and he felt immobile. Doing anything active gave him pain.*

This provided Beverly with a metaphor for the young man's apparent inability to take action towards positive change in his life. She found herself able to appreciate the extent of his stuckness and the constriction of his situation.

Another of Beverly's clients was a middle-aged woman who was a recovering drug addict. Her husband asked her to leave, as her behavior was threatening and dangerous to the children. She was homeless for a while and then entered a 12-Step program. Beverly recalled feeling fearful of this woman physically, although she attended counseling sessions regularly and was always on time. Beverly found it hard to listen to the woman's stories of violence towards her family.

When she started to write about this client's shoes, Beverly envisaged slip-on ballet shoes that were scuffed. They seemed comfortable but capable of falling off her feet easily. Beverly wrote that this client was careless with her shoes and often lost them. The soles of her feet were bloody and bruised.

The image of the flimsy shoes and damaged feet enabled Beverly to access feelings of empathy for this woman. She developed a deep respect for her client's commitment to recovery. She reflected:

> *Doing these exercises gave me back the unconditional positive regard and empathy required to be an effective therapist. I appreciated how vulnerable they both were despite the difficult behavior they exhibited as a result of their histories. By taking off my own shoes and putting on those of my clients I was able to explore feelings that had impeded the therapeutic relationship.*

CONCLUDING THOUGHTS

This technique can enable counselors to arrive at a more constructive view of their clients. It may enable them to consider new ways to support the clients, or it may lead them to accept that there may be little they or anyone can do. It can help to clarify the boundaries between clients and counselors, enabling counselors to see what they can and cannot influence.

The technique is adaptable to use with clients who are struggling to understand a relative's or friend's differing approach to grieving. Those who grieve cognitively may find they can understand the different grief reactions of intuitive grievers and vice versa; hence it may be of assistance in resolving tensions among family members, especially those between the different genders (Doka & Martin, 2010). Its use here, however, suggests it has a value from the perspective of the counselor and others providing bereavement support. In those cases where empathy is challenged by attitudes and behaviors that suggest values that are in opposition to the counselor's, the ability to step into someone else's shoes and walk a mile in them, before judging, can enable congruence and unconditional positive regard to be maintained.

References

Doka, K. J., & Martin, T. L. (2010). *Grieving beyond gender*. New York: Routledge.
Rogers, C. (1980). *A way of being*. Boston: Houghton Mifflin.

94

Degriefing Caregiver Burden

Lyn Prashant

CLIENTS FOR WHOM THE TECHNIQUE IS APPROPRIATE

Pastoral, funeral and humanitarian service providers working with the bereaved who are unable to regain their emotional equilibrium due to *compathy* (the physical equivalent of empathy), which causes the caregiver to experience the client's presenting physical distress. However, restoring basic routines and establishing a sense of safety, or other methods of promoting self-regulation may be a more appropriate focus for some in the initial phases of traumatic grief.

DESCRIPTION

In addition to raw emotional pain, grieving individuals resonate physical sorrow as well. A qualitative study examining the nurse–patient relationship has identified the contagion of physical distress or "compathy" as a significant but otherwise neglected phenomenon. Compathy occurs when one person observes another person suffering a disease or injury and experiences in one's own body a similar or related distress (Morse & Mitcham, 1997). Although this particular somatic aspect has yet to be incorporated into the common protocol for caregiver overload, Integrative Grief Therapy (IGT) provides direction for its inclusion. IGT's *degriefing* procedures utilize integrative therapies that enable caregivers to take primary responsibility for themselves in order to be ultimately responsible to their clients. The holistic approach transforms the caregiver's embodied grief by providing self-care techniques intended to ease emotional distress, mental anguish and physical discomfort by increasing self-awareness, fortifying their strengths and teaching new coping skills for ongoing caregiver stress. The degriefing protocol is usually organized into eight sessions, featuring several distinctive interventions. These often begin with timelines of personal and professional losses and a telling of the healer/client's story, which is engaged with active listening on the part of the *Degriefing* counselor (henceforth client and counselor, respectively). Additional points of entry may include the sharing of photographs related to the client's timeline, and the exploration of the client's emotional reactions, body language, and styles of communicating regarding losses. Middle sessions introduce the concept of "compathy" and symptoms of caregiver burden, which are reviewed in terms of various degriefing premises, as illustrated below. Various self-care options are discussed, including simple yoga postures, breath-focused relaxation, dance, stretching, walking, oils and bodywork for specific somatic complaints. Expressive arts interventions follow using paper and crayons and storytelling, after which clients explore the meanings of various emotion states and the needs associated with them. Finally, in the closing sessions, yoga exercises are extended into various spiritual practices and rituals, as clients formulate a plan for integrating greater self-care into their daily lives. Several of these features are illustrated in the case example that follows.

CASE EXAMPLE

Sue, 43, came to see me, saying her physical problems had gotten out of hand. Her physician had found no organic cause for her problems and suggested she seek counseling as physical pain often has an emotional component. Sue reported lack of focus, headaches, back and shoulder pain, upset stomach, and raspy throat. As the oldest of seven, with a working mother and an alcoholic father, she had assumed a parental role with her siblings since childhood, and continued a lifelong pattern of focusing on others at the expense of her own self-care. She was employed as a psychiatric nurse at a local hospital but refrained from telling her colleagues about her exhaustion, fearing they'd think less of her. She had stopped exercising, returning calls or socializing. After work she'd turn on the TV, eat dinner and fall asleep on the couch.

> *Session 1: Sue expressed shame that she could help others and not know how to help herself. While showing photographs of deceased loved ones she complained of anxiety and tears appeared without warning. Sue created two timelines. On her personal timeline she named each loss, where she felt it in her body, what her mind said and what her body felt about each. Her work timeline indicated places where professional and personal losses intertwined and overwhelmed her. As homework, I suggested she list her intentions with respect to managing her stress differently.*

> *Session 2: We reviewed the parameters of Degriefing, a holistic process approach to healing grief-related pain that combines verbal counseling therapies with individualized physical care. The premises that Sue resonated with most were that: the mind has a body and the body has a mind; in times of grief, your mind is not your friend; we don't get over our losses so much as we change our relationship to them. Sue said putting words to her physical discomfort helped her feel normal in the midst of her confusion. As homework she began to journal about her experience, enjoy a lavender bath each day, walk 20 minutes daily and engage in inspirational and self-help reading.*

> *Session 3: We discussed the concept of compathy and Sue's realization that she had been too hard on herself. She was emotional while talking about patients who died traumatically at work. She could not get their faces out of her mind and would often dream about them. Using ginger oil on Sue's feet and Neroli on her heart, we did progressive relaxation. She agreed to bathe in rosemary oil, and to continue reading.*

> *Session 4: Focusing on the somatic aspects of grief, we engaged in deep breathing to release tension, as I did bodywork on Sue's shoulders, arms, back, legs and feet. She talked about joining a yoga class, and walking more. She reported feeling better and waking up feeling clearer. As homework, Sue continued her inspirational reading.*

> *Session 5: We worked with Psycho Somatic Semantics, the use of language as a therapeutic tool to evoke a desired response in the body, in this case, a release of grief (Prashant, 2002). Sue reveled in the opportunity to role-play since she often shied away from direct communication. She had little feedback from colleagues now because she had not talked to anyone about her conflicted feelings. Sue reported that she had started using breathing exercises when listening to other's communications.*

Session 6: Our focus was emotional expression. Sue had been asked to bring her favorite music to the session, which we played. Tools for emotional expression included collage supplies, musical instruments, modeling clay, crayons and sketchpad, yoga mat, essential oils, and music selection. She chose to do collage and kazooed songs that evoked memories and tears. Sue decided that she would assign song titles to losses on her grief timeline, because she often remembered life events that way. For homework she read the book "Tear Soup," with its message that grief has a function.

Session 7: Sue built an altar with photos, sacred objects, flowers, candles and crystals; she made a list of everything she wanted to eliminate from her life, which we burned outside in the fire pit as a form of symbolic release. Sue also made a second list of her hopes and dreams, which she placed on her altar. I led her through a mindfulness meditation. As homework, she practiced belly breathing, journal writing and tratak, a form of concentration-enhancing meditation.

Session 8: We reviewed work accomplished, answered questions and tied up loose ends. I made recommendations for other integrative therapies such as acupuncture, dance classes and swimming. We discussed what had been the hardest to work through and what had been easier than expected. She agreed to write a summary of her work and to call in two weeks to touch base. When she did so, she reported much less burden than in the past.

CONCLUDING THOUGHTS

Caregivers engaged in compassionate service with grieving individuals are subject to caregiver burden, which profoundly impacts their body, mind, and spirit. Basic to the physical, emotional, and spiritual well-being of professional counselors are self-care strategies that promote resilience for the prevention of empathy fatigue (Stebnicki, 2007). *Degriefing* meets the specific needs of a caregiver currently suffering physical distress. It also primes caregivers to remain vigilant about how their work can continue to directly affect their own body, mind and spirit. By engaging in personally chosen self-care therapies Sue used the power of grief as fuel to transform the pain into a healing experience and obtained the tools to manage ongoing issues, truly representing *the caregiver's quest for healing*.

References

Morse, J. M., & Mitcham, C. (1997). Compathy: The contagion of physical distress. *Journal of Advanced Nursing, 26*(4), 649–657.

Prashant, L. (2002). *Transforming grief: Degriefing training manual.* San Francisco: Self-published.

Stebnicki, M. A. (2007). Empathy fatigue: Healing the mind, body, and spirit of professional counselors. *American Journal of Psychiatric Rehabilitation, 10*(4), 317–338.

Epilogue

Looking back on this massive project, with its compilation of nearly 100 distinctive practices in the field of grief therapy, affords a chance to close with a few observations about the nature of bereavement care as practiced in the early 21st century, and to hazard a guess—or perhaps a hope—about further developments to follow. As readers themselves will have perused those chapters that call to them, I will resist the temptation to reiterate the content of the foregoing chapters, and instead simply underscore a few themes and trends that invite comment. No doubt others might survey the same series of chapters (though with a less editorial eye!) and draw different conclusions. And that is as it should be, in a field as variegated and multidisciplinary as our own, which usefully resists what Foucault might have called the "normalizing gaze" of a single authoritative view that seeks to impose its own order on the chorus of voices contributing to this volume (Foucault, 1970). In contrast, I would celebrate the polyphony of voices that constitute bereavement care, and simply hope to invite dialogue among them, rather than to privilege any one voice over the others.

And so it seems appropriate to begin with a remark about the considerable variety of viewpoints, theories, practices and disciplines represented in this volume, which likely is rivaled by few others in the field of psychotherapy. Indeed, a scan of the initials that follow the names of contributors in the List of Contributors gives testimony to the diversity of disciplines and countries represented in this collection, hinting at the breadth of the chapters themselves. Adding to this the range of bereaved populations with which different authors characteristically work—child and adult, traumatized and non-traumatized, individuals and families, military and civilian—it is unsurprising that the techniques featured represent a cornucopia of methods that range widely in style and focus. And again, this is how it should be, as bereavement is itself as variegated as the lives of those people it challenges and changes. Hegemonic attempts to dictate or constrain practice to a few favored procedures therefore seem misguided or worse, and could only be seriously advocated by those most remote from the hurly-burly of grief therapy as practiced, or by those with the least imagination or most devout disposition to genuflect before the ascetic altar of science.

Does this celebration of diversity in the practice of grief therapy imply that all techniques have equal utility? Not in the least. Indeed, one salutary sign of humility in this regard is the recognition in each chapter that the authors' preferred methods, while indicated as a way of working with some of the bereaved, could be contraindicated in others. Thus, each contributor can be viewed as both advocate and critic of his or her own practices, and this openness to a recognition of limitations can be seen in the field as a whole as well, as reflected in its openness to empirical evaluation. For example, many of the techniques conveyed in these pages (a) are coherent with a testable theory; (b) are compatible with a growing field of basic research on grief processes and their complication; or (c) have been evaluated as part of systematic research on psychotherapy in general or grief therapy in particular. Indeed, it is my hope that one function of this book will be to offer clearer procedural guidelines for various techniques not only to practitioners interested in using them, but also to clinical scientists interested in evaluating their impact in controlled research. Clearly the methods described and illustrated in these pages greatly stretch the fairly narrow range of methods that have caught the attention of researchers to date. Encouragement for investigators to study therapy as actually practiced, in all of its creativity and contextual responsiveness, is but one of several strategies that could produce a sturdier bridge between the often distant shores of science and practice (Neimeyer, Harris, Winokuer, & Thornton, 2011).

Finally, it is worth noting that the techniques reviewed here are not typically competitive with one another, except in the important sense that they tend to nest within disciplines (e.g., psychiatry, psychology, social work, nursing, art therapy) that contend among themselves for legitimacy and power. At the level of the eclectic readership of this book, however—a readership often more identified with grief therapy or bereavement care than with any given professional discipline—the procedures between these covers are more complementary than in conflict. For example, the various rituals or resources for bereavement support in the near aftermath of loss can readily be supplemented by more intensive and individualized interventions in grief therapy for the subset of mourners who require them. Indeed, even the most evidence-based treatment protocols (Shear, Boelen, & Neimeyer, 2011) tend to be eclectic in their choice of techniques, even if these are organized within an overarching attachment and coping, cognitive behavioral, or meaning reconstruction framework, for example. I trust that the current compendium of methods will give rise to still more imaginative and useful hybrid forms of treatment.

In closing, I hope the reader has found in these pages a useful companion in serving the bereaved, with its trove of techniques bearing on various contexts, losses or therapeutic intentions (as suggested by my groupings of methods in the Table of Contents). While no volume can claim comprehensiveness in a field as broad-ranging as grief therapy, I trust that the ample selection of methods offered here provides something of value to practitioners in the field and the clients they serve, as well as ample grist for the mill of their clinical imagination.

References

Foucault, M. (1970). *The order of things*. New York: Pantheon.

Neimeyer, R. A., Harris, D. L., Winokuer, H., & Thornton, G. (Eds.). (2011). *Grief and bereavement in contemporary society: Bridging research and practice*. New York: Routledge.

Shear, K., Boelen, P., & Neimeyer, R. A. (2011). Treating complicated grief: Converging approaches. In R. A. Neimeyer, D. L. Harris, H. Winokuer, & G. Thornton (Eds.), *Grief and bereavement in contemporary society: Bridging research and practice* (pp. 139–162). New York: Routledge.

List of Contributors

Courtney Armstrong, MEd, LPC/MHSP, private practice, Chatanooga, TN.

Rafael Ballester Arnal, PhD, Department of Basic and Clinical Psychology and Psychobiology, Universitat Jaume I, Castellón, Spain.

Thomas Attig, PhD, Professor of Philosophy Emeritus, Bowling Green State University, OH.

Melissa Axler, MTS, Beneficial Living & Wellness, Oakville, Ontario, Canada.

Heidi Bardot, ATR-BC, Art Therapy Graduate Program, George Washington University, Washington, DC.

Christine Barrett, EdD, LCPC, Tamarack Grief Resource Center, Missoula, MT.

Barbara Barski-Carrow, PhD, Carrow Associates, Milton, DE.

Joan Beder, DSW, Yeshiva University, Wurzweiler School of Social Work, New York.

Joy S. Berger, FT, DMA, Director of Education and Special Projects, Hospice Education Network, Inc./Weatherbee Resources, Inc., MA.

Mel Berish, MA, Department of Educational and Counselling Psychology, McGill University, Montreal, Quebec, Canada.

Theresa L. Blakley, PhD, Union University, Jackson, TN.

Paul A. Boelen, PhD, Department of Clinical and Health Psychology, Utrecht University, the Netherlands.

Ted Bowman MDiv, Grief Educator, Universities of Minnesota and Saint Thomas, MN.

William Breitbart, MD, Department of Psychiatry and Behavioral Sciences, Memorial Sloan-Kettering Cancer Center, New York.

Laurie A. Burke, MS, Department of Psychology, University of Memphis, Memphis, TN.

Joanne Cacciatore, PhD, Center for Loss and Trauma, Arizona State University, AZ.

Cecilia Lai Wan Chan, PhD, Si Yuan Professor of Health and Social Work, The University of Hong Kong, Hong Kong.

Laura Copeland, MSc, Department of Educational and Counselling Psychology, McGill University, Montreal, Quebec, Canada.

Mieke De Preter, MPsy, Interactie-Academie Antwerp, Belgium.

Kenneth J. Doka, PhD, the College of New Rochelle and Senior Consultant, The Hospice Foundation of America, New York.

Alison J. Dunton, PsyD, The Family Center, Ellicott City, MD.

Bruce Ecker, MA, Coherence Psychology Institute, Oakland, CA.

Tina C. Elacqua, PhD, School of Graduate and Professional Studies, LeTourneau University, Longview, TX.

Maria M. Entenman, MEd, MS, Bereavement Coordinator/Counselor, Holy Redeemer Hospice, PA.

Stephen Fleming, PhD, Department of Psychology, York University, Toronto, Ontario, Canada.

Louis A. Gamino, PhD, Scott & White Healthcare® and Texas A&M Health Science Center College of Medicine, TX.

Nick J. Gerrish, Curtin University of Technology, Perth, Western Australia.

Nancy Gershman, BA, Prescriptive Artist, Art For Your Sake, Chicago.

Linda Goldman, MS, FT, LCPC, Adjunct Professor Johns Hopkins Graduate School, MD.

Stephanie Handel, MSW, Wendt Center for Loss and Healing, Washington, DC.

Darcy L. Harris, PhD, RSW, FT, Kings University College, London, Ontario, Canada.

Lorraine Hedtke MSW, LCSW, PhD, California State University–San Bernardino, CA.

Melissa Henry, PhD, Department of Educational and Counselling Psychology, McGill University, Montreal, Quebec, Canada.

Todd Hochberg, BA, photographer and educator, Evanston, IL.

Laura E. Holcomb, PhD, MS in Clinical Psychopharmacology, Health Psych Maine, Waterville, ME.

Lorraine Holtslander, PhD, College of Nursing, University of Saskatchewan, Canada.

An Hooghe, MS, Clinical Psychologist, Marriage and Family Therapist, Leuven University, Belgium.

Gloria C. Horsley, MFT, CNS, PhD, president of the Open to Hope Foundation, New York.

Heidi Horsley, MSW, PsyD, executive director of Open to Hope and Adjunct Professor, Columbia University, New York.

J. Shep Jeffreys, EdD, FT, Department of Psychiatry, Johns Hopkins School of Medicine, and Department of Pastoral Counseling, Loyola University, MD.

Mimi Jenko, MN, RN, CHPN, PMHCNS-BC, former Clinical Nurse Specialist, Palliative Care, Lakeland Regional Medical Center, Lakeland, FL.

John R. Jordan, PhD, FT, private practice, Pawtucket, RI, and Wellesley, MA.

Beatriz Gil Juliá, MS, Department of Basic and Clinical Psychology and Psychobiology, Universitat Jaume I, Castellón, Spain.

Jeffrey Kauffman, MA, MSS, psychotherapist, suburban Philadelphia.

Phyllis Kosminsky, PhD, FT, private practice, Pleasantville, NY and The Center for Hope, Darien, CT.

Lara Krawchuk, LCSW, MPH, Healing Concepts, LLC.

Jill Harrington LaMorie, DSW, LCSW, University of Pennsylvania School of Social Policy & Practice, PA.

Pamela Piu Yu Leung, PhD, Assistant Professor, Department of Social Work and Social Administration, The University of Hong Kong.

Wendy G. Lichtenthal, PhD, Department of Psychiatry and Behavioral Sciences, Memorial Sloan-Kettering Cancer Center, New York.

Daisy Luiten, art therapist, private practice, the Netherlands.

Christopher J. MacKinnon, MA, Department of Educational and Counselling Psychology, McGill University, Montreal, Quebec, Canada.

Ruth Malkinson, PhD, The Israeli Center for REBT, Tel Aviv University, Tel Aviv, Israel.

Doreen S. Marshall, PhD, Argosy University, Atlanta, GA.

D. "Dale" M. Mayer, PhD, Montana State University College of Nursing, MT.

Raymond McDevitt, MSS, LCSW, private practice, Wilmington, DE, and Council for Relationships, Philadelphia, PA.

Nita Mehr, MSSW, Union University, Jackson, TN.

Evgenia Milman, MA, Department of Educational and Counselling Psychology, McGill University, Montreal, Quebec, Canada.

David C. Mitchell, MA, ATR-BC, LPAT, Hosparus Grief Counseling Center, Louisville, KY.

Robert F. Morgan, PhD, University of Arkansas, Little Rock.

Jane Moss, MA, bereavement support volunteer, Cruse UK, writer and group facilitator.

Rebekah Near, CAGS, the Art 2 Heart Project, European Graduate School, Switzerland.

Robert A. Neimeyer, PhD, Department of Psychology, University of Memphis, TN.

Gail Noppe-Brandon, MA, MPA, LMSW, Find Your Voice, Inc./JBFCS, NYC.

Vicki Panagotacos, MTP, FT, CH, private practice and Hospice Grief Support Facilitator

Jordan S. Potash, PhD, Centre on Behavioral Health, University of Hong Kong, Hong Kong.

Lyn Prashant, PhD, FT, private practice, Grief Counselor, Educator, Consultant.

Therese A. Rando, PhD, BCETS, BCBT, Clinical Director, the Institute for the Study and Treatment of Loss, Warwick, RI.

Joanne C. Robinson, D. Clin. Psychol., Lancashire Care NHS Foundation Trust, UK.

Bronna D. Romanoff, PhD, The Sage Colleges, New York.

Susan Roos, PhD, private practice, Dallas, TX.

Simon Shimshon Rubin, PhD, Director, International Center for the Study of Loss, Bereavement and Human Resilience, and Chairman, Postgraduate Psychotherapy Program, University of Haifa, Israel.

E.K. Rynearson, MD, Clinical Professor of Psychiatry, University of Washington, Separation and Loss Service, Virginia Mason Medical Center, Seattle.

Diana C. Sands, PhD, Centre for Intense Grief, Sydney, Australia.

M. Katherine Shear, MD, Columbia University and New York State Psychiatric Institute, New York.

Jane A. Simington, PhD, Taking Flight International Corporation, Edmonton, Canada.

Harold Ivan Smith, DMin, FT, St. Luke's Hospital, Kansas City, Missouri.

Nathan G. Smith, PhD, Department of Educational and Counselling Psychology, McGill University, Montreal, Quebec, Canada.

Mariken Spuij, MSc, Department of Child and Adolescent Studies, Utrecht University, the Netherlands.

Sharon Strouse, MA, ATR, The Kristin Rita Strouse Foundation/Rita Project, MD.

Carrie Thiel, MA, Tamarack Grief Resource Center, MT.

Barbara E. Thompson, OTD, LCSW, Department of Occupational Therapy, The Sage Colleges, New York.

Nancy Turret, LCSW, Columbia University and New York State Psychiatric Institute, New York.

Jan van den Bout, PhD, Department of Clinical and Health Psychology, Utrecht University, the Netherlands.

Patsy Way, MSc, The Candle Project, St Christopher's Hospice, London.

Howard R. Winokuer, PhD, The Winokuer Center for Counseling and Healing.

Eliezer Witztum MD, Director of School for Psychotherapy, Mental Health Center Beer-Sheva, Faculty of Health Sciences, Ben-Gurion University of the Negev, Israel.

Index